Psychotherapy
for Children
and Adolescents

Psychotherapy
for Children and Adolescents

DIRECTIONS FOR
RESEARCH AND PRACTICE

ALAN E. KAZDIN

New York   Oxford

Oxford University Press

2000

Oxford University Press

Oxford   New York
Athens   Auckland   Bangkok   Bogotá   Buenos Aires   Calcutta
Cape Town   Chennai   Dar es Salaam   Delhi   Florence   Hong Kong   Istanbul
Karachi   Kuala Lumpur   Madrid   Melbourne   Mexico City   Mumbai
Nairobi   Paris   São Paulo   Singapore   Taipei   Tokyo   Toronto   Warsaw

and associated companies in
Berlin   Ibadan

Library of Congress Cataloging-in-Publication Data

Kazdin, Alan E.
    Psychotherapy for children and adolescents : directions for
research and practice / Alan E. Kazdin.
        p.   cm.
    Includes bibliographical references and indexes.
    ISBN 0-19-512618-1
    1. Child psychotherapy—Research—Methodology.   2. Adolescent
psychotherapy—Research—Methodology.   I. Title.
RJ504.K373   2000
618.92'8914—dc21   99-17112

9   8   7   6   5   4   3   2   1

Printed in the United States of America
on acid-free paper

To Bundle and Vugie—Ineffable sources of joy

Preface

Psychotherapy piques our interest in part because of the scope of problems it addresses. Psychotherapy is used for psychiatric disorders and mental illnesses, including schizophrenia, depression, alcohol abuse, to mention only a few. In addition, in everyday life, many stresses, strains, and traumas (e.g., experience of loss, problems of identity and meaning, and relationship issues) can be aided by psychotherapy. Although they are ordinary in the sense of being universal and commonplace, their impact can be extraordinary. Of course, psychotherapy is not just for "psychological" problems. Mental health is inextricably related to physical health. For example, fat consumption and lack of exercise predict heart disease, but so does depression. Moreover, psychotherapy can have significant impact on physical health, including length of survival among terminally ill patients. Although therapy is not a panacea, the scope of its application and beneficial effects is broad.

We are also interested in the seeming mystery of therapeutic change. How does therapy help? How does it work? We hear stories from therapists and friends about significant changes or personal transformations produced by therapy. Of course, personal transformations are fascinating whether effected by age, religion, or psychotherapy. Psychological research can inform us about basic processes of change. Such information can be put to use beyond the confines of therapy to aid in understanding development, interpersonal relationships, and other processes in which change is involved (e.g., teaching and training).

The problems for which psychotherapy can be helpful can emerge at any point over the life span. But the social, emotional, and behavioral problems in childhood raise special issues and special frustrations. Parents are often placed in a demanding, frustrating, and demoralizing position in coping daily with a seriously disturbed child. Yet, parents must mobilize efforts and resources to obtain the necessary help and to follow through with treatment that may make further demands. Psychotherapy is not the only solution to address the difficulties that children, adolescents, and their families experience, but it is one to which they can and do often turn.

Children and adolescents experience many types of social, emotional, and behavioral problems. Moreover, a large proportion of children and adolescents in everyday life are significantly impaired. The task of providing interventions, over the range of disorders and number of children and adolescents in need, is overwhelming. The mental health professions have been actively addressing the task in many ways. There are hundreds of different types of therapies and well over a thousand controlled outcome studies of their impact. Thus, much has been done to develop effective treatments.

Psychotherapy is the topic of this book. My focus is on what we do and do not know about its effects. The book examines the current status and future directions of psychotherapy research. I have two central theses. First, there are major limitations in contemporary research and its conclusions about the effects of psychotherapy. Limitations can always be identified in any area of study, so this thesis is not new or even necessarily important. Second, progress (or at least significant progress) in treating disorders of children and adolescents is unlikely to result from current psychotherapy research. Current research ignores central issues important both in the short and long term for providing effective interventions. I address the central theses by focusing on three questions: (1) What do we wish to know about therapy and its effects? (2) What do we already know? (3) What needs to be accomplished to fill in the gap between what we wish to know and what we already know?

The book covers the current status of knowledge, current limitations, needed knowledge about therapy, and a model for future research. The model is designed to chart a course that assures systematic progress in the accumulation of research. I make suggestions to redirect the questions, methods, and foci of both research and clinical practice. Research goals are to understand therapy and its effects and to advance the knowledge base so that clinical work has a strong empirical footing. The goal of clinical practice is the care of the individual client or patient. Both research and practice can be mobilized to fill the knowledge gaps. The book discusses the present but aims squarely at future progress.

The mental health professions are not at a loss for more books on psychotherapy. There are several genres of psychotherapy books, including those that propose and promote a particular treatment, those that serve as compendia to review research on many treatments as applied to many problems, and those that instruct one how to do some form of treatment (e.g., treatment manuals, self-help books). These are all valuable no doubt, but this book has a different purpose, namely, to guide future research and to accelerate or ensure progress.

The overall goal is to influence psychotherapy research. What is now regarded as "state-of-the-art," "cutting-edge," and "groundbreaking" (insert your favorite such term here) psychotherapy research simply will not lead us to understand how therapy works and what to do to make it more effective. The task of this book is to reconcile the present knowledge with the goals of therapy and to connect them with an explicit plan or course that plots future work.

I am pleased to acknowledge several sources of support provided during the writing of this book. I am grateful for the support for research on child and adolescent psychotherapy from the Leon Lowenstein Foundation, the William T. Grant Foundation, and the National Institute of Mental Health. Yale University is a very supportive environment and has provided colleagues—faculty and students—who have greatly influenced my thinking. My current work is conducted at the Yale Child Conduct Clinic, a clinical service for children and families. I am grateful for the work and collaboration of the staff at the clinic, where we daily confront the many problems toward which therapy research is directed. At the same time, clinical work has also taught us about the many problems and issues that research has eschewed.

The book is about the strengths and limits of therapy research. To that end, research design and methodology are pertinent topics, especially so in one of the chapters. A brief appendix on the topic of methodology has been provided to convey key concepts for the interested reader. Dr. Irving Quickie graciously agreed to serve as a guest author and to prepare a "quick" overview and brush-up course. I am grateful for his contribution. Several individuals, but especially Susan Breton and Tricia Zawacki, contributed to the appendix that identifies treatments currently in use. Their work is described and gratefully acknowledged further in that section. Finally, Michelle Kazdin assisted with the content and editing; I am grateful for her contribution and participation.

New Haven, Connecticut   A. E. K.
April 1999

About the Author

Alan E. Kazdin, Ph.D., is Professor and Chairman of Psychology at Yale University, Professor in the Child Study Center (Child Psychiatry) and Director of the Yale Child Conduct Clinic, an outpatient treatment service for children and their families. He received his Ph.D. in clinical psychology from Northwestern University in 1970. Before coming to Yale, he was on the faculty at Pennsylvania State University and the University of Pittsburgh School of Medicine. His research focuses on therapy for children and adolescents, including the treatment of aggressive and antisocial behavior, processes involved in therapeutic change, and barriers to participation in treatment. He has been a fellow of the Center for Advanced Study in the Behavioral Sciences, president of the Association for Advancement of Behavior Therapy, and recipient of the Distinguished Scientific Contribution and Distinguished Professional Contribution Awards in Clinical Psychology. He has been editor of various journals (*Journal of Consulting and Clinical Psychology, Behavior Therapy, Psychological Assessment,* and *Clinical Psychology: Science and Practice*). Currently, he is editor of *Current Directions in Psychological Science*, the *Encyclopedia of Psychology,* and a book series on *Developmental Clinical Psychology and Psychiatry*. He has written or edited over 30 books, including *Research Design in Clinical Psychology* (3rd ed.), *Conduct Disorder in Childhood and Adolescence* (2nd ed.), *Behavior Modification in Applied Settings* (5th ed.), *Child Psychotherapy: Developing and Identifying Effective Treatments, Methodological Issues and Strategies in Clinical Research* (2nd ed.), *Single-Case Research Designs: Methods for Clinical and Applied Settings,* and *Cognitive Behavioral Interventions* (with L. Craighead, W.E. Craighead, & M.J. Mahoney).

Contents

PART I

Background

Chapter 1

Introduction

PSYCHOTHERAPY IS CONSTANTLY in the public eye. Cartoons in magazines, newspapers, and greeting cards are omnipresent and invariably depict scenes in which a client on a couch speaks to a seated therapist. In this scene, the client conveys odd memories, dreams, and fantasies, each pregnant with significance about childhood. This image is a carryover from yesteryear and in fact does not represent most therapy. Nevertheless, the stereotypic image, however distorted, holds before the public the relevance of therapy for psychiatric disorders, personal problems, and life crises. The look and image of psychotherapy vary widely. Indeed, with advances in technology, communication, and information systems, therapy is now available through self-help books, computer software, videotape cassettes, and Internet web sites (Marks, Shaw, & Parkin, 1998; Newman, Consoli, & Taylor, 1997; Santrock, Minnett, & Campbell, 1994). With a mouse click or two, one can access a sympathetic ear or at least a pleasantly colored if not soothing computer monitor. Integration of therapy with technological advances in the media further reflects the public's keen interest in the subject matter.

Furthermore, there is often a mystique associated with therapy, also stereotypical. Through some wizardry, perhaps one can unlock one's early childhood to uncover amazing capacities or to overcome angst, foibles, or significant impediments to functioning. Perhaps if we have this or that insight or unlock some impacted memory, our problems and symptoms (e.g., anxiety, shyness, stuttering, hallucinations) will disappear or substantially improve. This prospect is intriguing, mystifying, and hopeful. It is also plausible enough. Perhaps (in my own case) if I did talk and relate to someone (a therapist), I could learn how to talk and relate to (and in conversation actually face) other people. Well, in my own case there may be little hope, but with less severely impaired cases, this prospect is hopeful.

Therapy has a novel history, some of which seeps out in ways that foster further interest in the topic. There are scores of fascinating treatments over the course of history. For example, self-suggestion (repeatedly making statements to oneself) was used by the nineteenth century psychotherapist Emil Coué (1857–1926) to treat all sorts of mental and physical conditions, including insomnia, depression, incontinence, alcohol abuse, hernias, tumors, myopia, pain, and paralysis (Coué, 1922, 1923). The assumption was that believing is a necessary and sufficient condition to change. Treatment consisted of suggesting that the patient's condition would improve and prescribing a program of self-suggestion in which individuals repeated that they would improve. The most common phrase that individuals were instructed to state daily and frequently was "Day by day in every way, I'm getting better and better" (Brooks, 1922, p. 27). By all accounts, autosuggestion was generally effective for a number of problems patients brought to treatment. Suggestion has played a role in many treatments over the course of history (e.g., Mesmerism, hypnosis) and no doubt plays a role not fully understood in contemporary treatments as well.

Therapy has its share of fascinating case histories with seemingly wonderful effects. For example, in the 1880s Joseph Breuer (1842–1925), a Viennese physician and collaborator of Sigmund Freud (1856–1939), treated Anna O (Breuer & Freud, 1957). Anna was 21 years old at the time and had several symptoms including paralysis and loss of sensitivity of the limbs, lapses in awareness, distortions of sight and speech, headaches, and a persistent nervous cough. These symptoms were thought to reflect anxiety rather than medical or physical problems. As Breuer talked with Anna and used a little hypnosis, she recalled early events in her past and discussed the circumstances associated with the onset of each symptom. As she made these recollections, her symptoms disappeared. This case is credited with marking the beginning of the "talking cure" and cathartic method of psychotherapy.[1] Such cases inform our views of therapy and often exert much more influence than the actual evidence about therapy's accomplishments.

Therapy is interesting to the public because in fact many people use psychotherapy in their lifetime. Many stresses and strains of living (e.g., marital discord, general relationship problems, loss of loved ones) as well as clinical disorders (e.g., depression, panic attacks) lead people to seek psychotherapy. Indeed, within a given year, between 3–6% of children, adolescents, and adults receive outpatient treatment for mental health (U.S. Congress, 1986). Over the course of childhood and adolescence, 10% of youths (ages 3–17) receive treatment for emotional or behavioral problems (U.S. Congress, 1991). By current census (U.S. Bureau of Census, 1993), this would translate to approximately 7 million youths who receive treatment. These percentages are likely to be underestimates because mental health services are provided by many professionals (e.g., psychologists, psychiatrists, social workers, pediatricians, general practice physicians, psychiatric nurses, school counselors, clergy) and are not easily tracked.

In addition, therapy can be very effective and have far-reaching impact. Controlled studies have shown that some forms of psychotherapy can affect mental and physical health and survival. For example, it is not surprising to learn that various forms of psychotherapy are effective in treating depression and anxiety—these are the traditional home turf of therapy. Perhaps more surprising is the evidence that therapy can have significant impact on physical health, such as decreasing the recurrence of heart attacks (Thoresen & Powell, 1992) and increasing the longevity of terminally ill cancer patients (Spiegel, Bloom, Kraemer, & Gottheil, 1989). These examples convey the interrelation between mental and physical health and the broad relevance of psychotherapy to the human condition.

There is also keen professional interest in psychotherapy. Mental health professionals, primarily psychologists, psychiatrists, and social workers, are involved in the delivery of treatment services to children, adolescents, and adults. In addition, therapy is an active area of research. Researchers and clinicians alike are interested in evaluating and understanding the effects of therapy.

This book is about research on the effectiveness of psychotherapy for children and adolescents and the challenges in developing and evaluating treatments.[2] Many intriguing questions about the effects of therapy immediately come to mind. Can psychotherapy ameliorate the many personal, family, and social problems humans face? Among the many different treatment techniques, which ones work? These are only initial questions that arise, not the deeper questions. Questions about how treatment works, for whom it does and does not work, and why treatment may work for some but not others are critical to developing and identifying effective treatments. These questions are central to this book.

PSYCHOTHERAPY DEFINED

What Is Psychotherapy?

It is not an idle exercise to define psychotherapy. Problems in specifying the central features and the boundary conditions (what is not psychotherapy) show how understanding more about therapy and how it might work is important. For a general definition, psychotherapy consists of a special interaction between two (or more) individuals in which one person (the patient or client) has sought help for a particular problem and another person (the therapist) provides conditions to alleviate that person's distress and to improve functioning in everyday life (Garfield, 1980; Walrond-Skinner, 1986). The interaction is designed to alter the feelings, thoughts, attitudes, or actions of the person who has sought, or has been brought to, treatment. Typically, very special conditions define the interactions of therapist and client.[3] The client usually describes his or her difficulties and life circumstances and the reasons for seeking help. The therapist provides conditions (e.g., support, acceptance, and encouragement) to foster the interpersonal relationship and systematic experiences (e.g., new ways of behaving through practice, role-playing, homework assignments, advice) designed to produce change.

The goals of therapy and the means to obtain them help clarify what uniquely defines psychotherapy. The *goals* consist of improving adjustment and functioning in both intrapersonal and interpersonal spheres and reducing maladaptive behaviors and various psychological and often physical complaints. *Intrapersonal* adjustment includes how one views or feels about oneself and courses of action one pursues. *Interpersonal* functioning refers to how one adapts to and interacts with others, such as relatives, significant others, peers, or colleagues. As a form of treatment, psychotherapy addresses identifiable problems that impair individuals' functioning in everyday life, unlike prevention, in which some effort is usually made to intervene before a problem is evident. Treatment and prevention too have blurry boundaries: often one intervenes with a person who has a problem (anxiety, depression) not only to ameliorate the present problem but also to prevent the onset of other problems (dropping out of school, substance abuse).

The *means* by which the goals are achieved are primarily interpersonal contacts; for most treatments, this consists of verbal interaction. In child therapy, the means can include talking, playing, rewarding new behaviors, or rehearsing activities with the child. Also, the persons who carry out these actions may include therapists, parents, teachers, or peers. A variety of therapeutic aids such as puppets, games, and stories may be used as the means through which treatment goals are sought.

Psychotherapy is restricted to psychosocial interventions in which the means rely primarily on various interpersonal sources of influence such as learning, persuasion, social support, discussion, and similar processes. The focus is on some facet of how clients feel (affect), think (cognitions), and act (behaviors). The definition is necessarily general because of the range of approaches and dizzying list of techniques that need to be accommodated, as I discuss later. Thus, the definition includes treatments subsumed under many general rubrics such as individual, group, family, insight-oriented, behavioral, and cognitive therapies.

What Psychotherapy Is Not

Certainly, it is very important to delineate the boundaries between therapy and other practices or enterprises that may look like or share the goals of therapy. Excluded from the definition are interventions that use biological and medical means of producing change, such as medication, diet, exercise, megavitamins, and psychosurgery. These interventions (e.g., medication to control hyperactivity, electroconvulsive shock to ameliorate recalcitrant depression, or exercise to cope with tension and stress) are often directed toward improved psychological functioning. However, the methods, theoretical rationales, and clinical research issues differ from those raised by psychosocial procedures. Also excluded are interventions directed toward educational objectives, such as tutorial and counseling programs singularly directed to enhance academic performance and achievement. Omitted from the standard definitions of psychotherapy are activities such as chatting with relatives and friends; engaging in hobbies, sports, or other individual or group activities (dancing, singing, fishing); participating in religious activities; and merely spending time with one's spouse or significant other. All of these can be *therapeutic* in the sense that they improve adjustment and functioning, but they are not formally regarded as part of psychotherapy. Of course, the reader may say that if these activities are therapeutic, perhaps they ought to be integrated better into scientific research and practice and delivery of mental health. Indeed, to address personal adjustment, functioning, and psychiatric impairment, we ought to understand how all of these interventions not considered to be psychotherapy work and when they ought to be deployed. I shall return to the reader's point in the final chapter.

The exclusion of biological and medical procedures, interventions with educational objectives, and daily activities that share many of therapy's goals (enhancing adjustment) and means (talking) does not in any way slight the significance or utility of these other methods and activities. However, by tradition the definition of therapy is restricted to a large class of psychosocial interventions. These interventions are also those studied by the mental health professions (psychology, psychiatry, and social work). Hence, the domain of psychotherapy is separated from related interventions that may involve other disciplines. This is a bit arbitrary, but boundaries often permit a more intensive focus on a given area of work.

GOALS OF PSYCHOTHERAPY RESEARCH

This book is about making advances in psychotherapy research for children and adolescents. Concrete suggestions are provided regarding the questions that ought to guide research, how these questions ought to be answered, and how to make progress in systematic ways, beyond the goals of individual studies. I shall examine the questions that currently guide research later; I only highlight them here. How questions are asked about therapy and of course how the answers are sought dictate the kind of progress that is made. Recommendations of new ways to make progress require that we state, challenge, and then reformulate the questions that guide treatment research. The following issues convey the basis of the book's focus.

The "Ultimate Question"

The goals of psychotherapy research ought to be straightforward. There are questions to which we want well-supported answers. Does psychotherapy work? Is psychotherapy effective? As meaningful and direct as these sound, researchers do not consider them to be very useful. They oversimplify psychotherapy its effects (Bergin & Lambert, 1978; Edwards & Cronbach, 1952). Psychotherapy is a general term that encompasses many different treatments. It is not particularly meaningful to lump them all together and ask a single, simple true/false question. That is like asking, "Does surgery (or drugs, or child-rearing) work?" There are many different types of surgery, drugs, and child-rearing practices that work in some conditions, for some people. And, of course, what does "work" or "effective" mean? Do people get all better or partially better, in the short term or the long term? These important questions will reappear later.

Many years ago, the global question was replaced by a more specific question: "What treatment, by whom, is most effective for this individual with that specific problem, under which set of circumstances?" (Paul, 1967, p. 111). This is often regarded as the ultimate question toward which psychotherapy outcome research should be directed. The question highlights the importance of examining the specific effects of various treatments for a particular clinical problem and acknowledges that the effects of treatments may depend on the characteristics of the patients and therapists and on the conditions under which treatment is provided.

"Challenges," if not insurmountable obstacles, make this question difficult to address. In fact, I do not believe this is the question we ought to address anyway. But consider the question on its own terms. The sheer number of available treatment techniques alone makes this question close to impossible to answer. Surveys have revealed a continued proliferation of techniques in use for adults. In the early 1960s, approximately 60 different types of psychotherapy for adults were identified (Garfield, 1982). In the 1970s the figure rose from 130 (National Institute of Mental Health [NIMH], 1975) to more than 250 techniques (Herink, 1980). By the mid-1980s, there were over 400 techniques (Karasu, 1985). There is no systematic tracking of the number of new treatments or variations, at least to my knowledge. Moreover, the purpose served by tracking new treatments would be unclear. Also, any count of treatments has serious boundary problems (e.g., is a variation of a treatment a new technique or just a variation?). In any case, determining the effectiveness of the 400 or so different therapies for adults is a task of considerable proportions.

The ultimate question implies that the different techniques ought to be evaluated in relation to specific clinical problems. Assume, for example, that there were 100 or 200 plausible treatments for anxiety disorders; each would need to be tested in relation to each anxiety disorder. The symptoms, maladaptive behaviors, target complaints, and dysfunctions now recognized as clinical problems have also proliferated. Consider, for example, the classification of psychiatric disorders over the last fifty years. In the United States, the list of recognized disorders is provided by the *Diagnostic and Statistical Manual of Mental Disorders* (the DSM). This document is updated periodically and delineates various disorders (e.g., mood, anxiety, eating, and sexual disorders) and criteria invoked for their diagnosis. The most recent edition (DSM-IV; American Psychiatric Association [APA], 1994a) includes over 300 recognized

disorders and related problems that can serve as the basis for distress in everyday life and that may warrant treatment. Over the years, as the DSM has
evolved, more and more diagnoses and disorders have been distinguished (from
slightly over 100 in 1952 to slightly over 300 in 1994). Even assuming that the
number of recognized disorders does not continue to increase with further revisions of the DSM, evaluation of treatment in relation to disorders currently
recognized is an obviously formidable task. Indeed, evaluating the effects of
the 400 or so techniques on each of the 300 or so disorders, including the comparison of treatments (e.g., two treatments at a time), would require several million studies. For those students struggling for dissertation topics, this might be
good news. Yet for the rest of us this is disastrous. Moreover, the number is a
gross underestimate because it omits other variables to investigate that are included in the ultimate question (e.g., types of therapists, ethnicity of therapists
and clients, severity of dysfunction). Therapy studies—even poorly designed
studies—are not easy to conduct, so a very large number of such studies is not
feasible.

An Alternative Formulation

The ultimate question has been largely accepted as the agenda of therapy research. Yet answering the question is really not feasible. This could explain the
limited progress in securing answers. For most clinical problems brought to
treatment, we do not know which technique will be effective for some but not
other types of clients. To cover the number of treatments, problems, and other
conditions would require an indefinite and slightly less than infinite number of
studies. Efforts to complete the requisite number of studies no doubt would be
interrupted by a distracting astronomical event, namely, the increased bright-
ness and heat from the sun, which is expected to boil the oceans away and burn
the rest of the earth (in approximately a billion years).

The ultimate question is objectionable on other grounds as well. The question, as formulated, emphasizes an empirical approach of mixing and matching
variables in assorted combinations (this type of patient, that type of treatment,
under those types of conditions). An endless array of variables might be added
to make the list and the research task even greater. For example, any relation
between the effectiveness of a particular treatment and a particular clinical
problem may vary as a function of other variables such as the age of the client
(adolescent vs. adult), ethnicity, personality characteristics of the client (or therapist), and so on rather endlessly. The search for such variables and their impact unguided by theory or conceptual views can be seen in the various meta-
analyses of therapy that look at the influence of one variable after another,
without regard to prediction, meaning, or interpretability of the variable.
Components of the ultimate question *are* very important, but the agenda for research ought to be formulated somewhat differently.

The goal for therapy research is to understand how treatment leads to change
and how various factors relate to change. The goal ought to be approached by
emphasizing theory that poses the processes (or mechanisms) through which

therapy operates. The benefit of this alternative formulation of the task is that it does not require several million studies. Also, the formulation begins with a parsimonious assumption: the many treatments available probably do not all work through different mechanisms or processes. Thus, therapeutic improvement likely results from changes in some limited number of psychological, biological, and social processes. For example, therapy may achieve effects because of changes in memory, behavioral repertoires, and cognitions. Identifying how therapy works, even for one or two forms of therapy, could reveal processes that have generality across many types of therapy and also apply to changes in other contexts, such as child rearing or schooling.

Two key concepts that clarify the reformulated research agenda are *moderators* and *mediators* (see Baron & Kenny, 1986; Holmbeck, 1997). A moderator is a variable that influences the relationship between two (or more) other variables. For example, the effects of treatment A may differ for boys and girls. That is, the relationship between treatment and therapeutic change is influenced (moderated) by child gender. In this example, gender is a moderator. We can readily identify variables that likely serve as moderators of treatment. Severity of the child's problem or adverse conditions in the family (e.g., family chaos, psychiatric impairment of the parents) could plausibly serve as moderators. A goal of therapy research is to hypothesize and evaluate factors that moderate treatment effects and, eventually, to understand why these factors serve as moderators.

A mediator is the process, mechanism, or means through which a variable operates or produces a particular outcome. For example, therapy may achieve its effects because of changes in cognitive processes (e.g., how cues from the environment or from others are coded, changes in specific beliefs and attributions) that therapy produces. Alternatively, changes might result from learning processes, alteration of memory, or reduction in physiological arousal associated with real and imagined events. When we know how change takes place, we can say the particular process mediates treatment.

Moderators and mediators are distinct but relate to each other. If a relation is moderated by a variable, different mechanisms are likely involved. For example, early signs of disruptive behavior in elementary school children (first grade, age 7) predict later delinquency in adolescence. However, this relationship holds for boys, not girls. In other words, the relation of early signs of aggression and later delinquency is moderated by child gender. Knowing the moderator, we can assume that the paths toward delinquency may involve different processes for boys and girls. That is, identification of a moderator may imply that different mechanisms are involved in the outcome.

The search for mediators and moderators does not make the psychotherapy research agenda easy. However, the shift from the ultimate question to this formulation focuses on influences and processes that may extend across many treatments and disorders and moves from describing to explaining therapeutic change. Also, the agenda underscores the importance of understanding theory and mechanisms rather than or in addition to demonstrating empirical relations among conditions on which treatment effects depend. I elaborate the steps toward understanding treatment in a later chapter that provides a model to guide treatment research.

Another advantage of this formulation is that it draws on a broad range of research strategies. Mediators of change can be studied in basic research (human and infrahuman laboratory studies) in addition to therapy studies. All of psychology (leaving aside other disciplines) may be relevant to understand change processes (e.g., learning, memory, information processing, persuasion, and attitude change). How humans (organisms) learn, change, adapt, and develop are not unique therapy questions; hence, the answers need not derive from treatment studies. We do wish to know whether therapy "works," but we also need to know *why* it works. Discovering why is not an intellectual exercise but a key to being able to influence the course and magnitude of therapeutic change.

Deciding Whether Treatment Is Effective

The questions that ought to guide psychotherapy research are challenging to say the least, as I note in later chapters. The answers are problematic too. As a general statement, questions concern the effects and effectiveness of therapy. The notion of "effectiveness" is rather slippery. Deciding whether treatment is effective is not a straightforward process. The effects of treatment can be measured in several ways, including the reduction of symptoms, improvements in adjustment at home or in the community, increases in self-reported happiness, and the evaluations of relatives and friends who may or may not see improvement. Which of these or other indices should define effectiveness? Perhaps one should look for changes in several measures to be sure that the treatment has really worked. Yet improvements on one measure or set of measures are not always associated with improvements on other measures. So whether treatment is considered effective may depend on the specific measure one examines.

Also, how much change on a measure is needed to define an effective treatment? Changes in symptoms, adjustment, and happiness are a matter of degree. Perhaps the client's depression or fears decrease only a little by the end of treatment. Would we say that treatment was effective? Consider this—for some persons who come to therapy, problems may be worsening; for example, one becomes more deviant, more withdrawn, more impaired. Treatment may slow or stop the process or downward trend. At the end of treatment, perhaps the client has not changed at all. Conceivably, no change could be a great success in therapy just as it is in medical treatment of serious disease (e.g., showing that an AIDS patient remains stable). In almost all cases, the goal of therapy is to reduce symptoms and improve adaptive functioning. At what point would an improvement be regarded as a sign that therapy is effective or successful? There are no definitive answers to such questions.

THE SOCIAL CONTEXT: WHO IS INTERESTED IN PSYCHOTHERAPY RESEARCH?

To this point, I have highlighted the research agenda in a somewhat idealistic fashion. The fact is that research occurs in a political and social context with multiple interests and consumers of therapy and therapy research. The consumers include those who

- are directly served (clients and their families);
- provide treatment (mental health professionals, including psychologists, psychiatrists, and social workers);
- refer others for treatment (pediatricians and other physicians, school personnel, the courts);
- advocate for special interest groups (legislators, patient advocacy groups); and
- pay for treatment (sometimes clients, but often third-party payers, including employers, insurance companies, and governmental agencies).

All of these parties wish to know whether therapy is a viable means to address mental health and physical health problems such as alcohol and drug abuse and coping with and surviving terminal disease. They are keenly interested in therapy, to whom it is applied, with what goals, and at what costs and benefits.

The different consumer groups have overlapping but somewhat different interests and priorities. For example, parents who seek treatment for their children want an intervention that is acceptable (palatable, reasonable, not painful or aversive), time-limited and effective. The goals of parents are to improve functioning and eliminate their child's problems to the extent possible. Agents for insurance companies and third-party payment plans are interested in the least costly intervention. The goal of reimbursement agencies may not be to make clients "all better," "happy," or "productive," but rather to return them to adequate functioning in everyday life: to return the child back to school, the college student to classes, the adult to work. Insurance agencies are likely interested in knowing the least costly treatment that can be provided to achieve some change. The courts wish to know whether any form of treatment can provide a viable alternative to incarceration as a way of interrupting the path of a child or adolescent heading toward a career of criminality.

Consumers of therapy influence the research agenda by inadvertently, or sometimes directly, setting or modifying the priorities of research. Advocacy groups routinely lobby for more research funds to address a particular problem (e.g., substance abuse) or type of program (e.g., prevention). Also, public alarm over events that receive heightened attention by the media (e.g., children killing other children with handguns) can lead to pressure on those responsible for policy, which in turn can influence funding for research on a particular type of problem and treatments to ameliorate it. Although research grants are often evaluated for their scientific merit, scientific merit itself is evaluated in the context of political agenda. Citizens and lobbying groups can very much influence that agenda. Also, managed care plans wish to know which treatments work quickly. Researchers respond to such matters and often evaluate applied questions that have some social urgency. Funds for research, whether from federal or state agencies or private foundations, are more readily available to address questions of social than of scientific interest.

Consumer interests also provide implicit boundaries for what is appropriate to study and to evaluate. Ultimately a treatment effective in research is intended to be applied in clinical work with "real" clients who come for treatment. It would make very little sense to evaluate a treatment that is aversive, not feasible, costly, politically incorrect, or even unethical because it has little chance of ever being used by people in everyday life. This point, of course, does not apply only to psychotherapy. An effective medicine is useless if taking it is too painful or costly or has side effects that are as bad or worse than the problem itself. Therapy research also has to operate within such constraints.

Research does not occur in an academic vacuum. Psychotherapy research often has to address quite different constituents. One must recognize this at the outset because it places treatment research in context. Also, the different interests of persons invested in therapy research lead to a broad range of questions that treatment research is compelled to address. If we ask which treatment is more acceptable to the clients or which is less expensive for society, this leads to studies that go beyond the ultimate question and the expanded formulation.

FOCUS OF THIS BOOK

Psychotherapy research has made enormous progress in the past fifty years. Interestingly, the vast majority of work has focused on adults. In general, research on psychiatric disorders and problems of adjustment of children and adolescents, including diagnosis, assessment, and treatment, has lagged behind. For example, as the DSM delineated various forms of psychiatric or "mental" disorders, the focus was almost exclusively on adult disorders. Only in the 1980s (APA, 1980, 1987) were the emotional and behavioral problems of childhood delineated in some detail. Prior to that, the range of disorders and forms of impairment were not formally recognized, barring severe forms of dysfunction (e.g., autism, mental retardation) and pervasive forms of disruptive behavior (e.g., hyperactivity, delinquency). Even these disorders, while recognized, were not well differentiated in terms of their various subtypes and patterns. In the current diagnostic manual (4th edition, APA, 1994a), a large number of childhood disorders are recognized. The delineation of childhood disorders vastly accelerated their investigation, including onset, course, and treatment.

Within the past twenty years, research on childhood and adolescent disorders and their treatment and prevention has increased. For example, numerous books have charted progress of treatments for various disorders (e.g., Hibbs & Jensen, 1996; Mash & Barkley, 1998; Morris & Kratochwill, 1998). Although this book discusses progress, its goal is not to review the evidence in behalf of therapy techniques. Rather, the focus is on how to make progress, what the research agenda ought to be, and how future research ought to depart from contemporary studies.

Although there are now many studies of child therapy, there has been limited progress in understanding how treatments achieve change and how to optimize the outcomes. A central thesis of this book is that the slow progress can be traced concretely to how treatment research is conceptualized, the limited ways in which individual investigations are designed and conducted, and the absence of a blueprint, strategy, and long-range plan to answer questions about child treatment.

Research on child psychotherapy is floundering. When considering the ultimate question (what treatments to apply to whom and under what conditions) or the reformulated research agenda (efforts to understand how therapy works), very little can be said about the accomplishments of child and adolescent psychotherapy research in the past five years versus the five years before those years. Moreover, given the focus of therapy research, there is no reason to believe the next few years will see the leap in knowledge we need. These statements are arguable, and hence it will be important to discuss current progress, strengths, and limitations of treatment research. More importantly, identifying how work might be done differently will be critical. Indeed, an overall goal of this book is to accelerate progress by examining the current status of the field, pointing to special issues that have thwarted progress, identifying promising leads and findings, and outlining new directions. The new directions will not echo the familiar refrain that ends literature reviews, namely, that "more research is needed." Quite different research is needed, and the quality more than the quantity of evidence in the next decades will determine whether progress is made in providing effective treatments to children and adolescents. This book is designed to provoke thought about what is needed and to promote action in the use of alternative research strategies.

The book is organized into three parts: (I) "Background," (II) "Evidence: Major Findings, Strengths, and Limitations," and (III) "Improving Therapy Research." The parts convey a progression that begins with identifying what psychotherapy is and continues by exploring the range of problems to which it is applied and the constraints and demands of delivering therapy and conducting therapy research. The second part reviews the evidence cited in behalf of child and adolescent psychotherapy. A portion of the review considers exemplary studies to convey characteristics and findings of superior therapy research. The third part is future-focused. Chapters within this part focus on what is needed to overcome the tremendous gaps in knowledge and to accelerate progress on key questions.

There are a few aids in the book designed to embellish the content and provide useful background. Further readings are listed at the end of each chapter. The readings elaborate key points or place issues of the chapter in a broader context. There are two appendixes. Appendix A lists current therapies in use for children and adolescents; appendix B covers methodology of psychotherapy research. Although methodology is covered within chapter 9, a discussion of the basic information would detract from the main themes and progression of the book; hence, a guest chapter (appendix B) provides a quick review of methodology and research design.

OVERVIEW OF REMAINING CHAPTERS

Chapter 2 addresses "Clinical Problems of Children and Adolescents." An overview is provided of the range of psychiatric disorders and social, emotional, and behavioral problems that emerge in childhood and adolescence. Prevalence of the problems and their interrelations and diverse facets of child functioning are also discussed. The chapter conveys the multiple foci of treatment and the need for identifying interventions that can be deployed early in childhood.

Chapter 3, "Approaches, Treatments, and Characteristics of Psychotherapy," considers the scope of therapy techniques. The chapter begins with an overview of major approaches to treatment and the vast array of treatments currently in use. Unique features and challenges in providing therapy to children and adolescents, as opposed to adults, are also discussed in this chapter. Associated with this chapter is appendix A, which lists current techniques.

Chapters 4, 5, and 6 review the evidence on the effects of therapy for children and adolescents in three different ways. Chapter 4 considers the "The Effects of Psychotherapy: Current Status of the Evidence" and examines the methods of evaluating the effects of psychotherapy and the conclusions reached from contemporary reviews. Essentially, this is a review of literature reviews. This chapter also covers limitations of the various reviews and their implications for what can be said about the effectiveness of treatment.

Chapter 5 examines "The Effects of Psychotherapy: Empirically Supported Treatments," those treatments supported by empirical research. The chapter considers the historical context of identifying empirically supported treatments, the different meanings of this term, and specific treatments designated for children and adolescents. Limitations of empirically supported treatments and how such treatments are conceived, identified, and evaluated are described.

In Chapter 6, "Treatments That Work: Illustrations of Exemplary Research," focuses on four treatments that have been carefully evaluated. These treatments are presented in detail to move beyond the more general literature reviews and to illustrate child and adolescent therapy research at its very best. The examples show the progress and strengths of superior research and preview several features to be emulated. At the same time, even the best research illustrates the limitations of current research and progress.

Chapter 7, "Characteristics and Limitations of Therapy Research," considers the evidence reviewed in the previous three chapters and identifies several limitations related to who is studied in treatment, how therapy is evaluated, and the types of questions that dominate research. The key characteristics of psychotherapy research demonstrate why the conclusions about the effects of treatment are quite limited and why progress is likely to be very stilted if research continues its current trajectory and focus.

It is easy to complain about current progress, yet identifying limitations is not sufficient to make changes or to improve research. Consequently, chapter 8, "Developing Effective Treatments: A Model for Clinical Research," presents a constructive alternative way of proceeding. The chapter presents a blueprint for how to develop and evaluate treatments. The model demonstrates the scope of what we want to know about child and adolescent therapy and provides a means of evaluating therapy research progress. Steps to develop effective treatments are delineated along with necessary improvements in the range of questions asked, the methods used to evaluate treatment, and the models of delivering treatment.

Chapter 9, "Designing and Conducting a Treatment Study," focuses more concretely on the demands of conducting a treatment study and discusses critical issues and decision points in relation to experimental design, assessment, data analyses, and ethical issues that influence treatment research. The goal of the chapter is to improve the methodology and quality of individual treatment studies. As a complement to this chapter, appendix B provides a brief refresher on methodology and covers basic principles and practices.

Previous chapters have assumed that research advances will inform clinical practice. Clinical practice can be a significant partner in developing the knowledge base rather than a mere recipient of findings obtained in other contexts. In chapter 10, "Implementing and Evaluating Treatment in Clinical Practice," recommendations are made for altering treatment implementation in clinical practice. The goals of the suggestions are to improve the quality of patient care and the inferences that can be drawn about the effects of treatment. Developing the knowledge base and answering critical questions about treatment can be greatly informed by clinical practice.

The final chapter is "Psychotherapy Research in Perspective." It provides an overall evaluation of progress and different perspectives on how the current status of theory, research, and practice might be viewed. Key issues are discussed in relation to where we are and where we ought to go in relation to the knowledge base. The chapter emphasizes the need to expand our views of social, emotional, and behavioral problems and the range of legitimate interventions that might improve adjustment and well-being.

FOR FURTHER READING

Selected readings below are intended to provide resources that place contemporary therapy research in context. These include the history and evolution of treatment research, different conceptual models, and current trends and influences.

Bongar, B., & Beutler, L.E. (Eds.). (1995). *Comprehensive textbook of psychotherapy: Theory and practice*. New York: Oxford University Press.

Freedheim, D.K. (Ed.). (1992). *History of psychotherapy: A century of change*. Washington, DC: American Psychological Association.

Kazdin, A.E. (1978). *History of behavior modification: Experimental foundations of contemporary research*. Baltimore, MD: University Park Press.

Mash, E.J. (1998). Treatment of child and family disturbance: A behavioral-systems perspective. In E.J. Mash & R.A. Barkley (Eds.), *Treatment of childhood disorders* (2nd ed., pp. 3–51). New York: Guilford.

Table 2.1 (*continued*)

CATEGORY	DESCRIPTION
Feeding and Eating Disorders of Infancy or Early Childhood	Persistent eating and feeding disturbances such as eating nonnutritive substances (pica), repeated regurgitation and rechewing of food (rumination disorder), and persistent failure to eat adequately, resulting in significant failure to gain weight or in weight loss (feeding disorder of infancy or early childhood).
Tic Disorders	Sudden, rapid, and recurrent stereotyped motor movement or vocalizations. Separate disorders are distinguished based on scope of the tics (e.g., motor, vocal) and their duration and include Tourette's, chronic motor or vocal, and transient tic disorders.
Elimination Disorders	Dysfunction related to urination or defecation in which these functions appear to be uncontrolled, beyond the age at which control has usually been established. Two disorders, enuresis and encopresis, are distinguished and require the absence of medical condition in which these symptoms would emerge.
Other Disorders of Infancy, Childhood, or Adolescence	A collection of other disorders not covered elsewhere including separation anxiety, selective mutism, reactive attachment, and stereotypic movement disorders.

The disorders within each category have multiple inclusion and exclusion criteria related to the requisite symptoms, severity and duration, and patterns of onset (see DSM-IV, APA, 1994a). Details of the diagnoses are beyond the scope of this chapter.

tant loss of freedom (APA, 1994a). The range of psychological dysfunctions or disorders that individuals can experience is enumerated in various diagnostic systems, such as the *Diagnostic and Statistical Manual of Mental Disorders* (DSM-IV; APA, 1994a) and the *International Classification of Diseases* (ICD-10; World Health Organization, 1992). The DSM, the dominant system in use (Maser, Kaelber, & Weise, 1991), recognizes several disorders that arise in infancy, childhood, or adolescence. These disorders are grouped into 10 categories listed in table 2.1.

Omitted from the table are many disorders that can arise over the life span and hence are not unique to childhood and adolescence. The diagnostic criteria for these disorders are similar across all ages. Major examples include Anxiety, Mood, Eating, Substance-Related, Schizophrenia, Sexual and Gender Identity Disorders, and Adjustment Disorders. Table 2.2 highlights specific disorders within these categories to illustrate some of the more common diagnoses, par-

Table 2.2 Examples of Disorders Evident at Any Point over the Life Span

DISORDER	DESCRIPTION
Major Depressive Disorder	The appearance of depressed mood or loss of interest that lasts for at least 2 weeks and is associated with at least four additional symptoms including a change in appetite or weight, sleep, and psycho-motor activity; feelings of worthlessness or guilt; diminished energy; difficulty thinking, concentrating, or making decisions; and recurrent thoughts of death or suicidal ideation, plans, or attempts.
Posttraumatic Stress Disorder	Development of symptoms of anxiety after exposure to an extreme traumatic event involving actual or threatened injury or witnessing an event that involves death, injury, or a threat to the physical integrity of another person, or learning about these events experienced by a family member. The events may include personal assault (sexual, physical, robbery-related), accidents, life-threatening illness, a disaster (loss of one's home after a hurricane or tornado). Key symptoms involve intense fear, helplessness, horror, re-experience of the event (in thoughts, dreams), avoidance of stimuli associated with the event, and numbing of general responsiveness (detachment, restricted affect), and persistent symptoms of increased arousal (difficulty falling or remaining asleep).
Eating Disorder	A disorder in which the individual does not maintain minimal normal body weight ($<$85 percent of normal body weight), is intensely afraid of gaining weight, and exhibits a significant disturbance in perception of his or her body. Many methods of weight loss may be adopted such as self-induced vomiting, misuse of laxatives, and increased or excessive exercise.
Substance-Abuse Disorder	A set of disorders (depending on the substance) characterized by a maladaptive use of the substance as evident in recurrent and significant adverse consequences, such as failure to fulfill role obligations at school, work, or home, and social and interpersonal problems. A period of 12 months of use and continued use after untoward consequences (in role performance, legal problems, school expulsion) are required for the diagnosis.

continued

Table 2.2 (*continued*)

Disorder	Description
Schizophrenia	A disorder that lasts at least 6 months and includes two or more of these symptoms: delusions, hallucinations, disorganized speech, grossly disorganized catatonic behavior, and negative symptoms such as flat affect, poverty of speech (brief, empty replies), and inability to initiate or persist in goal-directed behavior. Significant dysfunction occurs in one or more areas of functioning including interpersonal relations, work, school, or self-care.
Adjustment Disorder	Development of clinically significant emotional or behavioral symptoms in response to an identifiable psychological stressor or stressors. The symptoms develop within 3 months of the event and are associated with marked distress or a reaction exceeding expectations within the context or culture. The symptoms of many other disorders may emerge (e.g., anxiety, depressed mood, conduct problems).
Other Conditions	Problems included that are not mental disorders but may serve as the focus of clinical attention. These may include relational problems (e.g., between parent and child, between spouses), physical or sexual abuse of an adult or child, isolated anti-social behavior, bereavement, and many others not considered as mental disorders but treated by mental health professionals.

ticularly for children and adolescents. The information from both tables begins to convey some of the complexities in disorders. There are not just a few simple disorders to master. Apart from their sheer number, a given type of disorder (e.g., anxiety, eating) has different versions, depending on their onset. Some disorders may emerge at any time; others during childhood or adolescence. It is useful to consider the list as a way to identify various types of dysfunctions in childhood and adolescence.

To note that some disorders can emerge at any age does not necessarily mean that they are identical over the course of development. For example, depression can emerge during childhood, adolescence, and adulthood and can be diagnosed based on symptoms common across the life span. Yet this does not necessarily mean that all symptoms and associated features are identical for all age groups. Some rather stark differences in depression are evident over the course of development. For example, suicide attempt and completion, which sometimes accompany major depression, are rarely evident in children. The rates of attempt and completion increase significantly during adolescence and adulthood. Thus, a key feature associated with depression can change considerably across age groups.

It is useful to delineate broad categories of disorders because of the way psychiatric dysfunction is often studied in research and examined in clinical work. Table 2.3 includes five categories that represent broader domains of dysfunction and are widely recognized as useful because they do not depend on the vicissitudes and arbitrary cutoff criteria of diagnostic systems. For example, externalizing behaviors and learning problems (mental retardation) in children have been recognized since the beginning of recorded history. In recent years, the more specific disorders within these categories have been debated and researched, and diagnostic criteria continue to evolve. Although specific disorders will be mentioned in later chapters, the broad terms are useful as well. In

Table 2.3 Broad Categories of Problem Domains/Disorders

DOMAINS	DESCRIPTIONS
Externalizing Disorders	Problems directed toward the environment and others. Primary examples include oppositional, hyperactive, aggressive, and antisocial behaviors encompassed by the psychiatric diagnostic category, Attention-Deficit and Disruptive Behavior Disorders (in table 2.1).
Internalizing Disorders	Problems directed toward inner experience. Primary examples include anxiety, withdrawal, and depression.
Substance-Related Disorders	Impairment associated with any of a variety of substances including alcohol, illicit drugs, and tobacco. These disorders, while important in their own right, are also associated with other psychiatric disorders.
Learning and Mental Disabilities	A range of problems related to intellectual and academic functioning including mental retardation and learning disorders. Such problems are probably underestimated both in terms of prevalence and impact on behavior among children and adolescents referred to treatment because of the more salient problems that serve as the basis for referral.
Severe and Pervasive Psychopathology	Problems include disorders recognized as the more severe forms of psychopathology with pervasive influences in the areas of functioning they affect and in their long-term course. Examples include schizophrenia and autism.

most treatment studies, diagnostic assessment is not conducted. From the case descriptions, measures, or inclusion criteria, the best information one can glean is that the individuals were recruited for their externalizing or internalizing problems.

Of the categories listed in table 2.3, externalizing and internalizing disorders constitute the most frequent bases of clinical referrals in children and adolescents. Clearly, externalizing disorders dominate. Substance abuse and severe psychopathology (e.g., autism, schizophrenia) less frequently serve as the focus of therapy. For these latter disorders, interventions are often conducted in institutional settings (hospitals, day treatment facilities). Psychotherapy is used on an outpatient basis, sometimes to maintain gains achieved in institutional programs.

Learning-based problems are usually not the focus of treatment in the same way as the other problems. Educational interventions designed to remediate deficits or enhance skills in an academic area (reading, mathematics) are provided. Learning-based problems are inextricably related to mental disorders. They often co-occur with other disorders, such as conduct disorder, and serve as important factors in predicting long-term outcome. Indeed, learning-based problems often exacerbate the long-term outcome of mental disorders in children (Kazdin, 1995b). The organization and specialization of professions that are responsible for the care of children (e.g., mental health professions, medicine, education) limit the domains that are addressed. Thus, learning-based problems are not usually the focus of mental health practitioners.

Prevalence

In the 1980s, a large-scale, nationwide study of the prevalence of mental disorders among adults (18 years of age and older) was completed in the United States (e.g., Regier et al., 1984; Robins et al., 1984).[1] The study used rigorous sampling methods, large sample sizes, and multiple sites (locations); hence, one can be reasonably assured that the findings represented the population at the time. A wealth of information about the nature of mental disorders was revealed by this project, but the most general finding is especially noteworthy: approximately 20% of adults suffer from a mental disorder in a given year. Over the course of their lives, 32% can be expected to experience a disorder (Robins & Regier, 1991).

To date, there has been no large-scale, nationwide study of psychiatric disorders among children and adolescents. Yet several studies have provided estimates of the disorders using current diagnostic criteria and rigorous assessment methods. Moreover, these studies have been completed in several different locales (e.g., the United States, Puerto Rico, Canada, and New Zealand) and have yielded fairly consistent results. Studies included children and adolescents (4 to 18 years old) and found that 17–22% suffer significant developmental, emotional, or behavioral problems (Costello, 1989; Institute of Medicine, 1989; U.S. Congress, 1991; Zill & Schoenborn, 1990). There are approximately 68 million children and adolescents in the United States (U.S. Bureau of Census,

1993). Assuming for a moment a prevalence rate of 20% approximately 13.5 million of our nation's youths have significant impairment due to an emotional or behavioral problem.

The rates for specific disorders vary considerably. For example, prevalence rates of attention-deficit/hyperactivity disorder and conduct disorder have varied from 2–10% and 2–9% respectively (U.S. Congress, 1991). Also, within a category of disorders, rates can vary as a function of the specific type of problem. For example, substance abuse among adolescents varies widely, depending on the substance (< 1% for hard drugs, 1–3% for marijuana, and 1–15% percent for alcohol) (Weinberg, Rahdert, Colliver, & Glanz, 1998). The prevalence rates and patterns of dysfunction for psychiatric disorders are influenced by a variety of factors including, but by no means limited to, gender, poverty, race and ethnicity, parent education and marital status, and rural or urban settings. Large-scale multisite studies are so useful because they can often demonstrate the influence of these other factors on prevalence rates.

Important Considerations

VARIATIONS IN DEFINING AND IDENTIFYING DISORDERS. The prevalence rates ought to be viewed as general patterns rather than conclusions about the "real" rates of disorders among children. Diagnostic systems and definitions of disorders have changed considerably over the past two decades. The disorders that arise in infancy, childhood, and adolescence have been modified, sometimes markedly. The changes include the emergence and elimination of various diagnostic categories, as well as changes in the criteria for specific diagnoses (e.g., conduct disorder, attention-deficit/hyperactivity disorder). Also, different prevalence studies have drawn on different diagnostic systems or different editions of a particular system. With these variations, the consistencies among the different studies (approximately 20% as the estimate of prevalence) are remarkable.

Even when the diagnostic criteria are the same, different methods of assessment can lead to quite different results. Typically, diagnostic interviews are conducted with parents and children or adolescents. However, sometimes symptom checklists are used and only parents are queried about the presence of a child's symptoms. Changes in the methods of assessing disorder lead to changes in the prevalence rates and in who is identified as meeting criteria for a disorder (Boyle et al., 1996; Kazdin, 1989; Offord et al., 1996). There is no "gold standard" or means of unequivocally deciding if a disorder is present. Considerable differences exist among children or adolescents, parents, teachers, and clinicians who provide the information regarding presence and severity of symptoms.

CHANGES OVER THE COURSE OF DEVELOPMENT. Although it is useful to consider childhood and adolescence together to highlight the scope of the problem, there are major differences in disorders across the life span. The shift from childhood to adolescence, marked by pre- and postpuberty, is associated with a number of changes in symptoms and disorders. First, several disorders increase markedly after the onset of puberty. Among these are mood disorders, eating disorders (e.g., anorexia nervosa), conduct disorder, substance abuse, and schizophrenia. For many of these, one can identify precursors in childhood, but the prevalence rates for these disorders sharply increase with adolescence.

Second, a number of sex differences emerge or become more pronounced with the onset of puberty. For example, rates of depression are low in boys and girls (Hammen & Rudolf, 1996). With the onset of puberty, prevalence of depression is much higher for girls than for boys. Similarly, eating disorders, not very prevalent in preadolescence, emerge mostly after puberty and are much more common in girls.

Third, characteristics of the disorder or the constituent symptoms of a disorder may change. As mentioned previously, suicide attempt and completion, associated with depression, are quite rare before puberty. The rates increase with the onset of puberty, reaching a peak among 15- to 19-year-olds (Cohen, Spirito, & Brown, 1996). Attempted suicide is more common in girls, although completion of suicide is more common in boys. As another example, conduct disorder, evident in childhood, changes in nature with the onset of adolescence (Kazdin, 1995b). The prevalence rates of delinquent activity increase in adolescence, the types of activity change (e.g., more vandalism, breaking into property, violence), and the ways in which these activities are completed change (e.g. in groups rather than individually, under the influence of illicit substances). Also, in childhood, conduct disorder is much more prevalent in boys than girls; during adolescence, the proportions are more evenly divided. Changes in conduct disorder, as well as the other previously noted changes in psychopathology, have been fairly well charted, although they are not well understood.

COMORBIDITY. Highlighting disorders and their prevalence rates does not fully represent the scope of impairment among children and adolescents. Many individuals meet criteria for two or more diagnoses, a phenomenon referred to as *comorbidity* (see Caron & Rutter, 1991; Clark, Watson, & Reynolds, 1995). In principle, an individual could meet criteria for any two or more disorders. In practice, some combinations of disorders are much more likely to occur than others; disorders that often go together are attention-deficit/hyperactivity disorder and conduct disorder, conduct disorder and substance abuse disorder, anxiety disorder and depression, autism and mental retardation, and Tourette's syndrome and attention-deficit/hyperactivity disorder, to mention a few. Why some combinations of disorders are more likely than others, whether there are common features or simply definitional overlap and ambiguities of various disorders, and how comorbid disorders emerge are just some of the intriguing questions that guide research on comorbidity.

Among community samples, comorbidity rates are relatively high. For example, among 10- to 20-year-olds, approximately half of the individuals with a substance abuse disorder also meet criteria for another disorder, including primarily disruptive behavior disorders (Cohen et al., 1993; Greenbaum, Foster-

Johnson, & Patrila, 1996). Among clinically referred samples, the rates of co-morbidity are much higher; among adolescents with a diagnosis of substance abuse, most ($\geq$70%) meet criteria for other disorders, again primarily conduct disorder (Milin, Halikas, Meller, & Morse, 1991; Weinberg et al., 1998).

Comorbidity is significant in relation to providing treatment. Many individuals may suffer significant impairment in multiple domains and areas of functioning. Thus, treatment is not focused only on children or adolescents who present with a single problem or disorder. Comorbidity is the rule rather than the exception in clinical settings. For example, in the outpatient clinic where my own work is conducted, children may meet criteria for up to four or five different diagnoses and average (mean) slightly over two diagnoses.[2] Even if the children do not meet criteria for multiple disorders, they usually show symptoms from several different disorders (Kazdin, Holland, & Crowley, 1997). That is, they may meet criteria for attention-deficit/hyperactivity disorder but also have a few symptoms of conduct disorder, anxiety disorder, and depression—but not enough to meet these other diagnoses. In any case, treatment is often applied to diffuse and multiproblem cases. Without systematic evaluation before treatment begins, it is easy to ignore the secondary and tertiary diagnoses that are overshadowed by the referral problems. Yet the comorbid diagnoses and the range of symptoms across disorders can have significant implications for an individual's long-term functioning as well as his or her responsiveness to interventions (Kazdin, 1995a; Rutter, Harrington, Quinton, & Pickles, 1994).

SUBSYNDROMES.   A prevalence rate of psychiatric disorder of approximately 17–22% is rather high. Indeed, this means that one out of five or six youths meets criteria for a diagnosis. Surely this must be an overestimate. Alas, the prevalence rates likely significantly *underestimate* the range of mental disorders and impairment. Prevalence rates are determined by identifying children who meet diagnostic criteria for a disorder. The criteria or threshold for deciding whether an individual meets criteria for a disorder has not been carefully established. Consider the extreme cases. Children who show absolutely no symptoms of depression can be safely said not to be depressed. At the other extreme, children who show all of the symptoms or who meet diagnostic criteria can be said to be clinically depressed. Somewhere near this very extreme group is another group, namely, individuals who show a significant number of symptoms for an extended period. These individuals do not have all the symptoms possible but still meet diagnostic criteria for major depression. Extensive research available on children who meet criteria for major depression shows that it is a meaningful designation. Children who meet criteria for the diagnosis have a variety of common past, present, and future characteristics (e.g., family history and long-term course) (Hammen & Rudolf, 1996).

What about the group that we left out, namely, children and adolescents who show some of the symptoms? Consider those children who "miss" meeting the criteria but are close. *Subsyndromal* is the term that refers to a set of symptoms that fails to meet the diagnostic criteria for a disorder.[3] Individuals whose symptoms are subsyndromal may still show significant impairment and untoward long-term prognoses. For example, adolescents who come close to, but who do not meet, the criteria for major depression are much more likely to meet criteria for another disorder, to develop another disorder later, and to show impairment in psychosocial functioning than individuals with few or no depressive symptoms (Gotlib, Lewinsohn, & Seeley, 1995).

Similarly, children and adolescents who meet criteria for conduct disorder are clearly impaired, by definition. Yet conduct disorder is represented better as a continuum based on the number and severity of symptoms and degree of impairment rather than as a condition achieved at a particular cutoff (Boyle et al., 1996; Offord et al., 1992). Individuals who miss the cutoff criteria are likely to show impairment and poor long-term prognoses, although to a lesser extent as a function of the degree of dysfunction.

Overall, these results show that prevalence rates, when based on meeting criteria for diagnoses, may be conservative. Those children identified with disorders are likely to be impaired, but many children who do not meet the criteria are also impaired and may have a poor long-term prognosis. In fact, the already high prevalence rate of mental disorders in children and adolescents clearly underestimates the scope of the problem.

PROBLEM AND AT-RISK BEHAVIORS

Currently recognized psychiatric disorders, particularly those that reflect externalizing and internalizing behaviors, constitute the primary focus of therapy with children and adolescents. Other problems, which warrant intervention because they are related to current and long-term functioning, partially overlap with but can be distinguished from psychiatric disorders.

During adolescence, a number of activities referred to as *problem* or *at-risk behaviors* increase (see DiClemente, Hansen, & Ponton, 1996; Ketterlinus & Lamb, 1994; U.S. Congress, 1991). Use of illicit substances, truancy, school suspensions, stealing, vandalism, and precocious and unprotected sex, for example, are referred to as at-risk behaviors because they increase the likelihood of a variety of adverse psychological, social, and health outcomes. For example, alcohol abuse is associated with the three most frequent forms of mortality among adolescents: automobile accidents, homicides, and suicide (Windle, Shope, & Bukstein, 1996); approximately 90% of automobile accidents involving adolescents also involve the use of alcohol.

The problem behaviors obviously overlap with psychiatric diagnoses, especially subsyndromal disorders. The distinction can be difficult to make. As a guide, the psychiatric disorders refer to a pattern of functioning, the presence of multiple symptoms, and impairment in everyday situations. Many youths with problem behaviors might well meet criteria for a disorder, perhaps substance abuse disorder. However, a larger group would not. They may engage in problem behaviors, but they fit in with their peers and manage daily functioning—at school, for example.

The prevalence rates of problem behaviors are relatively high. A summary of several survey studies (Dryfoos, 1990) gave the following estimates for substance use among high school seniors:

- 12% engage in heavy cigarette smoking ($\geq\frac{1}{2}$ pack per day);
- 15% engage in heavy drinking (≥ 5 drinks in a row on three or more occasions within the past 2 weeks);
- 5% engage in regular use of marijuana (≥ 20 times within the past 30 days); and
- 3% engage in frequent use of cocaine (≥ 3 times within the past month).

A more recent survey found that 50.8% of seniors reported some alcohol use in the 30 days prior to the survey; 31.3% reported being drunk at least once; 4.9% reported using marijuana daily or almost daily (Johnston, 1996). Other studies paint a similar picture, even though estimates of substance abuse vary as a function of the age of the sample, the types of substances (e.g., inhalants), the time frame (use in past week, month, year), the assessment method (e.g., self-report vs. medical emergency visits), and the impact of many other factors (e.g., social class, ethnicity, neighborhood). Even so, the rates of abuse are alarming. Moreover, current data suggest that rates of substance use are increasing, a trend that began in the early 1990s (Weinberg et al., 1998). The direct and immediate health consequences and correlates of substance abuse (increased risk of death from overdose, injury and death while driving a vehicle, sexually transmitted disease [STD] through unprotected sex) are serious. The indirect and long-term consequences of substance abuse are problematic as well: school failure, poor occupational adjustment, crime involvement, and mental disorders (Newcomb & Bentler, 1988; U.S. Congress, 1991).

Substance abuse is merely one example of at-risk behavior. A number of other examples have been identified, including unprotected sexual activity and its risk for STDs (including human immunodeficiency virus [HIV]) and teen pregnancy; delinquent, antisocial, and violent behavior; dropping out of school; and running away from home (DiClemente et al., 1996; Dryfoos, 1990). Such behaviors are often associated with concurrent mental and physical health problems during adolescence as well as with subsequent problems in adulthood. The short- and long-term impacts of problem behaviors on the adolescent are influenced by a variety of factors, including severity and chronicity of the behavior or condition and a host of contextual factors (e.g., family constellation, support system). For example, the risk for adverse outcomes from substance abuse depends on the particular substance used and the frequency of use (Newcomb & Bentler, 1989).

Multiple problem behaviors often go together (see Ketterlinus & Lamb, 1994). This does not mean that drug abuse, delinquent behavior, and academic dysfunction invariably co-occur. Yet such behaviors often come in "packages." In the prior discussion of psychiatric diagnoses, the notion of a group of symptoms that occur together was described as a syndrome. The term *syndrome* is less often used outside of the context of disorder, illness, and disease, but the phenomenon is the same. A sample of youths identified with one of the behaviors—for example, early sexual activity—is likely to have higher rates of other problem behaviors (substance use and abuse, delinquent acts) than a comparison sample similar in age and gender. Stated another way, problem behaviors form a syndrome.

For many individuals, the syndrome includes many and more extreme levels of the behaviors. In an effort to estimate prevalence of problem or high-risk behaviors, Dryfoos (1990) delineated groups based on the number and seriousness of behaviors and estimated rates of adolescents with these problems in the United States: 10% were at very high risk (multiple and serious problem behaviors); 15% were at high risk (two or three problem behaviors); and 25% were at moderate risk (one problem behavior). The cumulative percent of youths at high-to-moderate risk was 50%, which, given the current census, would translate to approximately 17 million adolescents in the United States.

DELINQUENCY

Many of the problem behaviors mentioned previously are illegal, such as hard drug use. It is useful to discuss illegal behaviors more explicitly because the designation overlaps with, but can be distinguished from, problems already mentioned. *Delinquency* is a legal designation that includes behaviors that violate the law: robbery, drug use, vandalism, and others. Some acts are illegal for both adults and juveniles (referred to as *index* offenses) and encompass such serious offenses as homicide, robbery, aggravated assault, and rape. Other acts (referred to as *status* offenses) are illegal only because of the age at which they occur—that is, they are offenses only for juveniles.[4] Examples include underage drinking, running away from home, truancy from school, and driving a car before the legal age.

Delinquency is a weighty subject in its own right but warrants mention for at least three reasons. First, the delinquent acts overlap with psychiatric disorders and problem behaviors mentioned previously. Indeed, the distinction between delinquency and mental disorder is not always sharp, and individuals can readily meet criteria for both based on the same behaviors (e.g., conduct disorder symptoms). Second, individuals identified as delinquent often have high rates of diagnosable psychiatric disorders. Up to 50–80% of delinquent youths may show at least one diagnosable psychiatric disorder—with conduct, attention deficit, and substance abuse disorders being the most common (see Kazdin, in press; Otto, Greenstein, Johnson, & Friedman, 1992). Third, many of the interventions used for delinquent youths involve psychosocial procedures of the type covered here. One does not think of psychotherapy as a treatment for delinquency, but in fact many of the psychosocial interventions used for externalizing behaviors in patient samples are also applied to delinquents in outpatient and correctional settings. Variations of behavior modification, cognitive-behavioral treatment, and family-based treatment are among the common examples.

The prevalence rates of delinquency in the population at large vary as a function of how delinquency is measured. Arrest records, surveys of victims, and reports of individuals about their own criminal activities are among the most common methods. Because much crime goes unreported and detected, self-report has often been used and results in much higher rates than official records.

A few key points are pertinent to this discussion. First, a large percentage of adolescents (70%) engages in some delinquent behavior, usually status rather than index offenses (Elliott, Huizinga, & Ageton, 1985; Farrington, 1995). Most of these individuals do not continue criminal behavior. A much smaller group (20–35%) engages in more serious offenses (robbery and assault) and may be identified through arrest or contact with the courts. Third, a small group (5%) includes persistent or career criminals. They engage in many different and more severe delinquent activities and are responsible for approximately half of the officially recorded offenses (Farrington, 1995; Tracy, Wolfgang, & Figlio, 1990). There is a keen interest in this latter group and their characteristics. One goal of research is to identify and understand the paths leading to criminal careers. Psychiatric disorders in children are among the risk factors for career criminal activity (Elliott, Huizinga, & Menard, 1988; Moffitt, 1993). Career criminals are much more likely than less persistent offenders or normative samples to have prior and current attention deficit disorder or conduct disorder (Farrington, Loeber, & Van Kammen, 1990; Magnusson, Klinteberg, & Stattin, 1994). This raises the intriguing question of whether treating these other disorders could decrease (prevent the onset of) subsequent criminal activity. Some evidence suggests that this might well be the case (e.g., Satterfield, Satterfield, & Schell, 1987), but much more work is needed.

Delinquency can be distinguished from psychiatric disorders and problem behaviors, but clearly there is overlap among the three ways of categorizing behaviors. The distinctions are often made because they refer to different problems, including whether the problem is circumscribed or part of a larger pattern and whether the problem violates the law. Yet the arbitrariness of the distinctions is sometimes obvious. For example, if a 10-year-old child sets a neighbor's house on fire, the agency first called to intervene—police, mental health services—may dictate the designation and intervention provided to the child. The child may be taken to a police station or to emergency psychiatric services. From the standpoint of this book, the issue is child and adolescent dysfunction and what can be done about it rather than how the problem is categorized and the agency to which the child might be referred.

TASKS OF TREATMENT

The prior sections highlight the scope of the problems that children and adolescents experience and that can serve as the basis for providing some sort of intervention. The four most significant points are the most general:

- Children and adolescents experience many different types of problems;
- Children and adolescents often experience multiple problems concurrently (comorbid disorders, multiple problem behaviors, academic and learning problems);

- These problems can emerge at many different points over the course of development; and
- Several million children and adolescents need some intervention.

An overview of psychiatric disorders, problem behaviors, and delinquency yielded quite high rates of dysfunction among youths. One could add up the separate rates across these categories and, with hyperbolic misuse of the numbers, probably show extremely high rates of dysfunction, indeed, perhaps exceeding 100% of youths. Yet psychiatric disorders, problem behaviors, and delinquency overlap, and there is the equivalent of comorbidity among these categories. That is, individuals who experience a particular disorder may also be included among individuals with problem behaviors and delinquent acts. Yet the key point here does not require agreement on precise figures. I mentioned previously an estimate of prevalence of 20% of children and adolescents who evince some form of psychiatric disorder. This can be considered a quite conservative figure, even within the category of psychiatric diagnoses, for no other reason than the questionable and stringent cutoff point. Even without problem behaviors and delinquent acts, the scope of problems in need of intervention is great.

Psychotherapy is one of many interventions to address social, emotional, and behavioral problems. Other interventions encompass a variety of social services; home, school, and community-based programs; residential and hospital treatment; and medication. Also, given the scope of the problem, a multi-pronged approach is needed. Central to that approach are efforts at prevention and treatment. Preventive interventions themselves include many that may vary according to the disorder and points of intervention (early, middle, or late childhood). Although preventive interventions are beyond the scope of this book, a few comments can place the study of treatment in context.

Prevention, like treatment or other areas of research, has its own complexities. It is not obvious how to intervene to prevent many problems; the interventions used often are very well intended but not well understood. Also, identifying who will show the problem (e.g., conduct disorder, suicide) and hence serve as the appropriate target of the preventive intervention is not always easy. Many individuals not at risk for the problem may eventually show it and many who are at risk may not (Offord, Kraemer, Kazdin, Jensen, & Harrington, 1998). To whom ought preventive interventions be applied? How do we identify these individuals? These questions raise many issues. Often prevention is contrasted with and pitted against treatment. Yet both are critically important. Prevention may reduce the incidence (number of new cases) and decrease the magnitude, duration, or onset of other problems. Treatment, of course, focuses on those whose impairment is significant and requires some intervention.

The focus on treatment, and particularly psychotherapy, is of special interest for at least two reasons. First, psychotherapy, particularly if delivered on an outpatient basis, can preempt the use of more restrictive, costly, and disruptive interventions such as hospitalization and residential care. From the standpoint of child adjustment and family preservation, usually it is preferable to maintain the child in the context of his or her everyday life, except when remaining at home jeopardizes the child's mental or physical health, as in abuse or neglect cases. Removal of the child to an institutional setting can raise new problems, including the adjustment that such a dramatic change may entail. Second, conceptual models of psychotherapy and the specific treatment techniques that follow from them are used in diverse settings including schools, day-treatment and residential inpatient hospital services, and juvenile justice programs for both treatment and preventive purposes. Thus, intervention approaches within psychotherapy often bear the burden of producing the desired change. Consequently, research on psychotherapeutic treatments is critically important.

SUMMARY AND CONCLUSIONS

The importance of identifying effective interventions is underscored by the tremendous need among children and adolescents. This chapter outlined many of the problems that emerge in childhood and adolescence that warrant intervention. Psychiatric disorders refer to a range of currently recognized patterns of behavior associated with impairment in everyday life. As patterns including multiple behaviors, these disorders are different from isolated or circumscribed problems. For example, a child with attention-deficit/hyperactivity disorder is not merely overactive in the classroom but is also likely to show a pattern of excessive activity, other behavioral characteristics (impulsivity, poor attention, quite possibly aggressive behavior), and impairment in everyday settings like school or in peer groups. This is not the same as what a parent might mean in noting that a child is very active. Another point is that many disorders have no clear boundaries. The extremes can be readily identified (e.g., attention-deficit/hyperactivity disorder vs. sedentary child with highly focused concentration), but the specific cutoff point that designates a disorder is somewhat arbitrary for many psychiatric disorders.

In addition to a dizzying array of disorders, there are many problems and at-risk behaviors in which youths, particularly adolescents, engage: substance use (alcohol, drugs, tobacco), vandalism, theft, and precocious and unprotected sex, to mention a few. These behaviors are often associated with current problems in other domains such as poor school functioning and dropping out of school and portend later dysfunction such as psychiatric disorder, unemployment, and arrest. Problem behaviors clearly are worthy of intervention. Delinquency was also mentioned in this chapter. Delinquent acts often are not isolated and may reflect a pattern of criminal behavior that obviously warrants intervention. Delinquency also is often associated with psychiatric disorders.

From the standpoint of interventions, the question is, what can be done to avert, reduce, or eliminate the social, emotional, behavioral, and developmental problems of children and adolescents? Psychotherapy, conceived as an intervention in which the individual child or adolescent comes to treatment to meet a specially trained mental health professional, is not the answer. Yet this is a very narrow view of psychotherapy. It is much more useful—and accurate in light of clinical work—to conceive of psychotherapy as a body of theory and research used as the basis of psychosocial approaches to intervention. The interventions that can be used are methods to change emotions (affect), thought processes (cognitions), and actions (behavior). Psychotherapeutic interventions have direct implications for altering functioning and adjustment at home, at school, and in the community and are used in diverse residential, treatment, and rehabilitation settings. This chapter focused on some of the key problems toward which therapy is directed. The next chapter provides an overview of the historical and current contexts of child and adolescent therapy.

FOR FURTHER READING

Many resources are available that document the nature and scope of dysfunction in children and adolescents. The resources below provide details about several different types of problems, the factors with which these problems are associated, and the developmental course of the problems.

DiClemente, R.J., Hansen, W.B., & Ponton, L.E. (Eds.). (1996). *Handbook of adolescent health risk behavior*. New York: Plenum.

Ketterlinus, R.D., & Lamb, M.E. (Eds.). (1994). *Adolescent problem behaviors: Issues and research*. Hillsdale, NJ: Erlbaum.

Lewis, M. (Ed.). (1996). *Child and adolescent psychiatry: A comprehensive textbook* (2nd ed.). Baltimore, MD: Williams and Wilkins.

Mash, E., & Barkley R.A. (Eds.). (1996). *Child psychopathology*. New York: Guilford.

United States Congress, Office of Technology Assessment. (1991). *Adolescent health* (OTA-H-468). Washington, DC: U.S. Government Printing Office.

Chapter 3

Approaches, Treatments, and Characteristics of Psychotherapy

MANY MENTAL DISORDERS and other problems of children and adolescents would profit from intervention. In turn, there are also many interventions. This chapter considers the scope of available psychotherapeutic interventions. The chapter discusses approaches toward treatment and highlights the vast range of treatment techniques currently in use for children and adolescents, thus providing the context for what is feasible to accomplish in research. Applying psychotherapy to children and adolescents is not merely a matter of giving small doses of adult treatments to persons who are shorter and more playful. When children and adolescents are the clients, the entire process of providing treatment changes, with accompanying key challenges.

APPROACHES TO TREATMENT

Major Approaches

Traditionally, treatments have been organized into different approaches. *Approaches* to treatment refer to conceptual views and general statements about the focus or emphasis of the intervention. An approach is distinguishable from *treatment*, which refers more concretely to the specific intervention or method used to modify or alleviate clinical problems. Essentially, approaches are ways of categorizing many different treatments.

Of the approaches, the first and most influential is the psychoanalytic approach from which modern psychotherapy has emerged. Psychoanalysis, as developed by Freud, includes a theory of personality development, a method of studying personality and development, and a form of psychotherapy. The term also is used to refer to a more general approach that reflects an orientation toward treatment. Many different forms of psychoanalysis as a therapy technique have evolved; psychoanalysis as an approach encompasses all of them (see Eagle & Wolitzky, 1992).

As an approach, these are the key tenets that Freud proposed:

- Current symptoms are usually expressions of underlying conflicts and unconscious (out of awareness) processes;
- These underlying conflicts emerge over the course of early development, based on the satisfaction, expression, and resolution of various impulses and drives;
- Therapy sessions can reveal these processes and conflicts through various means of assessing unconscious processes (free association, dream interpretation, the nature of the relationship with the therapist); and
- Working through past conflicts and processes in the context of the therapeutic relationship can resolve clinical problems (e.g., anxiety, fear, physical symptoms that appear to have no underlying biological basis).

This is not an attempt to represent the richness of psychoanalysis as a theory, treatment, or method of study. Rather, the purpose is to draw attention to the broad assumptions that underlie psychoanalysis.

A contrasting conceptual view shows us precisely what an approach is and how it differs from a treatment or specific intervention. Behavior modification emerged as a competing approach to psychoanalysis. As an approach, behavior modification consists of the application of conditioning concepts to explain behavior and a methodological approach that emphasizes scientific research and empirical investigation. Among key tenets are these views:

- Learning theory (e.g., classical and operant conditioning, modeling) and research provide a useful basis for understanding how symptoms emerge and can be altered;
- Treatments provide new learning experiences based on direct training through modeling, practice, and repeated exposure to situations; and
- The focus of treatment is on current behavior and how it might be changed.

Psychoanalysis and behavior modification convey different conceptual views about the basis for clinical problems and for therapeutic change. Psychoanalysis emphasizes unfolding determinants early in life (internal processes, impulses) and how needs were met in relation to the environment. Be-

Table 3.1 Major Approaches of Psychotherapy

APPROACH	DESCRIPTION
Psychoanalytic Therapies	The focus is on psychological forces, impulses drives, and wishes within the individual that are presumed to emerge in infancy and early childhood, as elaborated in orthodox psychoanalysis or one of its many variants. Past experiences (early childhood psychosexual development) are considered determinants of current functioning. Insight and resolution of conflicts related to psychoanalytic themes serve as the goals of treatment.
Psychodynamic Therapies	The focus is in on psychological forces but with less adherence to one particular variant of psychoanalysis. Symptoms/problems are seen as expressions of underlying processes and their meaning (e.g., aggressive behavior may be expressions of displaced anger at a parent). "Dynamic" is drawn from the psychoanalytic view that conflicts, feelings, or impulses are underlying forces or sources of energy for overt problems and that these conflicts need to be resolved for therapeutic change. Psychodynamic is often used as a category to encompass psychoanalytic therapies too.
Family Therapies	The focus is on the family rather than, or along with, the child. The child is referred to as the identified patient insofar as the child's symptoms are considered to reflect problems in structure, function, communication, or other facets of the family. Treatment is addressed to these family issues.
Behavioral Therapies	The focus is on providing new learning experiences in treatment as a means of changing behavior. Psychology of learning serves as a conceptual view of how problems may have developed and how problems can be altered. Treatments focus on practice, training, learning new skills, and developing response repertoires in the situations in which behavior is problematic.
Cognitive-Behavioral Therapies	The focus is on cognitive processes (e.g., attributions, beliefs, problem-solving skills) as the basis for therapeutic change. Treatment attempts to alter these processes, usually through direct and active training. The training methods often use behavioral treatment techniques such as role-playing,

continued

36

Table 3.1 (*continued*)

APPROACH	DESCRIPTION
	practice, and homework assignments. In contemporary writings, cognitive-behavioral treatment usually encompasses behavioral treatments too, whether or not they rely on cognitive processes.
Experiential Therapies	The focus is on present rather than past experience and on the meaning of the experience to the client. Emphasis is on the relationship with the therapist, empathy, and the client's frame of reference. The focus is on providing conditions for the client's growth and development. Relationship-based and client-centered (nondirective) therapies are sometimes included in this class.
Existential/Humanistic Therapies	The focus is on the client's subjective experience including how the individual views and experiences the subjective, internal, and external world and meaning in the world. The relationship with the therapist and the processes of therapy are critical. This approach is rarely used in the context of child and adolescent therapy.
Integrative-Eclectic Therapies	The focus is on multiple treatment techniques that may derive from different approaches. The purpose is to use multiple procedures that appear to be suited to the complexities of the problems and individual characteristics of the case. This might include psychodynamic treatment, family work, and behavior therapy, as the therapist sees fit for the case.

havior modification emphasizes learning experiences (modeling, operant and classical conditioning) to explain how behavior was acquired and altered. Each approach underscores different processes to achieve therapeutic change (e.g., resolve conflict, redirect impulses vs. providing new learning experiences). Psychoanalysis and behavior therapy have been contrasted endlessly as competing treatment approaches (see Kazdin, 1978b). The contrast may be of historical interest but not particularly relevant to the research agenda that serves as the focus of this book.

There are many other approaches to treatment. Table 3.1 provides a list of major ones. Although there are different approaches, they are not equally popular among mental health professionals. For example, in relation to child and adolescent therapy, family therapy is a widely held conceptual approach to treatment. Family therapy adheres to the view that the family is a critical element in contributing to child dysfunction (psychiatric disorder, problem behaviors) and ought to be the central focus of treatment. As with any other approach, many different variations of treatment are included.

Approaches usually refer to conceptual views about the development of the clinical problem and the means of changing the problem. Other ways of categorizing and classifying treatment are important to mention because they provide another way of viewing treatments and also are invoked to determine which treatments are effective. Three separate categorizations have been used.

First, historically, *insight-oriented* and *action-oriented* treatments have been delineated (e.g., London, 1986). Insight-oriented treatments focus on processes within the individual as the means of achieving change. These treatments tend to be less directive—they evoke material from the client rather than advise the client on what to do—and focus on broad issues such as meaning. Major treatments encompassed within this larger grouping are psychoanalytic, psychodynamic, and experiential (e.g., client-centered) therapies. Action-oriented treatments focus more on overt behavior and cognitive processes. The treatments are more directive and engage the client in "actions," or things to do to change affect, cognition, and behavior. The therapist structures treatment in ways that provide a plan of action. Obviously, behavioral, cognitive, and cognitive-behavioral approaches are encompassed within this category.

Second, treatments have been categorized based on whether they are administered in *group* or *individual* format. Group versus individual therapy is not merely a matter of whether treatment is given to one person or more than one. Traditionally, group therapy has been considered unique because of the special processes that can emerge in this context (e.g., receiving feedback from others, viewing peers with similar issues and problems, modeling influences from the behaviors of others, forming alliances and relationships among group members). Group therapy can include psychoanalytic, behavioral, and other approaches and hence, as a category, masks conceptual differences among other approaches.

Third, treatment is frequently categorized at the most general level as one type versus all others: A versus non-A, where A = the particular approach of interest to an investigator or author, whose purpose is to draw broad conclusions about a particular type of treatment and to test whether one approach is better than another. Such general categorizations are used in behavioral versus nonbehavioral treatments or family versus nonfamily therapies. This method of categorizing obviously groups large segments of treatments together. More than that, a given type of treatment (e.g., psychodynamic, behavioral) might fall in both categories. For example, if family and nonfamily therapies were compared, some behavioral and psychodynamic treatment techniques would be used in both categories.

Cautions in Interpreting Approaches

The approaches in table 3.1 and the other ways of classifying treatments are useful as general descriptors of the focus of treatment. At the same time, it is critically important to note limitations of the categories. First and foremost, treatments *within* an approach, often are very different from each other and may reflect competing and indeed conflicting conceptual views and procedures. For example, family therapy can include structural family therapy, functional family therapy, and behavioral family therapy—all family therapy but each embraces discrepant views about the source of the problems within the family and what ought to be done in treatment. One might assume that all of the family therapies at least see the family as part of treatment. In fact, in some cases the family is *not* seen in family therapy. Family therapy is sometimes viewed as a way of conceptualizing treatment (emphasizing the individual's symptoms or dysfunction in the context of family interactions and process) and, occasionally, only the individual, rather than the family, is seen in treatment. When these two variants of family therapy are compared, evidence has suggested that seeing the individual is as effective as seeing the entire family (Szapocznik, Kurtines, Foote, Perez-Vidal, & Hervis, 1986).

Similarly, behavior therapy includes quite different conceptual views that address entirely different processes. Behavioral treatments for anxiety include many interventions, (e.g., flooding and systematic desensitization) with conflicting views about what treatment requires. In other cases, behavioral treatments focus on entirely different problems, such as anxiety in adults or feeding problems in young children, and draw on theories, such as information processing or operant conditioning that have only faint connections. In short, the meaningfulness of an approach in some cases is diminished by the multiplicity of its competing conceptual views and treatments.

Second, and related, a given treatment can be placed into different approaches and hence there is inconsistency in research reviews in the treatments encompassed by a given approach. For example, some behavioral treatments focus on the family and reviews of the effectiveness of family therapy may or may not include these techniques. Sometimes reviews of cognitive therapy include techniques that invoke behavioral techniques and other times they do not. Because treatments within an "approach" can vary conceptually and procedurally and because a given treatment may be placed in more than one category, one must be extremely wary about conclusions about the effectiveness of an approach to therapy. What does it mean to refer to behavior therapy as a general approach? The category is useful to organize professionals who share some common interests or for journals in which one can read about these interests. For example, many professional organizations, journals, and conferences are devoted to psychoanalytic, behavioral, cognitive, family, and humanistic approaches to treatment.

A difficulty emerges in discussions of the effectiveness of a treatment approach. The approaches have no specific referent, or a procedure or treatment whose effects can be evaluated. Often, reviews of therapy categorize treatments into one approach and then compare approach A to approach B or non-A. For example, some research, as discussed later, has suggested that behavioral therapy is more effective than nonbehavioral (i.e., all other) therapies. Such results are limited, given the remarkable variability and diversity of the treatments within a category. The key questions in treatment research pertain to the effects of particular treatments rather than the effects of approaches.

General Comments

Historically, approaches have served as a useful way of presenting and organizing different treatments in teaching, organizing books, and conveying the orientation or overarching philosophy of a training program (e.g., graduate program, internship). Beyond these uses, the utility of approaches is strained, particularly as a way of enlightening or guiding therapy research. Traditionally, each approach included multiple theories about the nature of a particular problem. For an approach to remain viable, it had to remain very general to accommodate the different theories. For example, proponents of one approach, perhaps psychoanalytic or behavioral, might attack key tenets of another approach. Yet, the criticisms were likely to be untrue, or inapplicable to, some theories or treatments within the approach.

The generality of the conceptual views that the approaches reflected has not been too helpful for therapy research. General conceptual views are not usually very useful in testing how disorders or clinical problems emerge or can be ameliorated. Much of treatment research became separated from any genuine theories about clinical problems or treatment processes, becoming instead atheoretical. Treatment effects are meticulously evaluated, but the basis of treatment or efforts to understand why treatment might work have been largely neglected. I shall return to this topic, but it is relevant here. Currently, general approaches to treatment are not discussed very much in the therapy research. We are left with multiple techniques, few of which draw on specific theories about the problems to which they are applied or are based on specific and testable hypotheses about the therapeutic change process.

THERAPIES CURRENTLY IN USE

Proliferation of Therapies

The problems and ambiguities in approaches are eclipsed by the chaos in the treatments themselves. *Treatment* in this context refers to the specific intervention used to improve the child.[1] Thus, family therapy might be the general approach to which the therapist subscribes in his or her practice, but structural family therapy might be the actual treatment he or she uses.

The number of treatments in use is enormous and continues to proliferate. At any time it is difficult to pinpoint the precise number of techniques in use, but surveys show a continuous growth. Indeed, I believe the evidence is consistent with a "big-bang" theory of psychotherapy, which closely parallels the cosmological theory that explains the expansion of the universe and why stars are moving away from each other. As applied to therapy, here is the view. At the beginning of time, or maybe a few moments before (I have not worked this part out yet), there was one swirling mix of suggestion, placebo effects, general relationship factors, learning, persuasion, and conflict resolution. These must have heated, formed a mass, and then exploded in an ever-expanding universe of more and more treatment techniques. Instead of expanding in space, each splits into more and more fragments and combinations.

As mentioned previously, there has been an informal tracking of the number of therapy techniques, beginning in the 1960s (approximately 60 different types of psychotherapies) and continuing through the 1980s (over 400 treatments). These were treatments used primarily in the context of adult psychotherapy. Child and adolescent therapies are less well charted. My own informal effort to document these therapies (Kazdin, 1988) revealed over 230 different treatments in use with children or adolescents. A more comprehensive search has revealed over 550 treatments. (A list of these treatments is provided in appendix A at the end of this book.) This count cannot be considered precise because there is no formal way of entering or registering a new technique into the world nor a way to look up all treatments in use. Researchers and clinicians do not formally patent their new therapies. When professionals publish or present their work—in a book, article, convention presentation, or workshop—the technique is available to be counted. No doubt there are many undocumented treatments. Consider the treatments in the appendix merely as an estimate, no doubt an underestimate because of the omission of undocumented treatments.

Other obstacles in interpreting the number of treatments in use reflect broader problems. Sometimes the name of treatment may be the same, but the procedures can be quite different. For example, social skills training often refers to quite different treatments. Often a name is used consistently, but the versions of treatment differ in format (group vs. individual, duration, and the use of adjunctive procedures). When does a variation become a distinguishable treatment? Further, the same or seemingly the same treatment occasionally may have different names. For example, parent management training refers to procedures to train parents to interact differently with their child and invokes several behavior modification procedures. Sometimes the intervention is referred to as contingency management in the home. To the extent that similar treatments are given different names, the treatment count can be "padded" with treatments that overlap in some way. (An effort was made to minimize this in constructing appendix A.)

Finally, the number of current treatments in use is difficult to capture because of how treatments are used. Eclectic treatment includes combinations of different therapies or different components (techniques) of therapies. All sorts of techniques can be combined in innumerable possibilities. In principle and practice, the number of treatments in use would be difficult to document; once documented, the count is likely already outdated.

The Research Agenda

The large number of treatments attests to the inventiveness of mental health professionals. Plainly, there are many treatment options from which to draw. Yet there are reasons for alarm. Well over 90% of the treatments in use (as listed

in appendix A) have never been subjected to controlled or uncontrolled outcome studies. That is, we have not even a morsel of evidence that these treatments work or help children or families. Consider, for purposes of simplicity,
three possible effects of treatments on the problems to which they are applied:
helpful, neutral, or harmful. These effects should be determined before application. Even neutral therapies might be considered harmful if their application
inadvertently prevented or delayed application of another viable treatment.

With many clinical problems to treat and many treatments available, the situation seems like a perfect match: A huge grid or table can represent the agenda
for researchers and clinicians. That grid lists clinical problems along the side
(labeling the rows) and treatments on the top (the columns) to find out what
treatments work with what problems. Now we have several thousand blank
cells, and each cell could represent a study or two. More concretely, if we assume 200 types of child clinical problems and conservatively say there are 500
treatments, we would *just* need to complete the 100,000 studies to have the answers—well, probably 200,000 studies because replication is pivotal in scientific research. The number is large but at least finite. As studies are completed,
we could fill in the cells, knowing that progress was made.

If the grid is even partially tempting to the reader, consider that a grid would
need to be made for children and adolescents at different points in development
because the effectiveness of a given treatment, as applied to a given problem,
could well vary with the age and the developmental stage of the child. So we
would need separate grids for different ages (although maybe not for all ages).
Still tempted by the grid idea? Well, forget it again—some treatments are more
effective with girls than with boys, so we would want a separate grid by sex of
the child. We could only hope that separate grids are not needed for different
ethnic groups, but this hope could prove to be false. The idea of filling out a
grid with empirical studies is pretty much the wrong focus. Even if this were
feasible, the grid idea ignores the need to *understand* how treatment works, for
whom treatment works, and the conditions under which treatment works.

Because there are many treatments and many problems to which they can be
applied, it is natural to address the obvious and important question of treatment
outcome. Does treatment A work (produce change) with clinical problem X? Is
treatment A or B more effective? If treatment A is modified in some way, will
its effectiveness be improved? These questions are important and have come to
dominate treatment research. These questions pose an endless research agenda
and divert attention from even more critical issues.

The large number of techniques currently in use ought to underscore the importance of understanding how treatments work. Do different mechanisms or
processes explain why or how each treatment produces therapeutic change? For
the treatments known to produce change, we have little idea about mechanisms
of change. Understanding the basis for treatment effects is not merely of academic interest. Once we understand how change occurs, treatments can be applied more effectively. Aspects of treatment that are responsible for, or directly
contribute to, therapeutic change can be fostered, maximized, or emphasized.

The number of available treatments presents a challenge for research and clinical practice common to child, adolescent, and adult psychotherapy. That challenge is to identify what is responsible for change and to determine whether a few key processes might unify or explain the many different variants of treatment. Understanding mechanisms of change may be more productive than evaluating the many individual treatments.

SPECIAL CHALLENGES OF TREATING CHILDREN AND ADOLESCENTS

Many challenges and obstacles to providing treatment are inherent in the enterprise itself. Clinical problems often include features (e.g., sadness, immobilization, panic, personality disorder) that make treatment delivery difficult in any given session or in general. (How much easier it would be if the people who came to treatment had absolutely no problems!) Beyond the usual tasks of therapy, special challenges emerge in providing treatment to children and adolescents. These challenges affect the administration and evaluation of treatment and have direct implications for research. Salient challenges include identifying what problems warrant treatment, assessing child functioning, providing therapy when the child or adolescent may not see any need for treatment, deciding the focus of treatment, and retaining children and families in therapy.

Identifying Dysfunction

The initial task of identifying problems worthy of treatment raises special issues. Extreme and pervasive departures from normative functioning, by definition, warrant special intervention. Examples include autism and more severe forms of mental retardation, as highlighted in the previous chapter. These pervasive developmental disorders are relatively easily recognizable, at least when compared to anxiety, depression, and hyperactivity. Yet the pervasive disorders are not usually the focus of various forms of psychotherapy for children and adolescents.

The social, emotional, and behavioral problems most frequently seen in treatment are externalizing (oppositional, conduct, and hyperactivity) and internalizing (anxiety, depression, withdrawal) behaviors. Most of the symptoms that comprise these problems are relatively common even in normative development. For example, fears, fighting, lying, difficulty in concentrating, and social withdrawal are symptoms of recognized disorders, yet they are also relatively common at different points in development. Of course, usually the clinically severe versions are more extreme, but this is not always easy to discern. Separation fears in young children, for example, can be very upsetting to the "normal" child and can disrupt the child's and parents' lives by interfering with attending or remaining in day care, adding to marital conflict, and increasing stress for a parent related to his or her job. Even so, mild problems of everyday life can be quite challenging. Identifying a pattern of behavior as a problem worthy of intervention is a problem that is difficult for parents, teachers, and physicians, who are often responsible for referring cases to treatment. There is no "psychological thermometer" to determine a social, emotional, or behavioral "fever."

Identifying a problem or dysfunction worthy of treatment is difficult because of a related obstacle: namely, the behavior or characteristic of the child may not be deviant or significant at all. Rather, the significance of the behavior may rest on when the problem occurs over the course of development. For example, the implications and long-term outcome of a behavioral pattern such as fighting or bedwetting depend on the age of the child (e.g., 2 vs. 10 years old). Bedwetting in middle and later childhood but not in early childhood (before age 5) is a risk factor for later psychopathology (Rutter, Yule, & Graham, 1973). One ought to evaluate and intervene in middle to late childhood but probably not in early childhood. The obstacle in identifying the problem is the absence of clear and readily available information about normative development and quite varied parental thresholds for identifying when there is a problem. In my own experience, I have seen many children younger than 4 punished for bedwetting and others older than 10 whose parents were not concerned at all about the complete lack of bladder and bowel control (enuresis and encopresis).

Identification of dysfunction among children concerns not just the appearance of a symptom or symptom constellation but rather the relation of that characteristic to expected development. Judgment comes into play. What to expect over the course of development may be clear to health professionals like pediatricians or clinicians working with children. However, parents and teachers who usually initiate the treatment-referral process may have aberrant expectations about normal development. I can cite examples from four separate families at a clinic in which I am involved, in which parents

- physically beat their infant for crying when he was hungry;
- whipped their toddler with a belt because he still was not fully toilet trained at age 2;
- awakened and beat up a 7-year-old boy in the middle of the night because he had not washed all of the dishes in the sink; and
- held down and repeatedly hit a 10-year-old boy because he forgot one item while completing the grocery shopping by himself.

In each case, parental expectations rather than child deviance or impairment were the central features of the problem. That is, none of the children's behaviors was developmentally unique, out of step, or otherwise remarkable. (And, of course, even if it were, abusive parenting practices would not have been appropriate.) The examples illustrate the strong role that parental expectations can play in designating behavior as appropriate or inappropriate, deviant or nondeviant. Decisions about whom to bring to treatment occasionally are based on a mismatch of child performance and parental expectations, rather than on clinical dysfunction or impairment on the part of the child.

With a child's maturation and socialization, many problematic behaviors, emotional reactions, and maladaptive cognitions subside. For example, most adults are toilet trained, do not suck their thumbs (or for that matter anyone else's thumbs), and do not cry themselves to sleep because of darkness or monsters in the bedroom. The specific age or point in development at which some problem behaviors emerge and subside can be identified only approximately. That is, both the age of onset and age of termination of the "problem" have a mean (average age at which children develop the behavior, average age of termination), and there are individual differences (variability about each mean). Some behaviors clearly are problematic and impair functioning, but others are not so easily identified. Thus, one of the challenges of child and adolescent treatment is deciding whether the qualitative or quantitative characteristics of the behavior are maladaptive or within the normative range for the child's age or development level. These can be subtle judgments for trained and untrained individuals alike.

Assessing Dysfunction

Measuring clinical problems in children and adolescents raises special challenges that affect treatment and treatment research. Children and adolescents are often asked to report on their own dysfunction. An initial issue is the extent to which children are capable of reporting, or willing to report, on their social, emotional, and behavioral problems. Measures often ask subtle questions about the onset, duration, and intensity of specific symptoms. Can children report on their symptoms and their functioning in everyday life? Clearly they can, but their ability to do so depends on the nature of the problem and characteristics of the children (LaGreca, 1990).

As a guideline, children younger than 5 are usually not considered to be reliable reporters on self-report measures (interviews, paper-and-pencil measures with items read to the child). The standard interpretation is that young children may lack the cognitive development necessary to identify the behavior as a problem, to see that it is leading to or associated with impairment, and to realize that something could be done about it. Plainly, many adults cannot do this either. Perspective taking and metacognitions (thoughts about thought processes) are not likely to be well developed in young children. Perspective taking requires seeing one's own behavior in context and relative to prior behavior or functioning. Perhaps even more critical, the perspective of the child is likely to be quite different from the perspectives of parents and teachers. For example, a child may be more likely to say that fighting is not his problem but rather a problem of others to whom he is responding in the setting.

A blanket statement about the utility of self-report in young children is difficult to defend. First, not many self-report measures are available that have been well validated for use in early childhood. This could be true because of an accepted belief that children cannot report well on their behavior or recognition that others are better informants. For children ages 8–9 and older, considerable research is available indicating validity of child report (LaGreca, 1990; Mash & Terdal, 1997). Second, the utility of self-report could depend on the presentation of the questions. The framing of the questions may be particularly critical. For example, one could readily find out if the child gets into fights by asking directly about it (Do others at school hit you? Do you hit them back?). More abstract or accusatory questions are likely to be less productive (Do you get into trouble or start fights at school?). Third, the focus or content of the questions no doubt contributes to the utility of self-report. Children may more easily report on some areas, and this could readily vary with age. For example, questions about subjective experience ("Do you get upset when your mom and dad argue?") or about events that have occurred often ("Do you ever go to the nurse's office at school [to evaluate health concerns and one of many signs that may pertain to depression]?") might be more easily answered than questions about changes in symptoms, about impairment, or about meeting role expectations.

Yet self-report in young children cannot be discounted because of age alone. Novelty in presenting the questions can make a great difference in the utility of self-report. For example, asking children to identify which of two puppets is more like them, as the puppets playfully self-disclose social, emotional, and behavioral problems, yields information unlikely to emerge from more direct questions (Measelle, Ablow, Cowan, & Cowan, 1998). Thus, the yield from self-report may in part be a measure of the ability of the investigator as well as of the child.

Parents are usually the primary source of information about child functioning because they know about the child's behavior over time and across situations and usually play a central role in the referral of children for treatment. Social, emotional, and behavioral problems often reflect a departure from a child's usual behavior (e.g., no longer interacting with friends, loss of interest in activities). Parents are in a unique position to comment on change. Parent evaluations usually are obtained on standardized rating scales such as the Behavior Problem Checklist and Child Behavior Checklist that assess several domains of child functioning (aggression, hyperactivity, anxiety, depression). Typically, parents are asked to rate the extent to which their child shows a particular symptom on a 3-point scale (0 = not at all, 1 = sometimes, 2 = often). Scores of studies have attested to the utility and validity of parent reports well beyond the confines of treatment research.

The information parents provide about their child's functioning raises further interpretive problems. For example, parent (usually maternal) perceptions of child adjustment and functioning are related to parent psychopathology (especially anxiety and depression), marital discord, stressors, and social support outside of the home (see Kazdin, 1994b). Parents with their own psychopathology or who are experiencing stress are more likely to rate their children as deviant, even when other, independently obtained evidence suggests that the children are no more deviant than children of parents with fewer symptoms or stressors. Thus, parent reports of child deviance are shaded by parent dysfunction (psychopathology, stress). This is a unique issue for child treatment and evaluation of child functioning. Child improvement at the end of treatment may reflect actual changes in the child, reductions in parental stress, or some combination of both. Similarly, lack of improvement on parent-completed measures may be the result of continued or increased parent stress, even though the child may have actually improved. In short, parent functioning may affect a child's level of deviance before and after treatment, at least on parent-report measures.

Since parent-report measures are the most frequently used measures to evaluate treatment, this is a concern within child therapy.

The use of multiple informants and multiple methods of assessment (e.g., self-report, other report, direct observation) is routinely endorsed as a wise strategy for psychological research in general. In the context of treatment, this strategy is no less important but raises another significant set of challenges. Parents, teachers, and children do not provide corresponding information about the child (Achenbach, McConaughy, & Howell, 1987; Kazdin, 1994b). Thus, children who appear deviant on measures obtained from one source (e.g., parents) may not appear to have problems on measures obtained from another source (e.g., teachers) (see Kazdin, 1989; Offord et al., 1996).

There is no gold standard, such as a laboratory test or solid criterion, to judge clinical disorders for most problems brought to treatment. Realistically, many children referred for treatment are clearly having significant problems, and these are readily detected on diagnostic interviews and parent-completed measures. It would be a mistake to imply that deviance is all in the eyes of the beholder. At the same time, once one omits extreme cases, a child who appears deviant in one context or on one measure may not be deviant in another. I shall take up assessment issues later. However, I mention them here because of the difficulties and challenges that measurement raises in child and adolescent psychotherapy.

Motivation for Seeking Treatment

Consider the paradigm for providing therapy to adults. An adult who is experiencing stress (from divorce or death of a relative) or a significant clinical dysfunction (perhaps anxiety or depression that interferes with work performance) comes to a clinic seeking relief. Although it may have taken some time for the individual to decide to seek treatment and then to take the initial step, the process was initiated by the client. In the vast majority of cases, children and adolescents do not refer themselves for treatment or identify themselves as experiencing stress, symptoms, or problems. Young children may lack the perspective to identify their own psychological impairment and its impact on daily functioning and may not know that therapy is a viable means to help. Also, problems most commonly referred for treatment among children and adolescents involve externalizing or disruptive behavior (e.g., aggression, hyperactivity) (Kazdin, Siegel, & Bass, 1990). In such cases, adults perceive the child as disturbing. Indeed, a cliché of child treatment is that the focus is on *disturbing* rather than *disturbed* behavior. Reports from adults (parents, teachers) serve as the impetus for treatment, so the focus may be in part someone else's stress rather than the child's. Children are less likely to report dysfunction or a problem in relation to their own experience. Of course, adolescents can self-report, although parents and adolescents might not agree about "problematic" behaviors (e.g., behaviors related to substance use and abuse, unprotected sex, vandalism, talk of killing oneself, or excessive concern with body image and extreme dieting).

The absence of a felt problem on the part of the child or adolescent affects the motivation for seeking and remaining in treatment and for engaging in the tasks that the particular treatment approach requires. The challenge for the clinician and researcher is to engage the child in treatment. Getting the child to come to treatment is a significant obstacle. Although the parent is "in control" of the decision to begin the treatment process, likely the child may be much more interested in staying after school for soccer practice than enduring therapy sessions. Occasionally, a child will throws tantrums or enact extremes of disruptive behavior associated with coming to treatment. In a case I recall, a mother arrived at the clinic in tears holding an audiocassette with most of the tape pulled out, badly tangled. The scene required some explanation, which she provided before I could comment. Apparently, on the way to the session, the boy tore the insides of the upholstery of the car (inside doors and roof) and destroyed the parent's nostalgia-filled audiotape (he pulled the cassette from the tape player while it was playing). Yet this episode demostrates the extremes of the challenge that bringing a child to treatment can entail. Even in less extreme circumstances, parents sometimes wonder if treatment is worth the challenge of getting the child to come to the sessions. Their perseverance is often challenged, and it is much easier not to come.

In treatment sessions, the therapist will employ various techniques to achieve the treatment goals. The techniques could involve talk, play, role-play, games, or a meeting with the entire family. Getting the child to participate in these activities is a challenge. Many therapists want the child to grasp the point of the activities. But the child may have little motivation, interest, or incentive to be in treatment, especially since he or she may be sacrificing more pleasant activities, such as hanging out with friends. Removing the child from school for the therapy sessions, when feasible, overcomes this objection for most children. Yet the parent is likely to ask, is treatment worth the loss of school time? In short, getting children to treatment and engaging them in the session present special challenges.

Focus of Treatment

Obviously, or so it would seem, the child is brought to treatment because he or she has a problem or significant impairment. The child is naturally the target of treatment. Yet children, and indeed all of us, function in a context or set of systems that influence what we do (Brofenbrenner, 1979; Lerner, 1991). *Context*, for purposes of this discussion, refers to the environmental factors in which the child functions and encompasses interpersonal relations (parents, peers, siblings), systems (family, school), and settings (neighborhoods). Although we all depend on the contexts in which we live and function, the dependence of children on adults makes them particularly vulnerable to influences over which they have little control.

Many adverse contextual influences can be identified that affect child functioning and have direct implications for child adjustment and psychopathology. Familiar examples include poor prenatal care and nutrition, maternal prenatal substance abuse, physical and sexual abuse, and neglect of the child. In relation to the delivery of treatment, some contextual influences are particularly important because they influence attendance to, participation in, and effects of the intervention. For example, among children and adolescents with externalizing problems, socioeconomic disadvantage, high levels of stress, and parental psychopathology can affect whether families will attend treatment and, among those who do attend, the extent to which the children will improve and maintain their improvements over time (Dadds & McHugh, 1992; Kazdin, 1995a; Kazdin & Wassell, 1999; Webster-Stratton, 1985).

The child's dependence on parent and family influences and evidence that many of these influences are somehow involved in the child's problems raise questions about the appropriate focus of treatment. To whom should the treatment be directed? Major options include the child, parents, the family (as a unit), teachers, peers, and siblings. Of course, at a broader level one might also target neighborhoods, cities, and society at large (e.g., through legislation or social policy) to reduce clinical dysfunction. In clinical work, treatment of child or adolescent dysfunction usually incorporates the parent, family, and teacher in some way (Kazdin, Siegel, & Bass, 1990; Koocher & Pedulla, 1977) perhaps involving parents in the sessions with the child, seeing parents separately, meeting with the family, and using the teacher to assess or intervene at school (as in a behavior modification program in the classroom). Point of intervention is especially complex for child treatment in general because of the range of options.

If children are particularly dependent on the parent and family, perhaps the parent and family are the best foci for intervention. This focus could be justified on one of two grounds. First, several of the forces or influences that promote or sustain the child's problems could be within the family or interpersonal context. In other words, contextual influences could be considered pertinent to the development of the problem. Second, changing contextual influences could a valuable way to alter child functioning. That is, no matter how the problem came about, changing aspects of the context might be an excellent way to effect change.

Contexts and their influence change over the course of development. Thus, in relation to treatment, it might make sense to involve the parents extensively in the treatment of young children. For adolescents, perhaps peers might need to be involved in treatment, given their critical influence on behavior. It is easy to say generally that treatment may need to consider contextual influences. From the perspective of providing treatment clinically or investigating treatment, involving others in the child's treatment raises its own obstacles.

Some facets of the parent and family context may warrant intervention as part of or as a precondition for effective treatment of the child. For example, marital conflict, spouse abuse, and substance abuse often affect children referred to treatment at the clinic where I work. Some of these problems may directly influence concurrent child deviance, for example, some of the child maltreatment and harsh discipline occurs in the context of marital conflict. Other facets of the context, such as substance abuse, may need to be incorporated into a treatment plan as well. Omnipresent contextual influences may be relevant to therapy for adults as well as children. Treatment for children may be a bit more intricate because many of these influences need to be considered directly in the treatment process (e.g., Cobham, Dadds, & Spence, 1998; Dadds, Schwartz, & Sanders, 1987; Henggeler, Schoenwald, Borduin, Rowland, & Cunningham, 1998). For example, any significant conflict between adults (marital partners, spouses, and live-in relatives) may need to be addressed directly as part of treatment because it could relate to the child's problem or influence execution of treatment prescriptions.

Remaining in Treatment

Retaining children and families in treatment is a significant challenge. Among children who begin treatment, 40–60% drop out prematurely, against the advice of the clinician (Kazdin, 1996b; Wierzbicki & Pekarik, 1993). Perhaps the reasons can be deduced from points already highlighted. Lack of motivation creates problems in attending and continuing in treatment. Indeed, as already mentioned, parent-child battles about going to treatment may occur because the competing activities for the child in that time slot (television, video games, hanging around, after-school sports, etc.) are a much stronger draw than treatment sessions. Many parents simply do not wish to fight these battles. Many parent and family problems (e.g., marital conflict, stress in the home, parent clinical dysfunction) or difficult living circumstances (e.g., socioeconomic disadvantage), provide further obstacles to remaining in treatment. Parents may disagree with each other about whether the child ought to be brought to treatment, and that too can make treatment a source of tension. These points do not exhaust the range of factors that might make participation in treatment difficult. For example, among oppositional, aggressive, and antisocial children, dropping out of treatment is predicted by many adverse contextual factors mentioned previously (e.g., socioeconomic disadvantage, high stress) as well as severity of child dysfunction, obstacles associated with coming to treatment, parental views that treatment is too demanding, and a poor relationship between parent and therapist (e.g., Kazdin et al., 1997; Kazdin, Stolar, & Marciano, 1995).

Retaining cases in treatment remains a special challenge. Contextual influences play a role in remaining in treatment. Consequently, if one is not focusing on the parents or family, one may be ignoring parent and family factors that may need to be addressed to retain the family in treatment (Prinz & Miller, 1994; Szapocznik et al., 1988). These challenges differ from those of adult therapy.

General Comments

Each challenge reflects the interface of theoretical and applied considerations. For example, identifying the appropriate or optimal focus of treatment is easier when one understands factors that contribute to or maintain deviance and factors that can be mobilized to produce change. Characteristics of child development and the role of contextual influences and variation of key influences over the course of development are among the topics essential to inform therapy. Thus, identifying effective treatments is not merely a matter of developing and testing an intervention that will reduce or eliminate the problems leading to clinical referral. Several other tasks and obstacles must be addressed that permit the intervention to be delivered, that consider how the child is brought to treatment (by whom, for what reason), and that recognize, account for, and integrate contextual influences in which treatment is embedded. This process is not very different from medical treatment. The intervention (e.g., surgery) alone does not determine whether treatment is successful (e.g., the outcome from bypass surgery, or organ transplant). In addition, patient characteristics (e.g., depression) and behavior (e.g., exercise, diet) also predict the outcome. Administration of treatment must take into account other factors that influence the desired long-term outcome. In child treatment, clearly the child's problems need to be addressed, probably directly. The overarching challenge is to figure out how. The factors that influence the child are not all *within* the child. Identifying, weighing, selecting, and altering the pertinent factors are major challenges.

SUMMARY AND CONCLUSIONS

There are many different approaches to treatment, including psychoanalytic, psychodynamic, family, behavioral, cognitive-behavioral, experiential, existential/humanistic, and integrative-eclectic approaches. These terms are meaningful because they convey the overall orientation of the treatments. When a clinician or researcher may identify with an approach, this does not necessarily convey the specific treatments used in daily clinical work. Hundreds of psychosocial treatments are applied to children and adolescents. Our research group identified over 550 (appendix A); that count may reflect our endurance in documenting the ever-expanding universe of "new" interventions. The extent to which they are all different is arguable.

There are many treatments and not much regulation of clinical practice. The result has been a proliferation of techniques applied to children and adolescents, with no initial information required about safety and effectiveness. Any informed citizen might want to ask some obvious questions of these treatments:

- Do any of the treatments work?
- Which ones work best?
- Do they all work for different reasons or through some common mechanism?

The researcher will refine and focus these questions and answer them in complex ways (e.g., with multiple outcomes). Yet the basic questions remain. One solution is to start evaluating the treatments as applied to specific problems. Obviously, research of this type is essential. Yet a pile of outcome studies, no matter how elegantly designed each study is, is in essence just a pile of outcome studies. Much more is needed to make progress, as I detail later.

Apart from the research agenda, there are major challenges in delivering treatments to children and adolescents: identifying and measuring child dysfunction, the motivation or absence of motivation of the children seeking treatment, identifying the target(s) or focus of treatment (e.g., child, parents, family), and retaining families in treatment. These challenges require a deeper understanding of clinical dysfunction, treatments, and the contexts in which they are provided.

I have suggested that progress will require understanding both the treatment and the mechanisms through which it operates. Before addressing some of the daunting questions that such understanding requires, we can begin by considering what treatments seem to be effective. Effective treatments are often developed with very little understanding of how they work. For example, many medications (e.g., stimulants for hyperactive children) and psychosocial interventions (e.g., hypnosis, suggestion) work for reasons that are not initially known. The basic question—does this treatment work?—often leads to study of the more complex questions. The primary focus of this book is on the evidence for the basis of providing therapy to children and adolescents. We need to evaluate the existing evidence, as well as identify the long-term goals of psychotherapy research and how to achieve these goals. The next chapters of the book evaluate the evidence.

FOR FURTHER READING

Several sources are available that convey approaches to treatment and specific treatments that are applied to children and adolescents. Over the years there has been a departure away from approaches. Reviews of the evidence are more likely to be organized by clinical problems (e.g., treatments for depression, anxiety), as reflected in some of the readings noted below.

Ammerman, R.T., Last, C.G., & Hersen, M. (Eds.). (1999). *Handbook of prescriptive treatments for children and adolescents* (2nd ed.). Needham Heights, MA: Allyn & Bacon.

Johnson, J.H., Rasbury, W.C., & Siegel, L.J. (1986). *Approaches to child treatment: Introduction to theory, research, and practice.* New York: Pergamon.

Mash, E.J., & Barkley, R. (Eds.). (1998). *Treatment of childhood disorders* (2nd ed.). New York: Guilford.

Morris, R.J., & Kratochwill, T.R (Eds.). (1998). *The practice of child therapy.* Needham Heights, MA: Allyn & Bacon.

PART II

Evidence: Major Findings, Strengths, and Limitations

Chapter 4

The Effects of Psychotherapy: Current Status of the Evidence

THE MOST FUNDAMENTAL QUESTION about therapy is whether it works. Do people get better? How great it would be if the question could be one question and a simple one at that. This fundamental question has been rejected long ago because it is much too simplistic. The simplicity can be conveyed by substituting another word for psychotherapy and asking the same question. For example, does *education* (or surgery, child rearing, medication, exercise) work? Psychotherapy and these other endeavors encompass many components (e.g., types of treatment or surgery or child-rearing practices) as independent variables and many consequences or outcomes (e.g., feeling better, actually showing fewer symptoms, performing better in one's relationships or at work) as dependent variables. At the very least, the conclusions about psychotherapy vary according to the type of treatment and type of outcome. Yet, the global question of whether therapy works continues to be of interest despite pleas to ask more specific and indeed entirely different questions. If one requires a quick answer—yes, it does work. But many of the treatments in use lack supportive evidence. Obviously, any statement about whether therapy works requires a number of qualifiers.

There are well over a thousand controlled studies that examine various forms of treatment for children and adolescents. From so many studies we ought to be able to draw conclusions about the effects of treatment, the extent to which children and adolescents improve, and the many nuances of treatment effects. This chapter and the next one consider the evidence and what can be said based on that evidence about the effects of therapy.

METHODS OF EVALUATING THE EVIDENCE

Although it might seem reasonable to start actually evaluating the evidence, the methods of evaluating the evidence warrant comment. How the evidence is examined and weighed can contribute to the conclusions reached. Methods of reviewing the evidence on the effects of psychological treatments have evolved along with the empirical studies themselves. First, the dominant review method had been the *narrative* or *qualitative review* in which reviewers sift through individual studies and summarize what conclusions can and cannot be supported. This method relies on an author's evaluation of the strength and merit of the individual studies and the patterns that emerge from them. Narrative reviews were the first to be used to evaluate the evidence for the effects of psychotherapy for adults (Eysenck, 1952) and for children and adolescents (Levitt, 1957, 1963). Narrative reviews remain the most commonly used method to evaluate the child and adolescent therapy literature, as many edited books and journal articles attest (e.g., Kendall & Chambless, 1998; Lonigan & Elbert, 1998; Mash & Barkley, 1998; Morris & Kratochwill, 1998).

Second, *quantitative reviews* recently have become more influential. Meta-analyses (Smith & Glass, 1977) and, to a lesser extent, box-score methods (Luborsky, Singer, & Luborsky, 1975) are efforts to codify and combine studies systematically and quantitatively. Box-score methods tally studies based on whether they support a particular finding (e.g., out of 10 studies, 6 show an effect, 3 do not, 1 is unclear). This method is not used too frequently because it neglects the characteristics of the studies and represents a rather gross level of analysis (see Kazdin & Wilson, 1978b). However, the box-score method is important to mention in passing because it reflects an interest in moving to quantifiable ways of integrating a large body of studies. Meta-analysis currently is the preferred way of reviewing the evidence because it provides a way to integrate a large number of studies systematically, using replicable procedures and explicit decision rules. Also, the method permits the reviewer to describe characteristics and patterns in the studies and to test hypotheses about influences those individual studies do not usually examine. Early meta-analyses focused on both adult and child treatments (Smith & Glass, 1977; Smith, Glass, & Miller, 1980) and child treatments alone (Casey & Berman, 1985; Kazdin, Bass, Ayers, & Rodgers, 1990; Weisz, Weiss, Alicke, & Klotz, 1987).

Third, a review of *validated* or *empirically supported treatments* has become another way to evaluate the literature. In this type of review, the evidence is examined from the perspective of a common set of criteria to select individual studies. Criteria are invoked to classify treatments based on the extent to which they are empirically supported (i.e., as showing that treatment produces systematic change in controlled trials). The reviewer asks the general question,

"What is known to be effective (i.e., empirically supported) for a particular clinical problem based on available studies that meet specific criteria?" Reviews of this type tend to be qualitative rather than quantitative (see Kendall & Chambless, 1998; Lonigan, Elbert, & Johnson, 1998), but the method of conducting the review is not as critical as is the focus or purpose of the review.

Each method of reviewing a body of literature contributes to the conclusions that one can reach about the effects of treatment. Each method relies on the same raw data: the individual investigations themselves. However, how these investigations are used, viewed, and selected is important. This chapter considers what qualitative and quantitative reviews say about the effects of child and adolescent therapy; the next chapter examines reviews of empirically supported treatments.

HISTORICAL CHALLENGE

Early Reviews of Outcome Research

Historically, evaluating the effects of psychotherapy began with narrative reviews. Well known in the adult psychotherapy literature is the review of Eysenck (1952), which invariably is a starting point in modern evaluations of psychotherapy. Eysenck's initial review focused on 19 studies of various psychoanalytic, psychodynamic, and eclectic therapies with adults. Eysenck revised and expanded the review in 1960 and 1966 and included children, adolescents, and adults across a wide range of contexts and clinical problems (e.g., soldiers who suffered stress reactions, adults and children with emotional problems). The conclusions were similar in each evaluation of the literature, namely, that approximately two thirds of clients who receive therapy improve over the course of treatment. More significantly, this is approximately the same rate of improvement among clients who do not receive therapy. In other words, there was no evidence to indicate that psychotherapy was effective.

The impact of Eysenck's review was enormous; rebuttals, critiques, and re-reviews, and other types of works were generated. The effects continue in contemporary writings (see Bergin & Garfield, 1994; Eysenck, 1995). The specifics of the review, the treatises that followed, and the impact of the exchanges need not be traced here (see Kazdin, 1978b). Suffice it to say that Eysenck's original review probably accomplished the most that one can hope for from an article: to provoke thought and discussion and to influence the quality of research that follows.

In the child literature, parallel reviews were completed in these early years of treatment research, although their impact has not been as jarring or productive in stimulating thought or treatment research. The reviews begin with Levitt (1957), who evaluated 18 studies of child psychotherapy. The review focused on youths whose problems could be classified generally as neuroses, a term no longer used. (Internalizing problems such as anxiety, depression, and withdrawal would be roughly parallel, but the key would be symptoms that are not sufficiently debilitating to warrant hospitalization or to constitute a pervasive type of disorder.) Studies with delinquents, mentally retarded persons, and psychotic patients were excluded. Levitt's analysis indicated that improvement among children who received psychotherapy was approximately 67–78% at posttreatment and follow-up, respectively. Children who did not receive treatment improved at about the same rate (73%). Thus, the general conclusion was that the efficacy of traditional forms of psychotherapy for children had not been demonstrated.

Levitt's review indicated that there was no evidence that therapy was effective. The clarity of the summary statement resulting from the initial review masked a number of problems. To begin, the "children" encompassed by the studies were quite diverse in age (preschool age to 21 years old) and clinical dysfunctions. Second, baseline or improvement rates of nontreated youths were derived from only two studies and from children who received treatment but terminated it early. Thus, the "control" or comparison groups to which treated children were compared were children who dropped out of treatment. Youths who fail to complete treatment likely differ systematically from youths who complete treatment and hence do not provide an adequate picture of the base rate of improvement without treatment. Third, improvement rates were based on evaluation of children by the therapists at the end of treatment. Therapist ratings alone, especially by current methodological standards, certainly are limited as a measure of treatment outcome. (Measurement will be discussed in a later chapter.)

As might be expected, Levitt's review generated a number of rebuttals and re-evaluations of the data (Eisenberg & Gruenberg, 1961; Heinicke & Goldman, 1960; Hood-Williams, 1960). The rebuttals raised cogent points that not only challenged Levitt's conclusions but also drew attention to important methodological issues in designing outcome studies. These included the need to consider variation of children's problems and family factors as moderators of treatment and the importance of using multiple measures to examine treatment outcome. Essentially, the rebuttals concluded that the original method of analysis, criteria, and research reviewed by Levitt did not permit clear conclusions about the effects of treatment or no treatment.

Levitt's (1963) subsequent review evaluated 22 additional studies and addressed a number of criticisms, such as consideration of different diagnoses or types of clinical problems. But the conclusions essentially remained the same. Summing across diagnostic groups, Levitt's analyses showed improvements in treated and untreated youths at approximately 65% and slightly below the rate of children who did not receive treatment (73%). Rebuttals and re-evaluations of these later reviews continued (Barrett, Hampe, & Miller, 1978; Heinicke & Strassmann, 1975).

Over the period of reviews and rebuttals, the need for greater specificity in evaluating treatment became quite apparent. One sign was the initial effort to distinguish different diagnostic groups. For example, Levitt (1963) noted that improvement rates were greater for neurotic patients than for those who were delinquent or psychotic. Delineating diagnostic groups, as a move toward more precise analyses of treatment effects, was a step in a needed direction. More recent evaluations of psychotherapy suggest that outcomes may depend on many different characteristics of treatments, patients, therapists, and outcome measures (e.g., Casey & Berman, 1985; Smith & Glass, 1977; Smith et al., 1980; Weisz et al., 1987).

Formulation of the Research Question

The early reviews not only prompted concern about the effects of psychotherapy but also about the questions that ought to guide psychotherapy research and the methods of studying therapy. The question underlying the early narrative reviews was, "Does psychotherapy work?" Very early after the reviews appeared, the question was regarded as much too general (Bergin & Lambert, 1978; Edwards & Cronbach, 1952). After all, psychotherapy is a general term that encompasses many different treatments. It is not especially meaningful to lump them all together and to provide a simple yes or no answer to the question, as noted previously. Similarly, there are many different mental disorders and clinical problems and it would not be very reasonable or meaningful to expect a simple answer in asking whether a given treatment is equally effective for all of the disorders and problems to which it could be applied.

An elegant criticism of the simplistic theory question was provided by Kiesler (1966, 1971), who introduced the notion of the *uniformity myth*. The myth refers to an assumption that the effects of psychotherapy will be the same (uniform) no matter to whom or how it is applied. The question, "Does therapy work?," assumes that most patients, therapists, and treatments are homogeneous, or at least more alike than different. Also, the assumption extends to various outcomes of treatment or domains that change. The uniformity assumption here is that therapeutic improvement is basically homogeneous across all measures and that one measure might just as well be substituted for another.

The simplistic question, riddled with uniformity myths, does not consider the complex factors that may contribute to outcome: individual differences of the patients and therapists (e.g., personality characteristics and other distinguishing variables), conditions of therapy administration (e.g., how treatment is applied), and the criteria used to evaluate treatment. Stated in more methodological and statistical terms, the simple question looks for a main effect of therapy, that it works equally well across a wide range of conditions. The uniformity myth raises the prospect that therapy effects are part of interactions. In other words, the effects will depend on characteristics of patients, therapies, and conditions of treatment administration. Furthermore, effective treatment may require carefully matching patient problems, therapists, and treatments to optimize therapeutic change.

Through similar discussions about how to evaluate psychotherapy, the global question (Does psychotherapy work?) was replaced by a more specific question. Here are two versions of the more specific question to guide research:

- "*What* treatment, by *whom*, is most effective for *this* individual with *that* specific problem, under *which* set of circumstances?" (Paul, 1967, p. 111); and

- "What kind of therapists administering what kind of psychotherapeutic treatments to what kind of patients produce what kinds of perceived effects, both immediate and ultimate?" (Fiske, 1977, p. 24).

These new questions, highlight the importance of examining the specific effects of various treatments for a particular clinical problem and acknowledge that the effects of treatments may depend on characteristics of the patients, therapists, and conditions under which treatment is provided.

Clearly the more specific question improves on the simplistic version it was intended to replace. And this question now guides contemporary research, even though there are clearly problems in answering it. As mentioned in the previous chapter, the task of evaluating therapy would be monumental if one were *merely* to address the effectiveness of many different treatments as applied to many different clinical problems. If one adds the type of clients and the type of therapist, the already unfeasible task begins to seem absurd. Moreover, the effects (outcomes) of therapy can be measured in an indefinite number of ways based on the area of functioning that is measured (e.g., symptoms, impairment, social behavior), the source of information (e.g., patient, relative, or therapist), and the type of measure (e.g., direct observation of the patient's behavior, ratings completed by others). Conclusions about the effectiveness of treatment or the relative effectiveness of two different treatments may be quite different depending on the outcome measures. Consequently, the guiding question may not be answerable. Later in the book, I shall return to the questions that can and ought to guide therapy research. At this point, let us consider the effectiveness of therapy across the various conditions in which it has been evaluated.

The brief historical comments identified early reviews and questions and provided a context for much of contemporary research and reviews of that research. I highlighted the early reviews to suggest the verdict on the effects of psychotherapy and to mention the question ("What works with whom . . . ?") that the reviews prompted. Early reviews focused on the paucity of studies, methodological shortcomings, and neglect of the range of variables likely to influence treatment outcome (e.g., child age, clinical problem). Rather than trace this history, later I shall discuss critical issues that mar contemporary research and ways to rectify them. Perhaps of even greater importance, in the last few years, the criteria for evaluating treatment outcome and for conducting outcome research more generally have changed. Early reviews did not focus on the level of specificity now considered essential, namely, evaluating different treatments as applied to different types of problems, across different measures, at different points in time.

CONTEMPORARY EVALUATIONS

Meta-analysis has become a preferred way of reviewing the body of treatment research for many reasons, including its ability to focus on the many variables on which treatment outcome depends. Indeed, a narrative review would not easily allow an author to draw conclusions systematically about the extent to which the effectiveness of a particular treatment depends on patient, therapist, and other characteristics. In some way, the what works with whom question requires a systematic method of examining the data. As there are now hundreds and hundreds of studies, drawing a few summary conclusions from this literature could be daunting because the studies vary along so many dimensions (e.g., age of the children, experience of the therapists, target problem or foci of treatment, and treatment technique). Meta-analytic reviews provide a systematic way to summarize the studies and to cull patterns in a quantifiable way.

Meta-Analysis

OVERVIEW OF THE FINDINGS. A major development in the evaluation of psychotherapy research was the emergence of meta-analysis, an alternative to the narrative and qualitative review. Narrative reviews have tended to draw different conclusions about the same literature (see Smith et al., 1980). Part of the problem with a narrative review is the absence of established rules for evaluating, combining, and weighing studies based on their merit or strength of effects or for drawing conclusions about the effects of a treatment when the results from several studies differ. Even more problematic, studies that use different measures or treatments or focus on slightly or completely different clinical problems are difficult to integrate. Trying to compare outcomes from different studies would be like comparing "apples and oranges," as the cliché goes. Meta-analysis in some sense permits such comparisons. Indeed, if one elects a more abstract metric (e.g., "fruit"), one can easily compare, combine, and integrate applies and oranges.

Meta-analyses are so commonly used in social and biological sciences that it is essential for any researcher to be familiar with their key characteristics, strengths, and pitfalls (see Cook et al., 1992). Meta-analysis refers to a set of quantitative procedures used to evaluate multiple studies. The essential feature is to provide an "analysis of analyses" (Smith et al., 1980, p. 809). Results of a given study are quantified to permit the combination and comparison of results from different studies. This quantification of the results extracts findings and integrates different studies more reliably and consistently than the usual narrative review permits. That is, how a study will be weighed and the strength of the effects are examined in a consistent fashion. Subjectivity is not removed, but the rules for evaluating and combining studies are consistent, explicit, and replicable.

EFFECT SIZE AND ITS MEANING. The most common way of evaluating the literature through meta-analysis is to compute *effect size* (ES), which provides a common metric across investigations. Effect size refers to the magnitude of the difference between two (or more) conditions or groups and is expressed in standard deviation (*SD*) units. In terms of statistical analyses in research, ES is a measure of the magnitude of an effect of a relation and is distinguished from statistical significance. Magnitude refers to how strong the relation is between (or among) variables; statistical significance refers to whether an obtained difference is likely due to chance. The concepts are quite different (see Kazdin, 1998b). There are many different measures of the magnitude of relations; the two most commonly used in psychology are ES and Pearson product-moment correlation (r).

Effect size is used in meta-analyses to evaluate the effectiveness of treatment and is illustrated here. When there are two groups in the study, ES equals the differences between means, divided by the SD or

$$ES = \frac{m_1 - m_2}{s},$$

where m_1 and m_2 are the sample means for two groups or conditions (e.g., treatment and control groups or two different treatments), and s equals the pooled SD for these groups. In meta-analyses, an ES is computed for each study. Because an ES can be computed for each measure or assessment device, usually a mean ES across all measures is used to summarize each study. Effect size constitutes the *dependent measure* for the meta-analysis and is used as a summary statistic to examine the impact of other variables. Characteristics of the investigations become the *independent variables*. All sorts of characteristics of individual studies can be coded and studied, including the type of treatment, duration of treatment, type of clinical problem, age of the participants, how well the study was designed, the types of measures included, and the allegiance of the investigator to one treatment rather than another. Hypotheses about the relations of these characteristics to treatment outcome can be tested.

Let us consider the meaning of ES for a moment. As an example, consider a two-group study that evaluates treatment for children who are experiencing anxiety. Assume the children are assigned to treatment or no-treatment conditions. After the study, children complete a measure of anxiety in which higher scores equal higher levels of anxiety. Suppose that treated children show a posttreatment mean of 20 on the scale, control subjects a score of 27. Suppose that the SD is 10; ES equals .70 (20 minus 27 divided by 10). So we have an ES of .70. What does it mean?

There are two useful guides to interpret ES. First, Cohen (1988) has conveniently provided us with an admittedly arbitrary but quite useful guideline noting small, medium, and large ESs, .20, .50, and .80, respectively. (If the measure were r rather than ES, small, medium, and large effects would correspond to correlations of .10, .30, and .50.) By convention, these magnitudes have become a way of speaking about ESs; that is, an ES of .80 is large.

Second, and related, an ES can be interpreted in relation to the differences in the distributions between two groups. Effect size is a measure in SD units. Figure 4.1 shows two distributions, one for the treatment group and one for the control group. The means of the group (vertical lines) reflect an ES of .70. That signifies the mean of the intervention group is .70 of an SD higher than that of the control group. One can refer to a table of the normal distribution and convert this information into how the intervention group fared relative to the control group in SDs. Given the ES of .70, the average subject (at the mean) treated

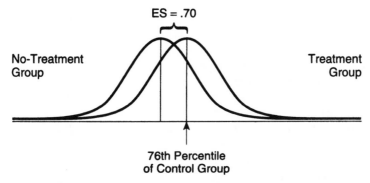

Figure 4.1 Representation of an effect size of .70 between intervention and control groups. Each group is reflected in its own distribution (normal curve). If the groups in fact were not different, the two distributions would be superimposed and would look like one distribution (same mean, same *SD*). With an effect size of .70, the mean of the intervention group is .7 *SD* units above the mean of the control group. The two distributions are discrepant.

is better off than 76% of the persons who did not receive treatment. This percentage was obtained by identifying the percentage of the population below +.70 *SD*s on the normal distribution (for a further discussion, see Kazdin, 1998b). Clearly, psychotherapy moves the mean of the distribution associated with no treatment. As a rule, children assigned to treatment are much better off than those who are not assigned to treatment.[1]

Effects of Treatment

There have been scores of meta-analyses of psychotherapy. In fact, the meta-analyses themselves often serve as the basis for reviews (see Brown, 1987; Matt & Navarro, 1997; Roth & Fonagy, 1996; Weisz & Weisz, 1993)—sort of an analyses of meta-analyses or, as some authors have noted, a meta-meta-analysis (Kazrin, Durac, & Agteros, 1979; Grissom, 1996). All of the work began with the seminal meta-analyses of Smith and Glass (1977) and Smith et al. (1980). In the 1980 study, the more comprehensive of the two, 475 controlled treatment outcome studies were evaluated. An ES was calculated separately for each dependent measure in each study, yielding a total of 1,761 different ESs. Across all of the studies and treatment techniques, the mean ES of psychotherapy was .85 (see Smith et al., 1980, p. 89). Of course, individual treatments and characteristics of the studies were richly elaborated, but two of the more general conclusions are particularly pertinent to this discussion. First, psychotherapies produced greater therapeutic change than no treatment; second, different treatment approaches, based on varied conceptual models (e.g., psychodynamic, behavioral) tended to be equally effective. The conclusions are not revolutionary or even particularly strong. Indeed, many professionals had believed that psychotherapy was effective and that specific approaches did not yield starkly different results. Yet many remembered Eysenck's review. A firm quantitative statement that psychotherapy in fact was better than no treatment would be very welcome indeed. The strength and value of the Smith and Glass evaluations derived from the method they provided rather than the conclusions themselves. Meta-analyses provided a method that seemed less subject to bias than the usual narrative review.

In the past two decades, scores of meta-analyses of psychotherapy have focused on therapy with adults; many are also available for treatment of children and adolescents and include reviews of therapy in general (all available treatments); specific treatment approaches such as cognitive-behavior therapy, group therapy, and family therapy; therapies conducted in special settings such as schools; and therapies that target a specific focus such as preparing children for medical procedures (e.g., tests and surgery). Also, meta-analyses have compared the effects of treatment conducted in controlled research settings versus clinical settings, a critical topic to which I shall return.[2] The list could easily continue because of the flow of meta-analyses generated with each month of journal publications.

Meta-analyses of child and adolescent therapy have sampled approximately 300 outcome studies. There has been little overlap in the studies selected for each of the analyses, so the repetitions are not merely reworking the same data. An excellent summary of the review of the meta-analyses was provided by Weisz, Donenberg, et al. (1995) and is reproduced in Figure 4.2. The figure portrays two adult and four child meta-analyses and summarizes the effects (ESs) obtained when treatment is compared to no treatment. There are comforting consistencies in the analyses. Based on the analyses in the figure and the reviews they reflect, two main conclusions are warranted:

- Psychotherapy appears to be better than no treatment, and
- The magnitude of the effects with children and adolescents closely parallels that obtained with adults.

The ESs for treatment versus no treatment hover in the .70 range for child, adolescent, and adult therapy. The broadest and most sweeping conclusion supported by the meta-analyses is that therapy is effective. This is an important conclusion because of the historical context in which the effects of therapy were repeatedly questioned.

Other, perhaps secondary, conclusions have emerged from the meta-analyses of child and adolescent therapy, for they are less consistently evaluated and demonstrated:

- Treatment differences, when evident, tend to favor behavioral rather than nonbehavioral techniques;
- The effects of treatment do not seem to vary from posttreatment (assessments at the end of treatment) and follow-up (approximately 6 months later);
- Treatments tend to be more effective with adolescents than with children, although both are effective;

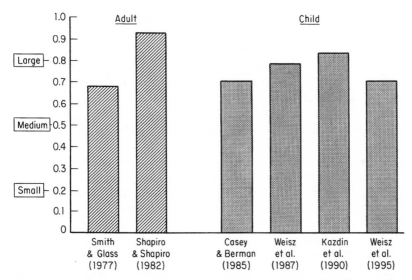

Figure 4.2 Mean effect sizes found in meta-analyses conducted primarily or exclusively with psychotherapy for adults (light bars on the left) or exclusively with children and adolescents (dark bars on the right). From Weisz, Donenberg, & Weiss, (1995). Copyright © 1995 by the American Psychological Association. Reprinted with permission.

- Individual therapy is more effective than group therapy; and
- Treatment is equally effective for externalizing and internalizing problems.

Other, highly specific conclusions might be mentioned (see Weisz, Weiss, et al., 1995), (e.g., statistical interactions that involve treatment technique × level of training of the therapist × sex of the child), but these are omitted here because they tend to be less well replicated across analyses, are not based on any a priori hypotheses, and are difficult to interpret meaningfully due to limitations noted later. Only the main conclusions have been replicated frequently and provide the information needed here. Reiterated simply, we know from the meta-analyses that treatment with children is worth doing, that children get better, and that some techniques tend to be more effective than others. Although early reviews focused on broad classes such as behavior therapy, contemporary reviews in addition provide effect sizes for individual treatments within the broad class. These latter effect sizes can vary substantially.

Limitations

When meta-analysis first emerged, many hoped that a quantitative method of reviewing the literature would be more definitive and provide the basis for stronger claims about the effects of treatment than those available in the usual narrative reviews. This hope has been realized in some important ways. The procedures of meta-analysis (how studies are selected, how dependent measures are converted to effect sizes, and whether coding of the studies is accomplished reliably) are explicitly specified by each meta-analyst. The narrative review method allowed an investigator more leeway in weighing individual studies and outcome measures within these studies; thus, a reviewer using the narrative approach might well combine studies inconsistently. Also, the narrative review method really did not afford opportunities to raise new questions and hypotheses and then test these questions using data from the studies (see Cook et al., 1992).

The benefits of meta-analysis are countered by significant limitations that are somewhat overshadowed by the prestige value and scientific benefits that statistical evaluation and quantitative evaluation engender. Meta-analysis as a method of conducting research has limitations that influence and partially determine conclusions. This is not the place to review all of the strengths and limitations of meta-analysis as applied to the evaluation of psychotherapy (e.g., see Matt & Navarro, 1997). At the same time, some absolutely critical issues qualify the conclusions and color our view of meta-analyses of child and adolescent therapy (or other meta-analyses). Consider a few salient points and their implications for evaluating the literature.

First, there are different ways of computing ESs, and the method selected can materially affect the conclusions (Matt, 1989). The usual method is to use all of the measures in a study to obtain a mean ES for treatment and control (or other) groups. Typically, a therapy study will include several measures (self-report, parent-report, direct observations of child functioning at home or at school, and measures of parent and family dysfunction). After an ES is computed for each measure in the study, a mean ES for that study across all measures is used as the measure of impact. However, all measures in a study do not invariably reflect improvement, and some measures may be more important or relevant than others. "What were the effects of treatment across all measures in the study?" is not a question of widespread interest, especially in light of the uniformity-myth warnings I noted earlier. We already know that the effectiveness of one or more treatments varies depending on the measure (e.g., Kazdin, Bass, Siegel, & Thomas, 1989; Szapocznik et al., 1989). Nevertheless, meta-analyses routinely combine measures within a study.

Second, the ES formula provided earlier assumes homogeneity of variance among all of the ESs combined (within and across studies). Studies with smaller sample sizes in particular may raise special problems when combined with studies of larger sample sizes; thus, some adjustment is needed in how ESs are computed. One solution is to give different weight to ESs. That is, rather than just combining all ESs from different studies (the usual method used), one can take into account the size of the sample (weighted effect size) (Hedges & Olkin, 1985).[3] Why mention a statistical digression? Because the conclusions about treatment can vary depending on which method is used to compute ESs across studies. Using the usual (unweighted) method, child therapy yields an overall ES of .71, but this effect is smaller (.54) for the weighted method (Weisz, Weiss, et al., 1995). Both estimates support the view that therapy is more effective than no therapy, but the magnitude of the effect varies greatly depending on how ES is computed. Also, a particular variable's influence on treatment outcome, as evaluated in meta-analysis, varies depending on how ES is computed. Thus, in one method of computing ESs, but not the other method, individual therapy is better than group therapy, adolescents do better in therapy than children, and girls do better than boys (Weisz, Weiss, et al., 1995). One of the methods does not always reveal an effect that the other does. One is not invariably more conservative than the other in determining that there is an effect. Yet it is important to bear in mind that the conclusions about treatment, particularly those about what factors influence outcome, can vary widely depending on how ES is computed.

Third, meta-analyses try to draw conclusions about the effects and relative effects of different types of treatment. For example, are family therapies better (larger ESs) or more effective than psychodynamically oriented treatments? The problem is that studies of different treatments vary systematically in other ways than the treatments they include. For example, behavior therapy, psychodynamic therapy, and play therapy typically do not study the same types of children, clinical problems, therapists, and type of outcome measures. Treatment technique is invariably confounded with one or more of these other variables (Matt & Navarro, 1997). Thus, when one is trying to draw conclusions, some other variable associated with the different treatments could explain the results.

Statistically, one can control for or attempt to remove the influence of confounding variables, but neither entirely solves the problem. When one exerts these controls, the landscape changes. For example, ESs for behavior therapies have been greater than those for more traditional therapies. However, when the type of problem is controlled, these treatments are not different (statistically) in their ESs (Weisz, Weiss, et al., 1995). Similarly, girls respond better to treatment than boys. Yet girls and boys bring different problems to therapy and come to therapy at different ages. When one controls for the type of treatments applied to girls and boys, the differences in treatment effects evaporate. In short, there are systematic differences in studies that evaluate different types of treatment, or different types of problems, cases, and so on. Statistical controls cannot disconnect the real confound, but they can help sort out likely influence or direction of influence. When such controls are invoked, some variables thought to influence outcome (e.g., treatment technique, child gender) no longer do.

Fourth, meta-analyses have emphasized *approaches* toward treatment, which are broad conceptual orientations or classes, such as behavior therapy, insight-oriented therapies, and so on. Broad classes are not too meaningful because many techniques encompassed by a given class often adhere to very different conceptual views and procedures and have very different effects. For example, in one meta-analysis, different behavioral techniques included one treatment that did not work at all (ES = .06) and another that worked extremely well (ES = 1.67) (Weisz, Weiss, et al., 1995). What value would there be in combining these? The effects of classes of treatment (e.g., behavioral, nonbehavioral treatments) are of interest in intellectual battles about whose general approach is better but do not inform us about therapy or which treatments help whom.

Fifth, scrutiny of the analyses themselves cautions us to be wary of the small number of studies that actually form the basis of conclusions about individual treatments. For example, the most comprehensive meta-analysis of child therapy included 150 therapy studies (Weisz, Weiss, et al., 1995). (For a meta-analysis, the number of studies becomes the sample size and is analogous to the number of subjects in an experiment.) For psychological research, whether a meta-analysis or a single investigation, a sample size of 150 is rather large. Yet, when one examines meta-analyses and the basis for conclusions, these sample sizes drop off sharply. For example, in researching the effectiveness of client-centered therapy, we learn that treatment is not very effective (ES = .11, but this is based on six studies); we also learn that systematic desensitization is very effective (ES = 1.86, but this is based on two studies) (Weisz, Weiss, et al., 1995). Both conclusions are suspect, especially as they are confounded by a host of other variables that cannot be separated from treatment technique. Statistical controls cannot address these confounds, particularly with so few studies.

There are other problems with meta-analyses of child and adolescent therapies. Most of the therapy research is omitted from current analyses. Although one cannot give a fixed, or precise count to the studies, we do know that the number of controlled treatment outcome studies is vast.[4] One search found over a thousand empirical studies completed up to 1990 for children ages 13 or younger (Durlak, Wells, Cotten, & Johnson, 1995). Obviously, extending this search by one decade and including youths through adolescence would yield an even more impressive figure. Meta-analyses of child therapy at best sample one to three hundred studies, perhaps 10–20% of the available literature. This percentage is difficult to estimate. Moreover, treatment outcome research based on single-case experimental designs is routinely omitted from meta-analyses and surveys of psychotherapy research. In any case, reviews represent only a fraction of the available research.

Another problem in meta-analyses is in defining a particular treatment. Two investigators may label treatment as cognitive-behavioral therapy or problem-solving skills training, but the treatment focus, procedures, and duration may vary. Grouping treatments by the same name is problematic, for different treatments may be counted together. Also, defining a treatment as similar enough to be combined with another is not always easy. I also noted in a previous chapter that identical names can occasionally be used for quite different techniques. Making sense of broad approach labels (e.g., behavioral therapies) is a problem in meta-analyses, but combining treatments with the same technique occasionally lends ambiguity as well.

On Balance

When meta-analysis first emerged as a way of evaluating therapy, it met controversy (see Garfield, 1983; Michelson, 1985; Prioleau, Murdock, & Brody,

1983). One commentator noted that if the therapy studies overall are not of very high quality, one cannot expect the results from meta-analyses to be very sound. As Eysenck said, "Garbage in—garbage out" (1978, p. 517). But this global criticism is much too extreme. There are excellent therapy studies available in child, adolescent, and adult research, and the "garbage in" comment is cute but not very helpful. In terms of "garbage out," clearly more needs to be said about what we are measuring by ES. A sweeping, overall rejection of meta-analysis is also misguided. As long as one grasps the strengths and limitations of meta-analysis, one can appreciate the conclusions but also know not to look for more.

Explicit and replicable procedures within science are essential. In a meta-analysis, the ground rules for inclusion or exclusion of studies, including how the different studies are evaluated and weighted, are made explicit. In fact, meta-analyses of psychotherapy can be replicated in ways we would not expect of more qualitative analyses of a body of literature. Meta-analyses have shown that therapy is more effective than no therapy. In an age of managed care and increased accountability, ES data showing that some treatments work is quite valuable. And if one were to recommend treatment to others, the information that ESs have been positive for some treatments but not for others is useful as well. Meta-analysis has been enormously helpful in other ways. Meta-analyses describe research systematically. From such research we have learned that sample sizes are usually small in therapy studies, that critical details of participants (race, gender, age) are often omitted, and that follow-up, which is infrequently studied, is evaluated generally for 5–7 months (e.g., Kazdin, Bass, et al., 1990; Weisz & Weiss, 1993: Weisz, Weiss, et al., 1995). These limitations have become increasingly conspicuous as a result of meta-analyses.

Meta-analyses often systematically evaluate variables that are not easily addressed in any single investigation. For example, one pertinent variable, allegiance of the investigator, refers to the extent to which one of the treatments in the study is preferred or consistent with the investigator's claimed conceptual approach. The study of investigator allegiance is not easily addressed in a single study. Meta-analyses have suggested that treatments more likely to be preferred or favored by the investigator produce stronger effects than other treatments included in the study (Hoag & Burlingame, 1997; Luborsky et al., 1999). This finding is enormously important and generates new research topics. In general, meta-analyses provide rich explanations of study data. The comments here focus largely on the evaluation of therapy and the somewhat limited conclusions that can be reached.

Meta-analysis, by definition, introduces higher levels of abstraction in evaluating a body of literature. The data become more removed from the direct impact of treatment on individuals and their functioning in specific contexts. One overall mean of all effects for all measures and all cases in a study illustrates this point perfectly. It is unfortunate that there is not a complementary quantitative method of study (perhaps called micro-analysis) that analyzes findings within studies. The focus would be on identifying who responded significantly within a study and would reach very specific conclusions that might answer the

"What works with whom?" question in ways that relate to real changes in individual clients.

Finally, one valuable use of meta-analysis has not been applied systematically to the child therapy literature: to propose and test conceptually driven hypotheses. The meta-analytic work to date has been largely atheoretical and exploratory; many complex, often unclear findings are reported (e.g., statistical interactions showing that ESs depend on combinations of multiple variables). Chance findings are likely to emerge in such explorations; indeed, meta-analyses rarely adjust for the enormous number of statistical tests conducted to reduce the likelihood of chance. Better to identify a few hypotheses, state their conceptual basis, and evaluate therapy studies to test them. Planned comparisons of conceptually based hypotheses might tell us even more about treatment and how it might work and for whom.

SUMMARY AND CONCLUSIONS

Reviews of psychotherapy research have taken different forms. The chapter began by mentioning narrative or qualitative reviews. The influential reviews by Eysenck and Levitt helped address the initial question: "Does psychotherapy work?" The answer was that the evidence did not suggest treatment was any better than no treatment. This verdict stimulated debates about the evidence, clarified the more complex questions that need to be addressed, and spawned more and improved psychotherapy research. In terms of the question to guide the field, we wish to know what treatment works with whom and under what conditions, rather than merely whether therapy "works."

Meta-analyses is regarded as the preferred method of reviewing research because of its explicit and replicable nature and because it can quantify estimates of effectiveness of treatment and the impact of other variables related to treatment outcome. Use of a common metric (effect size) among diverse studies permits quite different studies to be combined. Meta-analyses of child therapies have been consistent in their conclusion: therapy is more effective than no treatment. More specific conclusions suggest that ESs tend to be greater for behavioral than nonbehavioral treatments, for adolescents rather than children, and for individual rather than group therapies. These more specific conclusions are more tenuous.

Important cautions are necessary in interpreting the results of meta-analyses. The conclusions about the magnitude of the effects of treatment and whether a particular variable (e.g., type of problem, age and gender of the child) makes a difference in treatment can vary markedly depending on how effect sizes are computed. Different methods of computing ESs are defensible; hence, it is inappropriate or misleading to say one method is unacceptable or distorts the truth. There is no "pure" truth here; different methods of computing ES can generate different conclusions. This chapter noted other concerns as well, such as the global nature of ES as a summary of all measures in a given study and the confounding of type of treatment with other characteristics of the study (e.g., type of problem treated, type of outcome measures used, therapist training). Meta-analyses have focused on the effects of treatment approaches or broad treatment classes (e.g., behavior therapy), which may not be too meaningful, given the vast conceptual differences and actual effects of constituent treatments within an approach.

Meta-analyses shows that treatment is more beneficial than no treatment. This finding is very important in historical context, given the early challenges to the research and especially significant in today's debates about whether treatment ought to be reimbursed by third-party payers. However, the conclusions are too general. The research can be examined in another way that permits more specific conclusions. The next chapter addresses a different review focus and its findings.

FOR FURTHER READING

The readings below encompass narrative and meta-analytic reviews and the effectiveness of therapy more generally.

Bergin, A.E., & Garfield S.L. (Eds.). (1994). *Handbook of psychotherapy and behavior change* (4th ed.). New York: Wiley & Sons.

Eysenck, H.J. (1995). The outcome problem in psychotherapy: What have we learned? *Behaviour Research and Therapy, 32,* 477–495.

Mash, E.J., & Barkley, R. (Eds.). (1998). *Treatment of childhood disorders* (2nd ed.). New York: Guilford.

Weisz, J.R., & Weiss, B. (1993). *Effects of psychotherapy with children and adolescents.* Newbury Park, CA: Sage.

Weisz, J.R., Weiss, B., Han, S.S., Granger, D.A., & Morton, T. (1995). Effects of psychotherapy with children and adolescents revisited: A meta-analysis of treatment outcome studies. *Psychological Bulletin, 117,* 450–468.

Chapter 5

The Effects of Psychotherapy: Empirically Supported Treatments

RECENT REVIEWS of psychotherapy research have focused on identifying those treatments that have evidence in their behalf. At first, this focus does not sound unique. After all, narrative and meta-analytic reviews have the same goal. However, the search for evidence-based treatments begins in a different way, has a different agenda, and leads to different conclusions from those of other approaches to reviewing research. The central feature of these reviews is to delineate criteria defining supported treatments. Armed with these criteria, the reviewer then scans the literature, selects available studies, and draws conclusions about what treatments can be said to be effective or at least to approach the criteria. The vast number of other treatments that do not meet the criteria and studies associated with them are excluded.

The purpose of this chapter is to convey the findings of such reviews of child and adolescent treatment and to discuss the special contribution and limitations of this method of reviewing the literature. Many of the issues in identifying treatments that have evidence in their behalf raise concerns for research and clinical practice more generally. I cover the broader issues that extend beyond the specific method of reviewing the literature later (chapter 7).

A few prefatory comments are warranted on the terminology used to identify treatments that have evidence in their behalf. Separate and somewhat independent efforts to identify such treatments have been completed by different professional organizations and committees spanning different countries (e.g., *Evidence Based Mental Health*, 1998; Nathan & Gorman, 1998; Roth & Fonagy, 1996; Task Force on Promotion and Dissemination of Psychological Procedures [TFPP], 1995). These efforts have used different terminology to delineate these treatments: *empirically validated treatments, empirically supported treatments, evidence-based treatments, evidence-based practice,* and *treatments that work.* Even within a given professional group, the terminology has changed over time (e.g., Chambless et al., 1996; TFPP, 1995). The different terms are not completely interchangeable because the criteria of each of the groups have been slightly different. *Empirically supported treatments* is the term most commonly used in the United States and will be adopted here.

The search for empirically supported treatments has underscored a distinction between efficacy and effectiveness. In contemporary writings, *efficacy* refers to treatment outcomes in well-controlled studies in which several conditions depart from clinical practice; *effectiveness* refers to treatment outcomes in the context of clinical settings, where several conditions are much less well controlled and characteristics of the clients, therapists, and treatment usually depart from those in research settings (see Hoagwood, Hibbs, Brent, & Jensen, 1995). In the classification of empirically supported treatments, the focus is on findings from well-controlled research or *efficacy studies.* This reminder is important because conclusions obtained from treatment research might not apply to clinical practice. This is a serious enough concern to change one's career or at least to take up in another chapter.

BACKGROUND

The contemporary interest in identifying empirically supported treatments can be traced to early reviews of the literature (e.g., Eysenck, 1952), as discussed in chapter 4. However, there are more recent influences within the mental health professions as well as society at large (see Beutler, 1998; Nathan & Gorman, 1998; TFPP, 1995). First, there has been a long-standing hiatus between clinical research and clinical practice. Most mental health professionals (e.g., psychologists, psychiatrists, and social workers) enter career paths that focus on research or practice, even though occasionally one can find careers that combine both. Although there have been many efforts to bring research and practice together (e.g., Hayes, Follette, Dawes, & Grady, 1995; Stricker & Keisner, 1985), different priorities, criteria, and types of accountability drive the different activities and orientations. Lamentably, treatment research has had little impact on clinical practice and clinical practice has had little impact on treatment research (Kazdin, Bass, et al., 1990). Practitioners carry out diagnostic, assessment, and treatment procedures that are not based on the latest, or often any, evidence. As an illustration, psychodynamic and play therapies, for child dysfunction, are frequently used in clinical practice, yet each has very little empirical support in controlled studies. Indeed, the practice of these techniques has been cited as an example of many clinicians' "blatant disregard of the empirical literature" that supports other treatments (Ammerman, Last, & Hersen, 1999, p. 4).

From the practitioner's standpoint, the information from research is not clearly relevant to the "real world." For example, the evidence that treatment works pertains to studies conducted in well-controlled situations. Most of the treatments evaluated in research (e.g., pure forms of a particular treatment) differ from those used in clinical practice (e.g., eclectic combinations of treatments). Moreover, research and practice often treat different people (e.g., individuals with less severe and more circumscribed problems in research vs. individuals with more severe and comorbid disorders in clinical practice). Practitioners, alert to these issues, raise cogent questions about whether treatment research is relevant to clinical practice (e.g., Fensterheim & Raw, 1996). Hopefully, delineating empirically supported treatments will guide clinical practice and provide clear information to those in practice.

Interest in informing clinical practice is not new and by itself does not explain the recent urgency in identifying empirically supported treatments. A second impetus stems from concerns within society about the spiraling and seemingly uncontrollable costs of health care. These concerns have stimulated major changes in mental and physical health services. Third-party payers (e.g., businesses, insurance companies, federal and state governments) that cover the costs of diagnostic and treatment services for many individuals under their charge (e.g., employees and their families, veterans) have tried to reduce these costs. The proliferation of managed care and health maintenance organizations (HMOs) reflects efforts to control costs in health service delivery. These efforts have placed all health-care practices under the spotlight and have raised the question of whether a particular procedure, diagnostic test, or treatment ought to be provided at all.

Psychotherapy is used to treat all sorts of problems. Traditional forms of treatment have gone largely unscrutinized by the health-care system. A goal of identifying empirically supported treatments is to discern what can be justified for use in clinical work. Health-care agencies make decisions about reimbursement and in this sense control treatments. Professional efforts to identify empirically supported treatments are designed to inform not only practitioners but also decision makers about what treatments ought to be reimbursed for what problems.

A third impetus for identifying empirically supported treatments pertains to the training of mental health professionals. Given the numerous treatments in use and clinical problems to which they can be applied, what ought to be the focus of clinical training? It is unrealistic even to expose students and trainees to the vast array of interventions, let alone to train students to carry out these treatments competently. Identifying supported treatments for various clinical problems is one way to develop training priorities. Presumably, training ought to be provided in those treatments with known effects. That helps to reduce the number of options; the list of treatments in appendix A would be reduced by 80 or 90% if evidence were invoked as a criterion for training or use.

These contextual issues are weighty subjects in their own right, and many will emerge again in stating the need for entirely new foci and directions for research. However, they provide the background for identifying empirically supported treatments. Devising a list of empirically supported treatments is not merely an academic interest. Rather, the task itself and how it is accomplished take place in a highly charged sociopolitical environment. The efforts to identify what works influence what treatments can be used and, by implication, who gets to practice and who gets paid.

IDENTIFYING EMPIRICALLY SUPPORTED TREATMENTS

Multiple Proposals

Several responses have resulted from the influences mentioned in the previous section, including efforts to provide guidelines for clinical practice and standards of clinical care. These *practice guidelines* are based on reviews of the evidence and consensus opinions from panels of experts about the status of treatment and use of treatments in clinical work. Among these, the American Psychological Association (1995) and the American Psychiatric Association (1993, 1994b, 1995) have issued proposals for identifying effective treatments as well as practice guidelines for such clinical problems as depression, bipolar disorder, and substance abuse in adults. Within the domain of child and adolescent disorders, practice guidelines have been advanced by the American Academy of Child and Adolescent Psychiatry (AACAP) beginning in the late 1980s and continuing today (Dunne, 1997). The process is lengthy in part because guidelines are adopted disorder by disorder and involve multiple experts and committees. An updated statement provides practice guidelines for several child and adolescent problems (AACAP, 1997, 1998).

Efforts to identify empirically supported treatments tend to differ slightly from those that focus on clinical practice guidelines. Rather than aiming directly at practice, identification of empirically supported treatments begins by elaborating the criteria to evaluate the literature and then focuses more precisely on what the literature shows about treatment. These efforts have been less prescriptive about what ought to be used in practice and somewhat more cautious in drawing conclusions about which treatments produce change than many of the practice guidelines. Practice guidelines often reflect diverse conceptual views of panel members, clinical experience, and recommendations based on weak or nonexistent evidence when a clinician needs to act.[1] Nevertheless, the practice guidelines are explicitly intended to draw on treatment evidence.

Efforts to identify empirically supported treatments consistently seek rigorous scientific data as a basis for treatment selection. The reviews begin with a diagnostic category (e.g., attention-deficit/hyperactivity disorder) or more general label (e.g., anxiety, conduct problems) and review treatments within that domain. Different efforts have used somewhat different criteria for defining empirically supported treatments. Typically, the criteria include evidence in behalf of the treatment from studies that randomly assign subjects to conditions, carefully specify the client population, utilize treatment manuals, and evaluate treatment with multiple measures completed by "blind" (experimentally naïve) raters (if raters were used). Also, replication of treatment effects beyond an initial study is often included, especially replication by an independent investigator or research team.

Two efforts to identify empirically supported treatments illustrate the goals, methods, and yield from such reviews. The first effort has drawn the greatest attention and began in the early 1990s by the Task Force on Promotion and Dissemination of Psychological Procedures (TFPP) within the American Psychological Association. The charge of the TFPP was to "consider methods for educating clinical psychologists, third-party payers, and the public about effective psychotherapies" (TFPP, 1995, p. 3).[2] The group devised criteria to classify treatments as *well-established* or *probably efficacious*. Treatments with supportive evidence in either category were referred to as empirically validated treatments. Table 5.1 presents the criteria used to evaluate treatments. The members of the task force listed treatments they could identify that met crite-

Table 5.1 Criteria for Well-Established (Efficacious) and Possibly Efficacious Treatments

WELL-ESTABLISHED TREATMENTS

I. At least two good design studies, conducted by different investigators, demonstrating efficacy in one or more of the following ways:
    A. Superior to pill or psychological placebo or to another treatment.
    B. Equivalent to an already established treatment in studies with adequate statistical power (about 30 per group; cf. Kazdin & Bass, 1989).
    OR:
II. A large series of single-case design studies demonstrating efficacy. These studies must have:
    A. Used good experimental designs and
    B. Compared the intervention to another treatment as in I.A.
    FURTHER CRITERIA FOR BOTH I AND II:
III. Studies must be conducted with treatment manuals.
IV. Characteristics of the client samples must be clearly specified.

PROBABLY EFFICACIOUS TREATMENTS

I. Two studies showing the treatment is more effective than a waiting-list control group.
    OR:
II. Two studies otherwise meeting the well-established treatment criteria I, III, and IV, but both are conducted by the same investigator.
    Or one good study demonstrating effectiveness by these same criteria.
    OR:
III. At least two good studies demonstrating effectiveness but flawed by heterogeneity of the client samples.
    OR:
IV. A small series of single case design studies otherwise meeting the well-established treatment criteria II, III, and IV.

From Task Force on Promotion and Dissemination of Psychological Procedures (1995), tables 1 and 2 from pp. 21 & 22.

ria in an initial report (TFPP, 1995). Several recommendations were included to inform clinicians, third-party payers, and the public about such treatments and to draw implications for those beginning their professional training as well as for continuing education efforts for practitioners.

The initial report was viewed as the first effort of an ongoing project to identify treatments. The criteria and list of treatments included as empirically supported have continued to evolve (Chambless et al., 1996, 1998; Chambless & Hollon, 1998). For example, in the original criteria, to be well-established, a treatment needed supporting studies showing that it was more effective than another treatment or an attention-placebo condition (see table 5.1, IA). A more recent statement has been altered this requirement to evidence showing that treatment is more effective than no treatment. After all, if the treatment can be shown to be more effective than no treatment and this effect is replicated, then that treatment ought to be valuable clinically. Because most treatments have not been evaluated, this change to a less stringent standard seems reasonable.

In addition to evolution of the criteria, empirically validated was replaced by empirically supported because of concerns about the strength that the word *validated* implied (see Garfield, 1996). To say that treatment is validated may imply that it has been unequivocally established as effective. Later I discuss how, even among treatments considered to be empirically supported, many fundamental questions remain. In any case, the criteria were applied primarily to the treatments of adult disorders. A more systematic effort to apply the criteria was assumed by a separate task force (see Lonigan & Elbert, 1998). The treatments identified as empirically supported for children and adolescents are highlighted below.

A second effort to identify empirically supported treatments proceeded in a slightly different way. The general purpose of this project was to "present the most rigorous, scientifically based evidence for the efficacy of treatments that was available" (Nathan & Gorman, 1998, p. x). More specifically, the aim was to clarify "what treatments have been scientifically validated, what treatments are felt by a large number of experts to be valuable but have not been properly scientifically examined, and what treatments are known to be of little value" (p. x). The criteria used to identify treatments were based on the types of empirical support that might be applied to treatment. Six classes of studies were identified as on a continuum of degree of scientific rigor and methodological adequacy. Table 5.2 presents six types of studies. Treatments that had studies of the first two types in Table 5.2 could be considered to meet high standards of evidence and hence were identified as "treatments that work." For several different problem areas, as represented by psychiatric diagnostic categories (DSM-IV), reviewers were asked to examine the evidence. Although the primary focus was on disorders of adulthood, some disorders of childhood and adolescence were also covered.

Treatments Identified as Supported

Once the criteria are specified, the task of a reviewer is to examine the evidence that can be mobilized for specific treatments. The review proceeds usually by

Table 5.2   Classification of Types of Studies to Identify
▬▬▬▬▬ **Empirically Supported Treatments**

Classification	Key Characteristics
Type 1 Study	Most rigorous type of study to evaluate treatment; random assignment of clients to groups, clear specification of client inclusion and exclusion criteria and diagnoses, adequate sample size; analogous to a true experiment with optimal controls)
Type 2 Study	Some aspect of Type 1 missing (e.g., no random assignment, a flaw in assessment strategies, abbreviated treatment); analogous to a quasi-experiment where conclusions are less strong
Type 3 Study	Clearly methodologically limited; an open treatment study without a control group; pilot work to see if a more rigorous study is worth pursuing; naturalistic and retrospective studies that evaluate treatment
Type 4 Studies	Quantitative reviews of treatment research; meta-analyses of treatment studies; such reviews can encompass extensive evidence that includes studies with diverse designs (i.e., other types of studies)
Type 5 Studies	Narrative or qualitative reviews that are more subject to the opinions and subjective evaluations of the authors
Type 6 Studies	Reports that have marginal value such as case studies and opinion papers

In this evaluation system, empirically supported treatments would be those that have Type 1 and Type 2 studies in their behalf. The benefits of distinguishing the full range of studies is to characterize the status of a given treatment—what type of evidence *is* available for that treatment—and also to consider expert opinion and clinical experience that may suggest further study of a treatment (e.g., Type 6 studies) (see Nathan & Gorman, 1998).

specifying a problem area and the techniques that have been applied. Thus, the review begins with a specific question—what treatments work for this particular problem. By focusing on a problem and then only those treatments with evidence in their behalf, the reviewer will cover fewer studies than broad literature reviews do. Yet the studies included are likely to be those that are the most informative, well-controlled, and well-conducted.

Several reviews have identified empirically supported treatments for children and adolescents (see Kazdin & Weisz, 1998; Lonigan & Elbert, 1998). Committee work identifying such treatments and investigations of treatments are ongoing. However, there is value in enumerating and illustrating some of the current empirically supported treatments. I acknowledge, at the outset, the danger in listing empirically supported treatments. Such a list, out of context, could be misconstrued as definitive or complete. Also, any list of empirically supported treatments identifies treatments that meet rather specific criteria. A different set of criteria or slight modifications in the criteria could change the list.

Table 5.3 provides a list of empirically supported psychotherapies for children and adolescents. The list has been culled from reviews by problem domain (see Kazdin & Weisz, 1998; Lonigan & Elbert, 1998; Nathan & Gorman, 1988; TFPP, 1995). Because these different sources do not invoke the same criteria, I have selected any treatment identified as empirically supported by these reviews for the list.

A few points about the list are conspicuous. First, empirically supported treatments exist. This initial point is important information for professionals, potential clients, and society at large. Clearly, a child referred to treatment for severe anxiety ought to receive one of the empirically supported treatments as the intervention of choice. Other interventions, yet to be studied, might be very effective, but their use would be difficult to defend based on current evidence.

Second, the list of empirically supported treatments is not that long, especially when compared to the list of available techniques (in appendix A). Of course, the goal of psychotherapy research is not to identify long lists of effective treatment or to convert all of the treatments in use (appendix A) to empir-

Table 5.3 Treatments for Children and Adolescents That Are Empirically Supported for Key Problem Domains

PROBLEM DOMAIN	TREATMENT	REVIEW
Anxiety, Fear, Phobias	Systematic desensitization	Ollendick & King (1998)
	Modeling	
	Reinforced practice	
	Cognitive-behavior therapy	
Depression	Cognitive-behavior therapy	Kaslow & Thompson (1998)
	Coping with depression course	Lewinsohn & Clarke (1999)
Oppositional and Conduct Disorder	Parent management training	Brestan & Eyberg (1998)
	Problem-solving skills training	Kazdin (1998a)
	Multisystemic therapy	
Attention-Deficit/ Hyperactivity	Psychostimulant medication	Greenhill (1998)
	Parent management training	Pelham et al. (1998)
	Classroom contingency management	

The techniques noted here draw from different methods of defining and evaluating empirically supported treatments. The techniques would meet criteria for well-established or probably efficacious (Lonigan, Elbert, & Johnson, 1998) or those with Type 1 or Type 2 studies (Nathan & Gorman, 1998). Evaluation of treatments and identification of those that meet criteria for empirical support are ongoing; hence, the table is illustrative rather than exhaustive. Psychostimulant medication is mentioned because this is the standard treatment for attention-deficit/hyperactivity disorder.

ically supported treatments. Thus, identifying a small set of effective treatments as viable options for children and adolescents referred with a particular type of problem would be useful.

Third, the list is dominated by cognitive-behavioral treatments. This is no coincidence; approximately 50% of child treatment studies investigate cognitive-behavioral techniques (see Durlak et al., 1995; Kazdin, Bass, et al., 1990). Also, to be counted as empirically supported treatments, studies must include several methodological features (e.g., use of treatment manuals, random assignment). These characteristics are much more likely among contemporary studies than studies conducted twenty or thirty years ago, and cognitive-behavioral techniques are more popular in contemporary work.

ISSUES IN IDENTIFYING TREATMENTS

The goal of identifying empirically supported treatments is difficult to contest—who would not want to identify and advocate such treatments? Also, once the goal is stated, questions are raised that now seem obvious. For example, why have we not identified empirically supported treatments before? How have we allowed clinical practice to use treatments that have no evidence on their behalf? What has been the basis for deciding which treatments to train our students to use? There are answers to all of these, some perhaps embarrassing.

Reviews of empirically supported treatments begin with criteria that will be used to classify studies. This approach takes a stand on how studies ought to be conducted and alerts researchers to the methodological features that ought to be routinely included. For example, criteria focus on studies with random assignment (randomized controlled clinical trials), use of treatment manuals that document the procedures, use of clinically relevant measures, assessment of follow-up, and replication of findings from other research laboratories.

Consider just two of the practices of supported treatments and their implications. First, the criteria for empirically supported treatments require the use of treatment manuals. Such manuals document critical treatment components, provide prescriptions that other researchers and practitioners may follow, and permit replication of treatment and treatment outcome studies. Second, the focus on replication of findings is particularly important. Replication (i.e., independent efforts to reproduce the original findings) is routinely encouraged but also routinely ignored (see Kazdin, 1998b). In therapy research, we have learned that allegiance of the researcher, that is, the therapeutic approach to which he or she subscribes, may influence the results (Luborsky et al., 1999). (Of course, to say that an influence or bias *may* enter the findings does not invariably mean that it has.) A study by other researchers or a multisite study in which the investigation is simultaneously conducted in several locations can provide the requisite information.

Clearly, there are enormous benefits associated with identifying empirically supported treatments, notwithstanding the many concerns (see Kendall & Chambless, 1998) that highlight qualifications in evaluating the literature. Also, the concerns serve as a point of departure in later chapters for ways of advancing treatment research more systematically than has been the case to date.

Categorization of Treatments

The reviews identify empirically supported treatments (e.g., as well-established or probably efficacious) and by implication include another category that deserves comment: treatments not empirically supported. There may be good reason to make distinctions among treatments in this latter category. For example, some treatments that are not empirically supported have not been investigated at all; others have been investigated but do not seem to be effective; yet others have been shown to be effective but fall below the criteria or threshold for empirically supported (e.g., too few studies, no random assignment among the supportive studies). Delineating the status of such treatments would be valuable because of the implications for next steps in research and for clinical practice.

As an illustration, consider diet and nutrition as a treatment (biological) for the control of hyperactivity. For many years, there was a strong belief that children were hyperactive because of what they ate. Food additives (e.g., dye) and excessive sugar were blamed as causes for hyperactivity. Several studies were conducted to investigate whether reducing the intake of specific foods or food additives and increasing consumption of various "health foods" altered hyperactivity. The evidence indicated that nutritional interventions were not an effective treatment for hyperactivity (e.g., Ingersoll & Goldstein, 1993; Wolraich, Wilson, & White, 1995). One could say that nutritional counseling and diet changes are not empirically supported treatments (e.g., neither well-established nor probably efficacious). Several studies show that diet (or at least diet as investigated to this point) does not materially affect key symptoms. Several failed trials may foster stronger statements than merely noting "this is not supported." The availability of treatments with some proven efficacy (e.g., Barkley, 1998; Pelham, Wheeler, & Chronis, 1998) might make it even more important to caution the public about seeking dietary solutions for hyperactivity.

In some cases, evidence may suggest that a treatment in the nonempirically supported category may be potentially harmful. For example, several years ago, in one program delinquent youths were exposed to adult prisoners who described prison life and described their own untoward life experiences. The purpose was to identify youths early in their delinquent careers and to show them the consequences of criminal behavior. The treatment was designed to intimidate and to scare youths away from criminal activity. However, variations of these programs (referred to as "scared straight" or "stay straight") have shown deleterious effects. Subsequent rates of arrest for youths exposed to these programs *increased* in comparison to those for control youths (e.g., Buckner & Chesney-Lind, 1983; Finckenauer, 1982). Explanation of the results is that the programs brought delinquent youths together, and the peer bonding and friendships among youths in the treatment groups maintained or increased criminal behavior. Bonding with deviant peers can increase delinquent behavior, as attested to by other examples in the treatment literature (e.g., Feldman, Caplinger, & Wodarski, 1983; O'Donnell, 1992). In any case, for our purposes, the intervention is not empirically supported. Furthermore, evidence supports deleterious effects.

Empirically supported and even well-established treatments might warrant more precise analyses. Obviously, not all well-established treatments are necessarily equally effective. We want not only well-established treatments but also the best available treatment among empirically established options. imilarly, for a given treatment, a particular dose (10 vs. 20 sessions) or version (parents involved in treatment vs. not involved) may be more effective, even though both are effective and empirically supported.

It might be useful to evaluate treatments by placing them on a continuum that reflects the extent to which they have been evaluated and shown to produce therapeutic change. To illustrate, based on evidence, a given treatment might be placed on the following continuum:

1. Not evaluated;
2. Evaluated but unclear effects, no effects, or possibly negative effects at this time;
3. Promising (e.g., some evidence in its behalf);
4. Well-established (e.g., criteria used by one of the systems cited for identifying empirically supported treatments); and
5. Better/best treatments (e.g., studies shown to be more effective than one or more other well-established techniques).

The extra categories I have introduced could be divided further or framed differently. The purpose of embellishing among the categories (as in empirically supported or not) is threefold. First, it is important to address special situations such as well-investigated treatments that do not work and hence ought not to be practiced. Second, the status of a given treatment in relation to a continuum of supportive evidence provides a finer differentiation of all treatments. Some treatments may not meet rigorous evidential standards for empirically supported treatments but still be the best available. An example is the behavioral treatment for autistic children, which has on its behalf controlled outcome research (nonrandomized study) with long-term follow-up and clinical application with reports of success (Lovaas, 1987; McEachin, Smith, & Lovaas, 1993; Sheinkopf & Siegel, 1998). The evidence is not sufficient to warrant calling this a well-established treatment, but it may be the best treatment available and the treatment of choice, if empirical evidence is used as the criterion (Rogers, 1998; Smith, 1999).

Third, research might progress better if we demanded that studies of a treatment work to advance knowledge along the continuum. That is, if we know that treatment is probably efficacious, the next studies of that intervention ought to try to evaluate its efficacy more definitively. A continuum like the one cited helps to set a template by which studies and progress can be examined. We can evaluate studies according to where they fit on the continuum and whether another study is needed.

Invoking the Criteria

I have noted that narrative and meta-analytic methods of reviewing the literature include subjective decisions and often implicit decision rules. I did not mean to impugn any particular method but rather merely to note that the results or conclusions can depend on the methods used to study the phenomenon. Changes in assumptions or decision rules also change the conclusions reached. The search for empirically supported treatments too embodies critical issues that influence the conclusions.

First, as shown in table 5.1, a well-established treatment requires at least two "well-conducted group design studies." The definition of a well-designed study is not universally accepted. (For example—and sadly—I think *all* 100% of my studies are well designed, my close relatives have placed the figure close to 50%, and my dissertation committee members, when queried, were "unavailable for comment.") Also, a "large series of case studies" could support the effectiveness of treatment, but how many cases are needed? What if a few group and single-case studies show that treatment is effective but 10 other studies show that treatment is not effective?

Second, in evaluating treatment, multiple outcome measures are used. For example, separate measures may be used to assess symptoms, impairment, academic functioning, family interaction, and performance at home and at school. Invariably, not all of the measures yield the same results; however, in a given study it is conceivable, even likely that on some measures treatment, no treatment, or an alternative treatment will be similar. Which measures ought to be used to determine if treatment is well established when different measures yield different conclusions? A summary of all measures could greatly dilute or mask the beneficial effects. The benefits of treatment could be overemphasized if a few measures, but not the most important ones, show the effect and exert influence on some combined summary of all of the measures (e.g., effect size).

Third, an empirically supported treatment is usually based on evidence of group differences between treatment and control or alternative treatment conditions. This method is not very satisfactory because of the many objections to statistical significance (e.g., dependence on sample size, possibility of very weak effects being significant) (see Kazdin, 1998b). Demonstrating a statistically significant effect does not necessarily mean that the difference is important at all. Also, in a study that shows no difference, one treatment may have obtained stronger effects (magnitude of effects) than another. Statistical significance as a criterion for identifying empirically supported treatments is not entirely arbitrary because this is a criterion routinely invoked in contemporary research. At the same time, real (nonchance) differences and important differences, as reflected in effect size, for example, are not always reflected in statistically significant effects.[3]

Overall, the key issue in identifying empirically supported treatments pertains to the criteria. Whether one or more studies is required, the studies must be completed by independent investigators, must use one control group rather than another, and so on, to determine whether a treatment is or is not part of the "in group." Even if there were agreement on the criteria, their application is not entirely straightforward. The main obstacle is deciding whether two studies have evaluated the same treatment and hence can be combined as support and replication (Weisz & Hawley, 1998). Despite these issues, the more important distinction between those treatments with and without evidence is likely to remain intact.

Focus on Treatment Technique

A concern about the search for empirically supported treatments is its emphasis on treatment technique. Admittedly, the focus is on treatments effective for a given problem area (e.g., anxiety, attention deficits) rather than on a more global question about the effects of psychotherapy. Many concerns emerge from emphasizing treatment technique. First, over 550 techniques are in use for children and adolescents. No set of researchers could easily study this many techniques in relation to even a few of the clinical problems to which each treatment might be reasonably applied. The task is reminiscent of the grid notion pejoratively introduced previously (i.e., forming a large table of all treatments and all problems and trying to establish what works by filling in each cell of the table with a study or two). Also, as a new technique is invented or new combinations are formed, there would be the endless task of adding new treatments to the 550 and conducting a new set of studies—*not* a useful way to proceed.

Second, the criteria for establishing a technique are crassly empirical. That is, they focus on certain kinds of studies (treatment vs. no treatment or vs. treatment as usual) and look only at outcome. No effort is made to understand why a treatment works. The hundreds of available treatments do not likely work in hundreds of different ways. The mechanisms or processes through which treatments produce change are likely few in number (e.g., changing expectations, exposing individuals to new situations, repeated practice). Understanding these mechanisms may be more fruitful as a research agenda because one might focus how those mechanisms are invoked.

Finally, one cannot assume a given technique has a particular effect without considering other variables. Such an assumption—that treatment produces relatively homogeneous effects—would be a uniformity myth (Kiesler, 1966, 1971). The effectiveness of treatment can depend on many variables. For example, characteristics of the therapist can influence outcome. Different therapists administering the same treatment, even if they are all following the manual, can produce different outcome effects (Luborsky, McLellen, Diguer, Woody, & Seligman, 1997; Shapiro, Firth-Cozens, & Stiles, 1989). Also, treatment outcome depends on how well the therapy is conducted by the therapist. Well-executed treatment, as defined by adherence to a treatment manual or ratings of supervisors, influences treatment effectiveness (Frank, Kupfer, Wagner,

McEachran, & Cornes, 1991; O'Malley et al., 1988; Rounsaville, O'Malley, Foley, & Weissman, 1988). Whether an empirically supported treatment is effective may depend on how it is implemented and not merely on the content of the treatment.

Looking for effective treatments without considering possible moderators could be misguided. I have mentioned therapists' characteristics and therapists' adherence to treatment as two moderators of treatment outcome. Many other moderators can influence treatment outcome, including therapists' experience, developmental level of the child/adolescent, alliance and bonding with the therapist, scope of impairment of the child, and family dysfunction. These are not hypothetical influences. In the context of child and adolescent treatment, we know that these factors can influence treatment outcome (Kazdin & Crowley, 1997; Kazdin & Wassell, 1998; Weisz, Weiss, et al., 1995). Empirically supported treatments may have variable effects and can be ineffective when some conditions are not met. There must be a way to address these variables in identifying empirically supported treatments. I shall take up this topic again in much more detail in the context of directions for psychotherapy research.

Efficacy, Not Effectiveness

Empirically supported treatments are interventions shown to produce therapeutic change in well-controlled laboratory settings. Laboratory studies are important because they provide careful control over the phenomenon of interest. In relation to therapy, well-controlled research includes several conditions different from those evident in clinical practice. In research, investigators usually focus on less severely disturbed samples; utilize structured, manualized, and often inflexible treatments; train therapists well in the treatments they administer; monitor how treatment is administered to ensure therapists' adherence; and so on. These practices are important for research, but they depart from the practices of clinical work. Thus, empirically supported treatments may not have similar impact when applied in clinical settings. This is not a new concern in psychotherapy research (Borkovec & Rachman, 1979; Heller, 1971; Kazdin, 1978a).

Clearly, identifying empirically supported treatments requires some attention to what can work or has been shown to work in clinical settings. One would not want to identify empirically supported treatments without having some assurance that the effects can be evident in clinical work. More subtle concerns emerge than merely the generalization from laboratory research to clinic settings. It is quite possible that a minimally effective treatment in research might work very well in clinical practice. That is, treatments that work well in clinics may not generalize to the laboratory.

At the very least, the differences between research and practice limit what one can say about well-established treatments. In general, from reviews of empirically supported treatments, one can say that some interventions have worked in controlled studies. However, there is little or no evidence that these treatments work in clinical settings. That is, an empirically supported treatment, when applied to clinically referred children and families, as administered by clinicians in practice and under conditions where treatment delivery is not so well monitored, has unknown effects.

General Comments

More objections and concerns have been raised about the efforts to identify empirically supported treatments than those mentioned here (see Garfield, 1996, 1998; Weisz & Hawley, 1998). Some of the concerns raise fundamental issues about therapy research. For example, the search for empirically supported treatments emphasizes the need for randomized controlled clinical trials. Group studies with random assignment of individuals to conditions are fundamental. Randomized controlled clinical trials do not address many of the questions of interest in clinical practice, where efforts are made to match characteristics of clients to treatments (Persons & Silberschatz, 1998). Moreover, when compared, the results from randomized and nonrandomized controlled trials of therapy are not that different (Shadish & Ragsdale, 1996). Random is better for a variety of reasons, but nonrandom is far from worthless.

I have highlighted salient issues that will help point to new and needed directions in research. Yet it is important to reiterate that the search for and codification of empirically supported treatments are motivated by other influences, such as which treatments warrant reimbursement in clinical practice or ought to be included in the training of mental health professionals. Objections related to these other agendas are significant. For example, if we allow the practice of only those well-established treatments, then perhaps *your* favorite technique or, even worse, *my* favorite technique, cannot be used. This raises potential legal problems in the United States. If the techniques in which some professionals were trained cannot be used, then their ability to earn an income is restricted. They have legal grounds to object, especially if the criteria used to exclude their technique can be challenged. The criteria used to identify empirically supported treatments and their relevance to decision making in clinical practice could easily be challenged in court.

Efforts to identify empirically supported treatments represent an important advance. It is critical to identify which treatments work with which problems and to make a statement based on thoughtful deliberations among professionals. Professionals ought to evaluate the literature because others less qualified might do so without professional input. How professionals or others will make decisions about treatment is important too. Consensus (converging opinions of many) or clinical judgment (opinions of individuals) are not as firm as solid evidence, even though no method of reaching conclusions is flawless or nonjudgmental (see Beutler, 1998).

As a method of reviewing the literature, the study of empirically supported treatment provides a quite different yield from the general meta-analytic review. With the focus on empirically supported treatments, one can more readily consider the status of individual treatments as applied to specific problem areas. One can more easily consider what to do in clinical work. One might quibble about some of the criteria (e.g., for delineating well-established and probably efficacious treatments), but there are many efforts to identify empirically supported treatments. Singling out any particular effort misses the larger movement within treatment research and its contribution.

In terms of clinical application, if there are empirically supported treatments for a given clinical problem (anxiety or conduct disorder), a very strong rationale would be needed for not using one of these treatments in clinical practice. As an example, the most frequently used treatment in clinical work for oppositional and aggressive behavior in children is relationship therapy based on psychodynamic or relationship-based, nondirective therapy (Kazdin, Siegel, & Bass, 1990). These treatments may be effective, although there is no strong support in uncontrolled and controlled studies (Fonagy & Target, 1994; Kazdin et al., 1989). Defenders of psychodynamic and relationship-based treatments might well note that the treatments have not been well or carefully studied and that it is premature to impugn their effectiveness. Nevertheless, continuing to use these treatments in the absence of solid data to support them is problematic. There *are* well-established and probably efficacious treatments (see table 5.3). One of these treatments ought to be applied before any other would be justified. Alternatively, only a very special circumstance would prevent use of one of these (e.g., the child is allergic to these treatments and has uncontrollable bouts of sneezing). Certainly, if an empirically supported treatment has been tried and has failed, that too would be a reason to apply other treatments. Although researchers argue about interpretation of studies and criteria used to select the studies, in the day-to-day practice of therapy, unsupported treatments are being used when there is evidence for the efficacy of other treatments.

SUMMARY AND CONCLUSIONS

Among methods of reviewing the evidence, the review of empirically supported treatments is unique. Research in behalf of a given treatment must meet various methodological standards, such as controlled trials, use of treatment manuals, and careful assessment of outcome. The goals of these reviews have been manifold, beyond academic interests in identifying which treatments work with what problems. Social and political pressures regarding which treatments might be practiced and reimbursed, and who can practice (i.e., only those who know how to administer those treatments affirmed by research) have sparked keen interest and debate of the issues.

Reviews of empirically supported child and adolescent therapies have identified a number of procedures with strong supportive evidence. Since most therapies in use have never been studied, it is important to underscore the significance of treatments identified with supportive evidence. Although I have argued for the benefits of a more refined classification of treatments than empirically supported or not, the basic distinction is very important. The many different efforts to identify empirically supported treatments differ in criteria but not in their overall goal of distinguishing between supported and unsupported.

In terms of the research agenda, the reviews of empirically supported treatments show that we know much less than we wish to know. As mentioned, there is a vast number of controlled outcome studies of child and adolescent therapy. The yield from the available studies is actually modest if one considers the number of empirically supported treatments as a criterion. Hopefully, in the future the yield from research will be greater because criteria for establishing treatments as empirically supported, such as the use of treatment manuals and replications across researchers and research sites, are more explicit. In some ways, the criteria are particularly helpful in alerting us to how few studies might be needed to establish a technique. We do not need scores of duplicative studies for a given treatment; we do need studies that focus on specific questions, that replicate the answers, and that then systematically move on to the next questions.

This and previous chapters have examined the reviews of the evidence and their main conclusions. Interestingly, there are different methods of reviewing the same literature as well as different and complementary conclusions. These chapters have also considered unique characteristics and limitations of each method of reviewing psychotherapy research. Yet no method of reviewing the literature will yield significant conclusions if the individual studies that compose this literature are insufficient.

FOR FURTHER READING

The readings below include several reviews on empirically supported treatments. The reviews are organized by problem area or clinical dysfunction. Included in the sets of chapters and articles are discussions of obstacles and issues raised in attempting to identify empirically supported treatments.

Ammerman, R.T., Last, C.G., & Hersen, M. (Eds.). (1999). *Handbook of prescriptive treatments for children and adolescents* (2nd ed.). Needham Heights, MA: Allyn & Bacon

Hoagwood, K., & Hibbs, E. (Ed.). (1995). Special section: Efficacy and effectiveness in studies of child and adolescent psychotherapy. *Journal of Consulting and Clinical Psychology, 63,* 683–625.

Kendall, P.C., & Chambless, D.L. (Eds.). (1998). Special section: Empirically supported psychological therapies. *Journal of Consulting and Clinical Psychology, 66,* 3–167.

Lonigan, C.J., & Elbert, J.C. (Eds.). (1998). Special issue on empirically supported psychosocial interventions for children. *Journal of Clinical Child Psychology, 27,* 138–226.

Nathan, P.W., &. Gorman, J.M. (Eds.). (1998). *A guide to treatments that work.* New York: Oxford University Press.

Chapter 6

Treatments That Work:
Illustrations of Exemplary Research

Previous chapters have considered the reviews of therapy research for children and adolescents. Reviews, by their very nature, take a step back from the manifold details of treatment research in order to draw general conclusions. It is also very useful to illustrate in a more focused and analytic way the kinds of treatments being investigated. More than that, a goal of this book is to direct future research. To that end, examination of exemplary studies and treatments can be instructive. Such studies likely will provide guidelines for what is needed and exemplify features that ought to be emulated in research. The best studies are superior not merely because of their findings but rather because of how treatment is developed, conceptualized, and implemented. Exemplary research can provide other types of insights. If the very best research still suffers deficiencies, then one might want to consider new ways of conducting research or simply accept that research probably cannot get better.

In this chapter, I highlight four different treatment techniques. The treatments were selected if they were evaluated in a systematic program of research and if the effects were replicated in at least one, but preferably several, studies. Each treatment is identified as empirically supported, a term reviewed in chapter 5. The research also had to meet currently accepted methodological desiderata, such as the use of treatment manuals, measures of clinical significance, and evaluation of follow-up.[1] It useful to view this chapter as a set of "case studies," or close-up evaluations of individual treatments. There was no effort to select a representative or random sample of all treatments that might qualify. Certainly, this research does not represent all the literature, but it does represent the literature at its very best. I think few would disagree that the research included here and the investigators who completed the research are among the very best researchers in child and adolescent therapy research.

EXEMPLARY TREATMENTS AND RESEARCH FINDINGS

The following four treatments focus on internalizing disorders (anxiety and depression) and externalizing disorders (oppositional and aggressive behavior, delinquency) for both children and adolescents. There is a bias in selecting treatments for inclusion here. With a focus on research that invokes high methodological standards, programmatic studies, and replication, there is a greater bias against less traditional treatments (e.g., psychodynamic, client-centered, play therapy) and for cognitive-behavioral treatment. Perhaps this is not a bias—the focus on empirically supported treatments, reviewed in chapter 5, also invokes criteria that discriminates against treatments not sufficiently studied. The purpose here is not to promote any one treatment but to review the effects of some of the well-studied treatments.

Cognitive-Behavioral Therapy for Child Anxiety

BACKGROUND AND UNDERLYING RATIONALE. Cognitive behavioral treatment (CBT) for anxiety in children focuses on dysfunctional cognitions and their implications for the child's subsequent thinking and behavior (see Kendall et al., 1992; Kendall, Panichelli-Mindel, et al., 1997; Kendall & Treadwell, 1996). These key components of cognition are distinguished:

- cognitive structures—memory and ways in which information is experienced;
- cognitive content—ongoing self-statements;
- cognitive processes—how experiences are processed and interpreted; and
- cognitive products—attributions that result from the above.

Different types of distortions and deficiencies underlie internalizing (e.g., anxiety, depression) and externalizing (e.g., aggression) problems. Cognitive distortions are considered by play a central role among children with anxiety. Cognitive distortions are misguided information processes that lead to misperceptions of oneself or the environment. Treatment modifies cognitive processing to develop new schema or a cognitive coping template.

The therapy develops new skills, provides new experiences for the child to test dysfunctional as well as adaptive beliefs, and assists the child in processing new experiences. Strategies used in treatment directly focus on learning new behaviors through modeling and direct reinforcement. In addition, cognitive strategies such as the use of self-statements address processes (information processing style, attributions, and self-talk) considered to mediate anxiety.

CHARACTERISTICS OF TREATMENT. The treatment program consists of 16–20 sessions administered individually. The techniques that compose treatment are modeling, role-playing, in vivo exposure, relaxation training, and reinforcement. In addition, the child practices the learned skills at home and at school so that anxiety-provoking situations are confronted outside of the treatment sessions. Approximately the first half of treatment is devoted to learning steps for coping with anxiety and managing distress: recognizing the physiological symptoms of anxiety (e.g., internal signals for anxiety such as sensations of tension), challenging and altering anxiety-provoking cognitions and one's internal dialogue (e.g., expecting "bad" things to happen and generating alternatives for what else might happen); problem solving (e.g., devising a plan to cope with the anxiety, generating alternatives for what one can do and selecting one of the courses of action); and evaluating the coping plan and administering consequences (e.g., self-evaluation and self-reinforcement). These steps are taught to the children using the acronym FEAR, as summarized in table 6.1. (FEAR = Feeling frightened, Expecting bad things, Actions and attitudes that help, Rate and reword.)

The second half of treatment focuses on applying these newly learned skills. First, children are exposed to imaginary and minor anxiety-provoking situations and then later to moderate and more stressful anxiety-provoking situations. In all situations, the FEAR approach is used and the therapist helps to prepare the child, assists the child in coping with stress, and reviews the experience to help with future coping. In homework assignments the child rehearses application of the FEAR steps at home and at school. Rewards are earned for completion of these assignments. In the final session of treatment, the child makes a videotape describing the FEAR steps and their use in mastering anxiety-provoking situations.

OVERVIEW OF THE EVIDENCE. Treatment has been evaluated with children 9–13 years of age in both group and single-case experimental studies (e.g., Howard & Kendall, 1996; Kendall, 1994; Kendall, Flannery-Schroeder, et al., 1997). Children are included in the CBT program if they meet criteria for a DSM diagnosis for an anxiety disorder, primarily generalized anxiety, separation anxiety, and social phobia (see Kendall & Treadwell, 1996). In two initial

**Table 6.1   The FEAR Plan: Steps toward Mastering
Unwanted Anxiety Arousal**

PLAN	DESCRIPTION
F: Feeling frightened?	Clients ask themselves this question as they begin learning to recognize their internal and/or physical signs of unwanted anxious arousal. They also learn relaxation skills.
E: Expecting bad things to happen?	Clients ask themselves about the potential catastrophes that they worry about. Also, clients think about other likely outcomes. Clients learn to identify anxiety-related cognition.
A: Actions and attitudes that help	Clients are given a variety of actions and/or attitudes that they can use to reduce and master unwanted anxious arousal. Clients learn to use strategies to manage anxiety.
R: Rate and reward	After completion of the F, E, and A steps, clients learn to rate the outcome and to reward themselves for progress. Successful coping includes movement toward the goal.

From Kendall & Treadwell (1996). Copyright © 1996 by the American Psychological
Association. Adapted with permission.

randomized controlled trials, treatment was compared with a waiting-list control condition. The results indicated that treated children surpassed control children on child-, parent-, and teacher-report measures of anxiety, as well as other
symptom domains, including aggression, social problems, hyperactivity, and
depression, and on behavioral observations of child distress (Kendall, 1994;
Kendall, Flannery, et al., 1997). Many more youths (64%) who completed treatment, compared to waiting-list controls (5%) fell within the normative range
for anxiety at the end of treatment. Follow-up data at 1 year and over 3 years
later have indicated that treatment effects were maintained.

Another team of investigators (Barrett, Dadds, & Rapee, 1996) has replicated the effects of treatment. In a randomized controlled trial, children (ages
7–14) received CBT, CBT with an added family component, or a wait-list control condition. The family component provided training to the parents so they
could reward courageous child behavior, cope with their own anxiety stress, and
problem solve, i.e., address emergent problems in the family. CBT was effective, and the outcome was significantly enhanced by the addition of the family
component. The effects of the treatments were maintained at 6 months and 1
year after treatment. By the 1-year follow-up assessment, 70% of youths in the
CBT and 95% in the CBT plus family intervention no longer met criteria for an
anxiety disorder.

OVERALL EVALUATION.   The treatment research is exemplary in a number of
ways. First, the studies have included children who met criteria for a diagnosis
of anxiety disorder. In most studies of child treatment, diagnoses of the chil-

dren are unknown. Second, the impact of treatment has been strong and consistent across studies, including replication of the main findings by a separate investigative team. Third, there has been some search for moderators of treatment outcome such as severity of disorder, comorbidity, child gender, and ethnicity. Interestingly, presence of an anxiety in one or more parents moderates treatment outcome of the children. Children with one or more parent with an anxiety disorder respond less well to treatment (Cobham, Dadds, & Spence, 1998). Overall, exploration of treatment moderators is noteworthy and moves beyond demonstrations of effectiveness.

There are a few issues to note. At follow-up, a high percentage of children either fall within the normative range for anxiety or no longer meet criteria for an anxiety disorder. These data are difficult to evaluate because control conditions are not generally studied, and anxiety disorders, although probably not as episodic as depression, still have a high rate of improvement in untreated samples. Also, in the two initial outcome studies, the pre- to posttreatment assessment period for the wait-list control condition was much shorter than the interval for the treated groups. This was designed to reduce the time distressed wait-list cases had to wait for treatment. Consequently, direct comparisons of posttest performance for wait-list and treated cases must be interpreted with great caution. More critical is the interpretation of the follow-up results. At follow-up, control cases no longer were controls; by this time they had received treatment. One cannot infer that treatment effects were maintained without information on where untreated cases would be at the same point at follow-up. Notwithstanding these concerns, this treatment and the program it reflects are exemplary. For anxiety disorders CBT is one of the empirically supported treatments. The availability of a treatment manual (Kendall, Kane, Howard, & Siqueland, 1990) is useful for extension in clinical work and promotes further research.

Coping with Depression Course for Adolescents

BACKGROUND AND UNDERLYING RATIONALE. The coping with depression course for adolescents (CWD-A) draws on cognitive and behavioral conceptualizations of depression (see Lewinsohn, Clarke, Rohde, Hops, & Seeley, 1996). These reflect views that depression is associated with multiple cognitions (e.g., hopelessness, helplessness) and restricted behavioral repertoires (e.g., limited participation in pleasant activities, few experiences of reinforcement from the environment). The behavioral model that antedated CWD-A emphasizes multiple risk factors for depression that focus on the person-context interaction. Disruption of behavioral patterns in everyday life are accorded special importance in initiating depressive cognitions and the symptom patterns of the disorder (see Lewinsohn, Hops, Teri, & Hautzinger, 1985 for a more complete rendition).

The CWD-A is a cognitive-behavioral treatment that combines these different views and treatment components. To address the cognitive features of depression, therapists help individuals to realize their often pessimistic, negative thoughts and beliefs and self-blaming causal attributions. Adolescents learn to substitute more constructive cognitions for these and practice them outside of treatment. To address the behavioral features of depression, therapists teach specific social skills and help clients increase activities associated with positive reinforcement from the environment.

CHARACTERISTICS OF TREATMENT.   A group treatment, CWD-A is conceptualized as a "course" in part to emphasize the psychoeducational components in a way that eschews the stigma of treatment. The primary focus is on development of skills and the means to enhance the adolescent's ability to cope with problematic situations. Group activities and role-playing are central in the treatment sessions; between sessions there are "homework" assignments to extend the treatment beyond the classroom.

Treatment includes 16 2-hour sessions over a period of 8 weeks (see Lewinsohn et al., 1996). Up to 10 adolescents are included in the group. The course includes a workbook with brief readings, quizzes, structured learning tasks, and forms for the completion of practice (homework) assignments. The systematically planned sessions include skill training within the session and then extension to the home and focus on specific skills and themes, as outlined in table 6.2. Throughout the sessions, the skills noted in the table are taught and practiced in the session and at home. Early skills continue to be practiced over the course of treatment and are integrated with newly taught skills.

Other aspects of treatment have been included as well, but they are not necessarily central to the main treatment. A parent component has been added in which parents are trained to support and assist skills developed in the adolescent. During these sessions, separate from those provided to the adolescents, the parents are also taught communication and problem-solving skills. In addition, booster (additional) sessions for the adolescents have been provided at the

Table 6.2   Specific Skills and Themes of the Coping with Depression Course for Adolescents

1. Developing specific social skills (e.g., conversation, planning social activities, making friends)
2. Increasing pleasant activities (e.g., via teaching basic self-change techniques, setting goals)
3. Decreasing anxiety that may interfere with performance in social situations (e.g., by teaching relaxation)
4. Reducing negative cognitions associated with depression and replacing them with positive and more constructive cognitions
5. Resolving conflict through communication, negotiation, and conflict resolution skills (e.g., verifying messages, deleting nonproductive behaviors such as accusations and interruptions, brainstorming alternative solutions, reaching and verifying agreements, and others)
6. Planning for the future (e.g., integration of the skills, developing a life plan and goals, planning for relapse and developing an "emergency plan" of what to do).

For a further description of these themes, see Lewinsohn et al. (1996).

end of the 16-week course at 4-month intervals for a period of 2 years. These sessions address emergent issues individually tailored to each case through a brief assessment of the adolescent's functioning in everyday life, current target complaints, and use of skills from the prior training course.

OVERVIEW OF THE EVIDENCE. Two randomized controlled clinical trials of the CWD-A with adolescents provided direct tests of treatment efficacy (Lewinsohn, Clarke, Hops, Andrews, 1990; Lewinsohn, Clarke, & Rohde, 1994). These studies demonstrated that the course is significantly more effective in reducing depression than a wait-list control condition. Treatment effects have been maintained for up to 2 years of follow-up, although follow-up is difficult to interpret given the absence of an untreated control group at follow-up and the high recovery rate from an episode of depression. The studies have consistently in demonstrated the effects of the basic treatment. The parent component and booster sessions have not led to increases in effectiveness beyond the basic treatment without these features, although it may be premature to rule out these components (see Lewinsohn et al., 1996).

Apart from variations of the treatment, other factors have been studied that may influence outcome. Improvement in treatment has been associated with a number of characteristics of the adolescents. Those who respond better tend to be younger males and to engage in more pleasant activities before treatment (Lewinsohn et al., 1996). In contrast, characteristics of the trainers have not been found to influence outcome. For both adolescent and trainer characteristics, too little research has been competed to draw firm conclusions.

The treatment outcome research with adolescents must be viewed in a larger context to represent the status of the CWD-A. A large number (>20) of outcome studies, primarily with adult samples, have shown that this treatment significantly reduces depression (see Cuijpers, 1998). Indeed, effectiveness has been demonstrated across adolescents, adults, elderly adults and their caregivers, and minority groups, and in applications of treatment, as emphasized here, as well as prevention of depression. Thus, extensions to adolescents are reasonable because program efficacy has been established. Mentioning only those outcome studies that focused on adolescents misrepresents the broader empirical context from which these studies emerge.

OVERALL EVALUATION. There are several notable features of this treatment. First, the focus has been on adolescents with diagnosable depression. In many studies of other treatments for adolescent depression, the cases were less clearly significantly impaired or symptomatic to begin with (see Kazdin & Marciano, 1998). Second, the impact of treatment has been impressive across a range of outcome domains (e.g., symptoms, functioning in everyday life, coping skills). Third, the clinical impact or significance of treatment has been demonstrated by evaluating the extent to which youths continue to meet diagnostic criteria for depression. At the end of treatment, the perceptage of youths who still meet diagnostic criteria is significantly lower for treated than for wait-list cases (e.g., 33% vs. 52%, respectively) (Lewinsohn et al., 1996).

Fourth, the format of the treatment raises interesting prospects for dissemi-nation. The intervention is presented as a course and an academic or educational experience, rather than as psychotherapy or treatment. The course-like format may make the treatment disseminable to many depressed individuals who would not otherwise seek treatment because of any stigma, perceived or real, associated with seeking therapy or outpatient care. The availability of course materials, including a treatment manual, videotapes, and workbooks (Lewin-sohn et al., 1996) may also make the treatment disseminable among practition-ers. The course is quite structured in the focus of the sessions and in the tasks and activities that constitute the treatment. This too may make the treatment more disseminable than other forms of treatment and perhaps on a larger scale (e.g., in high schools).

Parent Management Training for Oppositional and Aggressive Children

BACKGROUND AND UNDERLYING RATIONALE.   Parent management training (PMT) includes procedures designed to help parents alter their child's behav-ior in the home. The parents meet with a therapist or trainer, who teaches them to use specific procedures to alter interactions with their child, to promote prosocial behavior, and to decrease deviant behavior. Training reflects the gen-eral view that oppositional and aggressive behavior is inadvertently developed and sustained in the home by maladaptive parent-child interactions.

Multiple facets of parent-child interaction promote oppositional and ag-gressive behavior. These patterns include directly reinforcing deviant behavior, frequently and ineffectively using commands and harsh punishment, and fail-ing to attend to appropriate behavior (Patterson, 1982; Patterson, Reid, & Dishion, 1992). Among the many interaction patterns, those involving coercion have received the greatest attention (Patterson et al., 1992). Coercion in this context refers to deviant behavior on the part of one person (the child) which is rewarded by another person (the parent). Aggressive children are inadvertently rewarded for their aggressive interactions and their escalation of coercive be-haviors, as part of the discipline practices that sustain aggressive behavior.

An excellent set of studies and conceptual models have elaborated the role of parent-child discipline practices in the development and maintenance of ag-gressive child behavior (Patterson, 1982; Patterson et al., 1992). The studies have included observation in the home of the sequences and progressions of family interactions in relation to children's aggressive behavior. In addition, PMT has been used to alter parent-child interaction patterns. Overall, the re-sults have shown that child-rearing practices directly foster and increase chil-dren's aggressive behavior and that altering these practices reduces that be-havior and related conduct problems (Dishion & Andrews, 1995; Dishion, Patterson, & Kavanagh, 1992; Forgatch, 1991). These powerful demonstrations show that parenting practices are causally related to aggressive behavior in chil-dren.[2]

The primary goal of PMT is to alter the pattern of interchanges between par-ent and child so that prosocial, rather than coercive, behavior is directly reinforced and supported within the family. This requires developing several different parenting behaviors, such as establishing the rules for the child to follow, providing positive reinforcement for appropriate behavior, delivering mild forms of punishment to suppress behavior, negotiating compromises, and other procedures. These parenting behaviors are systematically and progressively developed in the sessions with the therapist. The programs that parents eventually implement in the home also serve as the basis for the focus of later sessions in which the procedures are reviewed, modified, and refined.

The methods to alter parent's and children's behavior are based on principles and procedures of operant conditioning. Operant conditioning, elaborated by B.F. Skinner (1938) in animal laboratory research, describes and explains how behavior can be acquired and influenced by a variety of stimuli and consequences. Beginning in the late 1950s and early 1960s, extensions of this work led to applications across a wide range of settings (psychiatric hospitals, rehabilitation facilities, nursing homes, special education and regular classrooms, the military, business, and industry) (Kazdin, 1978b, 1994a). Experimental demonstrations have repeatedly shown that persons (parents, teachers, peers, hospital and institutional staff) directly in contact with others (patients, students, residents, and inmates) can be trained to administer consequences for behavior and to achieve therapeutic changes. Early applications with children focused on mental retardation, autism, and special problems in institutional or special education settings. Many extensions in the home focused on everyday concerns of parents (tantrums, thumbsucking, toilet practices, completing homework, complying with requests). But soon applications encompassed children with significant impairment in these and related domains. Applications in the home, begun initially in the late 1960s and early 1970s (see Hanf, 1969), stimulated a vigorous line of research that continues today.

CHARACTERISTICS OF TREATMENT. Although many variations of PMT exist, several common characteristics can be identified. Treatment is conducted primarily with the parent(s), who implement several procedures at home. The parents meet with a therapist who teaches them to use specific procedures to alter interactions with their child, to promote prosocial behavior, and to decrease deviant behavior. Parents are trained to identify, define, and observe problem behaviors in new ways. Careful specification of the problem is essential for the delivery of reinforcing or punishing consequences and for evaluating whether the program is achieving the desired goals. The treatment sessions provide concrete opportunities for parents to see how the techniques are implemented, to practice and refine use of the techniques (e.g., through extensive role-playing), and to review the behavior-change programs implemented at home. Parent-managed reinforcement programs for children's deportment and performance at school, completion of homework, and activities on the playground are routinely included, with the assistance of teachers, as available.

In most PMT programs, only one parent comes to treatment usually because the other parent is employed or because a single parent heads the household.

Whenever feasible, the therapist tries to integrate the parent who does not attend the sessions so he or she can participate in the behavior-change programs at home. Duration of treatment has varied depending on the severity of the child's dysfunction. Programs for young, mildly oppositional children usually last 6–8 weeks. With clinically referred conduct-disordered children, the programs usually last 12–25 weeks. Definitive statements about the required duration of treatment are not possible because of two competing trends: efforts to develop more abbreviated and more cost-effective variations of treatment, on the one hand (e.g., Thompson, Ruma, Schuchmann, & Burke, 1996) and to combine PMT with other treatment modalities (multimodal treatments), on the other hand (e.g., Webster-Stratton, 1996).

OVERVIEW OF THE EVIDENCE.   PMT is one of the most well-researched therapy techniques for children and adolescents. Treatment has been evaluated in scores of randomized controlled outcome trials with children and adolescents from 2 to 17 years old with a variety of oppositional and conduct problems (see Graziano & Diament, 1992; Miller & Prinz, 1990; Patterson, Dishion, & Chamberlain, 1993; Serketich & Dumas, 1996). Indeed, a recent review of treatments for conduct disorder identified PMT as the only intervention that is well-established (effective in independently replicated controlled clinical trials) (Brestan & Eyberg, 1998). The outcome studies support several conclusions:

- PMT has led to marked improvements in children's behavior, as reflected in parents' and teachers' reports of deviant behavior, direct observational measures of behavior at home and at school, and institutional records (school truancy, police contacts, arrest rates, institutionalization);
- The magnitude of change has placed conduct problem behaviors to within nonclinic levels of functioning at home and at school, based on normative data from nonreferred peers of the same age and gender;
- Treatment gains have been maintained in several studies 1–3 years after treatment, although one program reported maintenance of gains 10–14 years later (Long, Forehand, Wierson, & Morgan, 1994); and
- Favorable treatment effects also include reductions in problem behaviors of siblings in the home and in maternal psychopathology, particularly depression. Occasionally, marital satisfaction and family cohesion improve following treatment, but data on these outcomes are sparse.

Considerable attention has been devoted to identifying parental and family characteristics that contribute to outcome. Family socioeconomic disadvantage, marital discord, high parental stress and low social support, single-parent families, harsh punishment practices, parental history of antisocial behavior predict (1) who remains in treatment, (2) the magnitude of change among those who complete treatment, and (3) the extent to which changes are maintained at follow-up (Dadds & McHugh, 1992; Dumas & Wahler, 1983; Kazdin, 1995a; Webster-Stratton & Hammond, 1990). Those families at greatest risk often respond to treatment, but the magnitude of effects is attenuated by dysfunctional parent and family characteristics. Among children's characteristics, more severe and chronic antisocial behavior and comorbidity predict reduced responsiveness to treatment (Kazdin, 1995a; Ruma, Burke, & Thompson, 1996).

Characteristics of treatment also contribute to outcome. Providing parents with sufficient knowledge of social learning principles, rather than just teaching them the techniques, improves outcomes. Also, including mild punishment, such as a brief time out from reinforcement, along with reinforcement programs in the home enhances treatment effects (see Kazdin, 1985). These components are now standard in most PMT programs. Processes within treatment have also been studied to identify who responds to treatment. Measures of parent resistance (e.g., parents saying, "I can't," "I won't") correlate with parental discipline practices at home; changes in resistance during therapy predict changes in parental behavior. Moreover, a therapist's specific ploys during the sessions (e.g., reframing, confronting) can overcome or contribute to resistance (Patterson & Chamberlain, 1994). This work begins to identify ways to enhance the administration of PMT.

In much of the outcome research, PMT has been administered to families individually in clinic settings. Group administration has been facilitated greatly by the development of videotaped materials that present themes, principles, and procedures to the parents of children with conduct problems (see Webster-Stratton, 1996). Randomized controlled trials have shown that video-based treatment, particularly in group format and when supplemented with therapist-led discussions, leads to clinically significant changes at posttreatment and that these changes are maintained at follow-up 1 and 3 years later.

Now PMT has been extended to community settings to bring treatment to those persons least likely to come to or remain in treatment. It is effective and highly cost-effective when provided in small parent groups in neighborhoods where the families reside (Cunningham, Bremner, & Boyle, 1995; Thompson et al., 1996). Also, PMT has been effective in reducing conduct problems and increasing positive parenting behaviors when implemented on a large scale as part of early school intervention (Head Start) programs (Webster-Stratton, 1998). Occasionally, community-based treatment has been more effective than clinic-based. Of course, it is not clear that one form of treatment can replace another for all children. Yet community applications may permit dissemination of treatment to families that otherwise might not attend the usual mental health services.

OVERALL EVALUATION.   Perhaps the most important point to underscore is that no other technique for children with oppositional and conduct problems probably has been studied as often or as well in controlled trials (Brestan & Eyberg, 1998). The outcome evidence makes PMT one of the most promising treatments. Related lines of work bolster the evidence. First, the study of family interaction processes that contribute to antisocial behavior in the home and evidence that changing these processes alters children's behavior provide a strong empirical base for treatment. Second, the procedures and practices that are used in PMT (reinforcement and punishment practices) have been widely and effectively applied outside the context of children's conduct problems. For example, the procedures have been applied with parents of children with autism, language delays, developmental disabilities, medical disorders for which compliance with special treatment regimens is required, and with parents who physically abuse or neglect their children (see Kazdin, 1994a). Third, a great deal is known about the procedures and parameters of delivery that influence the effectiveness of reinforcement and punishment practices. Consequently, very concrete recommendations can be provided to change behavior and to alter programs when behavior change has not occurred.

Several resources are available to facilitate use of PMT clinically and in research. Treatment manuals are available for clinicians and convey the structure, content, and flow of treatment sessions (Forehand & McMahon, 1981; Forgatch & Patterson, 1989; Patterson & Forgatch, 1987; Sanders & Dadds, 1993). Books and pamphlets are also available for parents (Forehand & Long, 1996; Patterson, 1976) to convey basic concepts and to show how to apply various techniques. Videotapes can also be used by professionals to guide group PMT. In short, several training materials are available for professionals as well as their clients.

Several limitations of PMT can be identified as well. First, PMT makes several demands on the parents, such as mastering educational materials that convey major principles underlying the program, systematically observing deviant child behavior and implementing specific procedures at home, attending weekly sessions, and responding to frequent telephone contacts made by the therapist. For some families, the demands may be prohibitive. Interestingly, within the approach, several procedures (e.g., shaping parent behavior through reinforcement) provide guidelines for developing parent compliance and the desired response repertoire in relation to their children.

Second, perhaps the greatest limitation or obstacle in using PMT is the lack of training opportunities for professionals to learn the approach. Training programs in child psychiatry, clinical psychology, and social work are unlikely to provide exposure to the technique, much less opportunities for formal training. PMT requires mastery of social learning principles and multiple procedures that derive from them (Cooper, Heron, & Heward, 1987; Kazdin, 1994a). For example, the parent's administration of reinforcement in the home (to alter child behavior) and the therapist's administration in the session (to change parent behavior) requires more than passing familiarity with the principle and the parametric variations that dictate its effectiveness (e.g., need to administer reinforcement contingently, immediately, frequently; to use varied and high quality reinforcers; prompting; shaping). The requisite skills in administering these within the treatment sessions can be readily developed, but they are not trivial.

Finally, the applicability of PMT to adolescents, as compared with children, is less clear. Studies have shown that PMT has reduced offense rates among delinquent adolescents (Bank, Marlowe, Reid, Patterson, & Weinrott, 1991) and school behavioral problems and substance use among adolescents at risk for serious conduct problems (Dishion & Andrews, 1995). In the Bank et al. study, the impact of treatment, relative to intensive family therapy, group therapy, and drug counseling, was modest over posttreatment and 3-year follow-up. Analyses from other studies suggest that adolescents respond less well to PMT than preadolescents (Dishion & Patterson, 1992), but severity of symptoms at pretreatment may account for this effect (Ruma et al., 1996). Adolescents referred for treatment tend to be more severely and chronically impaired than preadolescents; once severity is controlled, age does not influence outcome. In light of limited applications with adolescents, the strength of conclusions about the efficacy of PMT rests mainly on studies of preadolescent children.

Multisystemic Therapy for Antisocial and Delinquent Adolescents

BACKGROUND AND UNDERLYING RATIONALE. Multisystemic therapy (MST) focuses on systems in which behavior is embedded and on altering these systems in concrete ways that can influence behavior (Henggeler et al., 1998). The adolescent is influenced by a number of systems, including the family (immediate and extended family members), peers, schools, and neighborhood. Multiple influences within these systems may be involved in development, maintenance, or amelioration of the problem. For example, within the context of the family, some tacit alliance between one parent and the adolescent may contribute to disagreement and conflict over discipline in relation to the adolescent. Treatment may be required to address the alliance and sources of conflict in an effort to alter adolescent behavior. Also, adolescent functioning at school may involve limited and poor peer relations; treatment may address these areas as well. Finally, the systems approach entails a focus on the individual's own behavior as it affects others. Individual treatment of the adolescent or parents may be included in treatment.

The primary focus of treatment has been with delinquent adolescents, including seriously disturbed, repeat offenders. The focus of treatment is influenced in part by the factors shown to relate to development and maintenance of delinquent behavior. MST is not very concerned with past determinants of behavior but considers risk factors (e.g., family discipline, child problem-solving skills, parental conflict) that may reflect current areas worth redressing as part of treatment.

CHARACTERISTICS OF TREATMENT. The goals of treatment are to help the parents develop behaviors of the adolescent, to overcome difficulties (e.g., marital) that impede the parents' ability to function as parents, to eliminate negative interactions between parent and adolescent, and to build cohesion and emotional warmth among family members. Emphasis on systems and contexts requires mobilizing many influences and aspects of the interpersonal environment, as feasible and available. Consequently, treatment is multifaceted and draws on several different techniques. Examples include PMT, contingency management, problem-solving skills therapy, marital therapy, and others. Domains may be addressed in treatment (e.g., parent unemployment) because they raise issues for one or more systems (e.g., parent stress, alcohol consumption) and affect how the adolescent is functioning (e.g., marital conflict, child-discipline practices). Much of the therapy is conducted outside of the treatment sessions in which parents and significant others engage in new strategies (e.g., reinforcement techniques) that alter behavior at home, at school, and in the community.

Treatment procedures are used on an "as needed" basis to address individual, family, and system issues that may contribute to problem behavior. The conceptual view focusing on multiple systems and their impact on the individual serves as a basis for selecting the different treatment procedures. Several principles guide treatment technique selection and activities, as listed in table 6.3. The principles, intended to convey the focus (e.g., action-oriented, direct involvement of the family) but to permit flexible application, underscore the key foci of treatment: concentrating on present behavior, aiming interventions to achieve concrete observable changes in the family and adolescent, treating specific and well-defined problems, and empowering parents in relation to family interaction, the school, and peers. In some cases, treatment consists of help-

Table 6.3 **Principles of Multisystematic Therapy That Serve as a Basis for Treatment**

PRINCIPLE	STATEMENT
Principle 1	The primary purpose of assessment is to understand the fit between the identified problems and their broader systemic context.
Principle 2	Therapeutic contacts emphasize the positive and use systemic strengths as levers for change.
Principle 3	Interventions are designed to promote responsible behavior and decrease irresponsible behavior among family members.
Principle 4	Interventions are present-focused and action-oriented, targeting specific and well-defined problems.
Principle 5	Interventions target sequences of behavior within and between multiple systems that maintain the identified problems.
Principle 6	Interventions are developmentally appropriate and fit the developmental needs of the youth.
Principle 7	Interventions are designed to require daily or weekly effort by family members.
Principle 8	Intervention effectiveness is evaluated continuously from multiple perspectives with providers assuming accountability for overcoming barriers to successful outcomes.
Principle 9	Interventions are designed to promote treatment generalization and long-term maintenance of therapeutic change by empowering caregivers to address family members' needs across multiple systemic contexts.

From Henggeler et al. (1998).

ing the parents address a significant domain through practical advice and guidance (e.g., to involve the adolescent in prosocial peer activities at school, to restrict specific activities with a deviant peer group).

Much of therapy is based on assessment and hypothesis testing. That is, a therapist evaluates an adolescent's activities in a particular context, generates a hypothesis about the factors influencing these behaviors, and tests it by intervening to alter the factor to discover any consequent concrete changes in adolescent behavior. Domains known to influence delinquent behavior, as mentioned before, alert the therapists to likely targets of treatment (e.g., parental marital discord, child-rearing practices, children's peer relations). Assessment, hypothesis generation, and hypothesis testing are sometimes said to characterize all clinical work. The approach is much more explicit in MST.

OVERVIEW OF THE EVIDENCE. There is strong evidence in behalf of MST. Treatment has been evaluated in multiple randomized controlled clinical trials with very seriously disturbed, adjudicated delinquent youths and their families, including chronic juvenile offenders, juvenile sexual offenders, youths with substance use and abuse, and maltreating (abusing, neglectful) families (see Henggeler et al., 1998, for a review). The benefits of treatment, in comparison to other treatment and control conditions, have been evident on measures of adolescent and parent psychopathology, family relations and functioning, rearrest rates, severity of offenses, drug use, and reinstitutionalization (e.g., incarceration, hospitalization). Cost-effectiveness data have also shown that the treatment is a bargain compared to alternative diversion and institutional programs to which such youths are ordinarily assigned.

Treatment influences key processes that purportedly contribute to deviant behavior (Mann, Borduin, Henggeler, & Blaske, 1990). Specifically, both parents and teenagers evince less verbal activity, conflict, and hostility and increases in support, and parents increase verbal communication and decrease conflict. Moreover, decreases in adolescent symptoms are positively correlated with increases in supportiveness and decreases in conflict between the mother and father. This work provides an important link between theoretical underpinnings of treatment and outcome effects.

Evidence suggests that the fidelity with which MST is carried out influences treatment outcome. Adherence to the principles in treatment predicts improvement on key outcome measures, including arrest, self-reported offenses, and psychiatric symptoms (Henggeler, Melton, Brondino, Scherer, & Hanley, 1997). Few studies of child and adolescent therapy have evaluated the relation of treatment adherence and clinical outcomes.

OVERALL EVALUATION. The evidence in behalf of MST has several strengths, including the focus on very seriously disturbed adolescents, replication of treatment outcomes in several randomized controlled clinical trials, evaluation of clinically and socially important outcomes (e.g., arrest, criminal activity, reinstitutionalization), and assessment of long-term follow-up. Another strength is the conceptualization of conduct problems at multiple levels, namely, as dysfunction in relation to the individual, family, and extrafamilial systems and the transactions among these. In fact, youths with conduct problems experience dysfunction at multiple levels, including individual repertoires, family interactions, and extrafamilial systems (e.g., peers, schools, employment among later adolescents). As a result, MST begins with the view that many different domains are likely relevant and need to be evaluated and then addressed in treatment.

Important challenges for the approach remain. First, the principles guiding treatment provide a novel way to manualize the intervention. Moving from the general principles to treatment within the session is not entirely straightforward, although several illustrations are available (Henggeler et al., 1998). Second, the administration of MST is demanding because of the need to provide several different interventions. Individual treatments alone are difficult to provide; multiple combinations of different treatments invite all sorts of challenges (e.g., therapist training, ensuring treatments of high quality, strength, and integrity). Third, MST is an intensive treatment. In some projects, therapists are available 24 hours a day, 7 days a week; sometimes a team of therapists is involved rather than only one therapist. This model of treatment delivery may be precisely what is needed for clinical problems that are multiply determined, protracted, and recalcitrant to more abbreviated interventions. However, the model of MST delivery will very much influence its adoption as a treatment. Outpatient care has been generally committed to 1-hour a week treatment (for most therapies), with occasional exceptions (e.g., 3–7 times a week for child psychoanalysis; Fonagy & Target, 1994). There has been little research on whether 1 hour a week is an optimal or desirable regimen. On the other hand, considerable evidence shows that the more intensive MST focus produces rather marked and dramatic results.

Fourth, further replications will be needed for this treatment. The treatment has already provided multiple replications across problems, therapists, and settings (Henggeler et al., 1998), but these have been completed mostly by the same team of researchers. Replications by others not involved with the original development of the program is the next logical step. Finally, the treatment already has impressive evidence in its behalf and is undergoing further treatment trials. The central issue is understanding what treatment components to provide to whom and how the decisions are made and identifying whether these rules can be reliably implemented across settings and investigators. These questions ought not detract from the superb evidence and consistency of the outcomes already established.

EVALUATION OF EXEMPLARY TREATMENTS

The four treatments cannot be fully described in a single chapter (see further readings section) because each is part of a program of research that extends beyond questions of treatment outcome (e.g., child, parent, family factors associated with the disorder, longitudinal course). This mere highlight of the treatments shows that the results are impressive and in many ways reflect the best research evidence in behalf of child and adolescent therapy. The research for each treatment focuses on samples with clinically severe dysfunction, uses treatment manuals, assesses clinical significance of change, evaluates follow-up, and replicates treatment effects. Most child and adolescent therapy research does not include any one of these characteristics. Several such features packaged into studies and programs of research are remarkable and exemplary. Needless to say, although the treatments highlighted here are exemplary, other treatments might have been presented too. Among the other candidates would be empirically supported treatments, as mentioned in chapter 5.

The excellent research is important to note for another reason. Even the best research illustrates weaknesses and lacunae in the literature. First, conceptualizations of the disorder (with supporting research) and conceptualizations of how change occurs (with supporting research) are scant. Many of the conceptual underpinnings are general orienting statements that suggest why the focus is on cognitions, behavior, or systems. Statements about mechanisms of therapeutic change and how these mechanisms may relate to the problem are included, but they tend to be general and lack empirical support. This characterization is true of the four treatments to varying degrees. The treatment program for depression is related to a long line of studies on cognitive processes and depression and restricted response repertoires as a critical part of the problem. Also, PMT has exemplary research on family interaction patterns and their causal relation to aggressive child behavior, as mentioned previously. The other treatments are more general in terms in specifying the mechanisms that might be causally involved in the problem and in change. Hypotheses regarding how treatments work and the mechanisms involved in therapeutic change are sparse in the treatment literature in general.

Second, the study of moderators is weak. Again, it is important to mention that the study of moderators is rare in child and adolescent therapy research. In the four treatments reviewed, the investigators focused on whether treatment was influenced by other factors such as child gender, severity of dysfunction, ethnicity, and socioeconomic disadvantage, to illustrate some examples. We certainly want to know about moderators, but research has not been inspired to focus on them. "Moderators of convenience" are selected, that is, readily available variables. A notable exception is evident in the context of cognitive-behavioral treatment for anxiety among children, reviewed previously. One study evaluated the role of anxiety disorder in the parent on the effectiveness of treatment with the child (Cobham et al., 1998). Parent anxiety is related to the onset of child anxiety and hence was hypothesized to limit the effectiveness of treatment of the child. Presumably parental anxiety in the home would attenuate the development of nonanxious behaviors and reactions on the part of the child. As expected, children with anxious parents responded less well to cognitive-behavioral treatment than children without an anxious parent.

In general, more attention is needed on the role of moderators in treatment outcome. If selection of treatment moderators is not driven by conceptual views of the clinical problem or treatment, this is not necessarily an indictment of the research. Exploratory work can lead to good theory but the step must be taken to move to theory. At this point, even the best research available gives little attention to moderators. When moderators are studied, the focus is on variables not usually connected to an understanding of the clinical problem or conceptual view of treatment.

Although more comments can be made about the studies, suffice it to say that the mechanisms through which therapy operates and the moderators of treatment (e.g., for whom, under what conditions, as administered by what type of therapist) are not evaluated very much, even among the better studies. In the research agenda for the next several years, understanding how treatment works and the conditions under which it works deserves more emphasis.

SUMMARY AND CONCLUSIONS

In this chapter, four treatments were highlighted, including cognitive-behavioral treatments for anxiety in children and depression in adolescents, parent management training for oppositional and aggressive children, and multisystemic therapy for delinquent adolescents. Each of the treatments has been subjected to programmatic research. Each would be included among the empirically supported treatments and has been so identified by at least one source (Lonigan & Elbert, 1998; Nathan & Gorman, 1998). Many excellent features of these studies were identified, including recruitment of clinical samples, use of well-specified treatments, assessment of outcome in ways that reflect significant changes, and evaluation of follow-up. Studies of this quality are exceptions rather than the rule.

The treatments and their supportive research were highlighted to illustrate concretely the accomplishments and benefits of child and adolescent therapy. The results demonstrate palpable effects of treatment on clinical problems, evident beyond posttreatment assessment. An objective of presenting these treatments was to illustrate the best research and to show what might be emulated in future studies and what still needs attention. Before I proceed to the directions this research might take, let us consider the characteristics and limitations of therapy research. Chapter 7 more systematically evaluates child and adolescent psychotherapy with a special focus on limitations that might serve as the basis for changes in future research.

FOR FURTHER READING

The readings provide further details and analyses of the treatment programs illustrated in this chapter. Each includes a review of multiple studies and hence also provides a bibliography of the primary investigations.

Cuijpers, P. (1998). A psychoeducational approach to the treatment of depression: A meta-analysis of Lewinsohn's "Coping with Depression" course. *Behavior Therapy, 29*, 521–533.

Henggeler, S.W., Schoenwald, S.K., Borduin, C. M., Rowland, M.D., &. Cunningham,

P.B. (1998). *Multisystemic treatment of antisocial behavior in children and adolescents*. New York: Guilford.

Kazdin, A.E. (1997). Parent management training: Evidence, outcomes, and issues. *Journal of the American Academy of Child and Adolescent Psychiatry, 36*, 1349–1356.

Kendall, P.C., Panichelli-Mindel, S.M., Sugarman, A., & Callahan, S.A. (1997). Exposure to child anxiety: Theory, research, and practice. *Clinical Psychology: Science and Practice, 4*, 29–39.

Chapter 7

Characteristics and Limitations
of Therapy Research

Previous chapters have highlighted the evidence in behalf of therapies for children and adolescents. The reviews encompass hundreds of studies and seem to provide a firm basis for concluding that psychotherapy produces therapeutic change and that a number of techniques are bolstered by strong empirical support. This chapter examines the body of evidence as a whole to determine key characteristics and limitations in relation to the goals of psychotherapy research. To reiterate prior comments, the goals of therapy research are to develop and identify effective treatments that can be used in clinical practice and to understand the bases of therapeutic change (mechanisms) and the conditions (moderators) that influence outcome. The overarching question of this chapter is how well does current therapy research address these goals.

Two related types of limitations can be identified. First, there are problems of commission, or characteristics of therapy study that limit generalization to clinical practice. Second, there are problems of omission, or lacunae in therapy research in which key topics, questions, and foci are neglected. Limitations in each of these domains warrant important qualifiers to the conclusions reached about treatment.

CHILDREN AND FAMILIES IN TREATMENT

Characteristics of the Children/Adolescents

In most investigations of therapy, children and families are actively recruited for participation in treatment. To recruit children, the investigator may advertise (newspapers, public service television), post notes on kiosks, and visit local schools to announce the availability of special programs. From the standpoint of research, recruiting cases is very helpful because one can usually obtain a larger sample of participants in a shorter period of time and also a more homogeneous sample (e.g., only boys 8–11 years old) than would be available in a clinic setting. Also, because the cases are volunteers who have not sought treatment, some of the demands of research can be more readily accommodated than would otherwise be possible. For example, volunteers and recruits can more readily be assigned to waiting-list control conditions than individuals urgently seeking treatment.

The primary concern is that individuals recruited for treatment research differ from those seen in clinical work. These differences may influence the extent to which the results of treatment in research apply to clinically referred cases. Many differences between recruited and clinically referred cases would be relevant to this concern. Foremost, children recruited for and included in research tend to be less disturbed than children referred for treatment. The "less disturbed" characterization is likely to be manifest in at least three ways: severity of the problem to be treated, chronicity of the problem, and presence of comorbid disorders. Obviously, conclusions from therapy research apply to cases included in the study; if they are less disturbed than patients usually seen in clinical work, the generality of the results can be challenged.

Child dysfunction (severity, chronicity, scope) is likely to be correlated with other areas of a child's functioning, including peer relations, school functioning, participation in prosocial activities (e.g., after-school group activities, lessons of some kind), and overall impairment. Thus, clinically referred youths, as compared to those recruited for treatment, may suffer greater dysfunction in areas other than their referral problems. These characteristics can influence long-term prognosis; children with more positive attributes and competencies in these other domains are likely to do better over time. In short, one might expect less severely disturbed children with greater competence and prosocial attributes in other domains to do much better in therapy than their more severely disturbed counterparts in clinical work. Hence, the conclusions obtained in research could be more promising and favorable than if obtained in clinical settings.

Often recruited children are screened (e.g., on a parent checklist) to ensure that they meet a criterion (e.g., >1 *SD* above the mean of nonreferred cases) that attests to the severity of their clinical problem. Assume for a moment that recruited cases are just as severely disturbed as those seen in clinical practice. It is still likely that recruited and clinically referred cases differ in important ways. Referral to clinical services is more likely to be related to impairment in everyday life than to symptoms per se (Bird et al., 1990). Indeed, we have learned from epidemiological studies of children, adolescents, and adults that up to 20% have a diagnosable clinical disorder, but very few of those individuals come to treatment. Individuals may come to treatment for a number of reasons (access to resources, insurance coverage, cultural views that permit seeking help outside of the family). However, one of the reasons is likely to be the degree of impairment. The difference in degree of impairment between recruited and referred children could influence the effects of treatment and the generality of findings from research to clinical practice.

It is important not to oversimplify the distinction between recruited and clinically referred cases. Variation is likely a matter of degree along multiple dimensions. For example, one might "recruit" children whose obesity or "tics" are extreme; hence, there is no question about the extent of their problem and the impairment with which it is associated. Also, clinically referred cases are not invariably severely disturbed or impaired. For example, at the clinic where I work, occasionally the children—all clinically referred—are functioning well in all or most domains, but the parents have odd expectations about child functioning. The behavior that parents interpret as problematic (e.g., mild noncompliance, separation fears, shyness) may fall well within the normative range. In short, not all clinically referred children warrant treatment or warrant treatment more than their counterparts who have been recruited and carefully screened for research.

These considerations notwithstanding, children treated in research are often much less severely disturbed and impaired and more competent in several domains (e.g., school, peer relations). At first, in reading a research article, it may be difficult to discern that the children are different from those seen in practice. For example, the title, abstract, and discussion of the research article may call the children anxious, noncompliant, hyperactive, or socially withdrawn. The method section of the article may reveal that the inclusion criteria were rather lenient or that the cases were specially recruited for the project. This qualification does not necessarily mean that the results would not apply to clinically referred cases, but it raises the issue. The findings from such studies might not apply to children with clinically severe versions of similar problems.

Parents, Families, and Contexts

Child dysfunction is likely to be correlated with parent dysfunction and characteristics of the situations in which children live, although these can vary by clinical problem areas. Consequently, recruiting mildly problematic cases for treatment research also will likely result in a sample of families who are less seriously impaired and who live in environments with fewer untoward influences on child dysfunction. For example, anxiety, mood, and conduct disorders tend to run in families (see Hammen, 1991; Klein & Last, 1989; Stoff, Breiling, & Maser, 1997). Parents of children referred for treatment with one of these disorders often experience the same disorders themselves, moreso than parents of nonreferred children.

If parents of clinically referred samples have higher rates of disorders than parents of nonreferred children with milder forms of the problem (e.g., anxiety), there may be a stronger family transmission of the disorder in clinically referred cases. That is, more factors that contribute to the problem could reside in such families, and that could well make the problem more enduring for the children. Stated another way, referred children might be more difficult cases because of the strong set of influences (biological, socioenvironmental, or some combination) in which their dysfunction is embedded.

No less significant is the role of greater parent impairment on treatment implementation. In clinical work, parents are usually involved in the treatment of their children and adolescents; they participate in the sessions and carry out therapeutic strategies at home. If parents of clinically referred subjects experience clinical dysfunction or impairment, implementation of and adherence to the treatment may suffer. The benefits of treatment could be commensurately reduced.

Apart from parent psychopathology, deleterious family and contextual influences (e.g., socioeconomic disadvantage, parent stress, low level of social support) are also likely to be greater among clinically referred children than children recruited for research, at least for some clinical problems. In fact, untoward parent, family, and contextual factors could impair parent adherence to treatment and influence treatment outcome. In general, investigating treatment effects with less severely disturbed children, children with fewer comorbid disorders, and families with less psychopathology could lead to results quite different from those obtained with clinic samples.

Are we just worrying about academic issues? I do not think so. The effectiveness of treatment, at least for externalizing disorders, varies as a function of severity and scope of child disorders, parent psychopathology and stress, and socioeconomic disadvantage (Dadds & McHugh, 1992; Kazdin, 1995a; Kazdin & Wassell, 1999; Webster-Stratton & Hammond, 1990). Children and families affected more severely in these domains show less change over the course of treatment. Since children and adolescents seen in most treatment research present with less severe problems than those seen in clinical practice, the results of treatment research may be much more positive or favorable.

The nature of the concern should be clarified here. The children and adolescents seen in treatment typically show some problem, as defined by a recruiting and screening criteria of the investigator. For example, the children may be in the top third of their peer cohort for a particular characteristic (e.g., anxiety, depression, hyperactivity) based on one or more measures (e.g., parent- and teacher-completed rating scales). Even though the children may be less impaired in several domains than clinic samples, they still should be treated. Improving the lives of children is important in its own right, whether they are clinically referred or not. Moreover, children whose deviance is not severe enough to meet diagnostic criteria may still have impairment and poor long-term prognoses. The cutoff for diagnostic criteria is rather arbitrary. Understanding how to reduce misery is an important goal, and any implication that the misery of nonreferred cases is of lesser significance is difficult to defend. At the same time, even if we are concerned about developing treatments for clinically referred cases, the bulk of contemporary research does not speak to this population.

To avoid perpetuating a uniformity myth, it is also important to state that not all clinical problems are alike in relation to concerns presented here. Recruited cases are not automatically easier to treat and less impaired than nonrecruited cases. For example, recruiting children or adolescents who meet diagnostic criteria (e.g., for autism, major depression, or substance abuse) blurs, if not eliminates, the distinction between recruited and clinically referred cases. Children and adolescents can be recruited because they show clinical dysfunction and impairment. That said, the fact is that the majority of research is with recruited cases, in which child, parent, family, and contextual dysfunction may be relatively mild. Conclusions about the efficacy of treatment must be appropriately tempered.

TREATMENT AND TREATMENT ADMINISTRATION

Types of Treatment

Conclusions about the effects of psychotherapy depend on those techniques studied and methods of study. As mentioned before, of the hundreds of techniques, only a small subset has been subject to investigation. Also, studies focus unevenly on the different types of treatment. Approximately half of outcome research for children and adolescents focuses on behavioral or cognitive-behavioral techniques (Durlak et al., 1995; Kazdin, Bass, et al., 1990). Many approaches commonly practiced in clinical work (psychodynamic therapy, relationship-based treatment, family therapy) have very little empirically supportive literatures (e.g., Barrnett, Docherty, & Frommelt, 1991; Shadish et al., 1993). Clearly, when we say to ourselves, other professionals, and to the media that "psychotherapy works" and cite comprehensive reviews (e.g., meta-analyses) as proof, it might be reasonable to state boldly (or at least to whisper) two qualifiers: "But relatively few treatments have been studied, and the techniques most commonly used in clinical practice are not the ones I am talking about." Of course, clinical practice ought to use the techniques shown to be effective in research, and research ought to focus on treatments used in clinical practice.

The type of treatment evaluated in research can be distinguished in another way. With few exceptions, research focuses on relatively "pure" (single type or modality) treatments. The investigator usually is interested in evaluating a particular type of treatment as applied to a relatively circumscribed problem. On the one hand, it is unfair to criticize research for isolating variables and focusing on narrowly defined interventions. This is what research does: answer focused questions and identify the basis of change. At the same time, methods of testing treatments in research depart considerably from methods of administration in practice. In clinical practice, therapists commonly mix and combine several different treatments; eclectic and combined treatments are the rule rather than the exception, whereas the reverse is true for clinical research. Thus, whether a particular treatment examined in research, when extended to clinical practice and combined with other interventions, will have an effect is in question. In general, we have little idea about the effects of treatments administered in clinical practice and little idea about whether the results we obtain in research apply to clinical practice. (Other than these problems, things are great!)

Characteristics of Administration

How treatment is administered in research is different from how it is administered in practice in ways that could readily influence outcome. In research, treatment is relatively brief (e.g., average of 8–10 sessions) and is administered in group format, which is convenient because many studies are conducted in school settings where children are recruited for participation. In clinical practice, treatment tends to be much longer and to be administered individually in clinics. One can only surmise what these differences between research and practice mean for generality of findings. Conceivably, the "same" treatment (e.g., cognitive-behavior therapy) administered in a group format in schools rather than administered in clinical settings might have quite different effects, all else (e.g., child's severity of dysfunction) being equal. Of course, we have discussed how all else is *not* equal. The inclusion of children and adolescents whose clinical problems may be relatively mild, as in many studies, may make brief group treatment effective. Such treatment might not be feasible or viable in clinical settings.

Treatments administered in research are often carefully described in treatment manuals. Manuals refer to written guidelines that delineate the nature of treatment and the method of administration. These guidelines can vary in degree of specificity. For example, a treatment manual may outline the general principles that guide the sessions; specify the themes, topics, skills, and tasks to be covered; and specify mini-speeches or key aspects of what the therapist says during each session.[1] The use of treatment manuals has several purposes. Manuals document the therapy itself and serve as the basis for training therapists, monitoring therapists' adherence to the treatment, and evaluating whether the treatment was administered as intended. Also, the manuals provide a way of specifying treatment to others, including researchers and clinicians who may wish to replicate the treatment or to understand what really was done in the session. Without a treatment manual, one really does not know what was done in treatment and whether a particular treatment (e.g., psychodynamic therapy) resembles another given the same name.

Being able to refer to a treatment manual to identify actual events in the sessions can be very important. For example, several years ago behavioral marital therapy and insight-oriented psychotherapy were compared in a study for the treatment of marital discord (Snyder, Wills, & Grady-Fletcher, 1991; Snyder & Wills, 1989). Immediately after treatment and later at a 6-month follow-up, both interventions had equally improved marital adjustment; at a 4-year follow-up the divorce rate was higher for the behavioral treatment. Examination of the treatment manuals after the study was completed suggested that the insight-oriented treatment really resembled a behavioral treatment (Jacobson, 1991). Having access to treatment manuals permitted one to move beyond general labels (treatment names). This analysis greatly altered interpretation of the study; findings of no difference in results at different points and of the inferiority of one treatment at a later follow-up period revealed variations of a particular technique rather than conceptually different techniques.

The use of treatment manuals is controversial in part because of the view that they may make treatment too rigid, limit clinical decision-making, or impose a structure that interferes with therapeutic rapport (see Addis, 1997; Gagnon & Gaston, 1996; Wilson, 1998). But manuals vary in structure and they are not necessarily rigid prescriptions of treatment. Moreover, one can build flexibility into treatment manuals, including options for special treatment sessions to handle unique situations and crises. It is useful to consider the treatment manual as a road map that specifies the main roads leading to a destination. Detours along the way are those many conditions and circumstances that will require the therapist to depart from the main path. This does not gainsay the advantage of the map, nor does it make the detours new trips with new destinations. The careful specification of treatment is important, and manuals represent a significant advance. At the same time, well-specified and manualized treatments are not the same as treatments used in clinical practice.

Research usually includes supervision of the therapists during the study to ensure adherence to the manual. Supervision may take many forms, but typically one or more of the following are used: (1) observing the treatment sessions (e.g., live through a one-way mirror or via audiotaping or videotaping); (2) reviewing the sessions with the therapists; (3) discussing cases in treatment on a regular (e.g., weekly) basis to identify any problems in administering treatment; (4) repeatedly practicing or conducting retraining sessions with therapists during the study; and (5) having therapists complete checklists or forms about what they did during the session to prompt adherence to the procedures. Such rigorous specification of treatment and oversight of its execution are not at all like clinical work. One would expect that well-specified and closely monitored treatment would lead to greater therapist adherence. Indeed, therapist adherence to the prescribed treatment can increase effectiveness (e.g., Dobson & Shaw, 1988; Henggeler et al., 1997). It is difficult to discuss "adherence to treatment" in the context of clinical work because treatments are often not well specified and cannot be evaluated easily or meaningfully. In other words, when there is no map or only a vague course, it is difficult to tell if one is lost. The key point here is that the findings from therapy research may have little or unclear relation to the effects achieved in clinical practice.

Therapeutic Agent

In administering therapy to adults, usually a therapist delivers treatment on a one-to-one basis. In the context of child and adolescent therapy, there also is likely to be a therapist. In addition, parents, teachers, siblings, and peers alone and in various combinations can play primary, complementary, ancillary, and supportive roles in administering treatment. Consequently, the term *therapeutic agent* is used here to encompass the range of persons who may be involved in the delivery of treatment.

In the context of adult therapy, therapists themselves have been studied as an influence on treatment outcome (see Beutler, Machado, & Neufeldt, 1994). As might be expected, some therapists are more effective than others, even when all of the therapists compared are administering the same treatments. Moreover, some therapists are consistently effective and more effective than others even when they administer different treatments (see Beutler, 1997; Luborsky et al., 1997). Clearly, the therapist can contribute to treatment outcome, even though not invariably or across all treatments and clinical problems.

The therapist, as a source of influence, represents many specific variables that can be identified and investigated. Among them are individual characteristics of the therapist (age, gender, training, experience, personality style) and characteristics in relation to those of the client (e.g., match or similarity in ethnicity, personality). As an example, in adult therapy, the relationship between the client and therapist, including alliance, bonding, and quality of the relationship, influences therapeutic change (Orlinsky, Grawe, & Parks, 1994). Better treatment outcomes result from therapy in which the quality of the relationship is better.

The therapist has been accorded very little attention in child and adolescent therapy research, even in cases where treatment is characterized by the traditional model of adult therapy, as in a therapist meeting individually with a child or adolescent. Attention to characteristics of other therapeutic agents and their role in treatment outcome may be important too. For example, if most therapy with children and adolescents involves a parent in the sessions, relationship issues involving the parents may play a role in treatment. Indeed, the quality of the relationship of the parent to the therapist can influence the child's treatment outcome. Children whose parents have a better relationship and alliance with the therapist do better in treatment than those who do not, when such potential confounds as severity of child impairment and parent psychopathology are controlled (Kazdin & Wassell, 1998, 1999). Clearly the role of the therapist or treatment agent and the relationship of the therapist and client warrant attention. The paucity of such work represents a major deficiency in current research.

ASSESSMENT OF TREATMENT OUTCOME

Characteristics of assessment warrant mention here because they introduce important qualifiers to the conclusion that therapy works and is more effective than no treatment.

Limited Outcome Focus

The impetus for seeking treatment usually is evidence of various symptoms or maladaptive, disturbing, or disruptive behaviors. Naturally, the effects of treatment are measured by how much the problems identified at the outset of treatment have diminished when treatment is completed. The reduction of symptoms is obviously central to the evaluation of outcome.

The effects of treatment are likely to be broad. More important, the problems the individual brings to treatment are likely to involve many domains other than just symptoms. For example, for a child who is clinically depressed or anxious or has a conduct problem, functioning in many domains (adult and peer relations, school performance, participation in activities, self-esteem) is likely to be problematic as well. In addition to symptom reduction, assessing these other domains is important. Conclusions reached about the effects of treatment on symptoms may differ from those that would be reached if a wider range of functioning domains was evaluated.

In the next chapter, I provide assessment recommendations to guide future research. Consider here, as a preview, the implications of a limited outcome focus. One domain relevant for diverse clinical problems among children and adolescents is prosocial functioning, which refers to positive adaptive behaviors and experiences, such as participation in social activities, social interaction, and making friends. With children and adolescents, adjustment depends heavily on positive adaptive behaviors or skills, given the significance of the peer group and prosocial experiences outside the home. Reducing symptoms no doubt can improve a person's functioning. Yet the overlap of symptom reduction and positive prosocial functioning is not large. For example, among clinically referred children, the initial level of symptom severity and the initial level of prosocial functioning as well as changes in each domain over the course of treatment are modest ($r = -.2$ to $-.3$; Kazdin, 1993a). (The minus sign reflects the expected inverse relation between symptoms and prosocial functioning—the greater the symptoms, the lower the prosocial functioning.)

Prosocial functioning as an important assessment domain is raised here merely to illustrate that a range of outcomes is relevant to evaluating therapy. Conclusions about a given treatment may differ according to the outcome domain. For example, two treatments can be equally effective in reducing child symptoms but differ greatly on measures of other constructs (e.g., family functioning) (Szapocznik et al., 1989). Conclusions about treatment based on symptom reduction alone give an incomplete picture of the benefits of treatment.

The argument can be extended to the effects of treatment across settings. Presumably, treatment effects can vary depending on the settings in which child performance is evaluated. Usually, the two most relevant settings are home and school. Measures of performance in these domains are not highly related, and conclusions about treatment might vary depending on which setting is used as the basis to evaluate treatment. For example, two treatments can be equally effective on measures of child functioning at home but differ on measures of child functioning at school (e.g., Kazdin et al., 1989). When we conclude that treatment is effective, or more effective than another condition, we may gloss over differences in functioning of children and adolescents across settings.

In passing, it is worth noting that meta-analytic reviews of child and adolescent therapy research often combine all measures of a given study into a single index. This solution skirts the problems noted here but creates other problems because not all measures are equally relevant or important. Summing multiple measures that may not be very well correlated is not really meaningful; the outcome tells us very little. Can you imagine having a blood test that evaluates several cell concentrations, enzymes, and biochemical agents, only to have the results provided as a single metric derived from all specific measures? Me neither. Summary measures that collapse across several different types of raters, domains of functioning, and performance in different settings have no clear meaning in terms of patient care, although they might be useful as abstractions for research purposes.

Clinical Significance and Impact of Treatment

Changes in symptoms *are* important, and the previous comments ought not to imply otherwise. Let us continue with symptom reduction as a legitimate and primary focus of treatment outcome and ask this question: Do therapy studies have impact on symptoms of the children and adolescents who are treated? Typically, conclusions about the effects of treatment or relative effectiveness of various treatments are based on statistical evaluation of treatment outcome. Occasionally within a study, measures of the magnitude of effects such as effect size are also reported as a supplement to statistical significance. It is important to show statistically that treated individuals change over the course of treatment and that groups (e.g., treatment versus control groups) differ. Yet no less crucial is evidence that the treatment provided some clear practical benefit to the child, adolescent, or family.[2]

Clinical significance refers to the practical value or importance of the effect of an intervention, that is, whether it makes any real difference in everyday life. Obviously, some index showing that treatment makes a difference is very important. As a illustration, years of research on interventions for obesity have shown that obese individuals, when treated with behavior modification strategies, show significantly greater reductions in weight than those who receive no treatment (see Blanchard, 1994; Brownell & Wadden, 1992). Follow-up data, a few years later, show that many of the gains are lost and reductions are a matter of relatively few pounds. It is unclear whether treatment leads to genuine health benefits over the long term. Obesity provides a relatively clear example because the health risks and benefits for different magnitudes of change are better studied and follow-up data are available. Assuming treatment has led to changes, do the changes make a difference to the persons who have been treated in any way that goes beyond changes on questionnaires, interviews, and measures of behavior in circumscribed laboratory situations?

Clinical significance is operationalized in many different ways (see Kazdin, 1998b). Table 7.1 highlights five of the most commonly used ways of evaluating treatment outcome. These methods are applied in addition to the usual meth-

Table 7.1 Commonly Used Methods to Evaluate the Clinical Significance of Therapeutic Change

METHOD	DESCRIPTION
Comparison with Normative Samples	Demonstration that at the end of treatment the scores of treated cases fall within the range of behavior (on a symptom measure) that is normative (characteristic of people not referred for treatment and functioning well in everyday life).
Comparison with Pretreatment Scores	Demonstration that the score for an individual at the end of treatment has departed substantially from his or her score at the beginning of treatment (e.g., 2 SDs based on the distribution of scores). A change this large suggests that the distribution of pretreatment scores of clinically referred individuals no longer well represents the individual's performance.
Psychiatric Diagnostic Criteria	Demonstrating that the individuals no longer meet diagnostic criteria for the disorder/problem for which they were referred to treatment. For example, children may have met criteria for major depression at pretreatment; after receiving treatment they no longer meet these criteria and hence would not be regarded as having the disorder.
Subjective Evaluation of Impact	Evidence that others in everyday life who interact with the individual or the individual himself or herself subjectively see a change that makes a clear difference in everyday life. Ratings are provided to assess if one can see a difference in or impact on critical or everyday areas of functioning (e.g., interacting at home, engaging in activities in the world).
Social Impact Measures	Demonstration that therapy has affected measures of functioning in everyday life that are important to society at large and to consumers of treatment. Decreases in rates of arrest, truancy, hospitalization, and use of and need for other treatments in the future and increases in grades and school attendance are examples.

A more detailed discussion of the assessment of clinical significance, including the range of measures, their strengths and limitations, is provided in other sources (Kazdin, 1998b; Kendall, 1999).

ods, such as showing pre- to posttreatment changes or statistically significant treatment and control group differences. Thus, measures of clinical significance complement these other methods of evaluating symptom changes.

Most studies do not evaluate clinical significance (Kazdin, Bass, et al., 1990). When clinical significance is assessed, the most frequently used measure is the extent to which treated patients are returned to normative levels of functioning. As noted in table 7.1, to invoke this criterion, a comparison is made between treated patients and peers (e.g., same age, gender) who are functioning well or without problems in everyday life. Prior to treatment, the patient sample presumably would depart considerably from their well-functioning peers in the area identified for treatment (e.g., anxiety, social withdrawal, aggression). After treatment, presumably on that measure the treated individuals would be indistinguishable from, or within the range of, this peer group.

Evidence that a clinically significant change has been made can be ambiguous (Kazdin, 1999). For example, consider the use of normative data as a criterion for clinical significance. There is very little solid evidence (validity data) that individuals who return to normative levels of functioning on a symptom measure are in fact doing better in everyday life (e.g., are viewed differently by their peers, are less impaired) or are doing better than others who have not entered into the normative range at posttreatment assessment.

The other measures of clinical significance can be challenged as well. For example, at the end of treatment, a significant proportion of children may no longer meet criteria for the psychiatric disorder that they evinced at the beginning of treatment. However, one or two symptoms can determine whether diagnostic criteria are met, so a slight change can lead investigators to conclude that a clinically significant change was made. Moreover, individuals who fall below diagnostic criteria can have significant problems (Gotlib et al., 1995; Offord et al., 1992). The criteria are rather arbitrary; meeting or not meeting them is interesting but not necessarily a measure of impact on the life of the child or adolescent.

Subjective evaluation as a criterion for clinical significance would seem to be especially vulnerable to criticism. To state that a clinically significant change occurred, we want something more solid than the opinions and views of the person being treated or others with whom he or she interacts. Yet, in psychotherapy research, there is long-standing recognition that evaluation of treatment effects entails many different perspectives, including those of the client, those in contact with the client (e.g., parents, teachers, peers), mental health professionals, and society at large (e.g., Kazdin & Wilson, 1978a; Strupp & Hadley, 1977). Clinical significance invariably includes a frame of reference or perspective. It is quite appropriate for many treatment goals to ask, "Clinically significant to whom?" It is likely that a treatment outcome would be significant to some parties but not to others. Nevertheless, subjective evaluation is quite useful; if the change achieved in therapy is important, this ought to be evident to someone in contact with clients or the clients themselves.

Social impact measures may be particularly interesting to mention. These measures often are more meaningful to the public and consumers of treatment (e.g., clients, policy makers) than psychological measures, whose relation to daily functioning is obscure at best. If treatment alters grades, school attendance, use of drugs, incarceration, or suicide rates, there is obvious significance to the outcomes. Unfortunately, for many problems brought to treatment (anxiety, depression, and adjustment disorder among children and adolescents), there are no clear indices of social impact. Treatment can have enormous impact on personal functioning without necessarily affecting a social impact measure. Measurement problems of social impact measures, such as unreliable recording or changes in definitions over time show that such measures are far from flawless (see Kazdin, 1998b).

I do not wish to quibble or to unwittingly discourage use of measures of clinical significance. These measures are important, ought to be used, and warrant further development to ensure that they in fact reflect differences for persons in treatment. Yet merely calling a measure or a criterion an index of clinically significant change does not automatically make it so. Whether clinically significant change, as researchers use that term, reflects an important change in real life, or in the perceptions of those who received treatment, is not at all clear.

Because of the few studies that evaluate clinical significance, we can draw only limited conclusions about treatment research. When we say (from the research reviews) that treatment has been shown to produce change, the effects of treatment do not necessarily signal that children and adolescents have changed in important ways or improved in their daily lives. We simply do not have the relevant information to make the claim. This is not a minor limitation of current research. Even empirically supported treatments may not clearly make a difference that affects functioning in everyday life. Research must evaluate the impact of treatment on dimensions that make a difference in everyday life.

Timing of Outcome Assessment

Assessment immediately after treatment is referred to as *posttreatment* assessment; any point beyond that, ranging from weeks to years, typically is referred to as *follow-up* assessment. Follow-up raises an important issue for psychotherapy outcome research: whether gains are maintained. Conclusions about the efficacy of a treatment or relative efficacy of different treatments may differ greatly depending on when assessments are conducted. All sorts of combinations and permutations have been found. Thus, sometimes treatments that are significantly (statistically) different from each other or from controls at posttreatment are not different at follow-up or vice versa; sometimes changes over the course of treatment are small and nonsignificant but increase over time or vice versa (e.g., Heinicke & Ramsey-Klee, 1986; Kolvin et al., 1981; Meyers, Graves, Whelan, & Barclay, 1996; Newman, Kenardy, Herman, & Taylor, 1997). Clearly, the conclusions about the effects of a given treatment relative to a control condition or another treatment may vary at posttreatment and follow-up.

Not all studies, or necessarily most studies, find that the pattern of results and conclusions about a given treatment relative to another treatment or control condition vary from posttreatment to follow-up assessment. The problem is that the majority of outcome studies do not report follow-up; among those that do, the duration of follow-up is a matter of months, perhaps 5 to 7 (Durlak et al., 1995; Kazdin, Bass, et al., 1990). Conclusions reached about the effects of treatment pertain mostly to effects obtained immediately after treatment is completed. Reviews have suggested that the gains are maintained at follow-up for those studies in which data are available (Nicholson & Berman, 1983; Weisz et al., 1997). However, the paucity of studies and the loss of participants during the posttreatment to follow-up interval weaken the strength of the assertion that effects are maintained. Also, we have seen that even among exemplary studies (chapter 6), follow-up assessment often omits evaluation of any control sample. Thus, the putative gains that are "maintained" at follow-up may not be different from the changes made over time among nontreated cases. That is, over time, nontreated control patients may "catch up" to the treated patients in level of functioning.

The possible dependence of conclusions on the timing of follow-up assessment has multiple implications. To begin, it is important to determine whether therapeutic changes are maintained and whether they surpass those that might normally accrue over time, even without treatment. More than that, it is important to identify the function, curve, or course of change on the outcome measures associated with different techniques. If a few assessment points were obtained during follow-up, the function might be extrapolated to infer whether and how change continues. In any case, when we refer to the effects of treatment, it is useful to bear in mind that these are generally short-term effects, although there are important exceptions with extended follow-up (e.g., Henggeler et al., 1998; McEachin et al., 1993).

QUESTIONS THAT GUIDE THERAPY RESEARCH

Therapy research is narrow and restricted in many ways. The limited focus is evident in the narrow set of clinical problems, treatment techniques, and outcome measures on which research draws. Arguably the most significant way in which research is restricted is in the questions that guide current research. As an illustration, table 7.2 is based on a review of child and adolescent therapy research. The review included an evaluation of the specific questions that guided each study. From the table, one can see that the bulk of the research has focused on evaluating some facet of the treatment technique (first four categories). Scant attention is accorded evaluation of nontechnique variables (e.g., child moderators). The oft-cited question of what types of therapy work, with whom, under what conditions draws attention to a variety of conditions other than treatment technique that might moderate change. Scrutiny of the studies suggests that the focus of research remains narrow—key questions continue to be neglected. Two areas, the focus on moderators and mechanisms of change, illustrate this neglect and its implications.

**Table 7.2   Types of Research Questions and Comparisons That Serve as the
Focus of Child and Adolescent Psychotherapy Research**

Research Question or Focus	% of Studies ($N = 223$)
Compare treatment vs. no treatment	51.6
Compare treatment vs. active control	39.5
Examine characteristics of treatment	38.6
Compare 2 or more treatments	60.1
Examine treatment processes in relation to outcome	2.7
Examine child/adolescent characteristics	9.0
Examine parent or family characteristics	2.2
Examine therapist characteristics	2.7
Examine characteristics of dysfunction	0.0
Match child/adolescent characteristics and treatment	0.4
Match family characteristics to treatment	0.0

A study could be classified as having more than one research focus, depending on range of hypo-
theses/predictions and comparisons included in the design. Consequently, the percentage can
exceed 100 percent (see Kazdin, Bass, et al., 1990).

Research on Treatment Moderators

Most child and adolescent therapy studies are designed to evaluate one treatment versus a control condition or to compare two treatments. This type of research is obviously important, but, by itself, unwittingly contributes to the uniformity myths. One could look for broad treatment differences but also predict
which conditions will influence treatment outcome and of course analyze the
data to test these predictions. There is very little research on moderators of treatment, that is, the conditions on which the effects of treatment depend.

CHILD/ADOLESCENT CHARACTERISTICS.   Many characteristics of the child
are likely to influence treatment outcome. Severity, chronicity, and scope of
dysfunction are obvious contenders. One might expect that treatment would be
less effective depending on how severe, chronic, and pervasive the problem is.
Other characteristics, such as child gender, ethnicity, and age may be interesting as well, insofar as they influence onset of clinical dysfunction. For example, several risk factors (e.g., early signs of aggression, separation from a parent early in life, parental child-rearing practices) contribute differently to
aggressive behavior for boys and girls. Some factors predict onset for boys but
not for girls and vice versa; others predict for both but vary in the strength of
that contribution (Stoff et al., 1997). Of course, gender differences in the factors leading to some dysfunctions do not necessarily predict gender differences
in response to treatment. Yet therapeutically planned influences may vary in
their impact as well.

Ethnic, cultural, and racial identity also are likely to affect treatment.
Ethnicity and race, for example, influence when and how children are identified for treatment, patterns of risk and protective factors, characteristic symptoms, age of onset, and course of symptoms (Gaw, 1993; Tharp, 1991). As one
type of dysfunction, consider substance use and abuse among children and ado-

lescents. The substances used, family rules and monitoring of children in relation to substance use, and the number and type of risk factors that predict onset of substance use differ according to ethnic status (e.g., Catalano et al., 1993; Maddahian, Newcomb, & Bentler, 1988). With differences in the factors that contribute to the emergence and maintenance of dysfunction, it may be reasonable to expect variation in responsiveness to treatment.

Gender, ethnicity, age, and developmental stage are samples of individual difference variables likely to moderate the effects of treatment. Obviously, these are not the only promising leads. Moreover, these variables are merely summary terms for a broad array of other influences and require further evaluation to pinpoint the basis of their influence. The task of research is not merely to identify or "toss into" the design one or two child characteristics. Theory and conceptualization of child characteristics and how they might relate to treatment are critically important; more will be said about this later. Yet the general point is worth underscoring: understanding treatment effects will require evaluation of children's and adolescent's characteristics that interact (subject $\times$ treatment effects) with the intervention to produce therapeutic change.

PARENT, FAMILY, AND CONTEXTUAL CHARACTERISTICS.   Clinical problems of the child and adolescents are often associated with parental, family, and contextual influences. As mentioned previously, many of these influences affect onset and long-term prognosis. The socioenvironmental influences to which the child is exposed prior to, during, and no doubt after treatment likely influence treatment effects. A familiar example regarding the importance of context on treatment outcome derives from the treatment of schizophrenia in adults. Treated patients who return to families with high *expressed emotion* (i.e., are highly critical, hostile, overly involved) are much more likely to relapse (show a return of symptoms and be hospitalized) than those patients who return to families with low expressed emotion (Falloon, 1988; Tarrier & Barrowclough, 1990). Treatment that focuses on the symptoms of schizophrenia alone is not as effective as treatment that also attempts to alter family interaction patterns. This excellent example focuses on a moderator variable (expressed emotion) that influences treatment outcome and shows that treatment effects can be improved by directly altering family characteristics.

In formulations of child dysfunction, there is increased recognition that multiple factors may increase the likelihood of occurrence of the dysfunction (risk factors) and attenuate the impact of such factors (protective factors) (Robins & Rutter, 1990; Rutter & Casaer, 1991). Parent psychopathology, family conflict, and socioeconomic disadvantage are factors mentioned earlier as related to selected disorders. These factors may operate differently according to the disorder. Parent dysfunction and these other factors may play a central role in maintaining a child's impairment or raising obstacles in the administration and delivery of treatment. Moreover, the influence of parent functioning on treatment outcome may vary for different types of treatment (e.g., family therapy versus individual child therapy). In child and adolescent therapy research, these parent influences are rarely assessed as potential moderators. With a wide range of moderators and treatments, theory becomes important as a guide to unravel these possibilities.

Family functioning, including interaction patterns, personal relationships, and system issues, are likely relevant to child treatment as well. For example, marital discord and interpersonal conflict influence child adjustment (Grych & Fincham, 1990). Treatment outcomes for children with similar clinical dysfunction might differ as a function of conflict in the home at the time treatment is provided. Such rudimentary tests of moderators that I raise in this example are rare in child therapy research. They would be remarkable additions.

A goal of treatment is to match cases and interventions. That means that the decision on treatment is based on knowledge of the problem as well as other pertinent aspects of the case (moderators). Toward this end, we need to identify sources of variance that contribute to treatment outcome and that interact with (moderate) the effects of treatment. In clinical work, the influence of parental and family factors on treatment is often conspicuous. For example, treatment administration and outcome may be influenced by whether parents are taking psychoactive medication, undergoing their own treatment, or experiencing multiple sources of stress. Some of these factors influence whether children drop out of treatment and the extent to which those who remain in treatment improve (Kazdin, Mazurick, & Bass, 1993; Kazdin & Wassell, 1999). The task is to measure parent and family factors in relation to treatment outcome. If these are neglected in treatment, the outcomes are likely to appear highly variable or diluted. Psychotherapy trials rarely assess factors that may influence onset or course of problems, address these factors during treatment, or analyze their impact as moderators of therapeutic change.

TREATMENT CHARACTERISTICS.   Even if one is interested only in treatment—rather than in child, parent, family or therapist influences on treatment—there is still a career's worth of moderators available for investigation. For example, parameters of treatment (i.e., those characteristics or dimensions of the intervention that can be systematically varied) can influence treatment outcome. Dose or amount of treatment (number or duration of sessions), concentration of treatment (number of sessions within a time period, such as one vs. three sessions/week), and duration of treatment (how many weeks, months) are all reasonable moderators of treatment outcome. Yet they have not been carefully studied in child and adolescent therapy. Actually, a few studies have systematically varied the amount of treatment (Heinicke & Ramsey-Klee, 1986; Lovaas, 1987; Smyrnios & Kirkby, 1993), but too few studies within a problem area or treatment approach are available to permit conclusions.

Two related lacunae in research can be identified. First, in general a narrow range of treatment intensities and durations has been sampled. Most studies remain within a fairly narrow range in which children receive brief, time-limited treatment (1 hour sessions per week for 8–10 weeks) (Casey & Berman, 1985; Weisz et al., 1987). The rationale for this regimen does not seem to be determined by evidence of clinically significant or durable changes, for most studies do not assess clinical significance or conduct follow-up assessment (Kazdin, Bass, et al., 1990). Also, most studies using relatively brief treatments were completed before any pressures to do so arose because of managed care. Given the long-term course of many clinical dysfunctions referred for treatment (e.g., conduct disorder, attention deficit-hyperactivity disorder), one might be skeptical of weekly (and weakly) treatments.

Second, individual studies rarely test parametric variations of treatment with longer versus shorter or more versus less intensive treatments. The paucity of direct tests of parametric variations of treatment means we know very little about treatment factors that influence outcome. From the standpoint of identifying and developing effective treatments, amount, concentration, and duration of treatment warrant much more empirical attention. Perhaps a first step to improve research would be to specify the rationale for a particular intensity or dose selected in a study. The rationale would reveal assumptions about treatment effects that could be subsequently tested.

GENERAL COMMENTS.   Characteristics that may moderate treatment effects have been sorely neglected. Characteristics of children, parents, families, contexts, and treatments were mentioned here to show classes of moderators likely to influence outcome. The specific factors and their relation to outcome may vary by type of disorder and treatment. For example, one would not want to say that parent stress and dysfunction influence the effectiveness of all treatments applied to children. Parent stress and dysfunction are associated with some child problems moreso than others. Also, some treatments make extensive demands on parents and others do not. For those treatments that do, parent stress and dysfunction may have greater impact on treatment effectiveness. Research that evaluates moderators requires more thought than the usual comparison of two or more treatments. The reward is deeper understanding of how and for whom treatment works.

Research Processes and Mechanisms

The question of how or why therapy works has seemed to be of little interest to researchers. Table 7.2 demonstrates the scant attention to processes (e.g., changes in cognitions, relationship factors between the therapeutic agent and child) involved in therapy that account for or contribute to therapeutic change. Over time, understanding how treatments work will provide the greatest benefits. Research ought to answer these questions: (1) What processes or characteristics within the child, parent, or family can be mobilized to foster therapeutic change? (2) What events, processes, activities, and tasks in treatment can foster therapeutic change? If we knew the bases of therapeutic change, we might readily optimize the effectiveness of treatment. As researchers, we cannot be faulted for our ignorance of the answers. Yet we probably can be faulted for not pursuing the questions. What could be a higher priority for treatment research than trying to understand how change occurs and can be optimized?

There are hundreds of available treatments but probably only a few common bases or mechanisms of therapeutic change. Perhaps such key factors as rehearsal and practice (e.g., symbolic via language, imagery, or behavior), catharsis (alleviation of the symptoms through expression and release), or the mobilization of hope explain how all or most therapies work. In child and adolescent psychotherapy research, it is easy to identify programs of research that focus on various treatments or disorders (e.g., Hibbs & Jensen, 1996). Yet it is very difficult to identify programs of research or indeed individual studies that focus on exploring the mechanisms of change.

Ideas for evaluating the basis of therapeutic change can come from all sorts of sources (various learning models, information processing, or social cognition views). Over the history of psychotherapy, many ideas and mini-theories have served as intellectual comets—they come around once in a while, the same ones after lengthy intervals. We like to look at them, although so far none has really had much impact on us. As we discuss future directions, the role accorded conceptual models of therapy and tests of the bases for therapeutic change will be elaborated.

IMPLICATIONS

Selected characteristics of therapy research were identified that have marked implications for conclusions about the effectiveness of therapy and for directions in future research. Consider two interrelated implications of the issues discussed previously.

Generalizing from Research to Clinical Practice

The very special conditions of research, as discussed previously, may limit generality of the results to clinical practice. This concern is by no means new, but still relevant. In contemporary discussions, efficacy and effectiveness research are used to denote the differences between research settings/conditions and clinical settings/conditions (Hoagwood, Hibbs, Brent, & Jensen, 1995). As noted before, the well-controlled and analogue conditions of research and less well-controlled and more "realistic" conditions of clinical practice are multidimensional and vary on continua. For example, research does not focus only on children with few or no problems or clinical work only on children who are very impaired. The severity, chronicity, and scope of dysfunction represent a wide range, and some research may well focus on samples exactly like those in clinical practice. Similarly, other characteristics, such as how treatment is administered, what treatment is administered, and the degree of rigor in administration, vary by degree. We do not know precisely which dimensions influence the effectiveness of treatment and whether the differences between research and clinical practice invariably influence treatment outcome (Kazdin, 1998b).

Do the results from therapy in more well-controlled laboratory-based research (efficacy studies) generalize to therapy in clinical settings (effectiveness studies)? The jury is still out. One meta-analysis suggests that treatment effects are stronger in controlled studies (Weisz et al., 1992), and another analysis suggests that the effects are similar in both contexts (Shadish et al., 1997). One can say only that the effectiveness of treatment in clinical practice is not at all clear, not just because treatments used in practice are not the ones investigated in research, although that, of course, is disturbing. The ways in which treatment is studied are the key issue. Treatments in clinical work are rarely evaluated systematically. We shall return to that topic in a later chapter.

Understanding Why and How Therapy Works

I mentioned the lack of attention to the bases of therapeutic change. Many complaints about therapy research focus on how research conditions depart from clinical practice; hence, generality from the former to the latter is in question. This is difficult to deny. Yet the main value of research is to test theory, propositions, and hypotheses to help understand the phenomenon of interest. Methodological practices that characterize well-controlled research may limit the generality of findings from research to clinical practice. Yet, rigorous methodology and experimental control are assets in the context of efforts to isolate variables and test factors that could not be evaluated in other, more naturalistic situations. Testing causal hypotheses about treatment and tinkering with parameters of treatment or moderators (by matching clients to treatments) to test such hypotheses would be the natural focus of research.

Conceptually driven therapy research to evaluate the mechanisms of change can draw on many resources. Theories and research on child and adolescent development and on the emergence of specific clinical dysfunctions provide rich opportunities. (More will be said about conceptualization of dysfunction and treatment in chapter 8.) Efforts to understand how therapy works may also draw on moderators. Specific hypotheses about why treatment works can be tested by predicting who will respond to treatment. For example, if cognitive therapy really works because of changes in cognitions, one might test whether changes in specific cognitive processes affect outcome.

Perhaps the greatest limitation of contemporary therapy research is the paucity of studies that attempt to explain why and how treatment works. Without such research, work is likely to hobble along. More techniques will be developed, there will be pressures to add to the list of empirically supported treatments, and more old techniques will be applied in new ways. If we knew how therapies worked, we might be able to select more reliable treatments. Research could explain the processes and how some treatments mobilized these processes better than others. Even the most effective treatments might be improved if we knew why they achieved their effects.

SUMMARY AND CONCLUSIONS

Prior reviews of the evidence have consistently concluded that treatment is more effective than no treatment and that some treatments, in particular, are supported by strong evidence (i.e., are empirically supported). This chapter examined characteristics of the therapy literature to place these conclusions in perspective. Many characteristics of child and adolescent therapy could be scrutinized. Indeed, they have been in other sources (Durlak et al., 1995; Kazdin, 1995c; Weisz, Huey, & Weersing, 1998; Weisz & Weiss, 1993). The goal of the chapter was to identify key features that might limit application of the findings to clinical practice and to consider significant or outstanding islands (continents?) of ignorance.

Clearly, therapy research departs significantly from clinical practice. Characteristics of children/adolescents, parents, families, and contexts included in treatment research distinguish research and practice. Moreover, the types of treatment and treatment delivery in research as a rule depart from their counterparts in clinical practice. Departure from clinical practice by itself is not necessarily important unless there is reason to suspect that one or more of the dimensions along which research and practice differ are related to treatment outcome. We have many reasons to believe this, based on studies cited previously. Stated in the most stark and anxiety-provoking fashion, the findings obtained in research may have little or no bearing on the effects of treatment in clinical work.

Apart from departures from clinical practice, contemporary research focuses on a limited range of questions about treatment and avoids the study of moderators and mediators of treatment outcome. Merely expanding the same old research paradigms to evaluate new therapies would continue uninspired and fairly noninquisitive research. We ought to be more curious about why treatment works, through what processes, and for whom and to pursue answers in a conceptually informed or inspired fashion. This chapter provides piecemeal hints about how to make research progress in the next decade. Chapter 8 presents a more systematic plan.

FOR FURTHER READING

The readings below provide further evaluations about characteristics and limitations of child and adolescent therapy research and the implications for drawing conclusions from research.

Durlak, J.A., Wells, A.M., Cotten, J.K., & Johnson, S. (1995). Analysis of selected methodological issues in child psychotherapy research. *Journal of Clinical Child Psychology, 24,* 141–148.

Kazdin, A.E. (1995). The scope of child and adolescent psychotherapy research: Limited sampling of dysfunctions, treatments, and client characteristics. *Journal of Clinical Child Psychology, 24,* 125–140.

Kazdin, A.E., Bass, D., Ayers, W.A., & Rodgers, A. (1990). The empirical and clinical focus of child and adolescent psychotherapy research. *Journal of Consulting and Clinical Psychology, 58,* 729–740.

Weisz, J.R., Weiss, B., & Donenberg, G.R. (1992). The lab versus the clinic: Effects of child and adolescent psychotherapy. *American Psychologist, 47,* 1578–1585.

PART III

Improving Therapy Research

Chapter 8

Developing Effective Treatments:
A Model for Clinical Research

CHAPTER 7 EXAMINED characteristics of child and adolescent therapy research that limit the conclusions one can reach about the effects of treatment and that reflect significant gaps in knowledge. The usual way to suggest improvements in research is to underscore redressing prior limitations. In principle, progress might be made in this way. However, pleas to overcome research limitations or to engage in new ways of studying a phenomenon rarely achieve clear results (see Amir & Sharon, 1991; Sedlmeier & Gigerenzer, 1989). Even if individual studies redressed the limitations and gaps in knowledge, long-term progress would not necessarily result.

The overriding issue for research on child and adolescent psychotherapy is whether we are moving toward the broad goals or objectives of research, not whether current studies are better than prior studies. Consider the task of research on child and adolescent therapy more broadly. There are the key questions:

- What do we want to know about child and adolescent therapy? That is, what are the goals of the research?
- What type of research is needed to obtain these goals?
- How can we evaluate that movement and determine whether we are making progress toward the goal(s)?

The most significant limitation of child and adolescent psychotherapy research, I believe, is not at the level of individual studies. Rather, it is the absence of an overall vision or plan that provides a systematic way of achieving the goals of research.

This chapter proposes a model or plan to guide psychotherapy research and to increase the likelihood of developing effective and clinically useful interventions. The central theses underlying the model are that (1) current therapy research is not moving very well or rapidly toward developing effective treatments for children and adolescents; (2) the ways in which studies are conducted limit the progress we can make; and (3) an overall plan is needed to guide the progression of research as well as the conduct of individual studies. For developing effective treatments, I propose a model, a general framework that encompasses the type of knowledge we need and the type of studies needed to obtain that knowledge.

STEPS TO DEVELOP EFFECTIVE TREATMENTS

To develop effective treatments, we cannot merely study treatment effects. There is a great deal we need to understand in order to make treatment effective and to ensure it is applied optimally. Knowledge is required along several fronts. Table 8.1 highlights the scope of research needed to explain treatment. Several steps are identified to evaluate different facets of treatment, how treatment relates to what is known about the disorder or clinical problem domain, and how and to whom treatment can be applied to achieve optimal gains. The steps emphasize theoretical development of treatment, so that there is some connection to processes that can be investigated and established in their own right. But steps and a progression of research do not necessarily entail a fixed sequence of studies. Rather, the steps refer to the areas that ought to be covered over a period of years of research so that the foundation of knowledge is systematic and builds in a unified way.

**Table 8.1   Model for Developing Effective Treatment:
Steps toward Progress**

STEP	COMPONENTS
1. Conceptualization of the Dysfunction	Propose key areas, processes, and mechanisms that relate to the development, onset, and course of dysfunction.
2. Research on Processes Related to Dysfunction	Efforts to test proposed processes in relation to the dysfunction.
3. Conceptualization of Treatment	Propose key areas, processes, and mechanisms through which treatment may achieve its effects and how the procedures relate to these processes.
4. Tests of Treatment Processes	Studies to identify whether the intervention techniques, methods, and procedures within treatment actually affect those processes that are critical to the model.
5. Specification of Treatment	Operationalize the procedures, preferably in manual form, that identify how one changes the key processes. Provide material to codify the procedures so that treatment integrity can be evaluated and that treatment can be replicated in research and practice.
6. Tests of Treatment Outcome	Direct tests of the impact of treatment drawing on diverse designs (e.g., open studies, single-case designs, full-fledged clinical trials) and types of studies (e.g., dismantling, parametric studies, comparative outcome studies).
7. Tests of the Boundary Conditions and Moderators	Examination of the child, parent, family, and contextual factors with which treatment interacts. The boundary conditions or limits of application are identified through interactions of treatment $\times$ diverse attributes.
8. Tests of Generalization and Applicability	Examination of the extent to which treatment can be effectively applied to different problems, samples, and settings and of variations of the treatment. The focus is explicitly on seeing if the results obtained in research can be obtained under other circumstances.

Conceptualization of Dysfunction

Conceptualization refers to the theoretical underpinnings and hypotheses about the likely factors and processes leading to the clinical problem or pattern of functioning. Many of the approaches to psychotherapy have originated from models of *treatment* that loosely explain how problems originated (etiology) and are to be ameliorated (treatment). Psychoanalytic, family, behavioral, cognitive-behavioral, and other approaches often begin with a view of key components about a problem, but treatment often focuses on processes thought to have wide applicability across many different problems. For example, family therapies are based on a view—depending on the variation of therapy—of how psychological problems emerge in the context of the family and are fostered by certain communications, roles, and so on. Similarly, cognitive-behavioral treatments often begin with a generic view that cognitions are important, sometimes deficient or distorted, and hence become the focus of treatment. There is little question that a domain of influences (e.g., the family, cognitions) may be critically important, but multiple influences from multiple domains are likely operative. Moreover, a given conceptual view, say, about the family or cognitions, cannot explain why the full range of problems emerges or how they might be effectively treated. In general, most treatments do not begin with clear or very specific views about the nature of the problem to be treated; fewer still, when a view of the problem is presented, follow up with a statement connecting treatment methods to those views.

Another way to develop treatment is to begin with a conceptualization of the dysfunction, concurrent correlates, antecedents, and causal factors. Any conceptual view may well be restricted to a particular dysfunction, such as major depression, or set of dysfunctions, such as mood disorders or anxiety disorders. Treatment ought to be connected with what we know about the factors related to onset, maintenance, termination, and recurrence of the problem. As we understand more about the clinical problem, we are much more likely to develop effective treatments. As a beginning, conceptualization of onset and course of clinical dysfunction or the specific problem domain is a critical step for the development of treatment. Treatment researchers are not often involved in research on the underpinnings of clinical problems, but they can draw more frequently on that research as a guide toward developing treatments or hypotheses about treatment.

Research on Processes Related to Dysfunction

Developing a conceptual view in the context of therapy research usually has meant that one proposes processes that play a role in emergence of the problem (e.g., the problem emerged because of underlying psychic conflict, deleterious family processes, limited social reinforcement, and so on). Conceptions that are not followed by research are incomplete and not very helpful. Consequently, a critical step for therapy research is direct tests of the processes hypothesized to be implicated in the clinical problem or direct tests of the conceptual view. For example, if cognitions are assumed to play a pivotal role in the onset or maintenance of a disorder or pattern of functioning, direct tests ought to be part of the foundation leading toward the development of effective treatment.

Tests of conceptual models about how problems develop are not usually treatment or intervention studies. Cross-sectional and longitudinal studies of child and adolescent development and animal studies can test models of clinical dysfunctions and developmental paths or trajectories. Research on the nature of the clinical problem is likely to identify subtypes, multiple paths leading to a similar onset, and key moderators that alter the profile of risk factors leading to the disorder. These findings can directly test the conceptual model about the problem and can identify factors that may warrant attention in treatment.

Treatment studies can also be used to evaluate the conceptual model of the clinical problem. In a treatment study, the investigator may include measures of processes (e.g., cognitions, family interaction) critical to development of the problem. If causes or influences on the clinical problem still operate at the time treatment is initiated, a treatment study may be able to show that, along with improvement, key processes of the problem have changed as well. That is, changes in the processes known to affect the problem may mediate therapeutic change. This is an infrequent focus of psychotherapy research.

Conceptualization of Treatment

I mentioned previously the conceptualization of the clinical problem, or the theory about what factors lead to the problem and how they operate. Conceptualization of treatment is different. Treatment ought to have conceptual underpinnings, explicit views about what treatment is designed to accomplish and through what processes. How will the procedures used in treatment influence the processes implicated in the dysfunction or counteract these influences by developing new repertoires? Treatment may directly address those processes believed to be involved in the development of the problem. For example, inept discipline practices influence the development of aggressive behavior in children (Dodge, Pettit, & Bates, 1994; Patterson, 1982; Patterson, Reid, & Dishion, 1992). Parent management training directly alters these practices and alters a child's aggressive behavior. That is, the conceptual model of contributory factors to the problem overlaps with the conceptual model of the treatment.

In other treatments, the conceptual model of treatment may be unrelated to the processes supposedly involved in the development of the problem. For example, an effective procedure to overcome agoraphobia (fear of open spaces) is to provide a graduated sequence of experiences that exposes the individual to diverse settings (e.g., shopping malls, public transportation). This treatment is not based on a specific conceptual model of how the problem emerged (e.g., when children were growing up, they were not exposed to open spaces in a graduated way). Rather, the conceptual view of the treatment encompasses these components: new learning needs to take place, repeated practice is important, and habituation (reduced arousal) results from repeated exposure in a controlled (gradual, small dose) fashion. The same might be said for many other problems brought to treatment, such as depression, hyperactivity, or enuresis. The focus of treatment may not be based on factors related to how the problem emerged. Illustrated another way, aspirin is effective as a treatment for headaches, but headaches are not due to the lack of aspirin in one's system. Nor does aspirin necessarily work because of the effects in getting at the underlying cause of the problem. A theory of onset or cause of a problem and a theory of how change occurs can be quite different.

This question guides the treatment conceptualization: how does this treatment achieve change? The answer may involve basic psychological processes (e.g., memory, learning, information processing) or a broader theory (e.g., motivation). Global conceptual views that foster a treatment approach or orientation are no longer sufficient. Rather, to ensure progress, specific conceptual models are needed to explain those processes (e.g., psychodynamic, cognitive, or familial) supposedly responsible for therapeutic change.

Tests of Treatment Processes

Do the intervention techniques, methods, and procedures within treatment sessions actually affect processes critical to the treatment model? These processes refer to those facets of treatment that are considered to produce or facilitate change. It may be that parenting practices are critical to change in the oppositional child. If so, these practices ought to change during treatment. The problematic practices and their change over treatment ought to relate specifically to child improvement. Among varied treatment models, relationship, alliance, and bonding between the child (or parent) and therapist may be viewed as critical processes to achieve change. Tests of such processes are essential to ensure we understand why and how treatment works.

Current research cannot easily begin by testing critical processes. Two steps are required to conduct the research: first, a conceptual view of the factors involved in treatment and, second, ways of operationalizing and measuring one or more of these during treatment. There has been relatively little work on conceptualizing the change process. How does change occur in therapy? Theories of therapeutic change and tests of these theories would be enormously helpful in moving research toward more effective treatments.

Specification of Treatment

Discussion of key processes in treatment raises the practical matter of ensuring that they are addressed in treatment. Specifying the focus of the treatment and what actually is done with, to, or for the child, adolescent, or parent during the sessions is relevant. Treatments ought to be operationalized, preferably in manual form, so that the integrity of treatment can be evaluated, the material derived from treatment trials can be codified, and the treatment procedures can be replicated. Manuals address all aspects of treatment that can be documented. Some of the information may seem relatively trivial, such as the materials to be used in a session, instructions to explain treatment, and forms used to document the sessions. The effective application of treatment may not require complete adherence to each point specified in the manual. At the same time, replication in research and clinical practice will require explicit knowledge of what was done. Any particular practice can then be researched if one doubts the importance of that facet of treatment.

There has been a movement toward and now, perhaps predictably, a movement away from the manualization of treatment because of the concern that manuals may make treatment inflexible or miss critical treatment processes (see Addis, 1997; Gagnon & Gaston, 1996; Strupp & Anderson, 1997; Wilson, 1998). At this time, there is no alternative to the manualization of treatment. It is a convenient straw man to argue that manuals are too rigid for clinical use or that they ignore individual differences of the patient (or therapist), but this claim is spurious. Manuals specify guidelines, session foci and content, the progression of treatment, and when and how to continue particular practices, tasks, sessions, and themes. The application can be individualized, but basic desiderata, guiding principles, and procedures should be in the manuals (Forehand & Long, 1996; Henggeler et al., 1998).

Manualization in some form is also essential in light of the likely alternative, namely, improvisation in clinical practice in which individual therapist differences in training, preferences for treatment, and judgment dominate. What is worrisome about clinical work is that a particular treatment, whatever it is called, may not be carried out faithfully. With evidence that therapists' adherence to procedures can influence the effectiveness of therapy (Dobson & Shaw, 1988; Henggeler et al., 1997), treatment execution is important. Manuals play a key role by codifying the procedures to which the therapist should adhere. The balance of manuals, improvisation, and individual therapist differences will remain important. Progress in developing treatments requires specifying critical facets of treatment and their implementation.

Tests of Treatment Outcome

Obviously, in developing treatment, direct tests of clinical outcomes are central. A wide range of treatment tests (e.g., open [uncontrolled, single-group] studies, single-case experimental designs, full-fledged randomized clinical trials) can provide evidence that change has occurred and that treatment is responsible for the change. Direct tests of treatment are the most common forms of research in child and adolescent therapy, so I need not dwell on this step. At the same time, there are several different types of outcome questions based on whether, for example, variations of parameters of treatment, components of treatment, or combinations of treatment influence outcome. A range of questions ought to be addressed, as discussed later in the chapter.

Tests of Boundary Conditions and Moderators

Tests of the conditions on which effective applications of treatment depend are critical. What are the conditions for effective application of treatment or the variables (moderators) that influence effectiveness? In child and adolescent treatment, influences related to children, parents, families, and contexts affect development of clinical dysfunction as well as the likelihood that critical treatment processes and child dysfunction will be altered. Our thinking in treatment development and research is dominated by the search for main effects. We look for the technique that will be "the answer." Indeed, one might argue that therapy has traditionally searched for main effects across multiple problem areas. Changing cognitions and family interactions, for example, is not just the solution to some clinical problems but the overall goal of therapy. What treatment works for whom and under what conditions has guided *discussions* of research but has not served as a basis for very many studies in child and adolescent therapy (Kazdin, Bass, et al., 1990).

Chapter 7 lamented the lack of studies on moderators and mentioned characteristics of children, parents, families, contexts, and treatments that are likely to influence outcome. I revisit the issue in this chapter in the context of a broader plan for developing treatment. The search for moderators is not a blind search for factors that interact with treatment (e.g., whether treatment is more effective with boys or girls, with younger or older children). Rather, the search moderators are, ideally, informed by conceptualization and empirical findings regarding the clinical problem of treatment. For example, we know that sexually abused children are likely to develop beliefs that the world is a dangerous place, that adults cannot be trusted, and that one's own efforts to influence the world are not likely to be effective (Wolfe, Gentile, & Wolfe, 1989; Wolfe, Gentile, Michienzi, Sas, & Wolfe, 1991). Based on this understanding of the problem, an investigator might make predictions that use this information to test moderators of treatment. One might predict that sexually abused youths with these beliefs would respond less well to treatment, as measured by posttreatment prosocial functioning. If these beliefs are not altered in treatment, the children's social activities may be more restricted than those of similar children who do not have those beliefs. Perhaps another study using this information might determine if the effectiveness of treatment could be enhanced by including a component that focuses on these beliefs. In general, the search for moderators ought to be guided by our understanding of the factors related to dysfunction or to the treatment. Of course, research on moderators need not wait until advances further our understanding of disorders or treatment; in fact, treatment can test moderators based on incomplete research evidence and in the process help inform conceptual views about disorders and treatment.

Clinical experience too is a good source of potential moderators of treatment. Practitioners who provide child and adolescent therapy believe that several factors influence treatment outcome, such as the degree of parent involvement in treatment, distress experienced by the child, duration of child dysfunction, and child motivation for treatment, to mention a few (see Kazdin, Siegel, & Bass, 1990). Although these proposed moderators are not theoretically based, their effects, if demonstrated in research, could prompt theory to explain how and why they operate. Connecting research findings to conceptualizations of treatment is, of course, a reciprocal process; where this process begins is not as important as where it ends, in theory with research support.

Tests of Generalization and Applicability

When a treatment is shown to produce change in a particular context, it is valuable to evaluate the generality of the findings across other dimensions and domains. Is treatment effective beyond the conditions in which it has been developed or already shown to be effective? Among the range of extensions, the most salient domains include types of problems, samples, settings, and variations of the treatment.

Generality across settings warrants special mention and includes the extension from research (efficacy) to clinical practice (effectiveness). Can this treatment be applied clinically and are the effects similar to those obtained in research? Generality across problem areas means that treatment can be administered in other areas and still achieve similar effects. The way in which treatment is administered too might provide a test of generality. For example, the treatment is effective when administered by a professional therapist, but is it also effective when administered via videotape, by a lay therapist, or by the clients themselves (e.g., self-help manuals for parents)?

Tests of generality of a treatment are similar to tests of moderators because moderators are the conditions that influence the effects of treatment. So, for example, showing that treatment works with one problem but not another is tantamount to showing that problem type moderates treatment outcome. Both tests of moderators (discussed previously) and tests of generality examine the conditions under which effective application depends. However, I have made the distinction for slightly different emphases.

Tests of generality are explicit attempts to extend and to evaluate treatment beyond the original focus. The results of such tests may well yield information about moderators. For example, if a test of generality showed that treatment was not effective with problem x but was with problem y, we would say that problem area moderated treatment. However, tests of moderators ideally draw on theory or prior research that elaborates the nature of the clinical problem or the treatment. Tests of generality are less conceptually inspired and more application-oriented. They ask whether treatment can be applied in different ways, to different people, and in different settings.

Whether a given study fits better as a test of a moderator or applicability may reflect how the study is conceived and presented. For example, an investigator may propose that ethnicity will moderate treatment effects, given cultural differences regarding the clinical problem or culturally relevant processes used in treatment. This study would emphasize a moderator. The same study might be presented as a test of generality or applicability of a prior finding to other ethnic groups. As a matter of course, it is useful to propose a reason why a particular variable was introduced as a moderator. Research designed merely to duplicate prior findings with another sample or setting is not highly regarded.

Clearly, there is a keen interest in current research to test generality of treatment to clinical practice. Too few studies evaluate whether a treatment effective in research is also effective in clinical applications (e.g., Shadish et al., 1997; Weisz et al., 1992). This step in the model proposed here focuses quite explicitly on tests of generality and application to other areas (problems, samples, settings).

General Comments

The steps of the model evaluate different facets of treatment, how treatment interfaces with what is known about the disorder and processes of change, and how and to whom treatment can be applied. Few examples in child and adolescent therapy research illustrate progression through some subset of these steps. One example already mentioned that illustrates several key steps is research on parent management training as a means of treating oppositional and aggressive children (Dishion & Patterson, in press; Patterson, 1982; Patterson et al., 1992). These steps include conceptualization of conduct problems, research on family processes (inept and harsh discipline practices) that promote the problems, and outcome studies that establish the central role of these practices. A progression of studies has shown the association and influence of inept discipline practices on conduct problems (Dishion et al., 1992; Forgatch, 1991). Also, many randomized controlled trials have shown that changes in parenting skills lead to reductions in children's antisocial behavior (e.g., Dishion & Andrews, 1995; Dishion et al., 1992). This research not only establishes an effective treatment but provides a model of how the problem may develop for many children, which domains of functioning are affected, what treatment techniques are needed in cases where inept practices are evident, and what to monitor during treatment (e.g., parent progress) if the outcomes are to be achieved. As a rule, the vast majority of studies ignore conceptual views or findings on the nature of the disorder or symptom pattern and do not test processes related to the disorder or therapeutic change.

These steps emphasize theoretical development of treatment, so that there is some connection to processes that can be investigated and established in their own right. Through steps and a progression of research, the literature can move systematically. Thus, the field can be evaluated in a quite different way from the usual qualitative and quantitative reviews. Current reviews focus on what has been done in research. The accumulated studies are haphazard, and what we can say is based on tracing the path through which the research has wandered. If we, as investigators, have ignored many critical questions or used design practices that limit the findings, the conclusions in the reviews will be limited. A better way to proceed is to begin with a model of what we need to know in moving from ignorance to knowledge about effective and disseminable interventions. Specifying some of the critical steps and movement from one step to another is likely to lead to greater progress and, just as important, to allow us to assess in subsequent reviews how much progress has been made.

EXPANDING THE RANGE OF QUESTIONS ADDRESSED IN RESEARCH

It is useful to consider the range of questions that treatment research ought to address. Table 8.2 presents questions about what we would like to know about treatment. Progress can be made by ensuring that, for a given treatment and clinical problem, these questions are addressed systematically. Surprisingly, very little attention has been devoted to the questions related to the components of treatment that contribute to change, the treatment combinations that optimize change, the role of treatment processes, and the impact of child, parent, family, and contextual factors on therapy outcome (Durlak et al., 1995; Kazdin, Bass, et al., 1990). As mentioned in chapter 7, the majority of research focuses on questions related to the treatment technique, an emphasis likely to continue in light of the keen interest in pressures to identify empirically supported treatments. However, the emphasis is shortsighted if it neglects other questions.

In the abstract, each of the questions in table 8.2 is important. However, I

Table 8.2   Range of Questions to Guide Treatment Research

---

1. What is the impact of treatment relative to no treatment?
2. What components contribute to change?
3. What treatments can be added (combined treatments) to optimize change?
4. What parameters can be varied to influence (improve) outcome?
5. How effective is this treatment relative to other treatments for this problem?
6. What child, parent, family and contextual features influence (moderate) outcome?
7. What processes within or during treatment influence (mediate) outcome?
8. To what extent are treatment effects generalizable across problem areas, settings, and other domains?

---

am arguing not only to expand studies to address these questions but also to track progress in a systematic way to ensure a full set of answers. If at this moment, we were asked to recommend treatments useful for, say, separation anxiety or adjustment disorder in early childhood or substance abuse in adolescence, what studies would we cite to provide answers? We would need initial studies to establish that treatments have an impact and then we would want the field to move to some of the other questions. Indeed, only a small number of controlled studies might be needed to address some of the questions, after which we could devote research to the more complex issues (e.g., therapy processes, boundary conditions). Deciding which treatments are empirically based, I believe, would require knowing much more about treatment than just a few studies designed to answer one or two questions could offer.

EXPANDING DOMAINS AND METHODS OF ASSESSMENT

Identifying questions inadvertently draws attention to answers. In treatment research, the "answers" involve measures used to draw conclusions about treatment, moderators, generality, and so on. The measures warrant scrutiny because the conclusion an investigator reaches may depend quite heavily on measures used to answer the questions. Three changes in assessment practices in research could greatly advance progress: (1) providing a comprehensive evaluation of the impact of treatment, (2) altering the way in which assessment is conducted so that it is more applicable to clinical work, and (3) evaluating characteristics of the treatments that can influence their adoption and use.

Range of Treatment Outcomes

Outcome criteria are important in developing effective treatment. Children and adolescents are referred to treatment because of dysfunction in some domain, and our attention as researchers is immediately drawn to symptoms (i.e., presenting problems and target complaints). Symptom reduction is usually the primary focus of treatment. All of the questions in table 8.2 could be answered profitably in relation only to carefully assessed symptoms and symptoms alone. Symptom measures are relevant, and I do not wish demean their importance.

At the same time, there is no need to restrict outcome to this focus alone, as there is no compelling evidence that symptom change (as opposed to improvements in prosocial functioning, family interaction, or adaptive cognitions) is the best predictor of long-term adjustment and functioning.

Many other outcomes are critically important because of their significance to the child, family, and, in many cases, society at large. Table 8.3 includes domains relevant for evaluating therapy outcomes, however; the relevance of any particular domain may vary depending on clinical problem (e.g., anxiety, hyperactivity) or indeed subtype of the problem within a given disorder. Yet, all or most of the domains likely are relevant most of the time and the conclusions about what techniques are effective will depend on the outcome criteria.

Among the many criteria, special emphasis might be given to impairment—that is, the extent to which the individual's functioning in everyday life is impeded. Impairment is reflected in limitations in meeting role demands at home and at school and in not interacting well or prosocially with others. Youths with a given disorder or problem can vary considerably in their degree of impairment. As I noted previously, impairment is related to, but distinguishable from, symptoms or a disorder (Sanford, Offord, Boyle, Pearce, & Racine, 1992) and contributes significantly to the likelihood that a child is referred for mental health services (Bird et al., 1990). A significant issue from the standpoint of treatment is initial level of impairment and how much it improves. Assessing impairment and moving individuals toward lesser impairment may be a considerable accomplishment of treatment.

By singling out impairment, I do not intend to imply that one criterion (impairment) ought to replace another (symptoms). Just the opposite, the full range of outcome criteria is relevant in developing and identifying effective treatments. One could make the case that other areas that tend to be neglected (so-

Table 8.3   Criteria to Evaluate Treatment Outcome

1. Child Functioning	a. Symptoms
	b. Impairment
	c. Prosocial competence
	d. Academic functioning
2. Parent and Family Functioning	a. Dysfunction (e.g., symptoms)
	b. Contextual influences (e.g., stress, quality of life)
	c. Conditions that promote adaptation (e.g., family support, quantity, and quality time)
3. Social Impact Measures	a. Consequences on systems (e.g., school activities, attendance, truancy)
	b. Service use (e.g., reductions in special services or needed services)
	c. Mental and physical health

cial competence, academic functioning) are central as well because they predict long-term adjustment and clinical dysfunction (Asher & Coie, 1990). Indeed, the importance of understanding development and psychopathology in part derives from understanding what outcomes at one point in development predict (serve as a risk or protective factor for) outcomes at a later point.

Pre- and Postassessment versus Continuous Assessment

A central feature of therapy research is assessment of the participants before and after treatment (pre- and posttreatment assessment). In relation to research design, there are many statistical and clinical advantages to assessing individuals before and after treatment (Kazdin, 1998b). However, there are a few difficulties with the focus on pre- and posttreatment assessment. First and foremost, the entire practice is odd because it does not provide the information needed to understand treatment effects and to develop treatments for clinical practice. What can we conclude from pre- and postassessment? At the end of the postassessment, we can say this child or adolescent improved, did not change much, or became worse. We do not only want posttherapy evaluation. We need to know how the patient is functioning while treatment is in process. To understand treatment, we need to see the pattern of data (function) and *how change is occurring*. In clinical work, we want to see *change occurring* either on the outcomes of interest or on putative processes that will lead to the outcomes of interest.

There are guidelines and examples for monitoring client progress over the course of treatment (see Barlow, Hayes, & Nelson, 1984; Clement, 1996, 1999; Kazdin, 1993b). The guidelines use ongoing (repeated) assessment through multiple observations for individual cases, so that one can describe patterns in the data and detect changes associated with treatment in key processes in therapy or outcomes of treatment. Outcomes refer to interim changes, such as previews, trends, progress in a therapeutic direction, that portend the desired outcomes at the end of treatment.

In the context of group designs to evaluate treatment, the use of pre- and postassessments ought undoubtedly to continue. At the same time, it would be helpful to integrate additional assessments over the course of treatment. As one example, the beginning of each treatment session (perhaps 10 minutes) might be used to evaluate any changes in key domains of interest. Or periodic but regular interim assessments could monitor progress in therapy. The purpose is to evaluate the change process and to provide measures that can be used clinically. In clinical work, the treatment cannot be evaluated at the end as posttreatment assessment is conducted in research. There usually is no formal end point because regimens of treatment are not fixed as they are in research. Rather, an effort is made to treat until progress is made. Also, in clinical work, one wants systematic information on which to base decisions about when to end treatment or to provide different treatment. If the results of research are to be applicable to clinical practice, interim assessments that can be used to evaluate progress would be very important to integrate into treatment research.

Evaluating Characteristics of Treatment

The prior comments pertain to the evaluation of therapeutic effects or impact of treatment on the child or adolescent. A rather neglected area is evaluation of characteristics of treatment related to adoption, use, or dissemination of treatment. That is, apart from patient change, are there characteristics of the treatment that we wish to know about? Obviously, evaluating characteristics of treatment becomes irrelevant if the treatment has not been shown to produce therapeutic change. However, can the treatments that *have* been shown to produce change be distinguished in important ways? Table 8.4 provides three criteria to evaluate treatment that are separate from the therapeutic changes produced in the clients. The following sections consider these criteria briefly and their relevance to establishing treatments as effective.

DISSEMINABILITY OF TREATMENT.   Some treatments, but not others, may be extended easily beyond the confines of the research study. Dissemination refers primarily to extending the treatment to others who provide treatment (therapists) and to those who seek treatment (children, adolescents, and their families). Ease of dissemination depends on the complexity of the treatment

Table 8.4   Criteria for Evaluating Treatment Procedures

CRITERIA	DESCRIPTION
1. Disseminability	Disseminability involves the extent or ease of extending the treatment widely to other clinicians and clients. This criterion may be related to complexity of the procedures, type and amount of training needed to implement the procedures, likelihood of adherence to those who implement the procedures, degree to which departure from the prescribed procedures is associated with loss of effectiveness.
2. Cost	The monetary costs of providing treatment and delivering services are pertinent measures of treatment. Cost is not usually a question of scientific interest in treatment evaluation but provides data that can influence dissemination, adoption, and policy. There are many ways to evaluate cost such as expenses in relation to obtained benefits or outcomes (e.g., cost-benefit analyses).
3. Acceptability of Treatment	The extent to which those who participate in treatment (e.g., children, adolescents, families, but perhaps mental health professionals as well) view the treatment as reasonable, justified, fair, and palatable. Among treatments that are equally effective, those viewed as more acceptable are probably more likely to be sought, adhered to, and executed correctly than those that are less acceptable.

procedures, type and amount of training needed to implement the procedures, likelihood of adherence to the treatment among those who implement the procedures, and the degree to which a departure from the prescribed procedures leads to a loss in effectiveness. Also, disseminability encompasses the efficiency of treatment, as reflected in how many persons in need can be served. For example, a familiar and long-standing distinction in treatment is delivery via individual or group therapy. If both were equally effective, group treatment might be preferred because it reaches more clients per therapist and treatment session.

Some techniques may be widely disseminated because they can be implemented by clients themselves or because they can be presented through mass media (books, computer, television). For example, many self-help manuals, also referred to as bibliotherapy, are designed to treat diverse problems, including overeating, cigarette smoking, depression, stress, anger, sexual dysfunction, anxiety, social skills deficits, and conduct problems (Rosen, 1987; Santrock et al., 1994). Often, extravagant claims are made about the effectiveness of "do-it-yourself" treatments without empirical evidence. Yet many treatments have supporting evidence. Indeed, a recent meta-analysis concluded that self- and therapist-administered treatments were equally effective when compared to controls and retained their benefits at follow-up (Marrs, 1995). Even if bibliotherapy were less effective, the self-administered treatment may be preferred because it is more easily disseminated to the public on a larger scale than therapist-administered outpatient treatment. Extremely severe cases (e.g., of depression, substance abuse) may not respond to self-help manuals, but many less severe cases may respond well.

Self-help is a matter of degree, and sometimes a therapist can supplement the self-help materials clients use. For example, the therapist/trainer can guide a group of parents for whom self-help manuals and materials serve as the main source of material and intervention (e.g., Webster-Stratton, 1996). The role of the therapist in supplementing self-help groups may require much less training than with traditional therapy. Some treatments may be more disseminable because less professional training and guidance are needed. Self-help is not new in developing treatment and as a basis for widely disseminating treatment. Self-help groups led by nonprofessionals have been used for some time in the treatment of alcohol and drug abuse and weight control (e.g., Alcoholics Anonymous, Synanon, and Take Off Pounds Sensibly, respectively).

Media and communication technology, such as the television, telephone, computer, and the Internet, provides opportunities to disseminate treatment widely (Meyers et al., 1996; Zhu et al., 1996). Access to the Internet through television as well as personal computers could reach a large number of individuals for a host of concerns (e.g., child rearing, coping with stress), problems of living (e.g., divorce, bereavement), and clinical dysfunction (e.g., anxiety disorders, depression). Computerized psychotherapy has been available in some form for decades and continues to develop in treatment outcome studies (Marks et al., 1998; Newman et al., 1997). Few applications are currently available in clinical practice, but no doubt others will appear with advances in software and software accessibility.

Under some circumstances, writing about one's problems, such as feelings about traumatic experiences, can have quite significant therapeutic impact, at least in adults (Smyth, 1998). Controlled studies have shown that briefly writing about one's thoughts and feelings can alter psychological and physiological functioning and overall well-being, measured at least one month after the writing task. In principle, structured writing tasks could be readily disseminated on a large scale, but this has yet to be tested. Presumably the processes through which writing achieves its therapeutic benefits in adults could be activated in other ways (e.g., structured speaking tasks or storytelling) in young children, whose writing skills may not yet have developed.

In discussing the ease of disseminating treatment, I must mention medication, because it often can be widely disseminated. For example, when a new drug for depression emerges from clinical trials and is approved for use, it is widely prescribed and quickly reaches millions of clients. An effective psychotherapy, if equally effective or indeed even more effective, is clearly less readily disseminated to others. Of course, disseminability of treatment is only one criterion for evaluating an intervention. The difficulty is that medication, although widely disseminable, raises other issues (e.g., adherence to treatment, side effects, restriction of other behaviors when combined with other medications or alcohol). The ease of dissemination may be counterbalanced by other issues related to use and effects.

There are no simple measures to assess the ease of disseminating a treatment. Several variables may determine disseminability, such as the cost of professional training, complexity of the procedures, need for ancillary equipment or apparatus, likelihood that the procedures will retain their effects when disseminated, and others. Some of these latter criteria should be assessed carefully in evaluating treatment. Disseminability is not an esoteric or incidental criterion and perhaps ought to be an initial consideration rather than an afterthought in developing treatment.

COSTS.   Disseminability of treatment is related to cost; in general, less costly treatments are more widely disseminable. However, cost is important to consider on its own as a criterion for evaluating treatment. Obviously, a less costly treatment is preferable to a more costly treatment, given evidence that both are effective. However, there are different ways of evaluating cost.

One can evaluate the benefits that derive from the costs for both large-scale social interventions and individual treatment. *Cost-benefit analysis* is designed to evaluate the monetary costs of an intervention with the benefits obtained. The benefits must be measured in monetary terms also. This requirement makes cost-benefit analysis difficult to apply to many psychological interventions, in which the beneficial effects might extend well beyond monetary gains (Yates, 1995). For example, providing programs to help parents rear their children may have monetary benefits (e.g., preventing some children from entering treatment, from being adjudicated, or from dropping out of school). Another gain of therapy may be to increase harmony in the homes of many families, an effect that cannot be so readily evaluated in monetary terms. Of course, many returns of treatment can be examined in terms of social benefits. In the treatment of adults, evidence that clients return to work, miss fewer days of work, have fewer car accidents, or stay out of hospitals or prison can be translated into monetary terms.

Cost-effectiveness analysis does not require placing a monetary value on the benefits and can be more readily used for evaluating treatment. Cost-effectiveness analysis examines the costs of treatment relative to a particular outcome and permits comparison of different treatment techniques when the treatment benefits are designed to be the same, such as reduction of drinking or increase in family harmony. Cost-effectiveness information would be very useful and address important questions independently of narrow debates about statistical differences that distinguish treatments. For example, one study compared two variations of parent management training for parents of kindergarten children with behavior problems (Cunningham et al., 1995). One variation consisted of individual treatment provided at a clinical service; the other consisted of group-based treatment conducted in the community (at community centers or schools). Both treatments achieved better results than a wait-list control condition. On several measures, the community-based treatment was more effective. Even if the treatments were equally effective, the monetary costs (start-up costs, travel time of families, costs of the therapist/trainer in providing treatment) of individual treatment were approximately six times greater per family than the group treatment. Clearly, this criterion is a significant one for evaluating the different ways of administering treatment.

Although monetary costs can represent an important criterion for evaluating treatment, psychological costs may be relevant as well, although obviously more difficult to quantify. For example, treatments for anxiety may induce varying degrees of stress (e.g., flooding versus graduated exposure for anxiety). The psychological and physical costs of completing treatment might be relevant to assess in evaluating therapy, particularly with techniques likely to be aversive to clients. The psychological costs of treatment may be too great to entice participants, no matter what the data show about treatment efficacy.

Within psychotherapy research, cost, cost-benefit, and cost-effectiveness measures are infrequently used. Estimating cost is not entirely straightforward because of the range of costs that can be included and the difficulty in translating benefits into monetary terms. Even so, efforts to describe costs of different treatments represent a worthwhile addition to intervention research. In fact, decisions about what treatments to use for individual services at clinics and hospitals and public policy are driven heavily by costs and related disseminability data. Lamentably, cost is often much more of a concern than evidence in behalf of the treatment.

ACCEPTABILITY OF TREATMENT.   Different treatments for a given problem may not be equally acceptable to prospective clients. Efficiency and cost considerations may contribute to the acceptability of a treatment, but there are other factors as well. Procedures may be more or less objectionable in their own right, independent of their efficacy. Indeed, many procedures readily acceptable to clients often have little or no demonstrated efficacy. For example, commonly advertised procedures to control diet or cigarette smoking are very acceptable because they are quick, easy, and inexpensive. Yet, the vast majority have no demonstrated efficacy, though that apparently does not detract from their appeal.

For various clinical problems for children, adolescents, and adults, several treatments are empirically supported. For example, various forms of psychotherapy and medication are viable options with supportive data for the treatment of depression. Although sparse research is available on the topic, some evidence suggests that forms of psychotherapy (e.g., cognitive therapy, behavior therapy) are viewed as more acceptable than medication for depression (Banken & Wilson, 1992). Thus, in addition to efficacy, it is important to evaluate how acceptable or palatable treatments are to clients. Acceptable treatments are more likely to be sought and adhered to once clients have entered into treatment (e.g., Reimers, Wacker, Cooper, & DeRaad, 1992). Also, highly acceptable treatments are likely to be adopted more by professionals and hence influence disseminability of the treatment (e.g., Arndorfer, Allen, & Alijazireh, 1999).

One challenge for child and adolescent therapy is obvious: treatments probably need to be acceptable both to the child or adolescent as well as the parent, because retaining the child in treatment may depend on evaluations of acceptability. Evaluations of acceptability may depend heavily on how the treatment procedures conform to participants' expectations from treatment. If talk and play are the medium of treatment, but the family is expecting some other intervention, or vice versa, treatment may be less acceptable. Although this discussion implies that acceptability is a property that adheres in the treatment, in fact it relates to the perception of the family about treatment. Even so, when full information is provided about treatment and parents and youths are exposed to the treatment procedures, still treatments are likely to vary in their acceptability (Kazdin, 1986; Kazdin, French, & Sherick, 1981; Tarnowski & Simonian, 1992). Information on the acceptability of treatment can greatly supplement data on effectiveness. Moreover, acceptability may be an important dependent variable for developing effective treatments. Understanding what can be done to make treatments more acceptable is crucial (e.g., Foxx, Bremer, Schutz, Valdez, & Johndrow, 1996).

EXPANDING MODELS FOR DELIVERING TREATMENT

The implicit model for much of therapy research is that a limited number of sessions ought to achieve change and that treatment can end when it has been in place for that period. Current treatment research emphasizes brief, time-limited treatments, usually 8–10 sessions. When innovations are made (e.g., new treatments or combined treatments), the brief, time-limited focus usually still obtains. Occasionally, studies include "booster sessions" during a maintenance period, but these are exceptions.

Considering current economic pressures, perhaps brief treatments are more feasible because only they are likely to be reimbursed in clinical practice. In addition, in child and adolescent therapy, attrition rates are high; between 40% and 60% of families that begin treatment terminate prematurely (Kazdin, 1996b). An implicit fear is that the rate of dropping out will simply increase with longer interventions. Neither argument is very cogent. Long before economic pressures of managed care, our models of investigating therapy emphasized brief treatments. Also, clients may not continue in longer treatment, but retaining cases in treatment is not an insuperable problem (e.g., Santisteban et al., 1996; Szapocznik et al., 1988). More likely, the pressure for brief treatments results from interest in completing timely investigations rather than interest in the clinical demands of the target problem. The net effect of this pressure is another uniformity myth: treatments of a relatively standard duration (8–10 sessions) are likely to be effective for most treatments and clinical problems. Probably no one actually believes this. Yet a review of the research suggests that the majority of studies reflect this duration, plus or minus a few sessions.

For purposes of discussion, let us call brief, time-limited treatment a *conventional model of delivering therapy*. In the conventional model, the number of sessions is fixed, as required by the research project. Table 8.5 presents a number of other ways of delivering treatment. These other ways are likely to increase treatment effectiveness as well as our knowledge about treatment.

High-Strength Treatment

In the conventional model, treatment obviously is intended to have impact, but rarely are the dose, strength, duration, and other parameters of treatment explicitly planned to maximize clinical impact. The high-strength treatment model begins with an effort to maximize therapeutic change. For severe or recalcitrant clinical problems in particular, it may be valuable to test the strongest feasible version of treatment to see if the problem *can* be altered and, if so, to what extent. The high-strength model tries to maximize clinical change but also to test the current limits of our knowledge.

For many problems (e.g., major depression, conduct disorder, attention-deficit/hyperactivity disorder), brief, time-limited interventions are likely to produce weak outcomes. Much longer treatments might seem more promising to maximize impact. Yet few studies test variations of treatment strength or try to evaluate high-strength treatments. As an exception, Lovaas (1987) treated autistic children for an average of 40 hours per week for 2 or more years and included an intervention in the child's home, school, and community using parents and aides. The benefits at follow-up (mean of 5 years after treatment) were evident in classroom placement, adaptive behavior, and measures of IQ, compared to control cases with less intensive treatment (McEachin et al., 1993). While this illustration of the model is extreme, it is also a good example because many professionals would say that the ability to achieve marked changes in autism is quite limited, given what we currently know. Few treatments for

Table 8.5   Models of Treatment Delivery

MODEL	DESCRIPTION
1. Conventional Model	Current model of research in which a time-limited, usually brief treatment is provided.
2. High-Strength Treatment	A test, a very strong intervention based on current knoweldge. An effort to see what can be accomplished with the strongest available treatment.
3. Amenability to Treatment	Identification of cases likely to vary in their responsiveness to treatment. The goal is to identify individuals for whom available treatments are likely to be very effective and, in the process, the factors that may moderate treatment response and hypotheses about what is needed for more recalcitrant cases.
4. Broad-Based Treatment	Use of multiple modalities, modules, components, or interventions to address the range of domains required to have significant impact on individual functioning.
5. Continued Treatment	Treatment that is ongoing in some form, even after an initial period of a conventional treatment may have been provided. If dysfunction is likely to continue, an ongoing maintenance phase may be continued, perhaps on a more intermittent schedule or with a different format of delivering treatment, such as group rather than individual therapy, or treatment in different settings, such as at school rather than at a clinic.
6. Periodic Monitoring and Treatment	After a initial period of treatment, the intervention is suspended. The patient enters into a phase in which functioning is systematically assessed on a regular basis. Based on the assessment results, treatment is provided as needed.

the disorder have any evidence on their behalf (Rogers, 1998; Smith, 1999). Consequently, the question becomes, what can we accomplish with a strong treatment based on the best available knowledge?

I am not advocating lengthy treatments for all or even most clinical problems. However, it is important to investigate much stronger versions of treatment for the range of problems usually seen in treatment. It is exceedingly important to learn in controlled studies what we can accomplish with a strong dose of our treatments. That dose may involve evaluating more intensive efforts to work with the child and family, involving others in the intervention, and encompassing more domains of the child's functioning, including academic performance and social behavior, for example. If the strongest version of currently available treatment produces change, then it is reasonable to study whether less protracted, less costly, and more easily implemented procedures can achieve similar outcomes and whether any loss in treatment gains is worth the savings in cost or ease of administration.

Amenability to Treatment

I mentioned previously the paucity of research on factors that may moderate treatment outcome, including the child, parent, family, context, therapist, and treatment. The information on moderators is pertinent to identifying children and adolescents who vary in the extent to which they can be improved by treatment, that is, who vary in their amenability or responsiveness to treatment. Identifying the subgroup(s) of individuals whom we can treat effectively on a fairly reliable basis would be extremely valuable to the mental health professions and society at large. For example, among children referred for the treatment of anxiety disorders, perhaps those who are doing well at school and those whose parents have no history of anxiety disorder are much more likely to respond to existing treatments than other children. Such identification can contribute to knowledge by raising hypotheses about why factors moderate outcome and contribute to practice by permitting better triage of cases to effective treatments.

Once subgroups of children who can be effectively treated are identified, research can turn to those less amenable and for whom effective treatments are unavailable. The approach of identifying children more or less amenable to treatment can be integrated into existing controlled outcome research. A study can identify children as more or less amenable to the intervention based on characteristics of the sample and hypotheses about the interface of treatment and these characteristics. Analyses of outcome effects can focus on planned or post-hoc comparisons of subgroups within the investigation to assess responsiveness to treatment.

Research on amenability to treatment can begin by identifying children with a given problem who are likely to be the most responsive to treatment. Hypotheses might target different subtypes of youths (e.g., those with early versus late onset), family loading for the problem (e.g., family history versus no family history of the disorder), and contextual influences (e.g., family adversity, untoward living conditions). Models of clinical dysfunction may also provide very useful guidelines regarding which factors (e.g., risk or protective factors, subtypes of the disorder) likely predict response to treatment.

Evaluation of amenability to treatment relies on empirically demonstrated or hypothesized moderators. An investigator may study several factors that have been studied in relation to a clinical problem and suggest who might be more or less amenable to treatment. For example, children referred for aggressive and antisocial behavior who are less amenable to treatment have more severe and chronic problems, have comorbid disorders, come from socially disadvantaged backgrounds, and live with parents who have current psychopathology and high levels of stress (Kazdin, 1995a; Kazdin & Wassell, 1999). These different variables can be combined to provide an amenability index. Both research on single or multiple moderators can be very useful in evaluating amenability of children to treatment.

Broad-Based Treatment

Many dysfunctions involve a broad range of symptoms, associated areas of dysfunction, and parent and family problems. Comorbidity among children and adolescents has received extensive discussion, but the range of problems that youths evince extends well beyond multiple symptoms and diagnoses. For example, attention-deficit/hyperactivity disorder may include impairments beyond the defining features: attention problems, hyperactivity, and impulsiveness. Academic dysfunction, poor peer relations, and aggressive and antisocial behavior are likely to be present as well. I propose systematic expansion of outcome criteria in treatment research partly because of evidence that symptoms are often associated with dysfunction in other domains. In current approaches to treatment, a particular intervention is implemented to alter an important facet (psychic conflict, self-esteem, family processes) of the child or the system in which the child functions. The targeted domain is considered, on theoretical or clinical grounds, to be central to the child's problem. Yet, for many dysfunctions, associated (correlated) features of, or consequences resulting from, the disorder may require a broader range of interventions than any one treatment approach can reasonably provide.

Treatments can be conceived as a modular system with separate components (modules) woven into an overall treatment plan. Implementation initially requires evaluating a child's functioning in diverse domains (home, school, community; deviance, prosocial, and academic functioning) and then providing multiple treatments or components of treatment to address these domains. An example is multisystemic therapy (MST), which I reviewed previously. This treatment consists of a package of interventions deployed with children and their families (Henggeler et al., 1998). The conceptual view is that multiple systems (family, school) impinge on the child as well as on each other. Domains (e.g., parent unemployment) are addressed in treatment because they raise issues for one or more systems (e.g., parent stress, increased alcohol consumption) and affect the child's functioning (e.g., marital conflict, child discipline practices). Several techniques (e.g., parent training, problem-solving skills training) and case management are combined to address these multiple domains. Obviously, MST is a broad-based treatment.

Broad-based treatment is not tantamount to a "shotgun" approach to treatment selection or justification for unspecified eclecticism. The shotgun approach is often evident in inpatient treatment programs for children and adolescents. As a matter of course, children may receive multiple treatments, including medication related to their primary symptoms, some form of psychotherapy (e.g., psychodynamically oriented, play-based sessions), group treatment (social skills, problem solving), and recreational (e.g., art, music) therapy, in addition to some wardwide therapeutic program (e.g., milieu therapy, token economy). I do not propose this model here, although, of course, it would be valuable to test whether any of these treatments are adding incrementally to treatment outcome. Rather, in a broad-based model, treatments are selected from those with available evidence. There should be evidence that the constituent modules or treatments produce change and, eventually, evidence that the combination of components is effective.

An assumption in therapy research is the more treatments applied to a clinical problem or client, the better the outcome. This is in part the rationale for eclectic combinations that often dominate clinical practice. But combinations of treatment are not invariably more effective. Squeezing multiple treatments within a fixed period of treatment, perhaps 10 weeks, can merely dilute the constituent treatments because no component is presented at full dose. There are cases in which combined treatments were actually less effective than treatments involving only one of the constituent interventions (see Kazdin, 1996a).

In many instances, combined treatments are likely to be more effective than their constituent treatments administered singly. Examples from medicine (e.g., for HIV, cancer, heart disease) can be readily cited. In the context of child and adolescent psychotherapy, broader-based treatments deserve more frequent tests, but selection of the components of treatment ought to draw from theory and prior findings about why the combination is likely to be important, useful, or warranted.

Continued Treatment

For several clinical dysfunctions or for a number of children with a particular disorder, the course of maladjustment may last a lifetime. Obviously, the more pervasive developmental disorders and more severe forms of mental retardation are in this class. Yet disorders more commonly seen in outpatient treatment (e.g., conduct disorder and attention-deficit/hyperactivity disorder) often are protracted as well (e.g., Robins, 1978; Weiss & Hechtman, 1986). For many such children, continued treatment in some form may be required.

The continued treatment model may need to emulate the model used in the treatment of diabetes mellitus, where ongoing treatment (insulin) is needed to ensure that the benefits of treatment are sustained. Clearly with diabetes, a conventional model of treatment (brief, time-limited) would not be very helpful in the long term. Analogously, with many children referred for psychological treatment, an ongoing intervention may be required to sustain treatment benefits. Perhaps after the child is referred, treatment can address the current crises and have an impact on functioning at home, at school, and in the community. After improvement is achieved, treatment can be modified rather than simply terminated. At that point, the child could enter maintenance therapy, which is continued treatment, perhaps in varying schedules ("doses"). Treatment would continue but intermittently.

There are a few examples of the potential benefits of continued treatment. In the treatment of adult depression, the benefits of providing maintenance therapy following a treatment course have been carefully evaluated in controlled trials in which the maintenance therapy has included different treatments (e.g., half-dose of the original medication, interpersonal psychotherapy, cognitive therapy) (Frank, Johnson, & Kupfer, 1992; Frank et al., 1993; Kupfer et al., 1992). Patients who received maintenance therapy were much less likely to relapse. Preliminary findings suggest similar benefits of maintenance treatment (cognitive behavior therapy) in reducing relapse in depression among adolescents (Kroll, Harrington, Jayson, Frazer, & Gowers, 1996).

Maintenance therapies can provide intermittent treatment or treatment as needed and hence are not merely more sessions of the same treatment regimen. Needless to say, ongoing treatment is not advocated in cases where there is evidence that brief, time-limited treatment is effective. Beginning with a model of brief, time-limited treatment may be quite reasonable, but heavy reliance on the conventional model will greatly limit what we can accomplish with treatment.

Periodic Monitoring and Treatment

An alternative to continued treatment is to provide treatment followed by systematic case monitoring. After initial treatment and demonstrated improvement in functioning in everyday life, treatment is suspended. At this point, the child's functioning begins to be monitored regularly (e.g., every 3 months) and systematically with standardized measures. The assessment need not involve an extensive battery but may reflect screening items to assess functioning of the child at home and at school and along salient domains. Treatment could be provided as needed, based on the assessment data or emergent issues raised by the family, teachers, or others. This is similar to the model for dental care in the United States, in which "check-ups" are recommended every 6 months; an intervention is provided as needed based on these periodic checks.

The novel feature of this model is monitoring of child functioning and the use of additional treatment sessions on the basis of the resulting data. The model may capture the advantages of continued treatment but specifically target individuals who need intervention. Many individuals who complete treatment may be functioning well; assessment can identify these individuals and not use resources for their continued treatment. Those functioning less well can be brought into treatment as needed. Some individuals may need maintenance therapy.

There is likely to be great value in this model. But assessing the value is difficult because of the few data on follow-up course for child and adolescent treatment. Indeed, the work on adult depression, as noted previously, came from evidence that some forms of depression are recurrent and that relapse is likely without treatment. With little evidence about how children are doing a year or two after treatment, there is no clear need for a maintenance therapy. We have learned from longitudinal rather than from treatment studies that many childhood disorders (e.g., depression, conduct disorder, attention-deficit/hyperactivity disorder) are recurrent, may continue into adulthood, or serve as precursors of other disorders even if they do not continue. These might be prime candidates for continued treatment or periodic monitoring and treatment.

General Comments

The varied ways of evaluating treatments consider different characteristics of clinical problems, the different types of treatment they may require, the differential responsiveness of some individuals, and the broad and enduring dysfunctions that clinically referred cases often bring to treatment. Typically, research on treatment of child and adolescent disorders is not conducted in ways likely to develop and to identify effective interventions. For example, the duration of treatment is relatively brief and thus probably not a test of high-strength treatment. Characteristics of the child, parent, and family are rarely examined to identify who is more or less amenable or responsive to treatment. Individual techniques are rarely combined to augment therapeutic change. Thus, broad-based treatments are not usually tested. Finally, treatment is usually terminated after the brief regimen, so continued care or treatment as needed is not evaluated. These characteristics of therapy research would not be problematic if effective treatments had been identified with the conventional model of treatment evaluation. However, the yield from research and the very severe and pervasive impairment of many disorders should compel us to reconsider the focus, design, and model of treatment trials.

Some of the models presented here raise the prospect of treatments more extended than those currently included in research. The recommendations for longer treatments in research for more protracted problems seem to oppose the move toward brief treatment prompted by managed care and cost-containment considerations. It is essential to be sensitive to pressures and trends in clinical service delivery. Yet the task for research is to identify what interventions can accomplish for the clinical problems of children and adolescents. More intensive and more extended treatments for some problems or some children will not necessarily mean more costly treatment. The costs to society, even purely monetary costs, are not merely those of treatment delivery. Cost savings and cost-benefit analyses are essential to consider as well. It may be premature to assume that using a broader range of models for treatment delivery would necessarily prove more costly. The previously discussed models also include better matching of cases to treatments so that extended treatments can be assigned to children for whom abbreviated treatments are not effective.

SUMMARY AND CONCLUSIONS

The proposed model for therapy research is intended to provide a blueprint for developing effective treatments. Studies are needed to understand how treatments work, how they interface with clinical dysfunction, and to whom they can be effectively applied. Impetus for proposing an overall plan stems from the directions and status of current research, which, by and large, has neglected to study how treatment is delivered, who is served, and so on. No doubt, further reviews of the treatment literature will continue to emerge in journal articles and books. However, further reviews or analyses of the literature, however quantitative, comprehensive, or scholarly, will not provide the essential information, if the requisite studies have not been completed.

The proposed model suggests several steps to develop the underpinnings of effective treatment: the conceptualization of dysfunction and tests of this conceptualization as a basis for developing treatment, conceptualization of treatment (the change processes) and tests of this conceptualization, specification of treatment, tests of treatment outcome, tests of the boundary conditions and moderators of treatment, and tests of generality and applicability of treatment. These steps do not prescsribe a fixed order, but research needs to address each of these bases.

Related recommendations in the proposed model focused on the need to expand the range of questions about treatment and treatment outcomes. Regarding outcome assessment, we need to know more about the scope of therapeutic change but also more about the treatments and their characteristics (e.g., disseminability, acceptability). Finally, the model included different ways of delivering treatment. The current model of therapy research, the conventional model, focuses on brief, time-limited treatment. Little thought is given to this model as it is routinely applied in even the best of the therapy studies. Other models, including high-strength treatment, amenability to treatment, broad-based treatment, continued treatment, and periodic monitoring and treatment as needed, are likely to augment what we learn about treatment and to enhance treatment outcome.

Major changes are needed in how treatment is developed, the range of questions asked, and the move toward progress in understanding process, outcomes, and the conditions under which the effects are obtained. The de rigueur conclusion that "more research is needed" is by itself hazardous. More is *not* what we need, or at least not just more research. We need different research, very different research from what characterizes current work, if we are going to make genuine gains. The model in this chapter attempted to outline salient ways to enhance progress and to accumulate research directed toward progress.

FOR FURTHER READING

The readings below address facets of the model proposed in this chapter and include overviews about the types of research needed in the future and comments on key issues.

Kazdin, A.E. (1997). A model for developing effective treatments: Progression and interplay of theory, research, and practice. *Journal of Clinical Child Psychology, 26,* 114–129.

Kazdin, A.E. (in press). Current (lack of) status of theory in child and adolescent psychotherapy research. *Journal of Clinical Child Psychology.*

Kendall, P.C., & Southam-Gerow, M.A. (1995). Issues in the transportability of treatment: The case of anxiety disorders in youths. *Journal of Consulting and Clinical Psychology, 63,* 702–708.

Mash, E.J., & Barkley, R.A. (1998). Treatment of child and family disturbance: A behavioral-systems perspective. In E.J. Mash & R.A. Barkley (Eds.), *Treatment of childhood disorders* (2nd ed., pp. 3–51). New York: Guilford.

Wilson, G.T. (1998). Manual-based treatment and clinical practice. *Clinical Psychology: Science and Practice, 5,* 363–375.

Chapter 9

Designing and Conducting
a Treatment Study

CHAPTER 8 DESCRIBED A MODEL for child and adolescent psychotherapy research. My goal was to underscore the importance of addressing neglected issues and to ensure a systematic progression in the knowledge base over years of research. Past evidence suggests that unsystematic accumulation of studies leads to continued neglect of critical areas and questions.

General research aims are important, but we also need concrete suggestions for conducting a psychotherapy investigation. Designing and conducting treatment research raises many challenges that must be addressed because the quality of the literature very much depends on individual studies. No analytic or statistical tools (e.g., meta-analyses, evaluation of methodology) can overcome poorly designed studies or well-designed studies that systematically omit critical issues. Obviously, well-designed studies that address critical issues are needed.

This chapter focuses on the design of treatment research and its special issues, decision points, and practices. I assume that the reader is familiar with basic research methodology, its many challenges, goals, and pitfalls. For those who are unfamiliar with basic tenets of methodology or who would like a quick review, an overview of key concepts and practices is provided in appendix B.

GOALS OF THE STUDY

Quality of the Study

The quality or value of a study is determined by the importance of the question(s) the investigator wishes to address. A study that is methodologically sound, or indeed even exemplary, still may not be important. Is the overriding question of the study really important? More cryptically, as stated by my dissertation committee at the beginning of my oral exam, "Who could possibly care about any facet of this study?" (I have edited some of the language in case children inadvertently pick up this book.)

One might reply that the quality of the study or importance of the question is a subjective matter and hence cannot generate consensus approval. But many people may share the same subjective opinion. The statement that "beauty is in the eyes of the beholder" is and is not true. Beauty *is* subjective, but people within a culture agree quite markedly on what is pretty, handsome, or generally physically attractive (Patzer & Burke, 1988). Quality of research, too, rests on opinion, but here too the judgment, far from arbitrary, depends on specific criteria.

The quality of the research question depends on whether the study advances existing literature. Research that draws on theory about the disorder, treatment, or characteristics of participants is usually more highly valued than simple comparisons of one treatment technique versus another or versus a control condition. As a general rule, research that seeks to explain, rather than merely to describe, at least in psychology, achieves higher status.

Sometimes the quality of the "same" study will differ depending on conceptualization or framing of the study. For example, studying treatment effectiveness with another age group (e.g., adolescents) after an initial demonstration with one age group (e.g., young children) is likely to be considered uninspired. This is a study of generality from one sample to another. Yes, generality of findings is of interest, but the premier journals would probably consider the question unimportant, perhaps rightfully so. The same study might be cast in a more coherent theoretical framework that suggests that key developmental characteristics (e.g., cognitive, interpersonal) of an age group will influence treatment outcome or the effectiveness of treatment. One could draw on the vast child and adolescent development literatures and predict therapy effects based on the identified differences in key processes. Moreover, the study might demonstrate that the proposed processes in fact mediate outcome differences between the age groups. This research would constitute a superior study.

The example helps to explain why we are discussing the questions that guide treatment research in a chapter on the methods and design of research. Design serves the research question. Who and what is studied and how it is studied are all intertwined. Methods need to match the question and vice versa. Evaluation of the quality of the methods should include the value of the research questions and how the methodology will serve these questions.

Questions That Guide a Study

As a general statement, it is useful for the investigator to ask what is the purpose of this study, why is it particularly important, and what advance does it make to this area of work. The specific questions are relevant to the design. Key questions dictate experimental and control conditions to be included in the study. Understanding how treatment operates and the factors that contribute to change can be translated into several specific treatment evaluation strategies that guide individual studies.

Table 9.1 presents major strategies used to evaluate treatment, the empirical questions they are designed to address, and the minimal treatment and control conditions the study will probably require. The questions associated with each strategy were noted in chapter 8 as those we want to answer for a given treatment. Going beyond these questions, the table includes the likely required comparison or control conditions for the investigation. The assumption in the table is that the question will be addressed in group rather than single-case designs.

As in chapter 8, one can see that the questions cover a range of factors that may contribute to treatment and represent a progression of research. For example, an initial study might examine treatment relative to a no-treatment control group (treatment package strategy) to determine the overall effects of the intervention. Further studies may consider how to vary the treatment to increase its effectiveness (parametric strategy), which factors (child, parent, family, or other) influence who responds to treatment (moderator strategy), and so on. Treatment mechanisms can be revealed within a portfolio of research that represents increasingly sophisticated questions about treatment. To judge the quality of research, one should consider the question an investigator has selected in relation to what is already known about the treatment or clinical problem. The

Table 9.1 Treatment Strategies, Questions, and Design Implications

TREATMENT STRATEGY	QUESTION	BASIC REQUIREMENTS
Treatment Package Strategy	What is the impact of treatment relative to no treatment?	Treatment vs. no treatment or waiting-list control group.
Dismantling Strategy	What components contribute to change, what aspects of the intervention are necessary, sufficient, or facilitative of therapeutic change?	Two or more treatment groups. One receives the full treatment package; other groups receive that package minus one or more components.
Constructive Strategy	What components or other treatments can be added to enhance therapeutic change?	Two or more treatment groups. One receives the full treatment package; other groups receive that package plus other components or treatment.
Parametric Strategy	What parameters can be varied to influence (improve) outcome?	Two or more treatment groups that differ in one or more facets (e.g., duration, intensity).
Comparative Outcome Strategy	How effective is this treatment relative to other treatments for this problem?	Two or more groups that receive different treatments.
Moderator Strategy	What features related to the child, parent, family, and context influence (moderate) outcome?	One or more treatment groups but divided by levels of a predicted moderator (e.g., severity of child symptoms).
Process/Mechanism Strategy	What processes within or during treatment influence (mediate) outcome?	One or more treatments with assessment on presumed processes that may be responsible for, lead to, account for, and cause therapeutic change.
Generality Strategy	To what extent are treatment effects generalizable across problem areas, settings, and other domains?	One treatment group but applied in a different context. Could be two (or more) treatment groups where the context is varied (e.g., examined as a moderator) to see if generality varies.

investigator ought to make the case that the study will add significant knowledge to the field.

METHODOLOGICAL ISSUES

The investigator's key decisions relate to the question or hypotheses and also reflect the care and thoughtfulness with which the study is to be carried out. Investigators who are interested in publishing the findings of their studies often are hoping for statistically significant results. An assumption is made that the suitability of the article for publication, especially in a prestigious journal, will depend on whether or not the results "come out." Perhaps this is true. Yet the publication fate of the study is partially determined before the first subject is ever run. Design decisions influence matters that reflect the quality of the study. Once these decisions are made, much can be said about the study, as well as its likely strengths and limitations, independently of the results that will follow. Consider some of the key methodological decisions and their implications.

Subjects

SELECTION OF THE PROBLEM AND SAMPLE.   An initial decision for designing the study is the clinical problem or focus (e.g., depression, anxiety, noncompliance, and family conflict). Obviously, this entails more than merely selecting a problem name. The first issue here is the sample itself, the subjects.[1] How will the sample be obtained? Will the participants be individuals recruited from schools, the community, or health centers, or will be they be individuals who have sought treatment? It is important to be explicit about how the subjects are obtained. The second issue is specification of the problem's severity, duration, and associated features. If depressed adolescents will be treated, what will be the extent of depression, as defined in what way (e.g., by psychiatric diagnosis? by parent- or adolescent-completed scale, and, if so, which ones?).

The question related to the problem reflects a broader issue: specifying the inclusion and exclusion criteria. What are the criteria for being included in this study? The inclusion criteria may cover severity of the problem, age, family characteristics, IQ, or whatever else. These must be explicit. Also, exclusion criteria are important because some individuals may have met the inclusion criteria but have other complications that the investigator wishes to avoid (e.g., are currently in another form of treatment, have a serious and debilitating medical disease, have other clinical disorders in addition to the one encompassed by the inclusion criteria). Even though an effort ought to be made to specify inclusion and exclusion criteria in advance, other, unforeseen considerations may emerge during recruitment. For example, in one of our studies, we excluded a single parent (mother), although she and one of her four children met our inclusion criteria for the treatment of conduct disorder. The mother was homeless; she and her four children lived in a car, did not have adequate provisions for basic care of the children (e.g., food, clothing, bathing facilities), and her school-age children were not attending school. We felt several other services were urgently needed before considering therapy and excluded the case. (We assisted in connecting the family to services to address housing and other needs.) None of these conditions was explicit in our exclusion criteria but seemed reasonable to invoke for clinical and research purposes.

Whether subjects are referred or recruited, some will meet criteria but still will not be included. Circumstances or unwillingness to participate may lead to less than 100% success in obtaining subjects from those who are eligible. It is important to state how many individuals were approached, screened, or considered and what percentage of these actually agreed to participate. Those who agree to participate are likely to be less disturbed and less dysfunctional and to show better social and academic functioning (see Frame & Strauss, 1987; Weinberger, Tublin, Ford, & Feldman, 1990). Specifying how many cases were considered may suggest how well the final sample likely represents the larger set of persons who were considered (see Betan, Roberts, & McCluskey-Fawcett, 1995).

HOMOGENEITY AND HETEROGENEITY OF THE SAMPLE.   Identifying the subjects and specifying inclusion and exclusion criteria raise another issue to guide decision making, namely, the homogeneity and heterogeneity of the sample. Consider homogeneity and heterogeneity as end points on a continuum (although they would reflect several different continua because samples can differ on multiple dimensions). A more *homogeneous* sample is similar on all or most dimensions (e.g., age, problems, gender, and socioeconomic status). A more *heterogeneous* sample would allow as many factors as possible to vary among the subjects. Homogeneity and heterogeneity have benefits and costs. Greater homogeneity minimizes extraneous variability in the data because there is a lower standard deviation and hence less error when computing statistical significance and effect size. But the trade-off is a rather restricted sample and results that may not be generalizable beyond this sample. Conversely, greater heterogeneity means more diverse types of cases are included and hence the results may be more generalizable, yet variability is higher and differences between groups or conditions will be more difficult to detect. Greater heterogeneity also may allow the investigator to analyze the results for a potential moderator that might influence outcome, because subjects vary on that characteristic.

Occasionally investigators select highly heterogeneous samples by admitting all cases that apply to treatment, by including different ages, and by not being too fussy about the presenting problems. The touted advantage is that such a study is really clinically relevant because all types of clients are included. However, sometimes a study is reported in which the sample was so heterogeneous that nonsignificant group differences at the end of treatment are very likely (e.g., Sloane, Staples, Cristol, Yorkston, & Whipple, 1975). When within-group variability (i.e., individual differences) is relatively large, showing that groups (treatments, conditions) are different will be difficult unless sample size is large or some other strategy is adopted to augment power.

There is no need to be a homo- or heterophobic, methodologically speaking.

There are options and compromises in identifying the sample for research. One option is to include very different subjects (heterogeneous) on one or two variables that may be conceptually important as potential moderators (e.g., child gender, presence of comorbid disorders). These variables then can be included in the hypotheses and their effects examined in the data analyses. By analyzing the variable, one can evaluate its effect rather than merely lump it with error variance. Also, subjects can be matched on a variable that makes them heterogeneous and then assigned to groups randomly. This does not solve the problem but permits some analyses that systematically evaluate key dimensions of the sample. The main points are to select the sample suited to the question, to demonstrate the effect of interest, and to minimize variability of the sample. This emphasizes questions of internal validity (see appendix B). If the goal is generalization, one wants a diverse sample and perhaps opportunities to evaluate whether the results vary as a function of that diversity.

SUBJECT ASSIGNMENT. Assignment of subjects to conditions is important to consider as well. Random assignment of all subjects to the various treatment and control conditions is the obvious, usual choice, and hence is not elaborated here. Other options serve different purposes. First, one might want to match subjects on one or more variables of interest (e.g., gender, severity of the problem) and then assign matched pairs (or triads, depending on the number of conditions) to treatment and control conditions (or to three conditions). When samples are not large and the subject pool is quite diverse, random assignment alone is too "chancy" to ensure that groups are equivalent on key variables (e.g., proportion of cases of boys or of a given severity of the problem). The option is to match cases on the variable of interest (gender or severity of symptoms within, say, one-quarter of a standard deviation on the measure of severity). If there are two groups (treatment A, treatment B), then two matched cases (e.g., two girls) are identified and then assigned randomly to each group. This continues with all of the subjects, who are matched and *then* assigned randomly. At the end of the assignment, the groups will be equivalent for the variables of interest.

Second, random assignment is not always possible, and this is not a catastrophe. One may wish to compare groups at two different clinics. For example, it may not be feasible to administer two different treatments at one clinic or to compare a new treatment with a standard treatment at the same clinic. Another clinic's patients may be useful for comparison purposes. If there are multiple clinics, which clinics receive treatment or control conditions can be randomly determined. But even with two clinics, there is still hope for drawing valid inferences. Random assignment is intended to make the groups equivalent before treatment and to ensure that possible threats to internal validity could not explain group differences. If cases at one clinic receive a special treatment but cases at another clinic receive standard care, one can evaluate both samples extensively to see if they are equivalent. Also, at the end of the study, through within-group analyses (i.e., analyses separately for each clinic), one can determine whether critical processes within treatment related to outcome.

Statistical analyses and evaluation of correlates and moderators of outcome within groups can help strengthen the interpretation that treatment differences were due to the treatment rather than subject selection (sample differences).

Random assignment *is* preferred, but it ought not to be worshipped. Indeed, random assignment does not guarantee group equivalence, especially when sample sizes are small (<20 per group) (see Hsu, 1989). The task of the investigator is to make the case that groups are equivalent and that nonequivalences do not explain the findings. If groups are not equivalent, the role of the variable(s) on which they differ can be evaluated to consider its relation to outcome.

Much can be learned from quasi-experiments in which random assignment cannot be used. Most of the sciences have proceeded without randomly assigning the "subjects" (e.g., planets, native tribes, volcanoes) to conditions to avoid confounds. Also, given the status of the evidence for child and adolescent psychotherapy (most treatments have not been studied, most treatments that have been studied have not been evaluated in clinical settings), findings from quasi-experiments could add considerably.

Assessment

Four areas of assessment are pertinent to a well-designed therapy study. Each one requires some decisions and, of course, relates to the overall purpose of the study.

DESCRIPTIVE INFORMATION. A measure is needed to provide detailed descriptive information about the subjects. The basic information includes subject and demographic descriptors such as age, gender, race, some measures of socioeconomic and occupational status (income, receipt of social assistance), and family composition (proportion of single-parent families, etc.). The characteristics noted here are probably the minimum needed to identify the sample. How the characteristics are measured can vary widely.

Other information can be quite useful as well, including diagnosis of the subjects, presence of multiple disorders, school functioning (IQ, grade level), and characteristics of the community and neighborhood (crime rate, population density, and so on). An indefinite number of characteristics can be listed here, but the point is to ensure that the basic ones are covered. Additional ones ought to have some rationale for inclusion. For example, in my own treatment research with antisocial children, we routinely measure and report IQ as a descriptor variable, because severity of impairment, long-term course, and response to treatment vary considerably as a function of IQ. It is important to report how any characteristic was measured (e.g., parent report, therapist interview). As a general rule, the method of obtaining information is potentially as important to report as the information itself.

Participants in a study also include the therapists. But they usually are not formally assessed through a measure because they are few and can be asked about key characteristics. Among therapist characteristics, it is useful to report age, gender, race, graduate degrees, experience, current status/occupation (e.g., graduate students, professional clinicians). As a matter of record keeping, it is helpful to develop a form that therapists can complete to collect this information systematically.

The consumers of research, including other scientists, ought to know precisely who was included in the sample. Furthermore, many therapy studies end up in secondary data analyses such as meta-analyses. An investigator has no special obligation to try to anticipate all the variables that future reviewers may wish to code. However, the frequent use of studies for secondary analyses reinforces the importance of ensuring that the basic information on subjects and therapists is included.

TREATMENT OUTCOME MEASURES. Obviously a central area of assessment pertains to measures used to evaluate therapeutic change. Chapter 8 discussed the range of relevant outcomes, beyond those related to the symptoms that may have been the impetus for treatment. A well-developed outcome assessment battery is sensitive to a key considerations.

First, any given construct or domain of interest (child psychopathology, depression, aggression) ought to be represented by more than one measure. As investigators, we are almost always primarily interested in constructs rather than measures. For example, we are interested in reducing adolescent depression or symptoms of depression, not in changing scores on a single scale (Center for Epidemiological Study-Depression Scale), even though we certainly view one as related to the other. As a rule, a single measure only imperfectly assesses a construct. One wants to be assured that the results are not limited to only a single measure of the construct. Needless to say, it is not always feasible to select more than one measure of all the constructs. For example, child symptoms, social behavior, school functioning, parent psychopathology, marital functioning, and family relations are among the reasonable outcome domains of child and adolescent therapy. Two to three measures from each of these areas might make the duration of assessment for the family longer than the treatment. Even so, the primary constructs ought to be represented with more than one measure.

Second, multiple methods of assessment are essential. As is well established, child, parent, teacher, and clinician evaluations of child functioning do not correlate very highly with each other (e.g., Achenbach et al., 1987; Kazdin, 1994b; Offord et al., 1996). So if child psychopathology is of interest, the separate measures used to represent the construct ought to use more than one informant. It is even better to draw on different methods of assessment such as informant reports, laboratory samples of behavior, direct observations in everyday life, archival records (e.g., school attendance), and psychophysiological measures, if relevant (e.g., anxiety). Multiple methods of assessment are just as important as multiple measures. Again, the goal is to ensure that the results are not restricted to a very specific way of measuring the outcome. When a construct is assessed by only one method, it is not clear whether the findings are restricted to that particular method.

MODERATORS AND MECHANISMS. An investigator may be interested in evaluating predictors of responsiveness to treatment or moderators on which the effectiveness of treatment depends. For example, there may be good theoretical reasons to believe that child gender or severity of symptoms at intake will influence the effects of treatment. Both of these variables are usually covered in the assessments I have mentioned.

Of course, many other moderators would require the addition of measures to the study. Characteristics of the child (e.g., temperament, self-esteem, self-efficacy), of the parents (e.g., parenting style), and of home relations (e.g., expressed emotion) might be of interest. The range of potential moderators is vast, as chapter 8 suggested. Methodological considerations, including the use of multiple measures and methods, apply to moderators as well. Also, previous comments about the goals of the study and the quality of the study certainly apply in selecting among the infinite range of potential moderators.

The investigator may be interested in processes or mechanisms of change, such as factors responsible for changes in the outcome measures. These processes might include cognitions of the child, parental execution of specific strategies or techniques in the home, or relationship (bonding, alliance) with the therapist. One usually needs to show that changes in the processes precede the changes in outcome. The time line is important because the proposed processes (e.g., cognitions) could change as, or indeed even after, the symptoms change. To evaluate such processes requires measures of the proposed processes, measurement occasions to establish the time line, and special data-analytic techniques to isolate the role of the process on the outcome (see Baron & Kenny, 1986; Holmbeck, 1997). Regrettably, very little therapy research examines why therapeutic change occurs. The model for therapy research in chapter 8 is an attempt to convey the importance and place of such research in the long-term goals of research.

TREATMENT INTEGRITY. I discuss methodological challenges associated with treatment delivery later, but one of them involves assessment, namely, the measurement of treatment integrity. It is important to ensure that treatment was delivered as intended. Development of clear procedures and treatment manuals are steps toward that goal, but they do not guarantee proper treatment implementation. Supervision of therapists during a study also advances the goal, but the question for the investigator is twofold: were the treatments administered as intended and how does one know that?

During the course of the study, some measure of the integrity with which treatment was administered is essential. The measure provides information about the extent to which a given treatment was followed as intended (*treatment integrity*) and the extent to which two or more treatments differed on critical procedures or components (*treatment differentiation*). There are no standard, widely available measures of treatment integrity that one can take off the shelf, but many examples can be obtained from published research (see Klosko, Barlow, Tassinari, & Cerny, 1990; Waltz, Addis, Koerner, & Jacobson, 1993). To assess integrity, investigators usually begin by specifying key components of treatment and then coding evidence of these components in a sample of sessions. Videotapes or audiotapes of the sessions often are coded so that one has a quantitative estimate of the extent to which treatment was carried out as intended. The results can be revealing and show, for example, that control subjects occasionally receive treatments they were *not* intended to receive and that treated subjects do not receive the treatment they *were* intended to receive (e.g., Feldman et al., 1983).

In assessment of treatment integrity, multiple methods and multiple measures are usually not used within a study. Any measure with some reliability that focuses on treatment fidelity is usually quite enough. Such measures are often difficult to use and are not the main part of the study. This is a procedural check rather than a test of key constructs within the study. Of course, conceivably one could conduct a study with the primary purpose of evaluating treatment integrity, in which case multiple measures and methods would become more important.

OTHER TYPES OF MEASURES. The investigator may wish to include yet other measures to elaborate some facet of treatment. One broad domain is referred to as *client reactions to treatment* and reflects dimensions not covered by outcome measures or processes, but which still distinguish different treatments. For example, rates of families canceling or missing sessions or dropping out of treatment, adherence to treatment prescriptions, untoward side effects, and satisfaction with and acceptability of treatment might be pertinent. Treatments might be equally effective on treatment outcome measures but vary on one or more of these other criteria. These other criteria may make one of the interventions the treatment of choice.

Other measures related to the *administration of treatment* may be of interest. These are not measures of treatment integrity, already covered, but rather such measures as the cost of treatment, requirements for training, ease of application of treatment, and perhaps acceptability of treatment to the therapist. These measures distinguish treatments in ways that may have implications for use and dissemination.

ASSESSMENT OCCASIONS. Assessment occasions focus on the outcome measures and when they are administered over the course of the study. Most studies administer measures at pretreatment and posttreatment. For purposes of research, pretreatment measures provide enormous benefits pertaining to the methodology (e.g., permits matching of subjects on pretreatment severity, evaluating equivalence prior to treatment), statistical evaluation (e.g., increased power), and clinical evaluation (e.g., one can examine who changed and how much each person changed) (see Kazdin, 1998b).

In addition to pre- and postassessment, knowing how well clients are functioning during treatment would be extremely helpful. As mentioned in chapter 8, the model implied by pre- and posttreatment assessment is that there is a specific regimen of treatment to be delivered, and once delivered, we must determine how well it worked. This is a clinically odd model: we want to know how well the child and family are functioning while treatment is in effect and to make decisions on the basis of that. Perhaps no more treatment is needed and treatment can be stopped; perhaps it needs to continue. The decision to end treatment ought to be based on therapeutic effects or change rather than on time served with the therapist. Assessment during the course of treatment will make research much more relevant for clinical practice, for which client progress along the way needs to be evaluated.

The assessment during treatment need not be comprehensive. First, it might be conducted only on some occasions (e.g., every third or fourth session or some other regimen, as feasible). Also, simple measures or clinically friendly measures that take a matter of minutes could be used (Clement, 1999; Kazdin, 1993b). Measures can be validated in research to ensure that in fact a highly abbreviated battery or measure relates to the larger outcome-assessment battery and can be used to reflect changes when administration of the full battery is not feasible (e.g., Kazdin & Wassell, 1998).

Assessment occasions also refer to the outcomes over the course of follow-up, which is an elapsed interval after treatment. The significance of follow-up stems from the prospect that conclusions about the effectiveness of treatment can vary over time. Treatment effects might not be maintained. Treatment may be better than no treatment at posttreatment, but this relation may not be evident at follow-up. Also, two treatments may vary in effectiveness at posttreatment but not at follow-up or vice versa. Follow-up assessment is important.

Many obstacles hinder follow-up, so investigators who do not follow their cases over time have plenty of reasons. First, loss of subjects from posttreatment to follow-up assessment can make interpretation of any results very difficult, and the investigator may have to, in the words of my dissertation committee, "Get rid of that section of the paper completely." I take up attrition later.

Second, obtaining follow-up data extends the duration of the study. Conducting treatment studies is a lengthy enterprise. Introducing a follow-up assessment interval of 6 months to a year adds time and generates more work: data, data analyses, more to write up, and so on. Depending on how an investigator operates, a 6-month follow-up could easily add a year to the study. Follow-up can be expensive too. Tracking families, repeatedly calling and mailing packets of measures, or scheduling visits to complete the measures (at a clinic, at home) requires person power, funds for reimbursement of families and postage, and investigator stress-management skills. Understandably, few investigators view follow-up with equanimity. Pressures to publish, to complete theses and dissertations, and to complete studies within time frames of grant agencies also may push investigators to collect the data as quickly as possible and omit follow-up. Yet the pain of follow-up assessment is important to endure. If one cannot wait for follow-up or does not want that data to jeopardize the study results, one should complete and write up the study after posttreatment data are collected. Investigators occasionally prepare follow-up reports separately from the original article in which the study was reported, as is routinely done in longitudinal studies. As for the time interval, longer is usually better, but even a 6- to 12-month follow-up assessment would be beneficial.

Unfortunately treatment studies are not part of large-scale longitudinal studies. Longitudinal studies typically follow a sample over an extended period to evaluate risk and protective factors, onset of disorders, or outcomes of interest; they are not intervention studies. In longitudinal studies, investigators make special efforts to establish long-term relations with participants to obtain extended assessments over time (e.g., 10–30 years). It would be very helpful to draw on the approaches used in successful longitudinal studies and to embed treatment groups into these studies (e.g., Luster, 1998).

Treatment

REPRESENTATIVENESS OF TREATMENT.   The treatment included in the study raises a host of methodological issues. The first issue is the need to ensure that the treatment fairly represents the intervention the investigator intends. The investigator may call the treatment cognitive behavior therapy or psychodynamically oriented treatment, but a name does not reveal what will actually be carried out or whether the name reflects the common or expected use of the term. In many studies in the adult therapy literature, the results are discounted because critics note that the treatments as studied did not represent the usual application of the intended intervention (e.g., Heimberg & Becker, 1984; Jacobson, 1991; Rachman & Wilson, 1980). Part of the problem is that there is no single accepted version of a given technique. Furthermore, techniques referred to by the same name (e.g., cognitive therapy) have many versions. It is important for the investigator to establish that the treatment to be delivered is a reasonable rendition of the standard treatment. Consultation with recognized experts in the field who might comment on the treatment manual would be one very good way to check on this (Sechrest, West, Phillips, Redner, & Yeaton, 1979). Consultants might comment on whether the procedures, strength, and dose of treatment are reasonable. Revisions could be made, if needed, to represent treatment better. If no revisions are needed, the treatment in fact reflects a reasonable rendition. If the investigator is the inventor of the treatment, the problem is moot. The task is merely to report the treatment and to make the manual available.

SPECIFICATION OF TREATMENT.   Any treatment ought to be described in a manual in some form. The manual guides the training of therapists, elaborates critical aspects of treatment, communicates to others what was done, and permits replication in research and clinical work. As highlighted in the chapter 8, manuals differ widely in degree of specificity, detail, and rigidity. They may include general guidelines, overarching principles, themes of the sessions, and scripts, mini-speeches, and sequences of activities (role playing, problem solving) presented by the therapist. Examples of the many available manuals were cited in chapter 8. Rarely can one take a manual "off the shelf" and merely start administering treatment (see "Therapists" section). Usually, it is necessary to see how the treatment is implemented and to practice implementing treatment, often extensively, in addition to consulting the treatment manual. These additional components do not detract from the main point: use of a treatment manual is essential for a superior treatment study.

STRENGTH OF THE MANIPULATION. Obviously, an investigator ought to conduct a strong test of the hypotheses or predictions (i.e., one that is likely to show an effect if there is one). At the design stage, one ought to consider whether the study, as planned, would provide a really good test of the hypotheses, predictions, or treatment. If the answer is no, then the task is to identify specifically how to improve this test.

For treatment studies, one first must consider basic parameters of treatment such as the number of sessions, their duration, and format (individual vs. group; individualized content vs. some generic treatment regimen applied the same way to all). Why was this duration and amount of treatment elected for the study? A practical answer (e.g., to finish the study within one academic term, to complete my dissertation) is a risky and inadequate, although understandable, justification.

Sometimes the investigator includes many different conditions or groups within the study, say, two or three treatment groups and one control group. If possible, can one or more of the groups be eliminated from the design? The strength of the manipulation can be improved by testing more extreme or sharply delineated groups among the conditions the investigator is contemplating. Also, the same number of subjects as originally intended deployed in fewer groups than originally planned can increase the power of the study.

ENSURING TREATMENT INTEGRITY. It is important to ensure that groups received the intervention as intended. Indeed, any inference (treatment was or was not effective) presumes that the treatment was well executed. The presumption needs to be documented. Treatment integrity focuses on the fidelity or faithfulness with which treatment was delivered. In addition, the investigator usually wishes to minimize the variability among the different therapists who administer the treatment(s). Large variation in how treatment is carried out can lead to the absence of statistical differences among conditions, when genuine differences exist.

The investigator must ensure a high level of integrity and provide some measure to evaluate or confirm this. Procedures to guarantee integrity of treatment include careful specification of the treatment to the therapists, special training of the therapists to administer the treatment, and ongoing procedures during the study to ensure that integrity is sustained. These ongoing procedures can include listening to or viewing tapes of selected sessions, meeting with the therapists to provide feedback, and conducting periodic review or training sessions whether departures of integrity are evident or not. Assessment of integrity requires some measure to quantify the extent to which treatment was carried out as intended. This means specifying how to carry out the treatment correctly, something addressed prior to beginning the study. To assess integrity, sample sessions can be videotaped randomly and evaluated by naïve raters who code the presence or absence or degree of particular characteristics. A particular score or set of a priori criteria on the measure, usually arbitrary but still helpful, defines an adequate level of integrity.

If two or more treatments are included in the study, it is also important to ensure that their key dimensions are different and that the treatments did not accidentally overlap. For example, if behavior therapy and relationship therapy are compared, they must differ on the dimensions intended to distinguish them and each group (e.g., relationship therapy) should not accidentally get the other treatment (e.g., behavior therapy). Such a spillover, referred to as *diffusion of treatment*, happens because sometimes therapists use what they know, and if they know both approaches, they may administer them both (see Austin, Liberman, King, & DeRisi, 1976; Feldman et al., 1983). The task of the investigator is to prevent this diffusion and to describe and conduct methods to show how it was done. There is no single, standardized way to supervise, ensure, and assess integrity. However, integrity is essential; statistical comparisons and conclusions of the study depend on it.

Therapists

I mentioned before that in child and adolescent treatment it is meaningful to speak of therapeutic agent because so many people (e.g., parents, teachers, or peers) are available to deliver treatment or play a significant role in the delivery of treatment. For this discussion, let us consider the therapist in the usual sense, as the professional agent who has primary responsibility for delivery of the intervention. Several decisions and issues emerge in relation to the therapists and the design of the investigation.

THERAPIST CHARACTERISTICS. The therapist can make a difference in treatment outcome, at least in adult therapy (e.g., Beutler et al., 1994). Less attention has been accorded the role of the therapist in child treatment, and the few available findings are too specific to provide insights at this time (e.g., therapist openness, assertiveness, and directness enhances the effectiveness of group therapy [Kolvin et al., 1981]). Who will serve as therapists? The usual alternatives are either professional therapists or persons in training such as graduate students. It is difficult to involve professional therapists because of the time commitment and inability of most research programs to pay therapists. Therapy projects are often short-lived; hence, the therapist is usually an individual in a temporary position such as a student.

How many therapists will be included? The answer is always at least two, and more are usually preferable. Some believe that if the therapist is "constant" (the same) across different treatments, the therapist is controlled in the design. Yet, if one therapist were to administer all conditions, he or she might be more effective with one of the treatments; consequently, the effects of the therapist and treatment cannot be truly separated (see Kazdin, 1998b).

Occasionally, the investigator may wish to study therapist characteristics within the design. If so, more than one therapist is needed to represent each level of the characteristic. For example, if warmth is the characteristic of interest, at least two therapists are needed at each level (high warmth, low warmth) so that the level of the variable can be separated from the characteristics or unique features of any particular therapist. If there is no interest in studying therapist characteristics, a minimum of two therapists is still needed to deliver treatment. One must be sure that any differences at the end of treatment can be separated from the impact of the therapist.

THERAPISTS AS A FACTOR IN THE DESIGN. If two or more treatments are administered, the investigator must decide whether all therapists will administer all conditions. If all therapists administer all conditions, therapists are said to be *crossed with treatment*. When therapists are crossed with treatment, the effects of therapists can be analyzed as a factor in the design (therapist × treatment interaction). The data analyses can identify whether some therapists were systematically more effective than others (no matter what treatment they administered) or whether some were more effective with the different treatments.

In some situations therapists administer only one of the treatments. For example, assume that there are two treatments (A, B) and four therapists. Two of the therapists, perhaps because of their expertise, administer only treatment A. Each treatment is administered by those individuals who are trained or expert in it. In this situation, the therapist is said to be *nested within treatment*. If therapists have identified skill or expertise, it would be unreasonable to train them to do all techniques. At the end of treatment, a potential problem can emerge. When therapists are nested, therapist differences rather than treatment differences could explain the results. Moreover, using more therapists between treatment conditions can increase variability and make detection of differences more difficult in the statistical analyses. Whether therapists are crossed or nested depends on the goals of the study, the type of treatment, and therapist availability.

THERAPIST TRAINING. Therapists must be sufficiently skilled to carry out the treatment. A common mistake is to confuse skills or competence with experience. For example, investigators occasionally report that therapists had 3, 5, or 10 years of experience, implying that they therefore know well how to deliver therapy. No doubt experience is valuable. But skill, not experience is the issue; experience and skill are not perfectly or necessarily correlated. The investigator must address three critical questions: are the therapists skilled to deliver this treatment? What training program, regimen, or procedure was used to ensure that they are? How was this competence evaluated in this study? (This last question pertains to treatment integrity and was already covered.)

Therapist training and treatment integrity assume increased importance when multiple treatments and multiple therapists are used. Obviously, the opportunities for large variability among therapists and departure from treatment as intended increase as the number of therapists and treatments increases. Also, because the resources to monitor all of the different therapists and treatments (usually just the investigator) are spread more thinly, a breakdown of integrity or slight departures from treatment more easily creep into the study. A practical recommendation helps with methodology here—keep the scope of the study small to address one or a few questions really well. Larger-scale studies with multiple treatments and therapists may be better left to multisite studies where the resources for monitoring everything really well are more likely available.

Statistical and Data-Analytic Issues

Of the many statistical and data analytic issues, only a few can be highlighted here. Statistical issues include the methods used to evaluate the data and also design issues that can affect the conclusions before any data are even collected. Let us begin with power as a fundamental issue.

POWER TO DETECT GROUP DIFFERENCES. Power is the probability of rejecting the null hypothesis when it is false. Stated differently, power is the likelihood of finding differences between the treatments when in fact their outcomes are truly different. Power is a issue in research in which statistical tests are used to evaluate the null hypotheses (no differences) or test for differences among conditions or groups. When a study shows that groups are not statistically different, this could be true or there could be real differences but this study could not detect them. There are many reasons why no differences might be found, but insufficient power is a main one.

Power (1-beta), the criterion for statistical significance (alpha), sample size (N), and the difference that exists between groups (effect size) are all related.[2] When any three of these are specified in a study, the other term is fixed. For example, in planning a study, assume that we will be testing group differences with an alpha of $p < .05$, that we will have medium effect sizes (e.g., .50), and we want power to be .80. With these three specified, we can consult various resources (noted later) to see how many subjects we would need to detect differences, if such differences exist. It is essential to conduct research so that individual studies are sufficiently powerful to detect differences.

Power is an issue in virtually all research and is important to consider here. In the context of therapy research, studies often have weak power for addressing two types of comparisons of interest. First, investigators often compare two or more treatment conditions, perhaps two or more types of therapy or two or more variations or combinations of treatments. It is common to find that treatments do not statistically differ from each other when compared on the outcome measures. It may well be that the effectiveness of the two treatments are not really different. However, most studies of therapy have too little power to detect treatment differences (Kazdin & Bass, 1989; Rossi, 1990).

Briefly, the problem pertains to the magnitude of effects when treatments are compared. As a guide, consider effect size as the measure of the strength of effects and delineate three points on a continuum as small, medium, and large effects (.2, .5, and .8, respectively) (Cohen, 1988). When treatments are compared, effect sizes tend to be in the small-to-medium range (e.g., <.50). To detect a difference in this range requires many subjects, approximately 70 subjects per group (i.e., for each group in the study [n] as opposed to all of the subjects in the entire study [*N*]. Most treatment studies include 10–20 subjects per group (Kazdin, Bass, et al., 1990). This is much too small a sample to detect differences, given the likely effect sizes, traditional levels of alpha (e.g., $p <$ .05 or .01), and reasonable power (.80). Indeed, a survey of therapy research over a 2-year period revealed that 55% of the therapy studies failed to meet power of $\geq$.80 in their comparisons of groups at posttreatment; approximately 70% fail to meet the power criterion for comparisons at follow-up (see Kazdin & Bass, 1989). In other words, most studies of treatment have insufficient power to detect differences. If one is interested in comparing treatments or variations of treatment, be sure to evaluate power in advance of the study. I discuss means of increasing power later.

Second, in therapy studies researchers are often interested in dividing the groups, conditions, or subjects into smaller units to conduct more precise analyses of the data. For example, the main comparison of interest may contrast treatment group A ($n = 50$) with treatment group B ($n = 50$). The investigator may plan several analyses that further divide the sample, for example, by gender (males vs. females), age (younger vs. older), intelligence (median IQ split), or some other variable. Such comparisons divide the groups into smaller units (or subgroups). Power is commensurately reduced as the comparisons entail subgroups with smaller group ns. A central reason to consider power in advance of the study is to ensure that comparisons of primary interest will be sufficiently sensitive.

The weak power of most therapy studies is not a minor annoyance. In psychotherapy research, the absence of differences (i.e., support for the null hypothesis) is, from conceptual and clinical perspectives often considered to be quite significant (see Frank & Frank, 1991; Luborsky et al., 1975; Stiles, Shapiro, & Elliott, 1986). Reviews of therapy research, as well as many individual studies, continue to show that treatments tend to differ from no treatment but that different treatments produce similar effects. Low power could readily explain this pattern.

There are two recommendations for conducting research. First, power ought to be computed before beginning a study. This is very easy to do because of the available books, articles, and computer software (e.g., Cohen, 1988, 1992; Gorman, Primavera, & Allison, 1995; Statistical Solutions, 1995). From these, power can be calculated within a minute or two without the use of a pencil, pen, or calculator. In some statistical packages for evaluating data, programs are included that compute power and that denote sample size required for a given effect. Once the investigator sees the likelihood of detecting an effect, he or she might want to redesign some facet of the study. One can presume that most studies with weak power were completed because the investigator did not realize in advance that a finding of no differences was likely to emerge.

Investigators ought to increase power of the study at the design stage whenever possible. Table 9.2 provides common methods of increasing power. The usual way of augmenting power is to increase sample size, but there are other ways as well.

Table 9.2 Ways of Increasing Power

What to Do	How This Helps
Use Pretests	To evaluate treatment, one needs only to administer measures at posttreatment and to compare groups. However, the addition of a pretest before treatment begins reduces the error term in the statistical analyses (e.g., repeated measures analyses of variance, analyses of covariance). The net effect is to enhance the obtained effect size by "removing" or taking into account the repeated measures across subjects.
Select Groups/Conditions to Maximize Differences	Select groups or conditions that maximize the effects that are likely to lead to the greatest between-group differences. Small differences between groups or nuances between treatments are less likely to be detected in statistical comparisons unless the sample size is very large.
Use Fewer Groups	If a fixed number of subjects is available or feasible for use, deploy them over fewer groups (e.g., two groups rather than three groups).
Use Reliable Measures	Unreliability of the measures introduces variability (greater error) in the results and this reduces the obtained effect size. Maybe combine measures (e.g., principal component analysis) to have more reliable measures (and also to reduce the number of statistical tests).
Minimize Sources of Error in the Study	Control, monitor, and carefully supervise how subjects are run, how assessments and treatments are administered, and the care and accuracy with which data are collected, scored, and entered. All sources of error (variability) in procedures and execution add to variability in computing effect size. Such variability reduces the obtained effect size and hence the power of the study to detect differences.
Change Alpha used for Deciding Statistical Significance	On a priori grounds, test comparisons at $p < .10$ or .20 rather than .05 or .01. If one knows in advance that a specific predicted comparison or two is likely to be weak, this is reasonable.
Use Directional Statistical Tests	This is a variation of changing alpha. Formulate predictions as direction (e.g., treatment A will be better than B) and use one-tailed tests for these predictions.

Further discussion of these alternatives is presented elsewhere (Kazdin, 1998b).

EVALUATING THE RESULTS.   The dominant method of data evaluation is the use of statistical tests (e.g., t, F) to evaluate whether the difference obtained in the sample is of a sufficient magnitude to reject the null (no difference) hypothesis. Statistical significance provides a consensually based criterion (e.g., $p < .05, .01$) that can be used to decide whether the results in a particular study are likely to be due to "chance," that is, to normal fluctuation, sampling, and the differences that such fluctuations likely yield. A statistically significant difference indicates that the probability level is equal to or below the level of confidence selected. Thus, for a significance level of $p < .05$, a significant difference means that if the experiment were completed 100 times, a difference of that magnitude found on the dependent variable would likely occur only 5 times on a purely chance basis. If the probability obtained in the study is lower than .05, most researchers would reject the null hypothesis and concede that group differences reflect a genuine relation between the independent and dependent variables. Of course, $p < .05$ does not necessarily mean that the findings are "real." Chance cannot be ruled out completely. Replications are so valuable because they reduce the likelihood of chance as an explanation of findings.

Diverse facets of statistical evaluation and null hypothesis testing have been challenged (Chow, 1988, Kupfersmid, 1988; Meehl, 1978), based on

- the arbitrary criterion that a particular level such as $p < .05$ represents;
- the all-or-none decision making based on that criterion;
- the absence of information regarding the strength or practical value of the relation between the independent and dependent variable, whether or not statistical significance is attained; and
- the likelihood that the null hypothesis on which tests are based is never really true.

Also, what is statistical significance measuring? As the most cynical interpretation, statistical significance is a direct function of sample size. That is, the larger the sample size, the smaller the group differences needed for statistical significance for a given level of confidence. Stated another way, a given difference between two groups will gradually approach statistical significance as the size of the samples within each group is increased. Indeed, statistical significance is virtually assured no matter what the comparison if a very large number of subjects is used (with the perplexing exception of my dissertation).

Although there are differing views on the value of statistical significance, there is consensus that measures of the magnitude or strength of effects of relations ought to be included in the data analyses. Magnitude of effect and statistical significance are not redundant. Two studies may show effects that are identical in magnitude (e.g., effect size = .70), but only one of these studies may show a statistically significant difference. This could easily occur if the sample size of one study is a little larger than the other. Similarly, two studies may show statistically significant differences at the same level of alpha, but the magnitude of effect (effect sizes) may be very different.

Magnitude of effect can be expressed differently, as mentioned in chapter 7. One measure we have already discussed, effect size, illustrates the informational yield provided beyond statistical significance. Effect size is familiar because of its frequent use in meta-analyses. Moreover, with effect size, the magnitude of effect is provided in a common metric that allows comparison (and combination) of different experiments using different outcome measures. The effect size is readily interpretable in terms of small, medium, and large effects, as these terms have come to be used (Cohen, 1988).

Statistical significance addresses whether the results are likely to be the result of chance and normal fluctuations in sampling. Effect size, r, or some other measure conveys the strength of the relation. What is left? For psychotherapy studies, measures of clinical significance or clinical importance of the change are left and ought to be included. A statistically significant effect and a large effect size may have nothing to do with clinical significance. If the large effect size is obtained on a measure that does not reflect functioning in everyday life, clearly a large effect size may have no bearing on client functioning. Even if the measure is relevant to functioning in everyday life, a large effect size still does not necessarily reflect clinical importance. Statistical significance, effect size (or other magnitude of effect measures), and clinical significance provide different information about the data, even though they are all quantitative methods of evaluating the results.

As mentioned in chapter 8, clinical significance focuses on the practical value of the effect of an intervention, that is, whether it makes any "real" difference to the clients or to others in their functioning and everyday life. Evaluation of the clinical or applied importance of the change usually supplements statistical methods of determining whether group differences or changes over time are reliable. Once reliable changes are evident, further efforts are made to quantify whether treatment has moved the client appreciably closer to adequate functioning, that is, whether the change is important. Several methods of evaluating the clinical significance of treatment effects were highlighted in the chapter 8. Some measure of impact of treatment that reflects functioning in everyday life and reports applied significance ought to be included.

Because of the difficulty of completing therapy studies, it is important that data analyses provide the maximum yield. Statistical significance, magnitude of effect, and clinical significance address three broad issues in data analyses. Statistical significance is routinely included in published studies of treatment research. Analyses of the magnitude of effect and clinical significance of the changes do not appear in the majority of studies; their inclusion would greatly improve the yield of treatment research.

CRITICAL ISSUES WITH METHODOLOGICAL IMPLICATIONS

Attending to the specific methodological practices discussed to this point is sufficiently demanding. Yet there are other challenges to completing therapy studies, including the loss of subjects over the course of a study and ethical issues in providing and evaluating treatment.

Attrition

Dropping out of therapy is a pervasive concern in treatment research. As a general rule, the rate of losing subjects over the course of a study is a function of the duration of treatment (Phillips, 1985). The longer the treatment, the higher the percentage of subjects who drop out. Most subjects who drop out do so early in treatment and then additional losses occur over the course of time. As usually defined, dropping out refers to terminating treatment prematurely and against the advice of the clinician. In child and adolescent therapy, 40%–60% of cases drop out of treatment, a rather high percentage (Kazdin, 1996b; Wierzbicki & Pekarik, 1993).

As a research topic, attrition raises interesting substantive questions. Why do people drop out? What are the predictive (risk) factors? What happens to those who drop out? There is a long-standing assumption that those who drop out prematurely from treatment do more poorly than those who complete treatment. The matter is not well studied; understandably, individuals who drop out of treatment are not usually asked to complete the outcome measures once they leave therapy. Consequently, little information is available about whether they have improved, in what domains, and to what extent. We have evaluated the outcomes of treatment among antisocial children and their families for those who drop out of treatment. Among the findings, 34% of those who drop out of treatment early and against our advice show quite definite therapeutic improvements (Kazdin & Wassell, 1998). Staying in treatment is associated with greater therapeutic change, but some families likely drop out of treatment because they have experienced improvement and see no need (or strong need) to continue. Of course, their change does not necessarily mean that the benefits can be attributed to therapy rather than to some other influence (e.g., end of a crisis that prompted treatment.) Dropouts, as a group, often are quite worse on outcome measures than those who remain in treatment, but perhaps because the more extreme or severely disturbed cases are more likely to drop out (Kazdin, Mazurick, & Siegel, 1994). The fact that a significant proportion of dropouts may improve underscores the importance of assessment during the course of treatment rather than just at the end.

Attrition is raised here in relation to methodological issues and the design of treatment studies. When cases drop out of treatment, there can be many methodological repercussions. First, the benefits of randomly assigning cases to groups can be lost. Because dropping out is not a random process, group equivalence fostered by random assignment is altered. Sometimes investigators report, with false security, that some small number or an equal number of cases dropped out from each condition. The implication is that attrition did not make a difference or was equivalent among groups. Yet the type of subjects who drop out of each group may differ in some way. When there is any attrition, comparing groups that received different treatments or control conditions might be a bit more difficult because any outcome differences could reflect selection factors.

Second, if there is attrition, the generality of the findings is potentially reduced. Dropping out means that the results will apply to fewer people because the characteristics represented in the study have been narrowed. That is, the results of the study now apply to those who met inclusion criteria, who did not meet exclusion criteria, and who did not drop out. Those who drop out are often more severely impaired, come from more disadvantageous contexts, and experience many more obstacles in coming to treatment. Characteristics of dropouts usually are difficult to evaluate because the number of subjects and dropouts is not large enough to generate sufficient power, so dropouts and treatment completers, compared statistically, look the same. Yet attrition means that the results may apply only to a select group of persons who can complete the study.

Third, the loss of subjects reduces the power of the study merely by reducing the sample size. As most treatment studies already have weak power, further loss of subjects exacerbates the problem. One can readily understand why most therapy has focused on relatively brief treatments, because longer treatments are associated with greater attrition. Also, most studies do not evaluate clinically referred cases who are also likely to have greater impairment and more adverse living conditions, two of many factors associated with dropping out of treatment.

As possible, the investigator ought to plan strategies to minimize the loss of cases over the course of treatment. If the initial pretreatment assessment is thorough, one can later at least identify characteristics of those who did drop out. As mentioned already, meaningful comparisons of dropout and treatment completers are difficult to make because of the small sample size and difficulty in detecting differences if any exist. Consequently, it is better to try to minimize the problem in advance. Among the many strategies are explaining to families at the outset of treatment what the duration will be, providing monetary incentives for completing treatment, addressing family stressors as part of treatment (which often interfere with coming to treatment), and engaging the family in decision making about treatment and its foci (e.g., Henggeler et al., 1998; Prinz & Miller, 1994; Szapocznik et al., 1988). The efforts can make a genuine difference. For example, in one study, all adolescent drug abusers and their families received treatment, but half were randomly assigned to receive an intervention to engage the family and to reduce attrition (Szapocznik et al., 1988). The engagement intervention included phone calls and contact with all family members and efforts to identify and address obstacles to treatment very early. More families who received the special engagement procedure (77%) completed treatment than those who did not (25%).

The investigator ought to be alert to the prospect of attrition and to its implications for evaluating the hypotheses of interest. During the study, some procedures might be used to foster completion of treatment. Grant-funded research often provides monetary incentives for completing assessments at the end of treatment or even for attending treatment sessions, but these options are not always available. Once the study is competed, it is important to evaluate the impact of attrition on the results. Beyond looking at dropout characteristics, various data-analytic strategies might be used (see Howard, Krause, & Orlinsky, 1986; Little & Rubin, 1987).

One procedure for handling the data is referred to as *end-state analysis*. In this method, dropouts are included in the data analyses. Where there are missing data, the last or most recent previous data point is entered. For example, if some subjects completed pretreatment but not posttreatment, the pretreatment scores for each measure would be used in both places on the database (e.g., before and after). If subjects completed pre- and posttreatment but dropped out during the follow-up period, then their posttreatment data would be used for the follow-up. In this way, all subjects are retained for all of the data analyses, thus preserving the random composition of groups. Every analytic strategy has trade-offs and limitations. In end state analyses, data points may not represent the best estimate of the current status of the subject. Even so, end state analyses can be useful as one way to analyze the data. In fact, the results can be analyzed with and without the dropouts. The investigator can evaluate whether the conclusions differ as a result of the analyses.

Ethical Issues and Design Interface

Ethical issues entail a variety of principles and practices designed to protect research participants, to govern the interactions of the investigator with the participants, and to address professional conduct more generally. The guidelines for ethical treatment of participants are overseen by professional organizations who provide ethical codes for research (e.g., American Psychological Association, 1992) as well as by federal law (e.g., U.S. Department of Health and Human Services, 1983). Investigators ought to be conversant with the codes of conduct that govern research and the expectations that many roles (teacher, mentor, investigator, collaborator, scientist) entail. Here I highlight a few issues particularly relevant to treatment research and the interface of ethical and methodological issues.

INFORMING CLIENTS ABOUT TREATMENT. Central to the research is informed consent from participants. Informed consent reflects an agreement that subjects are willing to participate in the study after being informed about it. The three elements of informed consent are competence, knowledge, and volition. *Competence* is an individual's ability to make a well-reasoned decision. *Knowledge* means understanding the nature of the study, the alternatives available if the subject does not wish to participate, and potential risks and benefits of participation. *Volition* is the will to participate. Participants must provide their consent free from constraint and duress.

In the treatment of young children, parents provide consent, but with older children (perhaps older than 7 or 8), consent may be sought from the children as well. There are obvious difficulties in ensuring knowledge, competence, and volition. Also, what if the child says he or she does not want to participate but the parent agrees to it? The investigator's task is to provide a good faith effort to convey the terms of the investigation and to proceed only with consent. And, of course, the consent can be withdrawn at any time to ensure full protection of the subjects, although this does not usually occur in treatment studies. Informed consent is a condition of research, is a reasonable constraint on the investigator, and ought to be approached willingly. Ethical issues take the highest priority; increased sensitivity to such issues is required because the treatment is for individuals in need and the focus is on children and adolescents who are especially vulnerable populations. Youths cannot be expected to make major decisions for themselves and hence may not be participating willingly. The coercion may come from the parents.

An important issue is the information provided to the client about treatment. Outside of the rationale and procedures themselves, the investigator is required to report the current status of the treatment, whether it has been effective or not in previous applications. Many treatments are experimental, and the subject normally can be provided with a statement to that effect. Information about treatment in a study may extend to the treatments the subject will not receive. Conceivably, families could be told that, of many different treatments, they will receive only one. They might want to know whether some treatments are more effective than others and whether they have been assigned to a "control" group. In addition, families may show a clear preference for an alternative treatment and react adversely or skeptically to the one they are assigned.

As part of informed consent, families must be informed at the beginning of the study that various treatments are offered and that assignment to treatment is random, assuming that this is true. Although subjects are rarely pleased to learn that their assignment to treatment will be random, the importance of randomness in assessing the impact of different treatments might be stressed. Only those individuals who agree to the conditions of the investigation can serve as subjects and be assigned to conditions. This process leads to selection of a special group that may have implications for the external validity of the results. Most clinical research must work within these constraints.

WITHHOLDING THE INTERVENTION.   Studies occasionally withhold the treatment and assign some of the subjects to no treatment or waiting-list control conditions. Although these conditions are essential to answer specific research questions, as discussed previously, their use raises obvious ethical questions. Assigning a client to one of these conditions withholds a treatment from which a person may benefit. Intellectually, one can say that we really do not know if the treatment is better than no treatment and thus may not really be withholding a "treatment." Yet the ethical issue stems from recruiting individuals and then assigning them to a condition in which no effort is made to help them.

An investigator is obligated to consider seriously whether delaying or completely withholding treatment is necessary for the questions addressed in the research. Because of the ethical problems, it may be more appropriate to reserve questions comparing treatment with no treatment to situations where subjects are willing to wait and are unlikely to suffer deleterious consequences. Obviously, volunteer clients solicited from the community may be more appropriate for a study in which a waiting-list control group is required than clients who seek treatment at a crisis intervention center. When clients have severe problems and warrant or demand immediate intervention, questions comparing treatment with no treatment may be difficult to justify and to implement.

In some cases, assigning subjects to a waiting-list control group will not really delay treatment. Waiting lists are common at many clinics, where clients may wait a few or several months before treatment. All subjects who are to serve in the study and who agree to participate can be moved up on the list. Those who are randomly assigned to the intervention condition are treated immediately; those who are assigned to wait can be assessed and then await treatment. However, ethical issues are not eliminated by rearranging waiting-list status. Moving some clients up on the list may delay the treatment of others who are not in the study. Some of the problems of delaying treatment can be alleviated by informing clients at intake of the possibility that they will not be assigned to treatment for a specified interval. As noted before, the investigation would use only subjects who agree with this stipulation and then randomly assign them to the various treatment and control conditions.

Withholding treatment emerges in another way in treatment studies. Once a study begins, families may need another treatment and may have to be withdrawn from the study. This can occur during treatment if another problem emerges (e.g., suicide attempt, evidence of psychoses) or was present but not previously detected (e.g., adolescent substance abuse, parental depression, marital discord). This need for other services can also emerge during a posttreatment follow-up period in which participants may seek additional treatment. From a very narrow methodological perspective, additional treatment can invalidate the inferences drawn (by introducing added variability among subjects, some of whom receive further treatment or by altering the random composition of groups if some subjects are selectively removed. Obviously, children, adolescents, and their families must receive the care and services that best judgment suggests. The investigator understandably wishes to ensure that the research goes smoothly but never ought to withhold potential benefits to continue a project.

For any extenuating circumstance that emerges in research, the investigator ought to seek additional input (e.g., formal evaluation of the child), recommendations about treatment needs, and assistance in reaching decisions on behalf of and with the family. Withholding potentially needed services from a participant cannot be justified and may be inadvisable as a model of professional care even if it could be. At the same time, families may seek treatment or care for which there is no clear evidence of need. An investigator is advised to seek outside counsel (from a human subjects committee and other professionals) to assure that the child or family is obtaining what they may need or information about alternatives. Other resources can affirm that the investigator does not favor a particular course of action that serves the research at the potential expense of the family.

USING TREATMENTS OF QUESTIONABLE EFFICACY.   Some treatments in a given study might be expected to be less effective than others. This expectation may derive from theoretical predictions, previous research, or from the nature of the design. For example, in a simple 2×2 factorial design, an investigator may study the effects of such variables as therapist experience (experienced vs. inexperienced therapists) and duration of treatment (1 session vs. 10 sessions). Subjects in one of the four groups resulting from this design will be exposed to inexperienced therapists for one treatment session, a condition likely to be less effective than the others. The use of treatments that have a low probability of effectiveness raises an ethical issue.

Sometimes groups are designed to control for "nonspecific" treatment factors, such as attending treatment sessions, meeting with a therapist, and believing that treatment may produce change. These groups are designed to provide a bogus intervention: procedures that appear to be therapeutic without specific treatment components expected to help the client. Providing a weak treatment or an ineffective control condition raises obvious ethical problems. First, the client's problem may not improve or may even worsen without an effective treatment. To withhold a relatively effective treatment renders these possibilities more salient. Second, clients may lose credulity in the process of psychological treatment in general. Clients expect to receive an effective treatment and to achieve change. If treatment is not reasonable in their judgment and does not produce change, clients may be generally discouraged from seeking help in the future. In general, the control conditions or treatments that may "fill out" the design warrant ethical evaluation by the investigator and review boards, including any special control condition in which the likelihood of improvement is unexpected or minimal. Other contextual issues such as who the clients are (patients seeking treatment, community volunteers) and provisions after the study is completed (free treatment and care) may affect evaluation of the issues.

GENERAL COMMENTS.   The ethical issues raised in intervention research depend on the precise research question and the control groups that form the basis of the design. Use of no treatment or waiting-list control groups is essential in research that asks "Does this treatment work?" The question usually requires assessing the extent of change without treatment. Similarly, use of a nonspecific treatment control group may be important in research that asks "Why does this treatment work?" Such research may require a group to look at the influence of "nonspecific treatment factors" alone.

The research questions that require ethically sensitive control conditions help us to understand treatment. The questions themselves cannot be abandoned. However, the conditions under which these questions are examined can be varied to attenuate partially the objections that normally arise. For example, studies requiring control conditions that withhold treatment or provide nonspecific treatment control groups need not be conducted in settings where clients need treatment and have sought a treatment to ameliorate an immediately felt problem. On the other hand, when volunteer subjects are solicited and can be informed about the experimental nature of all treatment procedures, a wider range of experimental conditions is more readily justified. In short, where patient care and service delivery are the higher priorities, the use of groups that withhold treatment or present "nonspecific" treatments expected to produce minimal change is generally unacceptable. Where research, rather than service delivery, has the higher priority and clients can be informed of the implications of this priority, the use of such groups may be more readily justified.

Some of the ethical issues of treatment can be ameliorated by providing all subjects with effective treatment after they have completed the treatment to which they were assigned. After treatment, clients who served as a no-treatment control group could also receive the benefits of treatment. Indeed, this is exactly what the waiting-list control group is intended to accomplish. In studies with several different treatments or a nonspecific control condition, clients who are not completely satisfied with their progress eventually might be given the most effective treatment. Thus, clients may benefit from the project in which they served by receiving the best treatment. From an experimental standpoint, this strategy is useful to further examine the extent of change in clients who continue in the superior treatment. Essentially, there is a partial replication of treatment effects in the design. From an ethical standpoint, providing all subjects with the most effective intervention may overcome objections against assigning subjects to variably effective treatments. Of course, at some point in the research, long-term follow-up studies need to determine whether the seemingly effective intervention is better than no treatment. One might conduct a randomized controlled trial or use nonexperimental designs where groups who have not received treatment are followed.

SUMMARY AND CONCLUSIONS

Psychotherapy research raises its own unique methodological challenges. Challenges for research derive from several characteristics, including the fact that subjects may come to treatment with significant clinical problems, want immediate benefit, and may be assigned to treatment or control conditions likely to vary in effectiveness. This chapter discussed several challenges in relation to the selection and assignment, assessment, and delivery of treatment. A few statistical and data-analytic issues were raised as well. As a rule, therapy investigations are not sufficiently powerful to detect statistically significant differences among groups that receive various forms of treatment. This critical issue can be addressed before the study begins. Also, in the design of the study, several practices can be included to augment power.

Attrition or loss of children and families during a treatment investigation was also a main topic here. Dropouts can affect all facets of experimental validity and introduce considerable ambiguity to the conclusions. The chapter discussed strategies to minimize and to evaluate attrition. Finally, ethical issues provide a critical context in which treatment research is conducted. Protection of participants' rights and, more than that, ensuring that the participants' interests are not sacrificed are central to the research enterprise. The very nature of the context of therapy research (i.e., providing treatment to people in need) compels the investigator to respond to family interests, needs, and concerns in ways that may compete with the design. Outside consultation with colleagues and mechanisms within the study for providing other services (referral for evaluation, additional treatment) are important.

Designing methodologically sound studies is obviously important. At the same time, methodology and methodologically sound studies should not be ends in themselves. The goal is to obtain incremental knowledge on key questions, which can be obtained in multiple studies, many not perfectly designed or true experiments. The task of the investigator is to choose an important question and provide reasonable means of finding answers. In this context, "reasonable" means that sources of bias, artifact, and other influences that could explain the results just as well as the treatment or intervention have been reduced, if not eliminated. This broader task is the ultimate goal of methodology; treatment research raises special challenges because of its responsibilities and constraints.

FOR FURTHER READING

A great deal has been written about the methodology of therapy research, including guidelines for designing, evaluating, and presenting studies. The readings consider desired methodological practices and how specific practices can influence inferences about the effects of treatment and conclusions related to clinical application.

Clarke, G.N. (1995). Improving the transition from basic efficacy research to effectiveness studies: Methodological issues and procedures. *Journal of Consulting and Clinical Psychology, 63,* 718–725.

Kazdin, A.E. (1998). *Research design in clinical psychology* (3rd ed.). Needham Heights, MA: Allyn & Bacon.

Linden, W., & Wren, F.K. (1990). Therapy outcome research, health care policy, and the continuing lack of accumulated knowledge. *Professional Psychology: Research and Practice, 21,* 482–488.

Peterson, L., & Bell-Dolan, D. (1995). Treatment outcome research in child psychology: Realistic coping with the "Ten Commandments of Methodology." *Journal of Clinical Child Psychology, 24,* 149–162.

Weiss, B., & Weisz, J.R. (1990). The impact of methodological factors on child psychotherapy outcome research: A meta-analysis for researchers. *Journal of Abnormal Child Psychology, 18,* 639–670.

Chapter 10

Implementing and Evaluating
Treatment in Clinical Practice

PREVIOUS CHAPTERS HAVE FOCUSED ON changing the way in which child and adolescent therapy *research* is conducted. So far, clinical practice has not been a focal point. But one must address central issues of clinical practice to develop the knowledge base of child and adolescent therapy, which is this book's objective. Of course, the priority of clinical work is to improve the client (child, adolescent, and family), rather than to develop knowledge. Even so, clinical practice can contribute in very special ways to the knowledge base. This chapter presents a model of clinical practice designed to contribute to the scientific knowledge base of child and adolescent therapy.

BACKGROUND: HIATUS OF RESEARCH AND CLINICAL PRACTICE

Delineating the hiatus or split between research and practice provides an important backdrop for key characteristics of clinical practice and ways that clinical work can contribute to the knowledge base. The hiatus represents differences in the foci, priorities, methods, rules of evidence, and goals of practice and research (see Barlow et al., 1984; Stricker & Keisner, 1985; Talley, Strupp, & Butler, 1994). Clinical research is designed to test hypotheses about treatment, to conduct methodologically sound studies (e.g., randomized trials) that permit one to draw valid inferences, to use standardized assessment methods, and to identify general principles about human functioning. Research, by design, consists of relatively fixed and prescribed procedures to maximize control and to minimize sources of bias that can interfere with drawing conclusions from the data. For example, all clients in a given treatment condition or group receive the same amount and type of treatment to standardize the intervention. Clients (subjects) are informed, via consent procedures, that the goal of the treatment is to obtain information but that there may be direct benefits (therapeutic change) as well. The benefits are incidental from the standpoint of the design.

Clinical practice is designed to help a client directly by improving functioning in everyday life. The pertinent data are qualitative; the therapist attempts to trace the convergence of multiple influences in the client's development, and to decide what facets of therapy can constructively contribute to this development. Therapy is individually tailored to the specific characteristics of the child and family, based on their presenting complaints and personal and interpersonal resources. Treatment is flexible and can be altered to help the client. Combinations of different treatments or selected facets of different treatments are likely to be used. From just the few differences noted here, one can readily understand the hiatus between research and practice.

The hiatus between research and practice is not absolute. Research and practice have drawn from each other. Indeed, clinical practice has drawn on basic research quite frequently. Extrapolations of models of learning to psychotherapy exemplify efforts to translate and to apply psychological theory and laboratory paradigms to therapy. Often, investigators who conducted basic research (e.g., Bechterev, 1933; Dollard & Miller, 1950; Pavlov, 1927) have been directly involved in extrapolations to clinical work. Also, professionals involved in practice frequently have drawn from laboratory research to develop specific treatment techniques (see Cautela, 1967; Salter, 1949; Wolpe, 1958).

Although clinical practice has drawn on psychological theory and laboratory paradigms, specific domains have not penetrated clinical practice as much as one would expect (Garfield, 1980). A major case in point is the negligible impact that the findings from therapy research have had on clinical practice. Surveys of practitioners have helped to identify self-reported reasons why some facets of research seem alien to clinical practice (Cohen, Sargent, & Sechrest, 1986; Haynes, Lemsky, & Sexton-Radek, 1987). The ways in which research is conducted, the focus on groups (group averages rather than the individual), the isolation of pure and narrowly defined (rather than eclectic and combined) treatment techniques, and the use of nonreferred cases are a few of the many reasons why research is not viewed as particularly relevant to clinical practice (see Barlow et al., 1984; Bergin & Strupp, 1972). The limited impact of psychotherapy research on practice is understandable.

The connections between substantive findings of psychology and clinical practice are critically important in their own right. A concern of arguably greater significance is the methodological tenets and rules of knowledge that separate clinical practice and clinical research. In clinical practice, the professional is called on to evaluate the nature and scope of client dysfunction, to ascertain the resources within the client and his or her life relevant to treatment, to determine the likelihood that various treatments will be beneficial, and to assess the impact of treatment as therapy unfolds. The professional relies on impressions, intuition, and seasoned experience to draw inferences. The clinician decides what the client "needs," how treatment is progressing, and whether therapeutic change has been achieved, usually based on unstructured and informal interviews.

In research, systematic assessment and evaluation are clearly defined and replicable. Key features of research are specification of variables, operational definitions of constructs through systematic assessment, and formal and specifiable methods of data evaluation. Certainly one should not accept scientific tenets and practices with unconditional positive regard. Epistemological tenets of scientific research and many specific practices derived from them (e.g., hypothesis testing, statistical tests) are laced with subjectivity and can be easily challenged (see Kazdin, 1998b). Even so, the weaknesses of scientific methods are not a sufficient reason to abandon systematic evaluation in clinical work.

There are objections to the methods of procuring "data" in clinical work. Usually interviews of and interactions with the client serve as the source of data on which the clinician draws to gather the details, themes, patterns, events, and other facets of the individual's life and to make a host of decisions (which treatments, which focus or problem, when to stop or change treatment). Unsystematic data and their informal integration are often unreliable, invalid approaches to decision making, as several researchers suggest (Dawes, 1994; Garb, 1997; Kleinmuntz, 1990; Meehl, 1954, 1997).

The problem lies in human information processing and "normal" biases in judgment. Humans organize incoming information in systematic but biased ways. A strong word such as *bias* is justifiable because one can be misled into invalid conclusions about the relations of various events (e.g., between factors in one's environment). Table 10.1 presents several biases, including the representative heuristic, availability heuristic, anchoring heuristic, confirmatory bias, illusory correlation, hindsight bias, and overconfidence (see Dumont, 1993; Kanfer & Schefft, 1988; Nezu & Nezu, 1989; Smith & Dumont, 1997). These biases are not necessarily mutually exclusive. In the abstract, one can readily acknowledge that a particular propensity to draw conclusions may exist.

Table 10.1 Sources of Bias in Reaching Judgments

Type of Bias	Characteristics
Representative Heuristic	This bias draws connections between events or characteristics based on stereotypes or expected relations. Expected relations assume that some present condition seems plausibly related to a past or current event. Less evidence or supportive information is needed when one relies on plausibility, stereotypes, and superficial resemblances between characteristics. An example in clinical work would be relating a child's current symptoms to some characteristic of a parent (e.g., rejection, withdrawal) that may have nothing to do with the problem.
Availability Heuristic	This is a tendency to draw from available information that may be vivid, recent, or salient. Judgments about a new case are made by inadvertently drawing conclusions about an individual based on similarities to another case. In clinical work, a previous case with a similar problem may lead us to false causal attributions about how this client's problem has developed.
Anchoring Heuristic	Often judgments are formed quickly based on initial impressions. The anchoring heuristic refers to these judgments. In the context of clinical work, judgments may be made about the client, about the causes of dysfunction or current problems, and about appropriate treatment. The initial judgment is "anchored" to initial impressions and does not adjust to, or sufficiently weigh, new information.
Confirmatory Bias	One tends to see information and to support hypotheses consistent with one's existing beliefs. Information that confirms one's beliefs tends to be more readily accepted and more heavily weighted than information that is contradictory. Attention to confirmatory information and neglect of contradictory information decrease the accuracy of predictions and judgments about outcomes. In clinical work, details that might refute the clinician's view about the client's functioning or relations to others (e.g., quite positive relations with others) are ignored or reinterpreted if they would disconfirm that view.
Illusory Correlation	Human judgment makes connections between events or characteristics when such connections are unwarranted in fact. Events may be seen as more related than they actually are. Conversely, the illusion may refer to seeing related events as unrelated.

continued

Table 10.1 (*continued*)

TYPE OF BIAS	CHARACTERISTICS
Hindsight Bias	This is a tendency to make sense of past events in light of the known outcome. The key to this bias is that the individual knows some outcome (e.g., patient improvement, divorce, rehospitalization). The bias refers to the perspective that one "knew all along" that a particular outcome would occur and looks to events in the past to explain the outcome. These events are accorded much more weight or significance when the individual knows the outcome. Case studies that explain the client's current problem routinely select the salient events to clarify the sequence of events.
Overconfidence	One overestimates the accuracy of one's judgment in comparison to the actual information or outcome. Confidence does not seem to be related to the actual accuracy of the judgment or to the complexity of the situation or outcome one is asked to judge. Once a judgment is reached, it seems coherent, relatively straightforward, and clear. This may promote confidence, which has no relation to the truth of the judgment.

Further discussion of these sources of bias and review of the pertinent research can be found in Dumont, 1993; Kanfer & Schefft, 1988; Nezu & Nezu, 1989; and Smith & Dumont, 1997.

However, these biases have been studied in the context of clinical situations. The biases operate when inferences are drawn about the likely basis of the client's problem, the personality of the client, likely behavior of the client in the future, and treatments that are needed.

The problem of judgmental biases is a strong reason to argue for more systematic assessment and evaluation in therapy. However, there is a related, more persuasive, clinically relevant reason to strengthen the case. Specifically, the priority of clinical work is to improve the functioning of a particular client. The questions for therapy practice ask how we can help this patient, with what strategies and procedures, how much progress is being made, in what ways this client has changed, and what further changes, if any, are needed or desirable? Evaluation in clinical work is designed to assess a client's functioning, to decide what interventions are suitable, to apply the interventions, to examine their impact on the goals of treatment, then to make decisions about the continuation, discontinuation, or modification of treatment. Giving priority to the individual client is not to argue against systematic assessment and evaluation. Indeed, given the importance of ensuring benefits to the client, systematic assessment and evaluation are essential.

EVALUATION OF THE INDIVIDUAL CASE

Interest in methods to study the individual is by no means new. For example, Allport (1937), a psychologist whose contributions to the study of personality were particularly notable, drew the distinction between *nomothetic* and *idiographic* approaches. The nomothetic approach studies groups and identifies laws that characterize people in general. The idiographic approach focuses on the study of individuals, particularly their unique characteristics. Allport emphasized that these approaches generate quite different types of research and different findings. The systematic study of the individual extends to several areas of psychology (see Barlow & Hersen, 1984; Davidson & Costello, 1969; Kazdin, 1982; Kazdin & Tuma, 1982; Yin, 1994). Not all of the different ways of studying the individual reliably produce replicable knowledge.

The Case Study

In the mental health professions, the case study has been the most popular method to evaluate clinical work. The case study, in its most general use, refers at once to a particular focus and a method of evaluation. As a focus, the case study consists of intensive evaluation of a particular instance. Within the context of therapy, the particular instance or case is an individual person. Within the context of other aspects of psychology and other disciplines, the "case" can also be a particular culture, city, school, or prison system (Stake, 1995). The goal is to learn about a particular case, not necessarily to learn about other cases or about a problem, setting, or people in general. Stated another way, the goal of the case study "is particularization, not generalization" (Stake, 1995, p. 8). No doubt insights from a case may well lead to generalities because people and situations are often alike. Yet this is not the usual goal of the case.

As a method of evaluation, the traditional case study has relied on anecdotal information, from nonstandardized observations and descriptions based on the views of the client and therapist. The descriptions are phenomenological, holistic, naturalistic, and qualitative. The therapist tries to capture the complexities and nuances of the full range of factors that may exert influence. The goal is a complete picture of the individual and the factors affecting him or her. Thus, the case report may include details of the role of others (parents, spouses, children) and contexts (e.g., living conditions). The process of obtaining that information emphasizes the importance of the client's reconstruction of his or her life and the therapist's interpretation from a particular theoretical and conceptual frame of reference. The clinician interprets connections between events and circumstances and identifies continuities and patterns over the life span.

The major weakness of the traditional clinical case study has been its heavy reliance on anecdotal information. Many inferences are based on clients' reports, which become the "data" upon which interpretations are made. The client's reconstructions of the past, particularly those laden with emotion, are often distorted, highly selective, and may bear little resemblance to the actual events. Unless subjective accounts are independently corroborated, they could be completely unreliable, influenced by the judgmental processes mentioned previously. The therapist then filters this information again to create coherent patterns of relations, causal paths, reasonable accounts, and so on. Although fascinating, credible, and provocative, such accounts may not accurately represent the phenomenon they are intended to explain.

Even so, anecdotal case studies, although unsystematic accounts, have contributed enormously to theory, research, and practice (see Davison & Lazarus, 1994; Kazdin, 1993b; Lazarus & Davison, 1971). Case studies have

- served as a source of ideas and hypotheses about human performance and models of development (e.g., case of Little Hans [Freud, 1933]; case of Little Albert [Watson & Rayner, 1920]);
- served as the source of new therapy techniques (e.g., talk therapy [Breuer & Freud, 1957]) and treatments for anxiety among children (Jones, 1924a, 1924b);
- permitted the study of rare phenomena (e.g., multiple personalities such as the well-publicized report of the "three faces of Eve" [Thigpen & Cleckley, 1954, 1957]) that could not otherwise be studied; and
- provided dramatic and persuasive demonstrations of otherwise abstract problems (e.g., convey vividly what it is like to suffer abuse, HIV, and so forth).

Notwithstanding these benefits, the anecdotal case study cannot provide the replicable knowledge needed to establish treatment or address the range of requisite questions about therapy. No less significant, the unsystematic means to evaluate patient progress can be challenged too as particularly vulnerable to biases in which causal relations (e.g., between treatment and therapeutic change) could easily be distorted. Worse, there may be no therapeutic change, but this could be difficult to discern without systematic observation.

Single-Case Research Designs

BACKGROUND. As a method of description, the case study is invariably interesting but does not provide evidence that could advance the theoretical, empirical, and clinical underpinnings of child and adolescent therapy. Other methods are needed to systematically evaluate treatment as it is delivered in practice. The methodology of single-case experimental research, mentioned in passing in earlier chapters, is usefully considered more fully here. The designs in their usual, unadulterated form are not likely feasible for clinical work. Yet the methodology provides feasible leads that advance the two goals we wish to address: improved patient care and development of the knowledge base.

Single-case research designs, as they are currently used, emerged from animal research on operant conditioning (Skinner, 1938, 1957). This research focused on individual organisms, rather than groups, to demonstrate basic processes (acquisition, extinction, generalization) (see Kazdin, 1978b). One or a few subjects were studied over time, with continuous assessment, and the impact of different experimental manipulations could be discerned from changes in ongoing performance (Johnston & Pennypacker, 1980; Sidman, 1960).

Usually rates of responding (number of responses within a time period) were represented graphically to show obvious changes as experimental manipulations were varied. Since that seminal work, the methods of evaluating individuals, animals or humans, in basic or applied research, have proliferated. Several specific research designs constitute true-experiments, which are rigorous ways of demonstrating causal relations and ruling out threats to validity discussed previously (see appendix B).

Single-case experimental designs have been proposed as one way to introduce systematic assessment and evaluation in clinical practice. One unique feature of these designs is their capacity to conduct experimental investigations with the individual case (e.g., Barlow & Hersen, 1984; Kazdin, 1982). The designs permit assessment of therapeutic change and "causal" inferences about the basis of the change. I mention the methodological approach here because some facets of it might be useful for clinical work.

OVERVIEW OF KEY COMPONENTS.   Single-case research methodology includes three essential components: assessment, design, and data evaluation strategies (see Kazdin, 1982; Krischef, 1991). Table 10.2 highlights the key components. These components act in concert to draw inferences about treatment and make single-case research designs unique.

First, in single-case research, assessment of the individual is ongoing, meaning that observations are gathered on several occasions, perhaps daily or several days each week in clinical work or intervention programs (Kazdin, 1994a). The purpose is to identify the *pattern of performance* before the intervention and then during the intervention. Baseline observations (before treatment) *describe* the existing level of performance and *predict* the likely level of performance for the immediate future if an intervention is not provided. The prediction is achieved by projecting or extrapolating into the future a continuation of baseline performance. Changes over the course of different phases (baseline, intervention) can be detected by comparing the data patterns to see if performance departs from the prediction extrapolated from baseline.

Second, single-case designs include several experimental designs to evaluate whether the intervention is responsible for change and to draw information about causal relations (see Barlow & Hersen, 1984; Kazdin, 1982; Krischef, 1991). Single-case designs, as true experiments, can rule out threats to validity (see appendix B). One can draw inferences about the effects of the intervention by comparing different conditions presented to the same subject over time. Continuous assessment provides the data to permit comparisons over time for the same subject. The design illuminates whether the intervention is responsible for change.

Finally, single-case designs provide novel methods of data evaluation. In group research, effects of an intervention are evaluated statistically, primarily by comparing groups that received different interventions. Data from single-case designs *can* be readily evaluated with statistical tests (e.g., Gottman, 1981; Kazdin, 1982). However, the evaluation in single-case designs usually is non-

Table 10.2   Key Characteristics of Single-Case
Experimental Research

PROCESS	CHARACTERISTICS
Assessment	Performance is assessed continuously over the course of the demonstration/experiment. The assessment usually begins before the intervention or experimental manipulation (referred to as baseline assessment). Measures from several occasions illustrate the pattern of performance, and any trends or fluctuation. After baseline assessment, the intervention or manipulation is implemented, as assessment is continued. The repeated measures on multiple occasions provide the basic data for the designs.
Design	The intervention or experimental manipulation can be presented in many ways. These designs are intended to rule out threats to validity and to establish the intervention as responsible for change. For example, in one variation, the intervention is presented after baseline observations for a time to see if performance changes. When change is evident, the intervention is withdrawn to check whether performance reverts to baseline (preintervention) levels. In other arrangements, the intervention is introduced in different settings (e.g., home, school) one at a time to address problematic behaviors (e.g., noncompliance, completion of homework). In this way, one can demonstrate that the intervention accounts for change.
Data Evaluation	The assessment information and the design reveal a pattern of performance that can help to verify whether the intervention led to change. Although the data can be evaluated statistically, single-case designs usually rely on nonstatistical evaluations of the data. There are guidelines for evaluating the data based on characteristics of the pattern of performance graphically displayed as changes in mean across phases, shifts in level of performance when phases are altered (e.g., from baseline to treatment), the latency of change once a shift in treatment is made, and changes in slope or trend lines across different phases.

This is a highly abbreviated characterization of single-case designs. See Barlow & Hersen (1984), Kazdin (1982), Krischef (1991) for details of the designs. Also, the designs have been used extensively to evaluate interventions in the home, at school, in business and industry, in the community at large and in diverse settings (hospitals; preschools; elementary, middle, and high

statistical (Baer, 1977; Parsonson & Baer, 1978). Nonstatistical evaluation of data has the same goal as statistical analysis: to identify whether the effects are consistent, reliable, and unlikely to have resulted from chance fluctuations. The method is sometimes referred to as *visual inspection*, which, unfortunately, suggests that the method is particularly subjective and unusually vulnerable to biases that statistics were designed to overcome. Actually, nonstatistical data evaluation depends on multiple characteristics of the pattern in the data to determine the reliability of change (see Kazdin, 1998b). These data characteristics include changes in mean (average performance on the measure across baseline and intervention phases), shifts in level of performance when treatment is initially introduced or altered (abrupt increase or decrease in performance), the latency of change once a shift in treatment is made, and changes in slope or trend lines across different phases in the single-case design. When the data converge in similar patterns, clear inferences can be drawn.

LIMITS OF THE DESIGNS FOR CLINICAL WORK.   Single-case designs provide a rigorous methodology that plays an important role in scientific research more generally. The designs have been proposed for use in clinical work because they focus on individuals, and some of them seem compatible with the process of implementing interventions and evaluating treatment progress (see Alter & Evens, 1990; Barlow et al., 1984; Bloom & Fischer, 1982; Kazdin, 1998b; Kratochwill & Piersel, 1983). In fact, the designs have been used in several clinical demonstrations of the effectiveness of diverse treatments. Clearly, when the designs are feasible and compatible with treatment, they should be used because they provide strong bases for inferences about treatment.

However, widespread use of the designs, at least as they are currently proposed, may not be feasible for clinical practice because the designs make very special demands on the administration of treatment. Typically, treatment and nontreatment phases are alternated or treatment is sometimes withheld or delayed. The demands of the design and the priority of clinical care of the individual client can conflict. Because single-case designs are true experiments, they can easily dictate priorities that compete with clinical goals. A methodology suitable for clinical practice must maintain the priority of quality patient care. Efforts have been made to identify selected elements (e.g., Hayes, 1981) and quasi-experimental designs (Kazdin, 1981) to make adoption of the designs more compatible with clinical work. Even so, in clinical work, isolating intervention effects and demonstrating causal relations do not necessarily advance individual client care.

In developing a methodology for clinical practice, one must first identify the central requirements. Clearly, the first requirement is recognition of the priority of clinical care. Unequivocally, methodological practices must work toward the benefit of the individual patient. Second, assessment and evaluation practices and other methodological requirements must harmonize with exigencies of the clinical situation. The assessment methods must accommodate a wide range of clinical problems and situations.

Although one can emphasize practices of assessment, design, and evaluation, methodology is also a way of thinking about phenomena and systematizing information to draw inferences. The thought processes reflect concerns about ways of operationalizing critical constructs, posing hypotheses about interventions and processes leading to change, and testing assumptions about interventions and their impact. Assessment, design, and evaluation are not alien to clinical practice. Invariably, practitioners always draw inferences, actively or passively making decisions on perceptions. A methodology for clinical practice does not introduce assessment, design, and evaluation. Rather, it would align these practices with tenets of science such as testing hypotheses, operationalizing critical concepts, and fostering replication. The special feature is evaluation concepts and practices that advance therapeutic progress of individual clients. To that end, the primary goal of a methodology for clinical practice is to assess, evaluate, and demonstrate change. Single-case research designs provide useful leads and, as an approach, is more relevant for clinical work than group methods. Assessment and evaluation, more than experimental design, are key features of single-case research that might be applicable.[1]

A MODEL OF ASSESSMENT AND EVALUATION FOR CLINICAL PRACTICE

Systematic assessment and evaluation of the effects of treatment in clinical practice aim toward quality patient care and contribute to the knowledge base on the effects of therapy. Quality care must come first, given the priorities of treatment in clinical work. Contributing to the knowledge base means answering important questions about the effects of treatment. Introducing systematic assessment to clinical practice is not merely the addition of a few measures to supplement clinical judgment. Table 10.3 summarizes several steps essential to evaluation in clinical work.

Specifying and Assessing Treatment Goals

Identifying treatment goals is a prerequisite to the selection of measures for assessment and evaluation. The goals refer initially to the objectives for the child and family (e.g., reduction of symptoms, improved functioning at home and at school, better parent-adolescent communication) that treatment is designed to address. Therapy can have many different goals, tailored in clinical work to individual clients. Consequently, prioritizing the goals is important as well. Treatment may be directed toward several interrelated areas, which should be prioritized to permit initial assessment as well as treatment decisions. Treatment will not likely affect all areas equally well or even in the same way or direction toward improvement. Assessment of treatment outcome often shows that different measures yield different conclusions (Kazdin, 1998b; Lambert, 1983). Hence, it is useful to identify the initial salient goals and to select measures to assess progress toward them.

The selection of one or a few initial goals does not limit the treatment focus. Rather, it means that assessment will sample critically relevant facets of child or adolescent functioning to examine progress and treatment impact. The goals may vary over time according to changing priorities and progress in treatment. For example, excessive dieting and maladaptive food consumption may serve as the initial treatment focus for an adolescent referred for an eating disorder. The focus may shift toward less immediate, but no less important, domains such as body image, management of stress, and relations with peers. Specifying

Table 10.3 **Key Steps for Systematic Evaluation in Clinical**
=============== **Practice**

STEP	DESCRIPTION
1. Specifying and Assessing Treatment Goals	Explicitly identifying the initial focus of treatment and the desired goals or changes. Selecting or developing a measure that reflects the current status of the individual on these characteristics (e.g., symptoms, functioning).
2. Specifying and Assessing Procedures and Processes	Explicitly identifying the means or processes (procedures, tasks, activities, and experiences) expected to lead to therapeutic change. Measuring the extent to which these means or their performance, execution, or implementation is achieved during treatment.
3. Selecting Measures	Identifying or developing the instruments, scales, or measures that will be used to assess progress over the course of treatment. This may require developing or individualizing a measure for the child, adolescent, and family. Identifying the measure of process or procedures depends heavily on whether the procedures are straightforward (e.g., execution of tasks in the session) or emergent processes (e.g., alliance, bonding) that require separate measures.
4. Assessment Occasions	Assessing performance on the measure of functioning toward which treatment is directed before treatment begins and then on a regular, ongoing basis over the course of treatment. Ongoing assessment may occur every session, every other session, or some other regimen that allows one to see any patterns or trends over time.
5. Design and Data Evaluation	Displaying the information obtained from the assessment to permit one to examine changes, patterns, or other features of progress that can directly inform treatment decisions (e.g., changing or ending treatment, shifting the focus of treatment). Graphical displays are especially useful.

goals does not mean that these goals become a destination toward which the course of treatment is irrevocably plotted. The goals of therapy are often multiple, and making them explicit is an initial as well as ongoing step. For our purposes, specification and operationalization of treatment goals are central.

Specifying and Assessing Procedures and Processes

In addition to making the goals explicit, we must also specify the means of achieving the goals: either, first, the procedures used in treatment, that is, what the therapist does and what the client (child, parent) is asked to do in or outside of the sessions, or second, emergent processes or relationship issues (e.g., experiencing emotions, developing a therapeutic alliance). Specifying procedures or processes will be useful in making key decisins about treatment.

Treatment integrity, mentioned previously, is relevant to evaluation of the treatment in clinical work. Ongoing assessment of child or adolescent progress may reveal no therapeutic change. Assessment of procedures or processes that the therapist believes are important may provide useful information about how to proceed. The information may reveal that treatment procedures (e.g., addressing certain topics, experiencing special types of insight, engaging in role-play during the sessions) were not implemented very well or goals within sessions (e.g., developing an alliance, dealing with a particular conflict) were not achieved. Hence, different strategies might be useful.

On the other hand, assessment of treatment processes or means may reveal that the processes have been evoked fairly well but without therapeutic change. Here, a different treatment approach might work better. In general, assurances are needed that the procedures were tried or that the processes identified by the therapist were achieved. Specifying the procedures or means in relation to the goals is an initial step toward this end.

Selecting Measures

Specification of the goals of treatment identifies the constructs of interest to the therapist and client. The next step is to operationalize the constructs by noting the specific measure(s) that will be used. Selecting the measure requires decisions about the source of information (child/adolescent, parent, teacher, clinician report) and assessment method (objective measures of personality or psychopathology, client diaries, card sorts, projective methods, interviews, direct observation, and others). In principle, the available measures include the full range of available psychological instruments. However, even though very few measures have been developed for repeated assessment and clinical work, one need not revert to clinical judgment as we saw in the anecdotal case study. Judgment can be codified and completed reliably. Systematic assessment is almost always preferred, even if the measure is not yet validated. Indeed, the process of validation and test development is all about collecting systematic data on measures not yet well developed.

Measures can be devised and individualized by incorporating items from a large symptom list, a standardized instrument, or an open-ended clinical interview. For examples, subscales from the Minnesota Multiphasic Personality Inventory (MMPI-A; Williams, Butcher, Ben-Porath, & Graham, 1992) for adolescents or the Child Behavior Checklist (CBCL; Achenbach, 1991) for children or adolescents might generate items for clinical use. Several items can be selected from a larger pool to provide an individualized measure specific to the child or family (e.g., see Kiresuk & Garwick, 1979; Shapiro, 1964).

In clinical work, measures need to be individually tailored to the client and treatment. Familiarity with scale development and available instruments will be useful. Measures useful in clinical work, based on different assessment methods and sources of information, have been identified elsewhere (see Alter & Evens, 1990; Bloom & Fischer, 1982; Epstein, Kutash, & Duchnowski, 1998; Faulkner & Gray, 1997). Rating scales represent a particularly useful format and offer numerous options that can be developed and evaluated (see Aiken, 1996). Such measures have been described and formatted to facilitate their use in clinical settings (see Clement, 1999; Wiger, 1999).

In addition to measurement of client functioning, measurement of the treatment methods or processes is important as well. The type of treatment and processes or features putatively leading to change dictate the assessment focus. The therapist proposes (hypothesizes) that specific criteria are central to therapeutic change. If these (e.g., quality of the relationship with the child, degree of parent participation in treatment) can vary with treatment administration, their assessment is likely to be useful because we wish to know whether treatment components were reasonably delivered and tested. Also, the therapist may want to try different interventions to alter the processes, perhaps to improve parent participation. The assessment priority is evaluating clinical outcome and systematically collecting information on whether the child, adolescent, or family is changing over the course of treatment. Other assessments may be peripheral. At the same time, there ought to be documentation of the methods of achieving change and sufficient description to ensure that the procedures (e.g., which treatment, number of sessions, content of the sessions) could be replicated.

Assessment Occasions

Before treatment begins, clinics often administer measures to obtain basic subject and demographic information, to evaluate broad domains of functioning, to attain information for diagnostic purposes, and to rule out conditions that might require other interventions or attention, such as medical diagnosis. Initial assessment identifies critical characteristics of persons who are treated. The variables important to assess were identified in chapter 10 as descriptive information. Descriptive variables do not burden delivery of services in treatment; indeed, many of the descriptors are required for administrative purposes (e.g., insurance). Presumably, a significant portion of the information obtained at pretreatment also determines the goals and foci of treatment. In addition, the information can help develop the knowledge base. As cases accumulate in clinical practice, treatment outcomes (e.g., dropping out, therapeutic change) can be evaluated in relation to moderators and predictor variables.

Central to evaluation in clinical practice, ongoing, continuous assessment before and during the course of treatment is needed. This critical component of single-case designs can be adopted for clinical work. Ongoing assessment can be used to chart functioning during baseline and over the course of treatment. Several data points help not merely to assess the mean level of functioning but also to indicate variability and trends. There are many opportunities for flexible application of continuous assessment. For example, pretreatment assessment for at least two or three assessment occasions (although more occasions generally are better) provides a baseline to help evaluate subsequent progress. Performance on the measure could be at an extreme level, because of stress or crisis, and marked changes from the first to second assessment occasion would be expected due to statistical regression, end of the crisis, and repeated testing on the instrument (see Kazdin, 1998b). Assessment on three occasions can help rule out such artifacts. Baseline assessment may even show improvement and suggest redefining the goals of treatment, the means to obtain them, and the selection of measures to evaluate treatment.

As in single-case designs, the initial assessment provides descriptive baseline information about the subject's level of performance and its variation. Only one assessment occasion may be feasible or indeed perhaps no assessment because of the urgent nature of the treatment. In most psychotherapy cases, it is not clear that intervention is absolutely essential at the first contact. Usually, assessment can begin while the therapist tries to manage the situation. In cases when treatment begins immediately, retrospective baseline, where an estimate is provided by the client and others in his or her life, may be an option. Apart from baseline assessment, assessment during the treatment phase is pivotal to evaluate change.

Typically, therapy does not involve ongoing systematic assessment. Consequently, an initial step is to integrate assessment and treatment as part of service delivery. Several practical decisions and options for implementing the assessments can serve the goals of empirical evaluation. Many of the options may be dictated by individual characteristics, problems, and circumstances of the patient; the nature and type of treatment service; and characteristics and preferences of the therapist. For example, among assessment options, therapists might conduct a brief assessment (e.g., 10–15 min) with the child or adolescent at the beginning or end of each treatment session. Or parents can complete measures and bring them to the sessions or leave recorded messages on a clinic answering machine if a log is kept. It would not be difficult for families to submit from their home computer coded information (e.g., responses to questionnaire items from an individualized symptom checklist) automatically recorded on a clinic web site. More readily perhaps, secretarial staff or assistants can conduct a brief telephone interview covering critical items or direct a client to a room immediately before a session so he or she can complete the measure(s). Similarly, a staff member or volunteer can sum scores or enter data on an office computer software program to summarize or to graph the information. A number of options for administering or assisting with assessment or summarizing the data are possible. Ethical protections for office information apply to all such options.

Whatever the assessment method, implementation requires discussion with the child, adolescent, or family. The therapist should tell the clients about the interconnectedness of treatment and evaluation so that they understand how important assessment is in the care and service provided. The rationale for assessment can be provided at the outset when treatment is explained. Salient points include the importance of an initial evaluation and goal selection. Goals as well as measures may change during treatment. Thus, the initial presenting complaints and their assessment would not preclude a subsequent shift in focus.

Even if goals do not change, evaluation of the assessment procedure is important. Before or early in treatment, it would be important to assess client functioning. Perhaps the assessment measure would show that the client is functioning well. For example, if depression were assessed in an adolescent and a low score on a standardized measure (e.g., Beck Depression Inventory) was evident in pretreatment, reconsideration of the construct or measure would be important. If further discussion and interview revealed depressive symptoms, another measure or an individualized measure might be needed.

Design and Data Evaluation

Research design and data evaluation could easily undermine adoption of systematic methods of evaluation in clinical practice. Yet each can be crafted to address the critical priorities and practical exigencies of clinical work. In clinical practice, the central design issue is whether therapeutic change has occured and to discern whether it is likely to be due to treatment. This does not require ruling out *all* of the threats to validity (see appendix B); indeed, designs that do often interfere with clinical priorities. Obtaining pretreatment (baseline) information, conducting ongoing assessment over the course of treatment, and documenting changes over time can lead to valuable conclusions about treatment impact. The assessment of therapeutic procedures also can assist in determining the likelihood that influences intended to achieve change contributed to outcome. The overall pattern of data contributes to the plausibility that treatment led to change. Also, in the clinical situation one can draw this conclusion from the history of the problem, other attempts to effect change, and the abruptness of the change (see Kazdin, 1981).

Data evaluation identifies change, its reliability and its departure from the fluctuations one would expect without the intervention. Ongoing assessment provides data before and during the course of treatment that serve as the basis for this evaluation. Several methods are available to evaluate single-case information. Of all methods, graphical display, like a simple line graph, is particularly useful for depicting the pattern in the data obtained over time (see Kazdin, 1982; Parsonson & Baer, 1978). Nonstatistical data evaluation methods, drawn from single-case experimental research, can be used for clinical evaluation. As I mentioned previously, several characteristics of the data (changes in means, levels, and trends, and latency of change across phases) can be useful in determining the reliability of the changes. These criteria do not require computations but follow directly from graphical presentation of the data. Also, if the data are entered regularly on a database, then graphical presentation and simple trends (e.g., regression lines) can be plotted automatically or with a couple of mouse clicks.

Graphical displays and nonstatistical data evaluation are examples of possible methods of evaluating change. Other evaluative aids varying in degrees of sophistication and complexity are available. For example, several methods of graphing data points for multiple subjects from group research (e.g., stem-and-leaf plots, box plots) might also be used for individual subjects as a means to describe and to evaluate progress (see Rosenthal & Rosnow, 1991). Also, descriptive and inferential statistical techniques are available for continuous data obtained from the single case (see Gottman, 1981; Kazdin, 1982).

The above methods suggest options for evaluating the changes in patient functioning to identify if improvements have been achieved. These methods, whether nonstatistical or statistical, focus on the reliability of the change. The importance of the change in terms in clinical work is obviously critical. In addition, therapists and their clients invariably are concerned with an important, noticeable, change that affects everyday functioning. Attaining clinically significant change is quite important. Although many methods have been identified to reflect clinical significance, there is no consensus on any particular measure. Presumably a measure of clinical significance of the change might be used in clinical work. Among the methods discussed, subjective evaluation of interested parties (parents, teachers, adolescent) and palpable effects on obviously critical measures (improvements in school attendance, grades) are probably most relevant. Of course, the nature of the client's problem dictates the evaluation of clinical significance. The goal is to make an effort to evaluate whether change is sufficient, helpful, or influential. Although clinically significant change is important, clearly the logical priority is introducing evaluation into therapy to discern any therapeutic change.

CONTRIBUTIONS TO THE KNOWLEDGE BASE

I have related systematic assessment and evaluation to the clinical priority of helping the individual in treatment. In itself, assessment is a sufficient reason to change clinical practice. However, systematic evaluation of individual clients can contribute significantly to the knowledge base.

First, individual therapy can provide evidence for the effectiveness of new techniques or technique variations. Currently, if an innovative technique emerges and is codified through an anecdotal case study or article without any evidence, the treatment is added to the ever-proliferating number of treatments. Techniques could be evaluated and presumably discarded or refined clinically if they were routinely evaluated in clinical practice. Furthermore, treatment effects can be replicated by clinicians as a treatment variation is applied to another case. Thus, innovative treatments could begin their entry into the knowledge base supported by preliminary evidence.

Second, the discussion has focused on treatment outcomes or intervention effects on the clients. Assessment and evaluation in practice could also examine processes of treatment and interim changes that may be important in their own right (Jones, Ghannam, Nigg, & Dyer, 1993). For example, measures of the therapeutic relationship, contextual events (e.g., relations at home), clients' thoughts during the sessions, and clients' views of the most recent session may help delineate the processes of therapy. Hypotheses could be generated and tested in this microscopic study of the individual.

Third, the accumulation of assessment data in clinical work can contribute enormously to the knowledge base. A database on intake variables and treatment outcomes would provide rich opportunities to study factors that influence treatment and variations of treatment effects for different types of patients and clinical problems (see Clement, 1994, 1996; Maletzky, 1980, 1991; Marquis, 1991). The descriptive research database can be examined with statistical models to test specific hypotheses about treatment (Leaf, DiGiuseppe, Mass, & Alington, 1993). It is not reasonable to expect that clinical practitioners would be interested in exploiting the database with sophisticated statistical models. Yet organizing the incoming information in systematic ways and accumulating a database is feasible (see Todd, Jacobus, & Boland, 1992). Researchers could collaborate with practitioners to draw from the rich findings that could contribute to the knowledge base. Some research too could be used for secondary analyses (e.g., meta-analyses) that combine information from multiple clinics.

Finally, evaluation in clinical work can test models of treatment studied in research and the generality of research results to different conditions (types of persons, therapists, settings) of clinical practice. I mentioned previously a concern about efficacy studies of therapy, that is, demonstrations of treatment effects under highly controlled conditions. There is reason to question whether treatment models and interventions apply in clinical practice, but they could be tested if systematic assessment and evaluation methods were introduced into clinical practice. This too would be a superb contribution to the knowledge base.

ISSUES AND LIMITATIONS

Methodological Issues

Earlier discussion has outlined generally how methodological practices and the underlying thought processes that methodology fosters can augment clinical work. Yet the methodology is not yet developed or in widespread use. One can readily identify obstacles yet to be resolved, such as the methodological tools available for clinical assessment. Several measures have been recommended for ongoing evaluation of treatment, particularly in the context of adult therapy (e.g., Clement, 1999; Sederer & Dickey, 1994). Unfortunately, these measures have not been validated in the usual ways; such validation would ensure that they measure the intended constructs and reflect functioning in everyday life.

Standardized measures (e.g., Beck Depression Inventory, MMPI, CBCL) might be used on repeated occasions. These measures have been validated by administering the instrument on one or two occasions (e.g., test-retest reliability or part of longitudinal studies) to large groups. Clinical evaluation will require repeated administration of the measure to the individual over the course of treatment. The basic questions are whether the measure can reflect change and will the correlates of the measure (i.e., evidence for validity) be the same on repeated use. Existing measures will be useful to provide relevant items of key constructs (e.g., anxiety, aggression, depression), but basic research will be needed to validate assessment strategies for ongoing assessment in clinical work.

In addition to measures, data evaluation methods are available but not well explicated for clinical use. Nonstatistical data evaluation in treatment research is generally unfamiliar beyond the cadre of researchers involved in behavior analysis. Descriptive statistics such as changes in means or slope can be used for inferential purposes. However, methods need to be developed for general use. Computerized data management programs could be used to enter data and to provide graphical displays with little effort. Computerized programs that provide documentation of progress in user-friendly ways (e.g., OPTAIO™, 1997) are available for use in therapy.

Clinical Issues and Concerns

First, those trained in traditional models are likely to object to the recommendations for systematic assessment and evaluation. These models focus on the importance of clinical judgment and clinical skill in the absence of systematic evaluation. Traditionally, objections to evaluation in clinical work were based on assumptions about the cognitive acumen of the clinicians and the deleterious influences of systematic evaluation of the client. First, we assume that, as clinicians, we can readily detect changes in the client; hence, no formal assessment is necessary. Clearly, for very dramatic changes (e.g., elimination of all obsessions, compulsions, stealing and vandalism, or symptoms of Tourette's syndrome), a complete shift might make formal evaluation unnecessary. Yet, in most cases, treatment effects are not so dramatic or unidimensional that they can be unequivocally determined without formal evaluation. Systematic evaluation of children, adolescents, and families is essential to identify the amount, scope, and stability of change.

Second, in clinical work, therapists are often concerned that assessment may interfere with the therapeutic relationship. The therapist is responsible for treatment; adding to that the roles of assessor or evaluator may seem antitherapeutic. Some models or theoretical conceptualizations of treatment might argue against the therapist as the person who provides treatment and who evaluates progress. Yet the presumption that evaluation harms is unsupported when alternative assumptions are even more plausible—not evaluating the patient can permit harm to occur, evaluation may have no impact, evaluation may help. How clients perceive systematic evaluation probably relates to the therapists' views of evaluation and how the evaluation objectives and methods are presented. If evaluation is presented as commonplace, central to treatment, and purposeful, then the clients' views are likely to be positive. Ongoing assessment can be presented similarly.

Third, some object to assessment because efforts to measure the problem or focus oversimplify the problem. This objection reflects a slight misunderstanding of assessment. A measure provides a key sign, correlate, or sample of the problem, as operational definitions. The measure is not the problem. As noted in chapter 9, we are usually not interested in measures but rather in constructs, that is, on the characteristics the measures are designed to assess. We use measures even though they may not encompass the whole problem.

Fourth, assessment seemingly may ignore the individuality or uniqueness of the child, adolescent, or family. Administration of standardized measures may ignore the individuality of the patient. Yet systematic assessment can be quite individualized (see Clement, 1999; Kazdin, 1993b; Kiresuk & Garwick, 1979; Shapiro, 1957, 1964). The clinician can designate the most relevant domains of functioning with the patient and build the assessment devices to reflect these. Clinical practice, unlike the usual research context, permits individualization of both assessment and treatment. The methods can be tailored to a patient's priorities, resources, and characteristics.

Standardized assessment does have a critically important role in therapy and complements individualized assessment. The profile of a child that a standardized measure provides along with his or her standing relative to a normative group of peers of the same age, gender, and ethnicity, for example, can provide meaningful data that may also guide treatment. For example, the data on the CBCL (Achenbach, 1991), a standardized measure, might be informative as a profile for domains of child symptoms and prosocial functioning. The standardized measure is not a threat to patient individuality but an opportunity to examine that individuality against a broader backdrop (Lambert & Brown, 1996).

Fifth, another objection against evaluation in clinical work is based on the dynamic nature of treatment. Specifically, in most psychotherapy no single, simple patient problem remains constant. Problems change and foci are redefined over the course of treatment. Indeed, evidence from adult therapy suggests that over half of clients add new target complaints over the course of treatment (Sorenson, Gorsuch, & Mintz, 1985). The changing focus of treatment is not a good argument against assessment. Rather, it makes systematic assessment all the more important because it can help to identify changes in problem domains and priorities of focus from the standpoint of the patient and therapist.

Systematic assessment is needed to evaluate change and patterns of change. If information indicates that the initial presenting problem no longer pertains or is appreciably less important than some other domain, different assessment and evaluation can be initiated. An excellent feature of clinical work and clinical evaluation, unlike most clinical research trials, is flexible assessment and treatment. Therapists and clients can set new goals along the way and present or withdraw assessments to reflect these changes. The changes in treatment do not conflict with assessment. In fact, changes are likely to be very important. We want more than just impressionistic information to chart these changes and to make informed decisions about treatment.

Professional Issues

Introducing systematic assessment and evaluation routinely in clinical practice will have dramatic implications in the professional training of the mental health professionals who provide psychological treatment: psychologists, psychiatrists, social workers, and counselors. Although the professions provide different training, none fosters systematic assessment and evaluation in clinical practice. Consider psychology as one example. Psychologists have, by training, common experience, and orientation, a concern for the methodological tenets of scientific research: assessment, evaluation, testing of hypotheses, and empirical de-monstration. In clinical work, this commitment to methodology cannot be abandoned merely because the situation is complex, individuals are unique, and therapy is demanding. Indeed, the complexities and richness of the treatment conditions require assessment and evaluation to counteract the limits of human information processing.

Other professional issues can be raised in this context. Teaching assessment and evaluation methods for clinical work to clinical students is obviously needed. Supervisors who can oversee internship experiences that incorporate assessment and evaluation as part of clinical care will be essential, but they will also be difficult to find. Discussions of clinical training now heavily focus on treatments that have empirical evidence in their behalf (Kendall & Chambless, 1998; Lonigan et al., 1998). This is a critical point, because many training programs do not focus on evidence-based treatments. I argue that training in methods to evaluate one's own clinical practice is even more important. Obviously, empirically supported treatments may be ineffective in a given clinical case. The therapist must try another variation of the treatment, another treatment, or a combination of treatments. Evaluation is the key to this decision-making process.

If the goal of clinical work is to help patients, then the case for systematic evaluation is easily made. Actually, in clinical work, where the individual is so important and direct benefits are a goal, *unsystematic* evaluation is hard to advocate. In clearly urgent circumstances such as disasters or suicide attempts, intervention must proceed immediately. These important exceptions certainly preclude collecting baseline data; they do not preclude evaluating impact after the crises have abated.

A professional issue that deserves comment pertains to accountability. In clinical practice for a given case, the practitioner cannot be held responsible for the client's outcome, progress, improvement, or lack thereof. Clinical dysfunction and problems clients bring to treatment are often multiply determined. Insufficient knowledge about the etiology, course, and risk factors for a given problem and about how to controvert such influences presents genuine limitations and indeterminacies of treatment. Also, the knowledge base is derived from the study of groups. Findings, even if well established, may not apply to a client's particular pattern of influences or set of determinants. For these reasons, we cannot be held responsible for the therapeutic changes that all parties involved would like. We can be held accountable for careful evaluation and for informed decision making, beginning with responsible evaluation of the problem and application of reasonable interventions. In addition, quantitative, ongoing assessment and evaluation of treatment are reasonable clinical responsibilities. Quantitative assessment and evaluation might be proposed as central to all mental health professions because the goals, accountability, and concerns for individual clients are shared in clinical work. At the same time, among the disciplines, psychological training is unique because of the strong commitment to the tenets of science during training. Hypothesis testing, assessment, and evaluation are relevant to both research and practice.

SUMMARY AND CONCLUSIONS

We need a methodology of clinical practice that encompasses assessment and evaluation of progress in treatment. Systematic methods will help to overcome the inherent limitations and biases of human judgment. The use of psychological measures and alternative methods of data evaluation does not eliminate biases but enters these biases in an empirical arena where they can be better studied. The clinician need not slavishly adhere to one or two measures and the data they provide. Qualitative and impressionistic information, now the main and usually sole source of information over the course of treatment, can still help to evaluate treatment progress. However, attention to more systematic information gathering may aid decision making to help the individual patient.

Clinical practice has very special goals, procedures, issues, and priorities. The tenets of science are not erased or abandoned by the exigencies of clinical work. Rather, they are adapted to serve the goals of clinical work. The tenets of science do not require the use of true experiments if the phenomenon of interest limits "control" and "experimental manipulation" of conditions. Systematic assessment of process and outcome, evaluation of correlations, development and testing of hypotheses, and creative use of data evaluation strategies can guide treatment and augment our understanding.

Of course, it is one matter to advocate systematic evaluation in the abstract but quite another to suggest a viable methodology for use in daily work. Methods are available, but they are not validated yet. Measurement strategies and individual assessment instruments must at once be feasible, valid, meaningfully interpretable over multiple assessment occasions, and able to reflect change. Individualization of goals and measures for clients in treatment is not new. The remarkable assessment and evaluation expertise in psychology, which has served the development of measurement theory and instrument development and validation, can be deployed to create individualized assessments for clinical use.

In principle, proposing systematic evaluation in clinical practice is not new either (e.g., Davidson & Costello, 1969; Shapiro, 1957, 1964). The opportunities are new. Research methods and practices have advanced. Development of measures of process and outcome, specification of treatments in improved form (e.g., manuals, guidelines), and concern with and assessment of treatment integrity, for example, can benefit applications of treatment for individual clients. Also, advances in technology, such as computerization of treatment plans and graphical displays of progress, can facilitate scoring and evaluation of clinically useful information. Besides opportunities, the social climate supports—indeed insists—on more systematic evaluation of treatment to justify reimbursement of services. Pressure from managed care can assist patient care insofar as it helps introduce evaluation of patient progress.

There are many obstacles to the integration of systematic assessment and evaluation in clinical practice, but the sacrifice of the quality of patient care must not be one of them. I suggest that using clinical work to develop the knowledge base is particularly critical. Now we need to develop methods to facilitate evaluation; we may also need further training of professionals to overcome trepidations about systematic evaluation.

FOR FURTHER READING

Methods to evaluate clinical practice are available in several resources, as reflected in the readings noted below. The goals of these sources are of course to enhance clinical practice and to provide concrete and user-friendly tools for evaluation. The books also are resources for research because they convey some of the conditions of clinical practice and methods of evaluation not usually considered in research.

Clement, P.W. (1999). *Outcomes and incomes: How to evaluate, improve, and market your practice by measuring outcomes in psychotherapy*. New York: Guilford.

Haynes, S.N. (Ed.). (1993). Special section: Treatment implications of psychological assessment. *Psychological Assessment, 5,* 251–301.

Jones, E.E. (Ed.). (1993). Special section: Single-case research in psychotherapy. *Journal of Consulting and Clinical Psychology, 61,* 371–430.

Kazdin, A.E. (1993). Evaluation in clinical practice: Clinically sensitive and systematic methods of treatment delivery. *Behavior Therapy, 24,* 11–45.

Lambert, M., & Brown, G.S. (1996). Data-based management for tracking outcome in private practice. *Clinical Psychology: Science and Practice, 3,* 172–178.

Sederer, L.I., & Dickey, B. (Eds.). (1994). *Outcomes assessment in clinical practice*. Baltimore, MD: Williams & Wilkins.

Wiger, D.E. (1999). *The psychotherapy documentation primer*. New York: Wiley & Sons.

Chapter 11

Psychotherapy Research
in Perspective

PREVIOUS CHAPTERS HAVE EVALUATED the strengths and limitations of psychotherapy research, provided a blueprint for progress to foster the systematic accumulation of knowledge, and recommended methods to improve the yield from clinical research and practice. This chapter considers current psychotherapy research more generally and begins with a discussion of recent progress. What progress has been made in child and adolescent therapy research, and what is the status of current knowledge? The discussion then focuses on clinical dysfunction and interventions beyond the confines of psychotherapy. Social, emotional, and behavioral problems are influenced by multiple factors (e.g., biological, sociological) beyond those ordinarily considered in psychotherapy research. I highlight such influences briefly to inform and expand conceptual views of treatment. Similarly, many interventions (e.g., participation in extracurricular activities, social policy change) are outside of the realm of psychotherapy but influence the social, emotional, and behavioral problems of children and adolescents. I provide examples to place therapy research in context and to raise questions about how therapeutic change occurs. Expanding perspectives about the nature of clinical dysfunction and how it can be altered raises opportunities for new theory and research. To ensure that this chapter goes beyond lofty and uplifting platitudes, I include specific recommendations as well.

WHAT PROGRESS HAS BEEN MADE?

Perhaps earlier chapters have not represented very well the different ways in which one can look at child and adolescent psychotherapy research. To underscore different aspects of contemporary research, I present contrasting views here. Sharply contrasting views of research accomplishments do not necessarily misrepresent the literature; both views have considerable merit. In the material that follows, I argue opposing positions to reveal different facets of current research and do so as if two advocates were debating their respective views.

Pro: Remarkable Progress Has Been Made

There has been remarkable progress in child and adolescent psychotherapy research, and the accomplishments are reasons to rejoice. First, the number of controlled treatment outcome studies is vast. Of course, one can fix no single number at a given point in time; the precise number depends on how the pertinent literature is searched (e.g., key words), the scope of the search (e.g., English-speaking and other language journals), and other factors (e.g., definition of therapy, age range of the children). As I noted previously, one review identified over 1,000 empirical studies completed up to the year 1990 that focused on children age 13 or younger (Durlak et al., 1995). Obviously, extending this search to today and including youths through adolescence would yield an even more impressive number of studies. By any count, psychotherapy research for children and adolescents has come a long way.

Second, several meta-analytic reviews of the research have led to the conclusion that psychotherapy for children and adolescents is effective. As a general rule, changes associated with treatment greatly surpass those achieved without formal treatment. Moreover, the magnitude of this effect (effect size) tends to be large ($\geq .70$). In other words, the research has shown reliable and strong therapy effects. Children who receive therapy are much better off than those who do not. Enough randomized trials have been completed to attribute the effect to therapy rather than to various artifacts and confounds such as subject selection or changes over time as a result of maturation.

Third, treatment is now available for a wide range of clinical problems, as evident in the many compendia that organize the treatment literature by clinical problem area such as anxiety, depression, attention-deficit/hyperactivity disorder, oppositional and conduct disorder, eating disorders, and autism, to mention a few (see Hibbs & Jensen, 1996; Mash & Barkley, 1998; Morris & Kratochwill, 1998). Never have more treatment options been available for a wider range of problems. As the cited references attest, the research advances continue in each of these problem areas.

Fourth, we now have a set of particularly well-investigated interventions, referred to as empirically supported treatments. The criteria for these treatments extend well beyond merely demonstrating efficacy in a single study (e.g., Chambless & Hollon, 1998; Nathan & Gorman, 1998; Roth & Fonagy, 1996). Several treatments for children and adolescents are empirically supported (e.g., Lonigan et al., 1998). To identify such treatments, particularly with the implications that identification might have (e.g., professional training, standards for clinical practice, patient care, and reimbursement of services), signals that child and adolescent psychotherapy research has advanced remarkably. Guidelines for clinical practice have begun to suggest that some treatments are clearly preferred and supported for the problems that children and adolescents bring to treatment (AACAP, 1997, 1998).

Fifth, the quality of treatment research has improved in the past decade or two (Durlak et al., 1995; Peterson & Bell-Dolan, 1995). Methodological practices such as evaluation of treatment integrity, assessment of the clinical significance of therapeutic change, and collection of follow-up data are used more often in current research. These practices clearly improve the research and the conclusions that can be drawn. Many treatment manuals are available that permit replication of treatment and in many cases extension of empirically supported treatments to clinical practice. Moreover manuals provide a way to codify revisions and improvements as clinical experience and research findings accumulate.

Overall, the progress within child and adolescent therapy research is remarkable. In addition, and no less significant, there are advances in allied areas. Research on child and adolescent psychopathology continues to advance at an accelerated pace (e.g., Mash & Barkley, 1996). These advances include research on various disorders, their interrelations, and subtypes, as well as studies of risk and protective factors and the many child, parent, family, and contextual influences that affect clinical dysfunction. Also, psychopathology research is elaborating multiple domains, as illustrated, for example, by research in genetics, neurobiology, and neuroendocrinology. Findings on the interaction of biological and social influences on development and clinical dysfunction are particularly noteworthy (e.g., Brooks-Gunn & Warren 1989; Graber, Lewinsohn, Seeley, & Brooks-Gunn, 1997). Research on the models of clinical dysfunction and advances in developmental psychopathology can serve as underpinnings for treatment research. Thus, the conceptual and empirical bases on which intervention research can build are progressing too.

Advances in assessment also are noteworthy because of their contribution to psychotherapy research and to basic research on psychopathology. These advances include standardization, or improved standardization, of many measures of constructs relevant to treatment research such as cognitive processes, family functioning, and peer relations (e.g., Mash & Terdal, 1997; Ollendick & Hersen, 1993). Constructs like impairment can now be assessed over a broader age range over the course of development. Also, specific modalities of assessment have progressed. For example, the range of available and valid self-report measures for children and adolescents, once a worrisome and suspicious method of gathering useful information, has advanced (see LaGreca, 1990). Assessment advances permit a more detailed analysis of child and adolescent functioning, the associated conditions (e.g., families, contexts), and, of course, the impact of treatment.

The characteristics highlighted here provide overwhelming evidence of progress and advances in child and adolescent therapy research. Of course, some critical and enduring questions, issues, and challenges need to be addressed. What can be accomplished for such severe problems as autism? Are treatment effects maintained over time (>5 years after treatment)? What are the mechanisms of therapeutic change? Some of the questions are prompted by and reflect the advances that have been achieved: Now that there are empirically supported treatments, can they be transported to clinical settings? Does combining two treatments, each with demonstrated efficacy, augment treatment outcome for a given clinical problem? The measure of progress is not how many questions remain to be answered—that number will always be somewhere between indefinite and infinite. Progress is better measured by the questions that have been answered and by the sophistication of those that are being asked.

These intellectual and scholarly questions about treatment and its effects must be seen in the context of the multiple interests of researchers, clinicians, consumers, and society at large. There are multiple perspectives on treatment (e.g., how much treatment ought to be provided, how much therapeutic change is needed or enough). They might view the same treatment quite differently, as effective by researchers, not feasible for everyday use by clinicians, too costly or not yet sufficiently proven by those who oversee reimbursement of services. But the remaining research questions or differing perspectives on critical issues do not detract from the progress that has been achieved. In summary, the case is clear about the progress of child and adolescent psychotherapy. [If this were a debate about that progress, I would end with the statement that any one who does not recognize the remarkable advances deserves to be diagnosed and given an empirically *unsupported* treatment!]

Con: Remarkable Progress? Hah!

Enthusiasm and optimism are always refreshing, and the preceding rendition of therapy research is indeed uplifting and enjoyable. I guess I just like reading fiction. Where to begin? There has been remarkable *lack* of progress in child and adolescent psychotherapy research. First, it would be a serious mistake to accept the large number of studies as a sign of progress. The majority of studies include features that limit the conclusions that can be reached about therapy. For example, patient samples are rarely studied and the "vast literature" becomes a minute literature if one includes those studies that examine therapy with clinical samples and in clinical settings (e.g., Shadish et al., 1997). Why is this important? Treatment effects are likely to be diminished when dysfunction is more severe, when individuals have multiple (comorbid) disorders, and when child or adolescent dysfunction is embedded in adverse family conditions (e.g., parent psychopathology, difficult living circumstances). The majority of youths studied in psychotherapy research are likely to be much less severely impaired and to come from circumstances less likely to exacerbate dysfunction than those cases referred clinically. We may know a lot about less severely impaired cases, and this knowledge may be valuable. However, this qualification should temper wholesale counts of therapy studies or overly ambitious conclusions about treatment.

In general, most treatment research consists of well-controlled laboratory-based (efficacy) studies, in which control is optimized and one can test theory, processes, or mechanisms rather than merely look at outcomes. Yet there is very little theoretical work. To tout the large number of studies as a cause to rejoice is merely a distraction. The issue is not the number of studies but rather whether we have answers to key questions. What clinical problems can be treated effectively? Are treatment gains maintained? What treatments work with whom and in what combinations? Does treatment prevent the onset of other problems or disorders or influence adjustment and functioning in adulthood? Those who tout progress tend to look away when these questions are asked.

The main conclusion from research reviews, meta-analytic or other, is that treatment is better than no treatment—a useful but disappointing finding. To begin, if the adult therapy literature is any guide, we know that placebos (inert substances provided as if they were medication) and psychological procedures designed to appear as a veridical treatment (attention-placebo conditions) are better than no treatment. In addition, most of the treatments used in clinical practice are not those studied in research and hence covered by the research reviews. The conclusion that treatment is better than no treatment could be followed with rather embarrassing qualifying phrases, such as "But this may not apply to clinically referred cases or to the treatments used in clinical practice, and may not be consistently better than placebo or placebo-like conditions." This is not merely an issue of looking at the literature as a glass "half empty or half full." In fact, therapy effects are not so clearly demonstrated.

With much of the research, investigators are communicating with each other and do not make much contact with the phenomenon of interest (i.e., therapeutic change among individuals who have problems, stress, or dysfunction). For example, many meta-analyses of therapy exist, and these are viewed as saying something about therapeutic change. Typically, all measures from a study are combined into a single number that is an effect size based on combining all cases that received treatment. Then multiple studies are combined further to get a grand mean (mean effect size). It is difficult to imagine a number further removed from what happens to individuals in treatment. The metric makes sense for specific research purposes but tells nothing whatsoever about what happens to individuals who receive a particular treatment.

A seeming counter to this concern is the fact that studies often report on clinical significance of the change. Look closely at measures of clinical significance. They are defined mathematically or statistically (see Kendall, 1999). Even with a generous interpretation, there is little evidence that individuals who have met a criterion that the investigator calls a measure of clinical significance are in fact functioning better in everyday life. More critical thinking is needed about the meaning of measures used to assess clinically significant change. For example, suppose a child is more deviant on a parent-rating scale of child deviance before treatment but then falls within the normal range at posttreatment (this is a commonly used measure of clinical significance). This does not necessarily mean that there is palpable improvement in everyday life for the child. Basic steps to validate indices of clinical significance have not been completed, and the meaning of such measures has yet to be elaborated (see Kazdin, 1999).

Overall, current treatment research for children and adolescents samples a very special set of nonreferred children, focuses on brief and time-limited treatment, and addresses a restricted range of questions about treatment, models of delivering treatment, and treatment outcome domains that are investigated. Other than this, the literature is fabulous. In characterizing the vast majority of studies, one must recognize exceptions. Programs of research such as those illustrated previously (chapter 6) are rays of hope—they are also great departures from how most treatment is usually evaluated.

So much of the literature focuses on nonreferred cases that it is important to recognize the genuine contribution that this makes. Improvement of symptoms and functioning of nonreferred cases *is* important and noteworthy. The differences between clinically impaired and nonimpaired youths for many problems seen in treatment (anxiety, depression, conduct disorder) are fuzzy and somewhat arbitrary (Gotlib et al., 1995; Offord et al., 1996). Many children and adolescents included in studies of psychotherapy, even if not clinically referred, likely would benefit from treatment. Outcomes with such youths are important insofar as any reduction in suffering and impairment is worthwhile. Yet, the extent to which treatments can be applied effectively in clinical settings is quite a different matter.

Will progress continue to be made? Well, more research is invariably viewed as progress, so there is a guaranteed *perception* of progress. But will there be efforts to move to new questions and to understand how therapy achieves its effects and for whom? The old question to guide therapy—what treatments work with what people, under what conditions—has not been addressed seriously. In one way, perhaps that is good. Prior discussions have shown that this question is not very feasible or useful in light of the extraordinary number of treatments, disorders, and moderators. New and better questions have yet to be substituted as a guide. The progress of psychotherapy research *is* remark-able—the *remark* one is *able* to make is that very little has been achieved to date in understanding which treatments are effective for clinically referred youths.

WHERE ARE WE AND WHERE OUGHT WE TO GO?

Anyone might well agree with aspects of both perspectives, my own position has a slightly different thrust. However one evaluates the past decades of research, the fact is we are here with a set of studies, treatments, clinical problems, investigators, methods, measures, and so on. We need to ask three critical questions:

1. What do we wish to know about therapy and its effects?
2. What do we already know?
3. What needs to be accomplished to fill in the gap between the prior questions?

We want to know more about treatment and its effects, including how, why, and for whom it works. We also wish to know how to make treatment optimally effective. Based on prior reviews and primary sources, as outlined in chapters 4, 5, and 6, we know little of what we need to know about these facets of treatment. This conclusion is not damning. By itself, the conclusion merely suggests that one ought to be patient. Yet there are no clear signs that we are moving along a path toward obtaining the knowledge we need.

Despite the progress, contemporary studies are not focusing on conceptualization of clinical dysfunctions, treatments, processes of change, moderators and mediators of outcome, and generality and applicability of treatment. The range of questions, treatment outcomes, and models of delivering treatment is restricted. Most studies focus on relatively brief treatments, with nonclinical samples, addressing questions about the treatment technique. There is a place for such research. But we need to ask deeper, broader, and more clinically relevant questions. By *deeper* questions, I mean research that focuses more on understanding and explaining treatment, including models of change and processes or mechanisms involved in improvement. By *broader* questions, I mean research that asks more varied questions about treatment than are currently being asked. By more *clinically relevant* questions, I mean research that addresses generality and disseminability of treatment and the facets of treatment that may influence them. If we wish to advance psychotherapy for children and adolescents, we must go much further than saying "more research is needed." In fact, more research is the last thing we need unless studies can move us toward a better understanding of treatment.

What are the goals of therapy research, or, as stated previously, what is it we wish to know? Because there are no agreed on or at least very explicit goals, it is very unlikely that any systematic progress will be made toward them. Scattered studies, unsystematically conducted and leading to no place in particular, cannot be expected to generate a systematic knowledge base. Neither leading meta-analysts nor magicians can derive the knowledge we need if the primary sources do not redirect and expand their foci. Rather than quibbling about whether analogue or efficacy studies are worthwhile, misused, overemphasized, and so on, as evident in the two contrasting views presented previously, let us chart the future. What vision does the field need to make progress? Surely it is more inspired than identifying a few more empirically supported treatments? I have outlined a plan for progress (chapter 8). No doubt other authors can generate different and better ones. Perhaps multiple blueprints will provide common themes that will lead us to better research.

ISSUES AND RECOMMENDATIONS

Basic Theory and Research on Child Dysfunction

Several specific areas deserve attention in order to accelerate the development and identification of effective treatments. Improved outcome studies obviously will be required to develop effective treatments, as discussed in chapter 9. However, such gains will depend on more fundamental areas. Theory and research on the nature of childhood dysfunction are greatly needed. In this context, theory means conceptualizations of the development of the clinical problem and factors that lead to its expression and amelioration. It is not reasonable to expect sweeping theories derived from a single conceptual model (e.g., psychodynamic, behavioral) to explain the development of "psychopathology" or even a particular disorder. Broad theories can provide coherent accounts or explanations of the problem, but they have rarely generated testable hypotheses.

What is likely to be more profitable are *mini-theories*, models or explanations designed to address one or more components of a specific type of dysfunction. At the outset, a mini-theory attempts only to explain a circumscribed set of influences and their effects. More restricted in scope, mini-theories are more likely to be directly testable and to be subject to refutation and revision. For example, the work on the role of child-rearing practices on aggressive and antisocial behavior in the home (Dishion & Patterson, in press; Patterson, 1982; Patterson et al., 1992) has posed separate models to explain how antisocial behavior begins in the home and how the child's antisocial behavior affects self-esteem, peer relations, and academic competence. Emphasis has been on early parent-child interaction, especially the progression from the child's mildly coercive noncompliance, whining, or teasing to more coercive parent and child exchanges (through shouting or hitting). Inept parental discipline, as reflected in excessive use of threats, physical abuse, attention to inappropriate behavior, among other practices, also contributes directly to coercive child behavior through modeling and direct reinforcement (see Patterson et al., 1992). The point here is that the important progress resulted from elaborating several facets of the model. Needless to say, the model does not necessarily explain how aggressive and antisocial behavior begins for all children. Nor is there a systematic effort in the model to incorporate all known risk factors and paths to aggressive behavior. Yet, from the model, effective interventions have been developed, specifically, training parents to alter their interactions with their children in concrete ways that promote prosocial behavior. We cannot expect all research on models of dysfunction to translate into effective treatments. Nevertheless, the best long-term investment in effective interventions is advances in understanding the problems treatments address.

Conceptualization of Treatment

Conceptualization of treatment can be distinguished from conceptualization of disorders, although, of course, we ought to rejoice whenever we can connect the two. Conceptualization of treatment considers how the treatment is intended to achieve change, through what mechanisms and processes, and perhaps for whom. Lack of conceptualization of treatments is perhaps the most critical deficit of current therapy research. We have procedures and techniques but few conceptual models that describe needed components of treatment and why and how these components interface with specific clinical dysfunctions. A notable exception, mentioned in chapter 6, was the work on parent management training, in which a conceptual view of onset and escalation of child deviance has been used as the basis for developing treatment (Dishion & Patterson, in press).

Conceptualizations often are at such a global level that they defy empirical evaluation. For example, comments about cognitive deficiencies, poor stimulus control, problems of attachment, or dysfunctional family communication, when discussed at the general level, merely convey an approach to treatment rather than a viable conceptual model.

The safety of a technique is assured in the short run by hiding behind global interpretations and clinical experience. However, the techniques and their interpretations will wither with changing times and fads if not subjected to and bolstered by empirical findings. The needed conceptualizations of treatment will propose methods to discover what we need to know.

Stronger Tests of Treatment

In addition to conceptualization, we need stronger tests of treatment than current treatment trials provide. Perhaps the most basic question of the field asks what we can effectively treat. An inventory of what can and cannot be accomplished with psychosocial treatments would be very difficult to create with a reasonable amount of consensus. Rather than an inventory of what is known, writings often enumerate various approaches to child treatment (e.g., family, behavioral, psychodynamic) or specific treatment techniques (e.g., play therapy, social skills training). More recently, there has been an emphasis on empirically supported treatments, a movement one must praise. At the same time, we are not interested merely in treatments that have evidence on their behalf. A treatment can be empirically supported by current criteria yet bear no evidence that genuine improvement has been achieved in the everyday lives of the children and adolescents who completed treatment. The distinction between statistical and clinical significance is worth mentioning here. Empirically supported treatments have evidence on their behalf and have been shown to produce greater change than no treatment. These differences are based on statistical comparisons. Such comparisons are not trivial, but we need to know much more. Clinical significance addresses the question of whether improvements make a genuine difference in everyday life. We do not know about the clinical significance of treatment effects in part because too few studies use such measures. Moreover, the meaning of measures of clinical significance currently in use is ambiguous. The measures have not been well validated against criteria related to actual functioning of the children in everyday life.

It would valuable to subject the most promising treatments (based on conceptual, empirical, or clinical criteria) to systematic experimental tests and to provide truly strong versions of those treatments. We need to know the magnitude of change we can achieve for a given clinical problem. The goal is not to determine the limits of treatment in a general sense, because presumably we can accomplish less now than we can in the future. But the lack of a clear idea of what we can accomplish now limits the vision we need to seek improvements. In general, strong tests are needed for many different treatments currently assumed to be effective in clinical work. Conceptualization of treatment, mentioned previously, is so important in developing strong treatments. Stronger treatment requires hypotheses about the mechanisms through which change is achieved.

Extratreatment Influences

We need to focus on diverse factors that can influence treatment effectiveness. Specific factors to consider depend on the conceptualization of the nature of the clinical problem and the treatment. However, the efficacy of treatment may depend on a host of other influences, some of which may be essential to harness to produce clinically significant changes.

There are obvious candidates for variables that interact with treatment to produce therapeutic change. In the adult therapy literature, patient, therapist, and relationship factors are well studied. Although these warrant study also in the context of child treatment, the general point is made here to entertain different sorts of influences. Factors in the parents' lives may warrant special attention, given their relation to deviant child behavior. For example, parental depression influences parent-child interaction and the social, emotional, and behavioral characteristics of infants, children, and adolescents (Hammen & Rudolf, 1996). Also, a mother's positive social contacts outside of the home influence the aversiveness of her interactions with her child and the level of her child's deviant behavior (Wahler, 1980). Child treatment may need to address features of the parent's life (e.g., psychopathology, social interaction) that extend beyond the child's specific problems and other facets of intrafamily life. This is not merely a restatement of the position that the child is an "identified patient" and reflects family problems. Rather, the suggestion is based on emerging evidence that specific aspects of the parents' lives have direct bearing on the child's functioning. Which features of parent functioning affect which problems and whether or how they ought to be incorporated into treatment remain uncharted. In principle, everything that impinges on parents as individuals, on parents as a couple, and on families might be studied empirically as moderators of therapy effects. The range of options underscores the importance of theory. Focused theoretical propositions are essential to ensure that the agenda for research is not expanded infinitely or mindlessly.

BROADENING THE PERSPECTIVES

This book has focused on child and adolescent therapy research and facets of clinical dysfunction that may inform or contribute to that research. Restricting the book to this narrow focus still leads to an extensive research agenda if we wish to identify, develop, and understand effective treatments. More topics for study are hardly needed. Yet, there are exciting opportunities to expand and enrich research. Consider a few examples in relation to conceptualization of clinical dysfunction and interventions.

Social, Emotional, and Behavioral Problems

A key theme has been that understanding clinical dysfunction (social, emotional, and behavioral problems) will lead to effective treatments. Knowing about onset, risk factors, and possible mechanisms leading to the problem, or indeed leading to termination of the problem over the course of development, may suggest foci for treatment or moderators of therapeutic change. Many domains are relevant to our understanding of clinical dysfunction.

Consider several examples of the many domains that might be relevant. Biological and physical factors are quite relevant to our understanding of the range of clinical problems to which psychotherapy is directed. There are many biological and physical correlates and antecedents of social and emotional problems in children and adolescents. As one example, temperament includes such characteristics as activity level, emotional responsiveness, quality of moods, and adaptability. Temperament is considered to be genetic or constitutional, in part because it can be identified very early in life. Assessed in early childhood, temperament predicts internalizing (e.g., anxiety) and externalizing disorders (e.g., conduct problems) in later childhood, personality characteristics (e.g., interest in avoiding harm, propensities to view the world as malevolent), and psychiatric disorders in adulthood (e.g., depression, antisocial personality disorder, alcohol-related problems (Caspi & Silva, 1995; Caspi, Moffitt, Newman, & Silva, 1996).

Nutrition too may influence children's social and emotional functioning. One has to be careful about this topic because there are so many fads and unsupported claims. Also, many beliefs are maintained (e.g., various food additives lead to hyperactivity), although, as chapter 5 notes, sometimes with little or no support after several empirical tests. Because biochemical influences play a role in functioning, nutrition is a reasonable area of influence (see Christensen, 1996). For example, recent studies suggest that consumption of some fatty acids (omega-3) found in fish and fish oil reduces symptoms of bipolar (manic depressive) disorder and schizophrenia in adults (Peet, 1998; Stoll, 1998). These fatty acids may affect neurotransmitters such as serotonin that are known to be implicated in symptoms of these disorders (see Hibbeln, 1998). This research is new and remains to be elaborated. Yet, to establish nutritional influences in relation to social, emotional, and behavioral problems, we need only one or two exemplars.

As another example, the ingestion of various toxins affects child functioning. As one example, lead is a heavy metal that can be ingested from breathing automobile lead fuel exhaust, eating lead-based paint chips, and drinking water that comes to the home through pipes that shed lead particles. Lead in school-age children predicts later hyperactivity and lower IQ (Needleman &

Gatsonis, 1990; Needleman, Schell, Bellinger, Leviton, & Alldred, 1990). Animal research has established that high doses of lead directly alter brain anatomy and physiology (Needleman, 1988). Cigarette smoke is another toxin. Cigarette smoking, particularly early in pregnancy, predicts aggressive behavior and hyperactivity in the offspring. These effects remain once other influences (socioeconomic status, parent psychiatric disorder, parent IQ) are controlled (Milberger, Biederman, Faraone, & Jones, 1998; Williams et al., 1998). Toxins such as lead and products from cigarette smoking connect biological factors to social, emotional, and behavioral problems.

Clumsiness in childhood is another example of a biological and physical factor implicated in social, emotional, and behavioral problems. Clumsiness is defined as difficulties in gross and fine-motor movements. Examples include performance on tasks involving hand movement such as picking up objects, catching a ball, and assembling objects. Clumsiness early in life is related to and predictive of disruptive behavior, lower self-esteem, lower levels of happiness, greater isolation from peers, and diminished participation in social activities (Sugden & Wright, 1998). I could cite other examples of biological factors related to social, emotional, and behavioral characteristics. Low birthweight, pre- and perinatal complications, and head injury in early childhood predict subsequent psychiatric disorders in children and adolescents (e.g., Rutter & Casaer, 1991; Rutter & Rutter, 1993). How fascinating it would be to conceptually connect the biological factors noted here with types or subtypes of clinical problems, impairment, and therapeutic change.

That mental and physical health are related is not a surprise, but it has not been exploited in the context of therapy. There are notable exceptions. For example, as discovered in therapy with adults, improvements in psychological symptoms (stress, anxiety) are related to improvements in physical health as well (Luborsky, Crits-Cristoph, Mintz, & Auerbach, 1988). The role of psychotherapy in improving physical status has been dramatic. Psychotherapy can improve quality of life and survival of terminally ill patients (Spiegel et al., 1989) and increase fertility rates among women having difficulty in conceiving (Domar, 1998). Clearly, the relation of mental and physical health in terms of conceptualization of mechanisms involved in dysfunction and moderators of treatment outcome might be pursued further in therapy research.

Socioeconomic factors are related to child dysfunction. Socioeconomic disadvantage in particular is a useful point of departure, even though it is a broad construct that encompasses an array of measures, including family income, occupational and educational status, and receipt of social assistance. In fact, socioeconomic disadvantage predicts a variety of untoward physical and mental health problems (Adler et al., 1994). Children and adolescents from socioeconomically disadvantaged environments show multiple problems of maladjustment from preschool through high school (see Luthar, 1999). The lower the income among children, the greater the prevalence of psychiatric disorder, poor school performance, and social impairment (Lipman, Offord, & Boyle, 1994). Socioeconomic disadvantage is associated with, and serves as a proxy variable for, many other factors: parent education, parent psychopathology, child-rearing practices, family disruption, and neighborhoods. These other factors may exert their own influence or serve as the basis for the connection between socioeconomic status and child adjustment. Many components such as those listed above individually contribute to disorders among children, and their precise impact may vary depending on the disorder, child gender, and other variables (e.g., Dodge et al., 1994; Lipman et al., 1994). Can an understanding of socioeconomic factors be incorporated into treatment trials?

If socioeconomic status relates to child and adolescent dysfunction, perhaps we could predict that academic functioning does so as well. Socioeconomic measures of the family relate to tested intelligence and a range of academic skills of the child (e.g., reading, school readiness). Yet academic functioning is worth mentioning in its own right because of its role in clinical dysfunction. Intelligence quotient, often used as one measure of mental ability, is a useful predictor of academic and school functioning and predicts later delinquency and antisocial behavior (Lynam, Moffitt, & Stouthamer-Loeber, 1993). Moreover, this effect is not due to the relation of socioeconomic status to intelligence; intelligence makes a separate contribution. Interestingly, among individuals with externalizing problems, IQ predicts long-term course as well. Antisocial youths higher in IQ have much better outcomes and are less likely to continue their dysfunction in adulthood than antisocial youths lower in IQ (see Kazdin, 1995b). Connecting mental abilities and cognition to treatment processes and outcome would be quite useful.

Finally, consider an influence far removed from the usual discussions of factors that relate to social, emotional, and behavioral problems: participation in religion. There is ample evidence, at least with adults, that religion can play a pervasive role in mental and physical health. The extent to which individuals are religious is assessed in many ways for purposes of research, including self-reports of belief in God, attending a place of worship on a regular basis, and being committed to religion. Among the many findings, participation in religion is associated with reduced rates of suicide, depression, and death from heart disease and higher levels of overall well-being (Levin, 1994; McCullough, 1995). The mechanisms through which these effects operate are not clear, but obvious confounds that might explain the effects are routinely ruled out (e.g., differences among participants and nonparticipants in religion in rates of cigarette smoking, obesity, prior history of disorders). Interestingly, some of the findings show a "dose-response" relation in which the mental and physical health benefits increase with greater orthodoxy or strictness of the sect to which one belongs. In short, participation in religion is very much related to adjustment and to the domains of functioning to which treatment is directed. One ought to understand more about beliefs, commitment, spirituality, and other facets that directly affect mental health. The issue here is not necessarily the study of religion per se but rather the mechanisms through which the effects operate.

Clinical problems to which psychotherapy is applied are related to and predicted by a host of biological, social, and psychological characteristics. The cited examples are provided merely to support the proposition that social, emotional, and behavioral problems are integrally related to other domains rather than to exhaust the domains themselves or to convey nuances of their relations. Obviously, I did not mention many domains (e.g., social competencies of the child, culture, and ethnicity).

I also omitted from the discussion the complex interactions of domains. Influences on social, emotional, and behavioral problems may operate together. The interactions of domains and influences illustrate the richness of development. For example, social and biological spheres interact in ways that relate directly to clinical dysfunction. Among children who live in socioeconomically disadvantaged situations, those with a relatively "easy" temperament—more good-natured, adaptable to change, affectionate—are less likely to experience negative outcomes associated with disadvantage that those with a more "difficult" temperament (see Luthar, 1999; Werner & Smith, 1992). Also, many relations among domains or influences are reciprocal, bidirectional, and dynamic and reflect sequences that unfold to influence the child. For example, the head injury of a child leads to stress among the parents, that combination of the disability of the child and stress can lead to marital and family problems, marital problems can affect parent health and child rearing, and so on (e.g., Miller, Dopp, Myers, & Fahey, 1997; Wade, Taylor, Drotar, Stancin, & Yeates, 1998).

Clearly, multiple influences are intertwined with clinical dysfunction. We do not need to embrace the full complexity of all influences to enrich therapy research. These influences could be important as a basis for understanding social, emotional, and behavioral problems and for identifying potential moderators of treatment outcome. Any systematic influences on the onset or course of adjustment or maladjustment warrant attention in our conceptual views of clinical dysfunction and perhaps should be drawn upon in our intervention work. Children do not come to treatment merely with *a* symptom (e.g., sadness), with a syndrome of multiple symptoms (e.g., major depression), or even with several (comorbid) disorders. They come as complex *gestalts* that we as professionals have carved into smaller units to isolate, investigate, and understand. In our efforts to understand, it may be useful to move into broader contexts occasionally to look for theory, hypotheses, common mechanisms, and potential treatment moderators. Of course, individual research investigations will always remain focused. Yet the conceptual domains and contexts from which hypotheses draw can be expanded greatly.

Interventions

Recall from the beginning of the book that the definition of therapy focused on efforts to improve adjustment and functioning and to reduce maladaptive behaviors and other psychological and often physical complaints. The methods to accomplish these ends are based on interpersonal influences and psychological processes (e.g., learning, persuasion, social support). Many types of interventions designed to improve functioning and to reduce maladjustment extend beyond the usual domain of psychotherapy. Consider a few examples.

Many medical and biological interventions are designed to alter social, emotional, and behavioral problems of children and adolescents. Perhaps the most familiar example is the use of medication for attention-deficit/hyperactivity disorder and major depression. Medication is widely recognized as a partner in treatments for child and adolescent disorders and need not be elaborated.

Participation in some activities may reduce social, emotional, and behavioral problems or the factors likely associated with such problems. For example, teenage girls who engage in sports are much less likely to use drugs, to suffer low self-esteem or depression, to be sexually active, and to get pregnant than similar girls who do not engage in sports (Lopiano, 1998). Interestingly, the findings showed that sports had no such influence on teenage boys. Of what relevance is this report to psychotherapy? Participation in such activities might be connected conceptually to treatment as a moderating influence, since social competence and clinical dysfunction are related. Also, understanding the mechanisms that explain why participation in sports operates in this fashion could inform conceptual views about treatment. The mechanism, once identified, might be activated through different interventions, including some variants of psychotherapy.

Substance use and abuse—alcohol, cigarettes—are often targets of psychotherapy. Economic interventions (control of the price of substances) influence usage. Increasing the prices of alcohol and cigarettes has been studied well in the United States and many other countries. The findings show that, as prices for alcohol or cigarettes increase, per capita consumption declines. Moreover, there tends to be a dose-response relation; higher increases in price lead to greater declines (see Horgen & Brownell, 1998). These findings show the responsiveness of specific target behaviors to economic manipulations, raise the prospect of treating significant health problems, and also raise questions about who changes and how.

I could list an array of interventions that focus on improving adjustment and psychological well-being. The examples I have illustrated so far have evidence on their behalf, but perhaps they are not exciting. Once we abandon evidence, the illustrations are more "fun." Here is one of my favorites. In addition to or maybe instead of psychotherapy, significant social, emotional, and behavioral problems might be improved if one gets a suntan. Are you skeptical? Do not take my word for this; let us appeal to higher authorities, namely, the bottles of suntan lotion. Such bottles (Coppertone™) promise that if you use the product, "You'll love the way you look and feel." Moreover, with a suntan, you will feel "vibrant, healthy, and confident" and, in general, "look and feel your best" (Schering-Plough, 1996). The claims are certainly relevant to adjustment—so many problems (mood disorders typically accompanied by low self-esteem and anorexia typically accompanied by poor body image) are obvious candidates for this intervention.

Although one might dismiss getting a suntan as an intervention as silly, there are reasons to withhold strong denials of it. After all, treatment research has demonstrated that exposure to sunlight improves some mood disorders (seasonal affective disorder; Lee et al., 1998). Establishing that sunlight can improve at least one clinical dysfunction makes this intervention more "legitimate" intellectually. Once the mechanisms of the change are identified, the intervention may move from legitimate to highly respectable. As mental health professionals, we hesitate to move too far afield in seeking interventions. A worry is that right behind this intervention might be others: the weather, sunspots, and full or not-so-full moon. Of course, as scientists, one can only welcome replicated news of any such influences. For now, without a set of studies to establish such influences, the broader question still has merit: what "interventions" other than those in psychotherapy have been shown to improve social, emotional, or behavioral problems?

The examples show that psychotherapy is only one way to improve adaptive functioning of children and adolescents and to ameliorate clinical dysfunction. It is important to identify other such efforts that share the same goals, especially if these efforts have supporting evidence. The application and effectiveness of psychotherapy might be improved with an understanding of other interventions and their effects. What mechanisms are involved when quite separate interventions (medication, education, psychotherapy) produce positive change in social, emotional, and behavioral adjustment? Different interventions (exercise, nutrition, psychotherapy) may not work through the same mechanisms. Just as many different influences can lead to a similar outcome (e.g., depression, anxiety), many different influences might also lead to change in social, emotional, or behavioral problems. Yet there may be common mechanisms among quite different interventions or similar moderators of change among the different influences and interventions. Models of change might be greatly informed with consideration of psychotherapy within the broader context of influences on clinical dysfunction and development.

SUMMARY RECOMMENDATIONS

Earlier chapters have discussed several issues that affect research, for example, the need for more conceptually based research, for a systematic model to chart a course for progress and accumulation of research findings, and for changes in clinical work to not only improve patient care but also contribute to the knowledge base. I present several specific recommendations to achieve research goals.

Table 11.1 presents three sets of recommendations summarizing prior discussions of what needs to be changed. First, the emphases and focus of therapy studies ought to change. The recommendations focus on the conceptual underpinnings of psychotherapy, the range of questions one can address, and novel models of delivering treatment. These recommendations emphasize expanding current research foci.

Second, we need research that provides the underpinnings for evaluation of treatment in clinical practice. The second set of recommendations presented in table 11.1 provide the tools essential for clinical work. Clinical practice ought to be changed to improve the quality of patient care. Key changes that can im-

Table 11.1 Recommendations to Improve Child and Adolescent Psychotherapy Research

Category	Recommendation
A. Treatment Research	• Improve and test conceptual models of treatment to relate treatment foci and procedures to what is known about the clinical dysfunction • Explore a broader range of models of delivering treatment (e.g., high strength, amenability to treatment, continued care) • Test a wide range of questions about treatment, particularly those related to predictors, moderators, and mediators of therapeutic change • Expand the range of outcome domains of child (e.g., symptoms, impairment, prosocial function) and family (e.g., parents, family functioning) • Identify whether changes affect functioning in everyday life • Evaluate treatment characteristics such as disseminability, cost, and acceptability • Improve methodology of treatment studies by assessing interim changes (rather than pre and post only) and follow-up, increasing power, evaluating adherence, and relating treatment delivery and therapeutic processes to outcome.
B. Underpinnings of Evaluation in Practice	• Develop measures that can be used in an treatment process as conducted in clinical practice • Validate the measures to ensure that their repeated administration is readily interpretable and that they reflect changes in everyday functioning • Establish measures that correlate with more comprehensive assessment batteries and measures of diverse domains • Record assessments for clinical use and data reduction methods in manuals
C. New Methods	• Explore $N = 1$ research methods as a way of evaluating treatment • Explore qualitative methods as a resource for models of change, new measures, and new techniques • Conduct focused status report reviews of the literature (rather than the usual narrative and meta-analytic reviews) that chart specific progress made since prior reviews in relation to concrete questions.

prove patient care and increase accountability can also serve to develop the knowledge base. Clinical practice is a critical resource we can draw from. Of course, in clinical work, we must move away from "clinical evidence" and "clinical experience," two terms just a step removed from "anecdotal evidence" and "in my opinion." There are methods for systematically evaluating clinical practice, although they are not available in valid or user-friendly forms.

Third, therapy research would benefit from expansion of the methods used to evaluate therapy. Our deep appreciation of group studies and the randomized controlled clinical trial is warranted, and these comments in no way demean current methods (even though de-mean and de-standard deviation from such studies say nothing about de individual). The third set of recommendations presented in table 11.1 fosters expanded methods of evaluating therapy. Qualitative research, $N = 1$, case-control studies that use databases from clinical services, and longitudinal studies of development might be used to elaborate the process of therapeutic or developmental change. Such research would greatly enrich the knowledge base about intervention effects. For example, qualitative research could greatly improve our understanding of the client's experience, the impact of therapeutic change, and the sequence of changes over the course of treatment (Webster-Stratton & Spitzer, 1996). Methodology is not merely a way to answer a question but contributes itself to the answer. Novel methods, just like novel questions, can lead to new insights about treatment.

Although research in the recommended areas would advance research, progress would benefit from periodic evaluation and status reports. We need a blueprint for treatment development to serve as a guide. I suggested one blueprint to address a range of conceptual issues and research questions in relation to a particular treatment. Clearly two qualifiers are essential. First, the particular model I have provided obviously is not the only one that can be proposed. Yet the meta-issue is the point, namely, that a systematic plan would be very useful for treatment development, progress, and evaluation. We expect periodic reviews of the literature to reflect progress, but they cannot unless the studies they include address the critical questions.

Second, not all research needs to follow a blueprint. There is no need for rigidity. Even with a model for research, there is always an important role for creative and innovative research that changes how treatment is conceived, presented, and evaluated. Indeed, such research may even compel changes in the blueprint itself. Adoption of an overall blueprint might generate trepidations. Perhaps a detailed plan would foster rigid or narrowly focused research. Yet the impetus for proposing a model of therapy research was the lamentable uniformity and narrowness of current research. The proposed model of research does not set the only path for research. Indeed, the model is intended to expand methods and topics of study.

Significant departures from current research paradigms will be very difficult to make. For example, one recommendation suggests expanding the methodology of treatment studies to include more single-case experimental studies and more studies using qualitative research methods. This is lofty but not realistic because most graduate training in clinical psychology, psychiatry, or social work, whether pre- or postdoctoral, does not expose trainees to such methodologies. We can continue with the current methods, but the questions we pose must become more inspired, theoretically informed, and novel. Very little in the recommendations is out of reach. Indeed, part of the frustration in evaluating the psychotherapy literature results from gross oversights, as in the absence of efforts to understand how change is produced or few tests of strong versions of treatment. Perhaps more frustrating is the trajectory. A decade or two has elapsed without real progress on key questions. Is there any reason to believe that the next two decades of progress will be very different?

CLOSING COMMENTS

I have outlined a research agenda for child and adolescent therapy research. On the one hand, the agenda could be conceived as merely a redirection of current efforts to expand the questions being addressed. That is, perhaps some might perceive the research advocated here as minor tinkering with current research priorities. Indeed, more theoretically informed and clinically relevant research, greater efforts to understand rather than merely to describe or demonstrate treatment effects, and more sophisticated questions about treatment would meet many of the concerns voiced in previous chapters.

On the other hand, the agenda could be conceived as a more radical departure. The research advocated here would be not a mere expansion of current work but a more systematic and thoughtful accumulation of knowledge. Charting progress is a task not merely for historians but also for planners. We could plan better the type of research we want or believe is needed and try to move toward that. More of the same research that characterizes current studies of child and adolescent therapy will not lead us very far, or at least will not lead us to the knowledge we need for effective treatments. There are three questions to guide us, as noted previously. What do we wish to know about therapy and its effects? What do we already know? What needs to be accomplished to fill in the gap between what we wish to know and what we already know? Without addressing these and periodically reevaluating progress, research may continue to wander.

Efforts to modify psychotherapy research in ways discussed in this book require changes in the infrastructure that supports the status quo. First, clinical practice ought to be revamped. Increased accountability for a client's individual care ought to emerge from concerns for the patient rather than for reimbursement issues. Accountability in clinical practice may also provide opportunities for increased candor about the status of treatments provided to the clients. Although most treatments in use have never been evaluated, I do not mean that they ought not to be used. For some problems, there are no empirically supported treatments; for other problems, empirically supported treatments may not be feasible or may have already failed. Clients might be informed that a given treatment is experimental because no firm data support it or the application the clinician is considering. Apart from the virtues and ethics of such candor, this approach sets the stage for the importance of systematic evaluation. Evaluation in clinical work begins with the priority of clinical care. Although the evaluative information can be used to make decisions that aid the client, the data from accumulated cases may also contribute to the knowledge base.

Part of the infrastructure that needs to be changed includes graduate and postgraduate training. Among the latest developments in training in clinical psychology, for example, is the focus on empirically supported treatments. Programs (e.g., predoctoral and postdoctoral internships or residencies, graduate training programs) pride themselves for being at the cutting edge if they endorse treatments that have evidence in their behalf. This certainly is an advance, but it raises the embarrassing question about what have we been doing before. Systematic evaluation of clinical practice is underdeveloped, and what has been developed is too new for us to expect widespread implementation (e.g., Clement, 1999; Wiger, 1999). Far too few measures have been validated for clinical work. Clearly, new methods for clinical evaluation should be introduced into graduate training.

There are many obstacles to making advances in research. Research is difficult to do, and treatment research has some added challenges. What is amazing is how much research is completed. This book calls for a broader look at what has been accomplished, what needs to be accomplished, and the intervening steps to meet the goals of research. There is no need to view this goal as rigid. Plans can change and ought to in light of new information. However, changing an existing plan to accumulate knowledge is quite different from proceeding without a clear plan at all. This book was designed to lobby for more systematic progress and to illustrate the form it might take in future research.

Appendix A

List of Child and Adolescent Psychotherapies

OVERVIEW

The list that follows consists of psychotherapy techniques in use with children and adolescents. The final count of the treatments included in the list (551 techniques) cannot be considered to be the "real" number of treatments applied to children and adolescents, for reasons described further later. The count merely suggest the plenitude of treatments. The search process itself suggested that the number continues to grow.

The list hints at broad issues discussed throughout this book. For example, I discuss the importance of the conceptual basis of treatment. Although the names of many treatments suggest their conceptual origins, others reflect different origins (e.g., television show characteristics) with less clear conceptual ties. Also, I discuss the questions that ought to guide therapy research. As the list of treatments shows, it would not be possible or indeed desirable to investigate the efficacy of all of the treatments currently available. Indeed, the number of treatments suggests, to me at least, that a better focus for research is models of change, that is, how treatments work.

METHODS

Treatments were included in the list if they were applied to youths (18 years of age or younger) and the application was documented in a publicly available source. The sources for identifying treatment were computerized databases, published books, and journal articles. For the computer database searches, key search words were drawn from meta-analyses of child and adolescent therapy. Among key terms included in the search were *child therapy, adolescent therapy, client-centered, counseling, cotherapy, insight-, intervention-, model-, modifica-, operant-, paradox-, psychoanaly-, psychodrama-, psychothera-, reinforce-, respondent, roleplaying, therap-, training, transactional, treatment.* In addition, several of us working on this list (see below) consulted many books that reviewed child and adolescent therapy. Although all sources could not be listed here, key texts from which many of the treatments were drawn are listed at the end of this appendix.

To be included in the list, a treatment had to be documented and applied to children and/or adolescents. When there was ambiguity about the treatment or the application, the material was read by more than one person. Treatments that were not clearly applied to children or adolescents or were insufficiently described were omitted. Ambiguities emerged in constructing this list in part because of similar and overlapping treatments. Several decision rules were adopted. Synonyms for a given technique were occasionally identifiable. When these seemed clear (e.g., assertion training and assertiveness training), only one term was used for the list, and the other name of the treatment was placed in parentheses. In some cases, one or more techniques (e.g., covert modeling, participant modeling) appeared to be subtypes of a broader category (e.g., modeling). In other cases, a broad category term (e.g., play therapy) included many different approaches, each based on and modified by a conceptual view (e.g., Jungian play therapy, Gestalt play therapy). We excluded most such variants unless the approach appeared to involve distinct procedures and conceptual views (e.g., sandplay therapy, family play therapy). As a general rule, we did not include all possible treatments and variants and made an effort to eschew redundancies. In keeping with the focus of this book, interventions were excluded if they were based on biological or medical techniques (e.g., nutrition, psychopharmacology) or focused exclusively on educational, academic, or communication (language, speech) objectives.

Dilemmas and ambiguities emerged early in identifying treatments from a vast literature, and these deserve further comment. We used various dilemmas as opportunities to reformulate guidelines and rules for coding the treatments. Yet, the absence of full details of many treatments made their evaluation difficult. Also, deciding when two variants of the same treatment ought to be distinguished, and when seemingly identical treatments with different names ought not to be, influenced the final count. Separate entries on the list that follows were included if a distinction could be made in the procedures. Because of the difficulties in distinguishing various techniques and the absence of data on interjudge agreement on the decisions, the specific count and entries must be viewed cautiously.

Presented as an indication of the vast array of interventions, the list very likely underestimates what is currently available and in use. Indeed, in the late stages of preparing this book for publication, I could still continue to identify newly proposed treatments (e.g., Metcalf, 1998; Rowan & O'Hanlon, 1999). The point made in chapter 3 about the proliferation of treatments is underscored by such entries. The list includes identifiable techniques and does not provide any indication of the extent to which any particular technique is in use.

The process of identifying treatments spanned 5 to 6 years. During this time, several individuals contributed significantly. Susan Breton and Tricia Zawacki oversaw critical facets of identifying treatments, coding and training others to code the resources, assisting with decisions about categories of treatment, helping to make distinctions among treatments, among related matters. I appreciate their remarkable efforts. Several others were pivotal in completing the reading of multiple sources, identifying treatment, and raising critical issues about treatments: Erica Atkeson, Todd DeSimone, Mara Folz, Gaby Grebski, Jonathan Hart, Jennifer Hoffman, Andrea Jones, Mimi Lin, Willis Sautter, Heather Slay, Joe Spinazzola, and Rachel Zucker. I am grateful to each person for their careful work.

PSYCHOSOCIAL TREATMENTS FOR CHILDREN AND ADOLESCENTS

1. Activation therapy
2. Active play therapy
3. Activities planning
4. Activity group therapy
5. Activity-intervention group psychotherapy
6. Activity-interview group psychotherapy
7. Adelaide Johnson's therapy
8. Adolescent relapse prevention
9. Adlerian family therapy
10. Adlerian group parent education
11. Adlerian group therapy
12. Adlerian psychoanalysis
13. Adlerian psychotherapy
14. Age game
15. Aggression replacement training
16. Aikido
17. Alf group
18. Analysis-reeducation therapy
19. Analytic play therapy group
20. Anger control training
21. Anger coping group training
22. Animal-facilitated child therapy
23. Anti-suggestion
24. Anxiety management training
25. Appropriate peer models in counseling groups
26. Art therapy
27. Assertiveness training
28. At ease therapy
29. Attribution retraining
30. Audiotaped group hypnotic suggestions
31. Autogenic training
32. Automated systematic desensitization
33. Aversive conditioning
34. Avoidance training
35. Awareness training
36. Background music bridge program (Background music)
37. Barb technique
38. Behavioral consultation
39. Behavioral contracting
40. Behavioral engineering
41. Behavioral family therapy
42. Behavioral group therapy
43. Behavioral rehearsal
44. Behavioral weight control therapy
45. Bell and pad conditioning
46. Bereavement counseling
47. Bibliotherapy
48. Biofeedback
49. Blindfold treatment
50. Boogeyman intervention
51. Brief focal therapy
52. Brief immobilization
53. Brief intervention
54. Brief parental counseling
55. Brief psychotherapy
56. Brief structural therapy
57. Brinich's therapy
58. Broad-spectrum behavior therapy
59. Caring community
60. Carkhuff-model counseling
61. Catalyst therapy
62. Chess therapy
63. Children's divorce groups
64. Children's feedback game
65. Child-centered education-support group
66. Child-centered therapy
67. Child-focused strategic therapy
68. Circle game
69. Classroom management (precision teaching)
70. Classroom meeting
71. Coaching
72. Cognitive and autonomic group

73. Cognitive behavioral program
74. Cognitive behavioral therapy for the treatment of anxiety
75. Cognitive control therapy
76. Cognitive developmental intervention
77. Cognitive emotion psychotherapy
78. Cognitive family therapy
79. Cognitive mediation
80. Cognitive perceptual treatment
81. Cognitive problem-solving approach (Problem-solving skills training)
82. Cognitive therapy
83. Color-your-life technique
84. Communication therapy
85. Community-based treatment
86. Community treatment groups
87. Companionship therapy
88. Compositional plays
89. Comprehensive family therapy
90. Computer games therapy
91. Computer-assisted behavioral health counseling
92. Concurrent family therapy (Concurrent parent/child therapy with same therapist)
93. Concurrent individual and family therapy
94. Conflict resolution therapy
95. Confrontational-educational group
96. Confrontational/reality therapy
97. Conjoint family therapy
98. Conjoint infant and parent treatment
99. Conjoint play therapy
100. Contact desensitization
101. Contingency contracting
102. Contingency management
103. Coordinated group psychotherapy of children and parents
104. Coping with depression course for adolescents
105. Cornerstone treatment
106. Corrective denouement play
107. Corrective social interaction therapy
108. Correspondence training
109. Court alternative program
110. Covert conditioning
111. Covert modeling
112. Covert response cost
113. Covert sensitization
114. Co-therapy
115. Creative aggression therapy
116. Creative characters
117. Creative drama groups
118. Crisis intervention
119. Cue-controlled relaxation
120. Cuento therapy
121. Dallas and Houston juvenile firesetters program
122. Dance movement therapy
123. Day treatment
124. Developing understanding of self and others
125. Developmental approach
126. Developmental facilitation groups
127. Developmental group counseling
128. Developmental play
129. Developmental therapy
130. Dialectical psychotherapy
131. Differential attention
132. Direct decision therapy
133. Directed daydream
134. Directive therapy
135. Discrimination training
136. Divorce therapy
137. Drama therapy
138. Dream content conceptualization
139. Dry bed training (bell and pad conditioning)
140. Duo therapy
141. Dyadic psychotherapy
142. Dynamic counseling
143. Ecosystemic approach to family-school problems
144. Ego-supportive child therapy
145. Elementary learning disability process group
146. Emotional imagery training
147. Emotive imagery
148. "Employer-employee" relationship treatment
149. Encounter therapy
150. Encouragement therapy
151. Eriksonian therapy
152. Essexfields social treatment
153. Exaggeration therapy
154. Excommunication

155. Experiential group treatment
156. Experiential psychotherapy
157. Expressing affection
158. Expressive arts therapy
159. Facial screening
160. Fair play therapy
161. Fairy tale therapy
162. Family art therapy
163. Family context therapy
164. Family contract game
165. Family council
166. Family crisis intervention
167. Family ecological treatment
168. Family enrichment programs
169. Family network intervention
170. Family play therapy
171. Family psychotherapy
172. Family reconstruction
173. Family scripts
174. Family systems therapy
175. Family theraplay
176. Family therapy
177. Family therapy lunch session
178. Fantasy communications
179. Fantasy manipulation therapy
180. Fantasy realization ceremonies
181. Feedback
182. Feeding program
183. Feelings are in
184. Filial therapy
185. Flooding
186. Florida parent education program
187. Focal treatment unit
188. Focusing technique
189. Fold-over approach
190. For instance
191. Fostering an authority dependency relationship
192. Free and sheltered space
193. Full cleanliness training
194. Functional analysis approach
195. Functional family therapy
196. Functional movement training
197. Game of insults (Talking the dozens)
198. Games analysis treatment
199. General alternative response
200. Gestalt therapy
201. Getting it together
202. Glasser's classroom meeting
203. Glove wearing therapy
204. Go-between process in family therapy
205. Graphing techniques (Cognitive-emotional psychotherapy)
206. Green stamp therapy
207. Greenhouse program
208. Group affection activities
209. Group anger control training
210. Group art therapy
211. Group assertiveness training
212. Group contingency
213. Group counseling
214. Group desensitization
215. Group hypnosis
216. Group progressive relaxation training
217. Group role-playing treatment
218. Group theraplay
219. Group therapy
220. Growth-centered group counseling
221. Guided fantasy
222. Guided group interaction
223. Habit reversal
224. Hakomi therapy
225. Handling death of a parent technique
226. Hierarchical implosive therapy
227. High schoolers as therapists therapy
228. Highfields community therapy project
229. Holistic counseling
230. Honesty pays
231. Horticultural therapy
232. Hospital-based treatment
233. Human development program
234. Human relations training
235. Hypnointrospection
236. Hypnotherapeutic intervention
237. Hypnotic relation
238. Imagery interaction play technique
239. Impasse/priority therapy
240. Implosive therapy
241. Incidental learning
242. Incompatible response training
243. Indirect hypnotic therapy

244. Individual education (Corsini, 4R system)
245. Information feedback
246. Initiative games
247. Inpatient family intervention
248. Insight-oriented psychotherapy
249. Instant print photography in psychotherapy
250. Integrative psychotherapy
251. Intensive psychoanalytic group therapy
252. Intensive psychoanalytic psychotherapy
253. Intermediate communication
254. Interpersonal problem-solving skills training with puppets
255. Interpersonal process recall
256. Interpersonal psychotherapy
257. Interpersonal skills training
258. Interpolated reinforcement
259. Interpretation Interpretive group therapy
260. Intervention with children who set fires
261. Keep it clean
262. Kinetic group psychotherapy
263. Kinetic psychotherapy
264. King tiger therapy
265. Kleinian technique
266. Konstantareas and Homatidis' group therapy
267. Letter writing
268. Let's pretend hospital
269. Levine's approach (to encopresis)
270. Life is for everyone
271. Life skills counseling
272. Life-space interviewing
273. Logotherapy
274. Long-term therapy
275. Magic circle program
276. Making life books
277. Managing suicidal children
278. Marathon therapy
279. Marionette therapy
280. Massed practice
281. Meditation
282. Mental imagery
283. Metaphor therapy
284. Milieu therapy
285. Mirror group therapy
286. Mirror image therapy
287. Modeling
288. Modeling with guided participation
289. Modifying impulsiveness
290. Morita psychotherapy
291. Mother as therapist therapy
292. Mother as therapeutic intermediary
293. Mother-infant games
294. Mother involvement
295. Multimodal therapy
296. Multiple family therapy
297. Multiple impact family therapy
298. Multisystemic therapy
299. Music therapy
300. Mutual storytelling (Story-telling reconstruction therapy)
301. Naikan psychotherapy
302. Narrative psychotherapy
303. Natural high therapy
304. Negative practice
305. Network therapy
306. New identity process
307. No-interview intervention
308. Non-aversive approach
309. Nurturing parent program
310. Obscene language as therapy
311. Ojeman's causal approach
312. Omission training
313. Oneness group
314. Oneness psychotherapy for parents
315. One-shot interview
316. Operant conditioning
317. Operant verbal mediation training
318. Operantly structured fantasies
319. Organic process therapy
320. Overcorrection
321. Pair therapy
322. Pal program
323. Paradigmatic psychotherapy
324. Paradoxical approach with family
325. Paradoxical intervention treatment
326. Paradoxical letters
327. Parallel group therapy
328. Paraverbal therapy
329. Parent adolescent relationship development
330. Parent and toddler training

331. Parent counseling program
332. Parent counseling-teacher consultation
333. Parent education
334. Parent effectiveness training
335. Parent group didactic training
336. Parent guidance
337. Parent involvement program with reality therapy
338. Parent management training (Parent training, Parent behavior management training)
339. Parent managing
340. Parent-mediated intervention
341. Parent-child interaction training
342. Parents' self-monitoring
343. Parent-tutor therapy
344. Passive play therapy (Relationship therapy)
345. Past lives therapy
346. Patient-selected photographs and positive self-statements
347. Peer group socialization therapy
348. Peer-mediated interventions
349. Peer therapy
350. Personal construct psychotherapy
351. Person-centered family therapy
352. Pet psychotherapy
353. Phenomeno-structural psychotherapy
354. Phototherapy
355. Physical challenge activities
356. Placebo plus reassurance
357. Planned activities training
358. Play group therapy
359. Play interview
360. Play process
361. Play therapy
362. Poetry therapy
363. Positive connotation
364. Prescription of an ordeal
365. Pretend play therapy
366. Pre-verbal play
367. Primal therapy
368. Primary relationship therapy
369. Problem-solving communication training
370. Programmed communication therapy
371. Programmed text
372. Project re-ed treatment
373. Provocative therapy
374. Pseudologia fantastica
375. Psychoanalysis
376. Psychoanalytic family therapy
377. Psychoanalytic group therapy
378. Psychoanalytic parent education
379. Psychoanalytically oriented milieu therapy
380. Psychodrama
381. Psychodynamic group therapy
382. Psychodynamic treatment
383. Psychodynamically oriented inpatient treatment
384. Psychoiconography
385. Psychoimagination therapy
386. Psychological competence-based therapy
387. Psychomotor therapy
388. Puppet therapy
389. Puppet therapy in groups
390. Pure reactor analysis family therapy
391. Rachman's group psychotherapy
392. Radical psychiatry
393. Rage reduction treatment
394. Rapid treatment
395. Rate
396. Rational behavior therapy
397. Rational emotive education group
398. Rational emotive family therapy
399. Rational emotive parent training
400. Rational emotive therapy
401. Reactor analysis family therapy
402. Reality group therapy
403. Reality integrative therapy
404. Reality therapy
405. Reattachment therapy
406. Reciprocity training
407. Reconstruction
408. Redecision therapy
409. Reduction in parental attention
410. Reevaluation counseling
411. Reframing
412. Regional intervention program
413. Rehm's self-control treatment
414. Reinforced practice
415. Reinforcement-and-strategy training

416. Relationship enhancement therapy
417. Relationship group treatment
418. Relationship therapy
419. Relationship-implosive therapy
420. Relaxation training/therapy
421. Release therapy
422. Repairing ego deficits
423. Response cost lottery
424. Response-cost procedure
425. Responsibility reinforcement
426. Restricted environment stimulation therapy
427. Restructuring role functions within a family
428. Retention control training
429. Rituals
430. Role play
431. Sandplay therapy
432. Satiation training
433. Say-then-do training sequence
434. Scared straight
435. School-home motivational system
436. Self-administered aversive conditioning
437. Self-concept group psychotherapy
438. Self-control therapy
439. Self-control strategy using song lyrics
440. Self-control training
441. Self-control triad
442. Self-hypnosis
443. Self-instruction
444. Self modeling
445. Self-psychological parent education
446. Self-punishment
447. Self-puzzle
448. Self-reinforcement
449. Self-selected adolescent peer group therapy (Office network therapy)
450. Self-verbalization
451. Sense-of-industry
452. Sensitivity training
453. Sensory deprivation
454. Sensory extinction
455. Sensory integration
456. Sensory integrative therapy
457. Separation (Treating the "mama's boy")
458. Separation-relevant play
459. Serial drawing
460. Shadow therapy
461. Shaping
462. Short-term family therapy
463. Sibling-mediated procedures
464. Silence treatment
465. Simultaneous semipermeable groups
466. Situation/transition group in school
467. (Slavson's) activity group psychotherapy
468. Social conception modification
469. Social learning–based family therapy
470. Social network family therapy
471. Social reinforcement
472. Social skills training
473. Social system therapy
474. Social work group
475. Sociodrama
476. Solution-focused group therapy
477. Solution-oriented therapy
478. Special kind of love
479. Sphincter-control training
480. Split-session co-therapy
481. Sports group
482. Squiggle-drawing game
483. Staggered wakening procedure
484. Stimulus control
485. Stimulus substitution
486. Stop and go play therapy group
487. Storytelling
488. Storytelling reconstruction therapy
489. Storytelling therapy
490. Strategic family therapy
491. Stress inoculation training
492. Stress reduction procedures (Palliative vs. Direct action)
493. Structural analysis
494. Structured approach
495. Structured fantasies
496. Structured learning therapy
497. Structured therapeutic game method
498. Student volunteers therapy
499. Suggestive therapy
500. Symbolic modeling
501. Symbolic-experiential family therapy

502. Symptom discouragement
503. Symptoms-as-healers therapy
504. Systematic desensitization
505. Systemic contracting
506. Systems family approach
507. Systems model (with family and schools)
508. Talking-feeling-and-doing game
509. Task-oriented group therapy
510. Teacher-mediated peer feedback
511. Teaching family model (achievement place)
512. Teaching mother
513. Televised feedback for parents
514. Theme-centered interactional groups
515. Therapeutic ally
516. Therapeutic community
517. Theraplay
518. Thou and I
519. Thought stopping technique
520. Time limits
521. Time-limited discussion groups
522. Time-limited psychotherapy
523. Time-out procedures
524. Token economy
525. Traditional group social work
526. Trance therapy
527. Transactional analysis
528. Transactional analysis in groups
529. Transference parenting
530. Treatment foster care
531. Triad therapy
532. Triadic behavioral approach
533. Turtle technique
534. Twenty-four hour therapy
535. Understanding dynamics between family members
536. Unstructured group therapy
537. Unstructured parenting group
538. Use of two houses in play therapy
539. Values clarification group
540. Verbal group therapy
541. Verbal sharing
542. Video therapy
543. Whittling away
544. Wholistic family therapy
545. Wild and crazy interventions
546. Work box
547. Work penalty system
548. Year-long observational group
549. Yoga and awareness training (Body cathexis)
550. Zaraleya psychoenergetic technique
551. Z-process attachment therapy

SELECTED LIST OF SOURCES

Bellack, A.S., & Hersen, M. (1985). *Dictionary of behavior therapy techniques*. New York: Pergamon.

Bernard, M.E. (Ed.). (1991). *Using rational-emotive therapy effectively: A practitioner's guide to applied clinical psychology*. New York: Plenum.

Brems, C. (1993). *A comprehensive guide to child psychotherapy*. Needham Heights, MA: Allyn & Bacon.

Brown, D.T., & Prout, H.T. (Eds.). (1989). *Counseling and psychotherapy with children and adolescents: Theory and practice for school and clinic settings* (2nd ed.) Brandon, VT: Clinical Psychology Publishing.

Budman, S.H. (Ed.). (1981). *Forms of brief therapy*. New York: Guilford.

Cath, S.H., Gurwitt, A., & Gunsberg, L. (Eds.). (1989). *Fathers and their families*. Hillsdale, NJ: Analytic Press.

Chess, S., Thomas, A., Hertzig, M.E. (Eds.). (1989). *Annual progress in child psychiatry and child development*. New York: Brunner/Mazel.

Chethek, M. (1989). *Techniques of child therapy: Psychodynamic strategies*. New York: Guilford.

Clarizio, H.F., & McCoy, G.F. (1983). *Behavior disorders in children* (3rd ed.). New York: Harper & Row.

Cohen, R.L., & Dulcan, M.K. (Eds.). (1987). *Basic handbook of training in child and adolescent psychiatry*. Springfield, IL: Charles C. Thomas.

Coppolillo, H.P. (1987). *Psychodynamic psychotherapy of children: An introduction to the art and the techniques*. Madison, CT: International Universities Press.

Corsini, R.S. (Ed.). (1981). *Handbook of innovative psychotherapies*. New York: Wiley & Sons.

Diel, P. & Rosenthal, R. (1961). *The psychology of re-education*. Boston, MA: Shambhala.

Dobson, K. (Ed.). (1988). *Handbook of cognitive-behavioral therapies*. New York: Guilford.

Feldman, L.A., Caplinger, T.E., & Wodarski, J.S. (1983). *The St. Louis conundrum: The effective treatment of antisocial youths*. Englewood Cliffs, NJ: Prentice-Hall.

Finch, A.J., Jr., Nelson, W.M., III, & Ott, E.S. (Eds.). (1993). *Cognitive-behavioral procedures with children and adolescents: A practical guide*. Needham Heights, MA: Allyn & Bacon.

Forehand, R., & McMahon, R.J. (1981). *Helping the noncompliant child: A clinician's guide to parent training*. New York: Guilford.

Gaynor, J., & Hatcher, C. (1987). *The psychology of child fire-setting: Detection and intervention*. New York: Brunner/Mazel.

Gumaer, J. (1984). *Counseling and therapy for children*. New York: Free Press.

Guerney, B. (1969). *Psychotherapeutic agents: New roles for nonprofessionals, parents and teachers*. New York: Holt, Rinehart and Winston.

Haworth, M.R. (1990). *A child's therapy: Hour by hour*. Madison, CT: International Universities Press.

Heap, M., & Dryden, W. (Eds.). (1991). *Hypnotherapy*. Milton Keynes, England: Open University Press.

Herink, R. (Ed.). (1980). *The psychotherapy handbook*. New York: New American Library.

Hersen, M. (Ed.). (1989). *Innovations in child behavior therapy*. New York: Springer.

Hersen, M., Kazdin, A.E., & Bellack, A.S. (Eds.). (1991). *The clinical psychology handbook* (2nd ed.). New York: Pergamon.

Hibbs, E., & Jensen, P. (Eds.). (1996). *Psychosocial treatment research of child and adolescent disorders: Empirically based strategies for clinical practice*. Washington, DC: American Psychological Association.

Hoghughi, M., Lyons, J., Muckley, A., & Swainston, M.A. (1988). *Treating problem children: Issues, methods, and practice*. London: Sage.

Hollin, C.R., & Howells, K. (Eds.). (1991). *Clinical approaches to sex offenders and their victims*. Chichester, England: Wiley & Sons.

Johnson, J.H., Rasbury, W.C., & Siegel, L.J. (1986). *Approaches to child treatment*. New York: Pergamon.

Kazdin, A.E. (1988). *Child psychotherapy: Developing and identifying effective treatments*. Oxford: Pergamon.

Keller, P.A., & Heyman, S.R. (Eds.). (1988). *Innovations in clinical practice: A source book* (Vol. 7). Sarasota, FL: Professional Resource Exchange.

Kratochwill, T.R., & Morris, R.J. (1991). *The practice of child therapy* (2nd ed.). New York: Pergamon.

Kratochwill, T.R., & Morris, R.J. (Eds.). (1993). *Handbook of psychotherapy with children and adolescents*. Needham Heights, MA: Allyn & Bacon.

Lahey, B.B., & Kazdin, A.E. (Eds.). (1989). *Advances in clinical child psychology* (Vol. 12). New York: Plenum.

Lankton, C.H., & Lankton, S.R. (1989). *Tales of enchantment: Goal-oriented metaphors for adults and children in therapy*. New York: Brunner/Mazel.

Lewis, M. (Ed.). (1991). *Child and adolescent psychiatry: A comprehensive textbook*. Baltimore, MD: Williams & Wilkins.

Lewis, M., & Miller, S.M. (Eds.). (1990). *Handbook of developmental psychopathology: Perspectives in developmental psychology*. New York: Plenum.

MacLean, G., & Rappen, U. (1991). *Hermine-Hellmuth: Her life and work*. New York: Routledge.

Mandell, J.G., Damon, L., Castoldo, P.C., Tauber, E.S., Monise, L., Larsen, N.F., & Hall-Marley, S. (1989). *Group treatment for sexually abused children*. New York: Guilford.

Mash, E.J., & Barkley, R.A. (1989). *Treatment of childhood disorders*. New York: Guilford.

Mash, E.J., & Barkley, R. (Eds.). (1998). *Treatment of childhood disorders* (2nd ed.). New York: Guilford.

Matson, J.L. (Ed.). (1988). *Handbook of treatment approaches in childhood psychopathology: Applied clinical psychology*. New York: Plenum.

Miller, A., & Eller-Miller, E. (1989). *From ritual to repertoire: A cognitive-developmental systems approach with behavior-disordered children*. New York: Wiley & Sons.

Morris, R.J., & Kratochwill, T.R. (Eds.). (1983). *The practice of child therapy*. New York: Pergamon.

Noshpitz, J.D. (Ed.). (1979). *Basic handbook of child psychiatry* (Vol. 3: *Therapeutic interventions*). New York: Basic Books.

Ollendick, T.H., & Hersen, M. (Eds.). (1989). *Handbook of child psychopathology* (2nd ed.). New York: Plenum.

Parkes, C.M., Stevenson-Hinde, J., & Marris, P. (Eds.). (1991). *Attachment across the life cycle*. London: Tavistock/Routledge.

Prout, N.T., & Brown, D.T. (Eds.). (1983). *Counseling and psychotherapy with children and adolescents: Theory and practice for school and clinic settings*. Brandon, VT: Clinical Psychology Publishing.

Rapoport, R.N. (1987). *New interventions for children and youth: Action-research approaches*. Cambridge: Cambridge University Press.

Schaefer, C.E. (Ed.). (1988). *Innovative interventions in child and adolescent therapy*. New York: Wiley & Sons.

Schaefer, C.E., Briemeister, J.M., & Fitton, M.E. (Eds.). (1984). *Family therapy technique for problem behaviors of children and teenagers*. San Francisco: Jossey-Bass.

Schaefer, C.E., Johnson, L., & Wherry, J.N. (Eds.). (1982). *Group therapies for children and youth: Principles and practices of group treatment*. San Francisco: Jossey-Bass.

Schaefer, C.E., & Millman, H.L. (1977). *Therapies for children: A handbook of Effective treatments for problem behaviors*. San Francisco: Jossey-Bass.

Schaefer, C.E., Millman, H.L., Sichel, S.M., & Zwilling, J.R. (Eds.). (1986). *Advances in therapies for children*. San Francisco: Jossey-Bass.

Schaefer, C.E., & O'Conner, K.J. (Eds.). (1983). *Handbook of play therapy*. New York: Wiley & Sons.

Seigel, E.V. (1991). *The psychodynamic treatment of affectively disturbed children*. Hillsdale, NJ: Analytic Press.

Shirk, S.R. (Ed.). (1988). *Cognitive development and child psychotherapy: Perspectives in developmental psychology*. New York: Plenum.

Spiegel, S. (1989). *Personality, psychopathology, psychotherapy: Theoretical and clinical perspectives*. New York: Columbia University Press.

Strayhorn, J.M. (1988). *The competent child: An approach to psychotherapy and preventive mental health*. New York: Guilford.

Trad, P.V. (1990). *Treating suicide-like behavior in a preschooler*. Madison, CT: International Universities Press.

Varma, V.P. (Ed.). (1990). *The management of children with emotional and behavioral difficulties*. London: Routledge.

Wester, W.C., II, & O'Grady, D.J. (Eds.). (1991). *Clinical hypnosis with children*. New York: Brunner/Mazel.

Wright, L., Everett, F., & Roisman, L. (1986). *Experiential psychotherapy with children*. Baltimore, MD: Johns Hopkins University Press

Appendix B

Methodology
in a Nutshell

DR. IRVING QUICKIE[1]

Methodology: Quick Overview
Rationale behind It All
Basic Major Designs
Commonly Used Control Groups
Guidelines for Making Your Study Great
Quickie's Rules
Tell Yourself a Story
Answer the Questions
Final Comments

Some psychologists spend much of their lives studying and writing about methodology, and as a result there are always lots of books written on the topic (Kazdin, 1998b; Kendall, Butcher, & Holmbeck, 1999; Rosenthal & Rosnow, 1991). Think about it; would any rational person want to spend much of life that way? I wouldn't. At the same time, methodology is important if one is a scientist, so one cannot neglect its many critical lessons. Admittedly, it is useful to grasp its many lessons but equally essential to avoid the drudgery of long hours, life-long study, and extensive reading. You may think this is impossible—like it *seems* impossible to eat rich desserts without gaining weight. But it *is* possible (e.g., do not swallow, use a fistula), and this appendix conveys how.

In the material that follows, my methodology course is presented in full. Several professionals have mastered this material as part of my workshops. While no one from one of my workshops has ever been able to get one of their studies published, no one has been sued either. In the United States, this is a terrific accomplishment. (Also, publication is slightly different from good science and my Instant Publication workshop is designed to address that topic. Be on the lookout for my combined 2-day workshop, "Methodology and Publication in the Social and Not-so Social Sciences." This is 2 days of continuing education credit but the whole business lasts 3 hours—$1\frac{1}{2}$ without lunch.)

METHODOLOGY: QUICK OVERVIEW

Rationale behind It All

We conduct research to uncover relations between variables that otherwise could not be readily detected and to test hypothesized relations. Without controlled research, potential relations between variables are usually too difficult to decipher. Research methods serve as a tool to help unravel the relations of interest. *Methodology* consists of those principles, practices, and procedures used in the study to help draw inferences about the variables of interest. *Research design* as part of these practices consists of the ways in which the conditions are arranged so that the specific comparisons of interest or predictions can be tested. The design helps to structure and to simplify the situation in which the influence of many variables, often operating simultaneously, can be separated from the variable(s) of interest to the investigator. Experimental designs are often used in which conditions are carefully controlled and varied by the investigator to maximize clarity. Without such simplification and isolation of variables, many, if not an unlimited number, interpretations could explain the results. Research is designed to help rule out or make implausible different interpretations that might explain a particular phenomenon. From a methodological standpoint, the better the design of a study, the more implausible it makes explanations of the results that compete with the explanation the investigator wishes to advance.

The purpose of research is to reach well-founded (i.e., valid) conclusions about the effects of a given intervention and the conditions under which it operates. Several domains of influences can interfere with drawing valid inferences. The main influences have been codified as types of experimental validity (Cook & Campbell, 1979). Four types of experimental validity have been identified: internal, external, construct, and statistical conclusion validity. Table B.1 lists each type of validity and some of the problems that can threaten each. The task is to use methodology, research design, and statistical evaluation to

Table B.1   Types of Experimental Validity and Questions They Address

TYPE OF VALIDITY	QUESTIONS AND ISSUES ADDRESSED
Internal Validity	To what extent can the intervention, rather than extraneous influences, be considered to account for the results, changes, or group differences? Validity is threatened when the results can be explained by history, maturation, repeated testing, changes in the measure in some way, regression toward the mean, selection differences/biases among groups, attrition, special influences affecting one group but not another, diffusion of treatment, and special treatment or reactions of control participants.

continued

Table B.1 (*continued*)

TYPE OF VALIDITY	QUESTIONS AND ISSUES ADDRESSED
External Validity	To what extent can the results be generalized to people, settings, times, measures, and characteristics other than those in this particular experimental arrangement? Validity is threatened when the results are restricted because of special characteristics of the sample, stimulus conditions of the experiment or setting, reactivity (awareness of participating in a study or of the measurement procedures), the way in which the intervention was presented (e.g., in the context of multiple treatments), novelty effects, and test sensitization (the results due in part to the measures that influenced receptivity to the intervention).
Construct Validity	Given that the intervention was responsible for change, what specific aspect(s) was the causal agent; that is, what is the conceptual basis (construct) underlying the effect? Validity is threatened when group differences could be explained by differential attention and contact with the subjects, experimenter expectancies, cues of the experimental situation, single operations (e.g., one therapist) and narrow stimulus sampling that cannot be separated from the intervention.
Statistical Conclusion Validity	To what extent is a relation shown, demonstrated, or evident, and how well can the investigation detect effects if they exist? Validity is threatened by low statistical power, variability in the procedures, subject heterogeneity, unreliability of the measures, restrictive or lenient error rates due to multiple tests.

Many readers no doubt would like more detail. See Cook & Campbell (1979), Kazdin (1998b), Rosenthal & Rosnow (1991).

address, rule out, or make implausible many alternative interpretations that these types of validity represent.

Threats to validity vary in their subtlety and ease of control. For example, internal validity threats include a variety of influences that might explain those differences the investigator attributes to the intervention. Historical events, maturational processes, repeated testing (where there is a pre- and posttreatment assessment), regression toward the mean, and related factors lead to changes over time and possible group differences. These factors generally can be controlled experimentally by assigning subjects randomly to groups, assessing subjects in the same way, and including a group that does not have the intervention so that influences occurring over time and experiences can be separated from the intervention. These are rather basic requirements and are met in most studies of psychotherapy.

Other types of validity raise more subtle influences. For example, statistical conclusion validity refers to those factors related to evaluation of the data. Many such issues such as selection of measures, sample size, and selection of statistical tests too can influence conclusions. Each type of validity raises critical points; not all potential threats to validity can be addressed in a given study because attention to one often has direct implications for another. For example, selecting homogeneous subjects (rather than all who volunteer to receive treatment), delivering and monitoring treatment in a rigorous way, and using therapists who are carefully and uniformly trained in the treatments may provide an excellent test of the treatment. As rigor, control, and monitoring procedures increase, the generality of the results (external validity) may be raised as an issue. Can the results be obtained when certain constraints, controls, and rigor are relaxed? The answer may be important depending on the purpose and research questions underlying the original study. In any given study of therapy, the priority accorded a particular type of validity and threat to validity may vary. For this reason, methodology requires appreciation of the underlying concepts rather than application of design prescriptions and practices.

Types of experimental validity also illustrate the critical interplay between methodological and substantive issues in psychotherapy research. Consider the notion of construct validity, as highlighted in table B.1. An investigator may propose that cognitive therapy is effective for depression and complete a study comparing this treatment with a no-treatment control. At the end of the study, assume that the treatment group is significantly (statistically) different from the no-treatment group. The investigator may wish to discuss the impact of cognitive therapy and perhaps even how cognitive changes lead to changes in depression. With the usual procedures and controls (e.g., random assignment, group equivalence prior to treatment), the threats to internal validity are largely controlled. Given the design, issues of construct validity (interpretation of the basis for the differences) emerge. The treatment group may have changed for a variety of reasons (relationship with the therapist, catharsis, behavioral "homework" assignments) that have little to do with cognitions. Other groups added to the design (that include these other components so their impact can be separately evaluated) and various assessment procedures (the study of cognitive changes over the course of treatment and their relation to outcome) could clarify construct validity. In short, the substantive questions and conclusions about treatment very much depend on the control conditions and assessment procedures of the study.

Basic Major Designs

The design involves how the conditions are arranged and presented to the participants. Almost all studies of treatment are based on group designs and are true experiments. *Group designs* are—guess—when there is more than one group in the study and the results are based on comparing groups. Typically, statistical comparisons are made by testing whether groups that received different treatments or different treatment and control conditions differ statistically. *True experiments* include all designs in which the investigator has maximum control over the situation and can assign participants to conditions randomly. When, how, and to whom treatment is delivered can be controlled. In group experimental designs, random assignment is pivotal because it increases the likelihood that groups are equivalent on a number of variables that might influence the results. When groups are compared after receiving treatment or control conditions, any differences do not likely reflect differences evident before treatment was given. That is, groups probably are equal on all sorts of things that could threaten validity. Sometimes conditions can be assigned randomly to settings such as clinics or schools, rather than assigning subjects to conditions, and that works too.

Usually, group designs that are true experiments include administration of a pretest in which all cases are assessed on a battery of measures. Participants are assigned to conditions, complete treatment, and then complete the posttreatment assessment. The investigator can compare groups on the pretreatment assessment to determine whether they are equivalent. A true experiment does not require measures provided at pretreatment, but this is the most common version.

True experiment is a term used in research in general. In the context of intervention research (treatment, prevention), *randomized controlled clinical trial* (or RCT) is a term used for a group design and true experiment. An RCT is considered to provide the strongest basis for drawing inferences about treatment. This design is used routinely in treatment research for all sorts of disorders (depression, cancer, and heart disease) and all sorts of treatments (psychotherapy, drugs, and surgery).

Well, if there are group designs and true experiments, this means there must be something else.[2] There is. In addition to group designs, there are *single-case designs*. These designs are characterized by investigation of a given individual, a few individuals, or one group over time. There are many variations (ABA designs, multiple-baseline designs, changing-criterion design), and many are really useful for evaluating treatment. Because these are true experiments, they can lead to strong inferences. There are many books on these designs (Barlow & Hersen, 1984; Kazdin, 1982; Krishef, 1991).

The underlying approach toward research for group and single-case designs is identical, namely, to implement conditions that permit valid inferences about the independent variable. However, single-case research accomplishes this goal somewhat differently. Typically, one or a few subjects are studied. The dependent measures of interest are administered repeatedly over time (e.g., days or weeks). The manner in which the independent variable is implemented is examined in relation to the data pattern for the subject or group of subjects over time.

Single-case designs can be used to evaluate the impact of a given intervention or multiple interventions experimentally. Although single-case experimental designs can look at the effects of treatment with the individual case, the designs can be readily extended to handle large groups of subjects. Like group designs, there are many different single-case designs, with their own requirements, advantages, and obstacles. Methodologically, these designs are every bit as rigorous as any group experiment in ruling out threats to experimental validity. Unfortunately, the designs are underused in the context of treatment research and clinical practice (see Hayes, 1981; Kazdin, 1993b).

In addition to true experiments, there are *quasi-experiments*. Occasionally the investigator cannot control all features that characterize true experiments. Some facet of the study such as the assignment of subjects to conditions or of conditions to settings (e.g., to schools, communities) cannot be randomized. Quasi-experiments are designs in which the conditions of true experiments are approximated (Campbell & Stanley, 1963). For example, an investigator may compare two different treatments (e.g., special new and improved treatment versus standard treatment), but they are conducted at two different clinics. Families cannot be randomly assigned because the clinics draw on different segments and locations within the community. Even if similar screening criteria to recruit cases for the study exist at the different clinics, this is not the same as random assignment.

Quasi-experiments often have several advantages because they are in settings or under circumstances where key hypotheses need to be tested. However, they are obviously not as strong as RCTs. The investigator conducting a quasi-experiment has to be more methodologically skilled and knowledgeable because the strength of the designs depends more heavily on using additional controls, comparison conditions, and data analyses to extract valid inferences. Make no mistake, quasi-experiments can draw truly strong inferences. In fact, most sciences (e.g., astronomy, geology, economics, anthropology, sociology, political science, and proctology) come up with new knowledge without using true experiments, random assignment, and the like. Quasi-experiments can be important.

Commonly Used Control Groups

Control groups include some conditions to address one or more interpretations of the results that the investigator wishes to eliminate. These groups usually address some of the threats to validity—especially internal or construct validity. There are four commonly used groups in treatment studies: no-treatment, waiting list, nonspecific treatment, and standard or routine treatment groups.

First, in the *no-treatment control group*, participants assigned to this group receive—you guessed it—no treatment during the period in which other participants are receiving treatment. Treated subjects usually receive pretreatment assessment, treatment, and posttreatment assessment. No-treatment subjects receive only the two assessments. Thus, if the passage of time or merely taking the measures on two occasions, before and after, leads to improvement, the no-treatment group will control for this effect. Two assumptions are made: (1) participants were initially assigned randomly to treatment or no-treatment groups so that the groups did not start out differently, and (2) the time between pretreatment and posttreatment assessment was the same for the two groups. Assume for a moment that the treatment group shows a much better outcome than the no-treatment group. The no-treatment group provides sort of a baseline against which treatment can be evaluated. The group is interesting for other reasons as well. Does a no-treatment group improve? Perhaps it does for some clinical problems more than others. This is useful to learn too. Use of a no-treatment group as a basis for comparison permits the investigator to address the most fundamental question about a treatment. But the group is difficult to use with genuine clinical samples and raises ethical issues because treatment is withheld.

Second, a variation of the no-treatment group is the *waiting-list control group*. This group completes preassessment and postassessment and receives no treatment during the intervening period. So far, of course, this is just the same as the no-treatment group. But, this group is promised that after the second assessment is completed ("post" treatment), treatment will be provided. This group handles some of the ethical concerns of the no-treatment group. Instead of not providing treatment, the group has delayed treatment. Also, methodologically, a waiting-list group raises other good and bad news. The good news is that after this group finally receives treatment, measures can be repeated to see if the group changed. Thus, there are three assessment periods for this group: pretreatment assessment (followed by no treatment), "posttreatment" assessment (and the end of the no-treatment period; after this assessment treatment is now given) and postassessment 2 (after the treatment is completed). If treatment is effective, one would expect little or no change between the first two assessments and a lot of change between the last two assessments. The downside of using this group is when the investigator wants to evaluate follow-up. At follow-up this group now is in the treatment condition, and one can no longer compare treated and nontreated cases.

Third, a *nonspecific treatment control group,* also called *attention-placebo control group,* is sometimes used. This group is designed to control for many common factors associated with coming to treatment such as attending sessions, believing one will get better, and hearing a therapist say or do good or reasonable things. The group is not intended to provide "real" treatment, but to give the appearance of a "real" treatment—interesting distinction. Usually the investigator invents some procedure that may seem credible but is not intended to produce therapeutic change. Examples might include just talking about daily activities, listening to tapes of some kind, and completing some bogus procedures or tasks. These are presented to participants as if they were therapy and designed to improve the problem. The group is intended to address construct validity issues and help the investigator explain why treatment does and does not work. If the treatment group is better than the nonspecific treatment control group, so the thinking goes, then there must be something quite special about the treatment. Merely attending sessions or believing one is receiving therapy is not enough.

There are problems with this group. The main one is no universal agreement about what a fake treatment would be and hence what to give to this group. In fact, in designing a fake treatment that is believable to the participants, one has likely stepped on the conceptual toes of several colleagues who consider the "fake" therapy a *real* intervention. In addition, a major view of therapy is that nonspecific features *are* the therapeutic ingredients—meeting with a therapist, hearing an explanation about one's problems, and working on a plan of action to solve them could be the essence of treatment (Frank & Frank, 1991). For individuals in crisis or experiencing stress, engaging in procedures delivered by a credible source (e.g., therapist) might mobilize hope and initiate a process of therapeutic change.

Not many investigators like this group. There are obvious ethical issues in providing a "fake" treatment to subjects. How to present informed consent to this group also is problematic. Can you imagine telling the prospective client that "one of the conditions to which you may be assigned is not a real treatment, but we have worked hard to fool you"? Me neither. Actually, the next group is an alternative way to address and to control for the influence of common factors associated with treatment.

Finally, *standard care*, also referred to as *routine treatment* or *treatment as usual*, is often used as a control condition. This group refers to the treatment that is routinely provided for the particular clinical problem under investigation. For example, if the investigator wishes to treat childhood depression or adolescent substance abuse, he or she finds out locally what the usual treatment is (e.g., in local clinical settings or nationwide) and then uses this intervention as part of the study. The interest of the investigator is in some other treatment, so the standard intervention serves as a comparison. Standard care controls for changes over time (and threats to internal validity to which no-treatment and waiting-list control groups are directed) and also the nonspecific factors associated with treatment (to which the nonspecific treatment control group is directed). Standard treatment participants come to treatment, receive a "real" treatment, and any related components that can lead to change as part of the treatment (e.g., relationship with a therapist).

Standard care is a great comparison group because it overcomes most of the problems raised by each of the previous groups. First and foremost, the group handles the main ethical issues mentioned previously. (It raises a new ethical issue—what is used as standard care in many places might be very hard to justify.) No treatment is withheld, nor is a fake treatment being couched as a real treatment. Also, use of the group answers a critical treatment question: Is my new and improved treatment better than business as usual (i.e., standard treatment)? Finally, routine treatment is a much better baseline for evaluating interventions than no treatment. If a family seeks treatment, the standard treatment is what they are likely to get. We want to know if standard treatment leads to any changes and if some other treatment is any better.

Methodology, like so much of life, is a matter of trade-offs. So there are obstacles in using standard treatments as a comparison group. To begin, standard treatment is actually unstandardized. In clinic settings, there is no monitoring, regular supervision, treatment manual, treatment integrity, and so on. Standard or routine care is an umbrella term for "what we do here" (at this clinic) or, worse, "what I do" (in private practice). In an experiment, the investigator will have difficulty in specifying the standard treatment so that others might replicate the procedure. Routine care at many clinics is a conglomeration of many different elements of different treatments, as the heart may prompt. Others could not replicate this standard care. Those who would want to replicate that might want to attend a few sessions of MA (Masochists' Anonymous) in advance.

A second and related problem is the variability in administering this treatment. There is a lot of leeway among therapists administering routine care in terms of the range of procedures that are used, how they are used, and in what proportions. Variable procedures can easily undermine an investigation and obscure treatment differences (i.e., reduce the likelihood of statistically significant differences) when such differences really exist.

A third problem is that when this condition is used, the study often is a quasi- rather than true-experiment. In an investigation, therapists at a clinic who do the "what we do here" treatment are compared with other therapists who do the main treatment being evaluated. In this situation, it is often hard to determine whether group differences are due to therapist, setting, or treatment differences. If standard care is one of the conditions in a true experiment, this concern is of course surmounted.

GUIDELINES FOR MAKING YOUR STUDY GREAT

The above is background but is too abstract to help you do your study. There are three sets of guidelines presented below that are intended to improve your treatment studies and, if I may say so myself, to make them great. Although they overlap slightly, use of any two of them is guaranteed to improve the quality of your research. (In fact, in my workshops for the past 10 years, I am so sure of this that I provide a full money-back guarantee to any one who has taken my workshop gratis and has applied these guidelines to a longitudinal study lasting at least 12 years. The success of these guidelines is a matter of public record; after 8 years of litigation, I have not had to return a cent.) Remember, of the three guidelines, use two. (Some workshop attendees have used all three guidelines, and their studies have been rejected for publication for being too well designed for the journals to which they were submitted.)

Quickie's Rules

The first set of guidelines consists of several simple rules to follow in thinking about, planning, executing, and writing up the results of your study. Table B.2 presents these rules. An acronym can be formed from the first word of each rule to provide a clever mnemonic to remember these rules—that acronym is TMTE (pronounced "Tum-tee"). (The reader will immediately recognize that this term is drawn from the mythological god Humpty Tumtee, who was responsible for all methodology and data evaluation in the underworld.) The rules are straightforward.

Tell Yourself a Story

Another set of guidelines begins by acknowledging that a study—an investigation—is a story. That is, it has a beginning and an end and a consistent theme

Table B.2   Quickie's Rules for Improving Your Study

STEP		DIRECTIONS
T	1. Tell the What and How	Operationalize everything and be explicit about any working definitions, what you will do (or in the write-up, what you did) and how you do it. This will make explicit many issues, including key concepts or constructs and whether some are better than others. Also, others need to know the underlying concepts and what they mean in your study.
M	2. Measure as Much as You Can	Carefully assess to describe the sample and to evaluate what happened during (characteristics of the procedures) and after treatment (outcome). Measure components to describe (what, who) and to explain (why, how), and think of your measures as serving one or more of these purposes.
T	3. Tell the Why	Give the rationale for all decisions, including the hypotheses as well as selection of the design, sample, measures, and conditions. All should serve the purpose of the study. Explaining why is the conceptual glue that binds different facets of the design. If there is no well-founded rationale, have a compelling back-up excuse; otherwise, rethink the study.
E	4. Evaluate and Analyze Only What You Need to	Stay focused on the analyses of the results—test specific hypotheses and predictions—and do not wander or give all the data analyses and address unrelated topics. Who needs it? If there is some provocative or fascinating accidental finding, toss it in, of course, but keep the original focus clear.

or set of themes throughout. Planning, executing, and writing up a study all reflect the story. Doing a good study is telling a good story. Many of us are not good storytellers, but we could be if much of the story was written and we had to fill in key parts of the story. Another way to design a good study is to tell the story.

Table B.3 presents the story. Here is how it is used. Take the story in a private room and you can talk out loud without being threatened with hospitalization or heavy medication. As you talk, merely complete the multiple-choice questions (circle the choices in parentheses) or fill in the options (as indicated by a blank space underlined in the text) to complete the story. The completed story will consist of a well-designed study.

The storytelling procedure is designed to be self-administered privately. The storytelling procedure has been useful for extremely shy and withdrawn individuals who complete this in the privacy of their own homes or extremely extraverted and outgoing individuals who do this in the presence of others (colleagues or advisors). Private and public uses seem to work equally well, although admittedly the right comparative study has not been done.

Table B.3   Tell a Story: Guidelines for a Well-Designed Study

Directions: The story is designed to be read aloud by the investigator in a private setting. Read each sentence slowly and complete the questions. There are multiple-choice questions, indicated by parentheses, where you are required to circle or underline one of the options and fill-in questions, indicated by a blank underline, where you are required to write in what you will do. Years of use of these guidelines have shown that the quality of the final study is deleteriously affected if the answer format is violated (i.e., if the investigator writes in answers for the multiple-choice parts and circles the blank underlines). Please begin reading slowly and mellifluously now.

Well, I am finally going to begin a study. This is going to be an important study because other studies that even come close to this have not _____ [fill in]. Probably this study, if I ever get it done, will contribute to (the knowledge base, science, humanity, my career [circle one]) in at least two ways: (1) _____ and (2)_____, and I know I am being modest. The field is really fortunate to have me to do this study. I am a pretty amazing (gal, guy, person with an identity problem). Basically, I have these (2, 3, 4) (predictions, hypotheses) and they are:

   1) _____
   2) _____ [add 3, 4 as needed]

I even imagine how I shall analyze the data to test these. Probably to test these I shall use _____ [list some statistical tests or analysis]. Of course, this is just tentative, but I am pretty cool to even think of the data analyses at this point.

The subjects for this study are going to be _____. I chose this sample, not because they are just convenient or because my advisor or colleague has them around—everyone does that and I actually was tempted. But hey, no, not me, *these* subjects are important because _____. I am going to use lots of subjects and in fact my sample size (God willing) will be _____. Of course, I did

continued

not pull this number out of the air. I looked at a book on power. The first book (*The Power Broker*) did not help, but one on statistics did. I estimate I will need a sample of this size to have a chance to find differences if they exist. To be honest, I hope this sample helps me find differences even if they don't exist. A big sample can't hurt either of these goals. For the subjects to be *included* they have to meet these (2, 3, 4) criteria: (1) _____, (2) _____, and (3) _____. I will *exclude* them if they meet these (2, 3, 4) criteria: (1) _____, (2) _____, and (3) _____ or have an "attitude problem." To measure these criteria, I will look at them, ask them a few questions, or give them these measures _____.

Speaking about measures, I am going to use a lot. Actually, I care about these constructs: _____, _____ [add _____ as needed]. For the first construct, these measures will be used _____; for the second construct, these measures will be used _____ (etc.). I am also throwing in these measures because they (are interesting, are used a lot in this area, may explain why the results come out the way they will, are being a pushed by my advisor, colleague, mother).

The main treatment I will be using is _____. I will be using (guidelines, manual, book on treatment) that I (got from a researcher who developed this treatment, a credible imitator; or I invented myself). This is a reasonable version of the treatment. Treatment will be given to participants for a period of _____ hour(s), for _____ weeks for about _____ sessions per week. I am going to train the therapists, establish criteria to decide when they are trained, and then monitor the delivery of treatment during the study. How am I going to do the monitoring? Well, I plan to _____ and _____. I will get some measures of treatment integrity to see that my efforts are not in vain and to see if I or anyone else ought to believe the results. I plan on a measure that consists of _____.

Oh. I almost forgot. This will be a (between-group study, single-case study) and I plan on having [fill in no.] _____ (groups or subjects). As applicable, if a group study, the treatment groups include _____. There will be (0, 1, 2) control groups and these include _____, _____. Many people just throw in a control group without being to clear as to why. Not me. My control groups are designed to control for threats to _____ validity and of course are essential to test the hypotheses.

Here is what happens to a subject when he or she comes to this project. First, we give a big (interview, welcoming speech, assessment battery) then of course seek informed consent. Yes, my study has already been approved by the ethics committee and I have the forms finally resolved to pass muster. My God, getting the wording right and final approval for the consent forms was (bizarre, no picnic, a breeze because I copied my advisor's forms). Then the subject will (complete, come back for) assessments. I will then assign subjects (randomly, as the heart may prompt) to conditions. Treatment begins, is then completed, and then followed by posttreatment assessment (right after the last session, on the same day, within one week).

As is my style, I shall probably analyze the data with every statistic I have ever learned and no doubt click my mouse on a few that I have no idea about. Hey—

continued

Table B.3 (*continued*)
<hr>

how can one learn without trying new things? But I shall provide very specific tests of my hypotheses with focused statistical tests and present these so the reader can see the hypothesis, the tests, and my conclusions. Clarity is not my forte, and people have been on me for that. If the results show anything else interesting, including possible confounds, I shall present that too but probably sequester that (whatever that means) from the section that gives the main findings.

There will be so much richness and depth to my study, and my work in general, that I probably ought to begin my discussion of the results with a brief overview or statement of the main findings. Then I shall try to (describe, explain) a key finding or two in more detail. As soon as I can, I shall make comments about (how this relates to, builds on) other work. If there is any (theory, other areas of research outside my topic) to which I can relate the study, I shall (toss, squeeze) that in as well.

I also will make a few comments about the limitations of my study. Given how I have designed this study and my own personal skills, this could be a very brief section. But no study is perfect and real limitations are always present. In writing this section, I shall try not to (get too defensive, righteous about how I chose to design the study). In the remote chance that there *are* serious limitations of the study, more likely than not I shall (blame my advisor, remind readers of my difficult childhood, use a small font when this section is run off on my printer).

Finally, if space allows, I shall talk about the next study that ought to be done to build on my work. This future work ought to be an important study and not merely a test of generality to a different sample or setting. Something really (meaty, inspiring, conceptually interesting) in this paragraph will suggest a new "story" that needs to be told. Who knows, maybe I'll even (do that study, rest on my laurels) after completing this study.

The End
<hr>

Answer the Questions

The third and final set of guidelines is in the form of questions. Frankly, I prefer this method the least, because I always get defensive when questions are fired at me. Also, all the questions to follow are essay or short-answer questions. This is intimidating. The previous (tell a story method) has multiple-choice and fill-in questions and is more in keeping with my own ability. Nevertheless, the answer-the-question-method is great all by itself, and my personal limitations ought not to hamper use by others.

A well-designed study has to answer many questions. Table B.4 presents the key questions. Some of the answers are obvious. So, for example, for the question that asks about who the subjects are, the investigator cannot simply say, "I don't know" and go on to the next question. Also, the question about why this study was done or the purposes of the study has some wrong answers (e.g., "no one has done this before" or "I think this is an important clinical problem"). Compelling answers are needed. The advantage of the questions is that they raise most of the issues that need to be adequately resolved. Once they are adequately resolved and addressed, the study ought to be terrific.

Table B.4 Questions to Guide Planning a Treatment Study

Directions: Answer each of the questions on a separate sheet. They are short-answer essay questions and answers like "true," "false," "yes," or "no," are frowned upon.

PURPOSE AND GOALS OF THE STUDY

What is the background and context for the study?

What in current theory, research, or clinical work makes this study useful, important, or of interest?

What is different or special about the study in focus, methods, or design to address a need in the area?

Is the rationale clear regarding the constructs (independent and dependent variables) to be assessed?

What *specifically* are the purposes, predictions, or hypotheses?

Are there ancillary or exploratory goals that can be distinguished as well?

METHODS

Participants

Who are the participants and how many of them are there in this study?

Why was this sample selected in light of the research goals?

How was this sample obtained, recruited, and selected?

What are the subject and demographic characteristics of the sample (e.g., gender, age, ethnicity, race, socioeconomic status)?

What, if any, inclusion and exclusion criteria were invoked, that is, selection rules to obtain participants?

How many of those subjects eligible or recruited actually were selected and participated in the study?

Was informed consent solicited? How and from whom (e.g., child and parent), if special populations were used?

Design

What is the design (e.g., group, true-experiment) and how does the design relate to the goals?

How were participants assigned to groups or conditions?

How many groups were included in the design?

How are the groups similar and different?

Why are these groups critical to address the questions of interest?

Procedures

Where was the study conducted (setting)?

What measures, materials, equipment, or apparatus were used?

What is the chronological sequence of events to which participants were exposed?

What intervals elapsed between different aspects of the study (e.g., assessment, treatment, follow-up)?

If assessments involved novel measures created for this study, what data can be brought to bear regarding pertinent types of reliability and validity?

What checks were made to ensure that the conditions were carried out as intended (treatment integrity procedures, measures)?

What other information does one need to know to understand how participants were treated and what conditions were provided?

continued

254

Table B.4 (*continued*)

<hr>

RESULTS

What are the primary measures and data upon which the hypotheses or predictions depend?

What analyses are to be used and how specifically do these address the original hypotheses and purposes?

Are the assumptions of the data analyses met?

If multiple tests are used, what means are provided to control error rates (increased likelihood of finding significant differences in light of using many tests)?

If more than one group is delineated (e.g., through experimental manipulation or subject selection), are they similar on variables that might otherwise explain the results (e.g., diagnosis, age)?

Are data missing due to incomplete measures (not filled out completely by the participants) or due to loss of subjects? If so, how are these handled in the data analyses?

Are there ancillary analyses that might further inform the primary analyses or exploratory analyses that might stimulate further work?

DISCUSSION

What are the major findings of the study?

Specifically, how do these findings add to research and support, refute, or inform current theory?

What alternative interpretations, theoretical or methodological, can be placed on the data?

What limitations or qualifiers are necessary given methodological and design issues?

What research follows from the study to move the field forward?

Specifically what ought to be done next (e.g., next study, career change)?

<hr>

FINAL COMMENTS

A well-designed study means that the question(s) was important, the methods get at the question in a reasonable way, and the analyses and interpretations relate directly to the questions. This means that there is a common focus throughout. This is why it is useful to ask oneself throughout, why am I doing this? Once answered, the next question is, will this way of doing it serve the goal?

Methodology can be abstract and otherwise uninteresting. Guidelines were provided to help design a good study and included three methods: Useful Rules, Tell Yourself a Story, and Answer the Questions. As a reminder, use any two of the methods for designing your study. Why two? Because a basic lesson of methodology is that any one method is likely to be imperfect; two or more begin to overcome the limitations of any one method. Good luck in your research, but now you do not need to rely so much on luck.

Notes

Chapter 1

1. The case has many nuances that make its historical use as the basis for the development or effectiveness of talk therapy a bit odd. For example, talk therapy was combined with hypnosis and rather heavy doses of medication (chloral hydrate, a sleep-inducing agent) used on several occasions when talk did not seem to work (see Dawes, 1994). Thus, the therapy included more than just talk. Also, the subsequent hospitalization of Anna O raises clear questions about the effectiveness of the combined talk-hypnosis-medication treatment. Yet the historical influence of the example still stands. There is, of course, no reason to select case examples from any particular treatment approach to convey the impact of a dramatic case in the absence of consistent empirical support. The famous case of Little Albert, in which fear was induced in an 11-month-old infant, advanced the view that fears could be conditioned (learned) (Watson & Rayner, 1920). The case had great impact even though there was great difficulty in replicating the effects of this demonstration (see Kazdin, 1978b).

2. The focus of the book is on therapy for children and adolescents. Throughout the book, the term *children* will be used generically to refer to both children and adolescents. I will address age and stage of development more specifically and use separate terms as appropriate.

3. The terms *client* and *patient* are occasionally distinguished in discussions of psychotherapy. The differences reflect varying approaches and views of the entire enterprise of therapy, the nature of the problems that participants experience (e.g., problems of living or mental "illnesses"), and the manner in which they should be conceptualized and treated. I use the terms interchangeably to refer to the person who comes to or is brought to treatment and is identified as needing intervention.

Chapter 2

1. *Prevalence* refers to the number of persons with the problem (e.g., psychiatric disorder) at a given point in time. *Incidence* refers to the number of new cases within a given period of time. Prevalence is highlighted here to convey the scope of the mental disorders and other problems among children and adolescents.

2. Occasionally, I shall refer to a clinic where I work, the Yale Child Conduct Clinic, an outpatient treatment service for children and families. Children seen at the clinic are between 2 and 13 and are referred for oppositional, aggressive, and antisocial behavior. Treatments provided at the clinic include variations of cognitive problem-solving skills training and parent management training (see Kazdin, 1996c).

3. A *syndrome* is a constellation or group of symptoms that go together. For example, major depression includes many individual symptoms such as sad affect, loss of interest in activities, changes in eating and sleep, feelings of worthlessness, and so on. Depression can be delineated as a syndrome because a particular set of symptoms go together. *Subsyndromal* means that individuals may have only some of the symptoms that define a disorder and do not meet diagnostic criteria. In some sense, one could say that all people who do not meet diagnostic criteria are subsyndromal because they likely have some symptoms of some disorders to some degree. Yet the point of identifying subsyndromes is to delineate individuals who experience impairment or untoward consequences even though they do not quite meet the diagnostic criteria. This delineation assumes special importance because the cutoff point for meeting diagnostic criteria is rather arbitrary.

4. Status offenses are usually referred to as delinquent *acts*, index offenses are usually referred to as *crimes* or *criminal activity,* with the implication of greater severity of the act. *Offense* is a more generic term used to encompass any of these illegal acts (U.S. Congress, 1991).

Chapter 3

1. *Approach* (general conceptual orientation) and *treatment* (the intervention used in therapy) are two of the three concepts often used in describing therapy. The third concept is therapy *technique*, which refers to concrete and more circumscribed practices that are applied. For example, in child therapy, using play, role-playing, or games in a session might be referred to as technique. Although techniques often are associated with particular treatments and approaches, they often have general applicability. Thus, the use of games and play is a technique that spans different treatments and indeed different approaches. The terms *approach, treatment,* and *technique* are not used carefully or consistently among mental health professionals. The most consistent of the terms probably is treatment, which usually conveys much about the conceptual orientation and the procedures or techniques used to produce therapeutic change. If the reader is slightly confused, then he or she may have grasped the field perfectly.

Chapter 4

1. It is important to mention in passing that "much better off" here refers to magnitude of the experimental effect as measured in standard deviation units. It does not follow that these differences are translated into clinically important differences. A large ES might result in a study of obesity, if everyone in the treatment group lost 3 pounds (1.35 kilograms) and everyone in the control group did not change at all. If everyone in the study were 50 pounds overweight (22.50 kilograms), then no one would have necessarily improved in an important way. Clinical significance is different from statistical significance and effect size. Among the three concepts, effect size and clinical significance are the most often confused (e.g., Matthey, 1998); although both refer to magnitude of effect in some way, clinical significance is intended to consider whether treatment makes a difference and includes its own methods of calculation (Kazdin, 1998b). The topic of clinical significance is addressed later.

2. The number of meta-analyses is large and growing constantly. In the comments made here, I have several examples in mind (e.g., Baer & Nietzel, 1991; Casey & Berman, 1985; Durlak, Fuhrman, & Lampman, 1991; Hazelrigg, Cooper, & Borduin, 1987; Hoag & Burlingame, 1997; Kazdin, Bass, et al., 1990; Prout & DeMartino, 1986; Prout & Prout, 1998; Saile, Burgmeier, & Schmidt, 1988; Shadish et al., 1993, 1997; Weisz, Donenberg, Han, & Kauneckis, 1995; Weisz, Weiss, & Donenberg, 1992; Weisz et al., 1987; Weisz, Weiss, Han, Granger, & Morton, 1995).

3. The statistical issues, rationales, and formulas underlying the different methods of computing effect size are elaborated elsewhere (Hedges & Olkin, 1985). The impact of using one method (weighted or unweighted) on the conclusions reached about the effects of treatment has been nicely elaborated by Weisz, Weiss, et al. (1995), who evaluated a set of studies using both methods. Conclusions vary considerably regarding factors that influence treatment outcome. Examples of this variation are highlighted in this discussion.

4. Of course, there is no single number that one can fix at a point in time; the precise number depends on how the pertinent literature is searched (e.g., key words), the scope of search (e.g., journals in English and other languages), and other factors (e.g., definition of therapy, age range of the children).

Chapter 5

1. As an illustration, practice guidelines for the treatment of child and adolescent depression note that, in clinical experience, psychodynamic psychotherapy is useful (AACAP, 1998). This conclusion is mentioned in the context of treatments (medication, cognitive-behavior therapy) that have supportive evidence. On the other hand, the guidelines also note that much of the evidence for empirically supported treatments for childhood depression has focused on mildly depressed children and has provided little follow-up data. These points qualify the conclusions about the effectiveness of some treatments that might meet criteria for empirically supported therapies. Stated another way, research reviews of treatments are unfettered by the concerns of clinical practice.

2. The American Psychological Association, the world's largest organization of psychologists, consists of over 155,000 members. Within the organization, groups or divisions focus on areas and themes within the discipline. The Division of Clinical Psychology formed the TFPP, which completed the initial report for the division (TFPP, 1995) and has continued this work (Chambless et al., 1996, 1998). The findings, recommendations, and listed procedures that are empirically supported are not endorsed with any official imprimatur of the American Psychological Association.

3. Quite unrelated to the evaluation of therapy, there have been extended discussions about the use of statistical significance as the primary basis for drawing inferences in research (see Kirk, 1996; Schmidt, 1996). Although not discussed here, the issues are very relevant to identifying empirically supported treatments because the absence of significant differences between groups does not mean that two treatments are equally effective and—maybe even more misleading—the presence of significant differences does not necessarily mean that one treatment is better (more effective) than the other (see Kazdin, 1998b).

Chapter 6

1. I kept changing these selection criteria in order to include my own work. No matter how low the standards were set, my own work never qualified. I am hoping to prepare an article on uncontrolled studies and empirically checkered treatments, which will feature my work prominently.

2. Additional comments are warranted because of the care with which the term *causal relation* must be used. The research has shown that inept parenting practices are not merely a correlate or antecedent (risk factor) for conduct problems. Rather, they are causally related insofar as they lead directly to the behavior. Also, when specific parenting practices are altered, child behavior improves. To state that inept parenting is a cause of conduct problems in children does not mean that this is the only cause or that such parenting practices are a necessary or sufficient cause of the behaviors (see Kazdin, Kraemer, Kessler, Kupfer, & Offord, 1997).

Chapter 7

1. Scores of treatment manuals are available within the public domain for such treatments as individual psychotherapy (Lord, 1985), psychoanalytic and psychodynamically oriented therapy (Kernberg & Chazan, 1991), parent management training (Forehand & Long, 1996; Sanders & Dadds, 1993), cognitive-behavior therapy (Clarke, Lewinsohn, & Hops, 1990; Finch, Nelson, & Ott, 1983; Kendall et al., 1990), multisystemic therapy (Henggeler et al., 1998), functional family therapy (Alexander & Parsons, 1982), social skills training (King & Kirschenbaum, 1992; Michelson, Sugai, Wood, & Kazdin, 1983), as well as combined treatment packages such as reinforcement practices and cognitively based treatment (Horne & Sayger, 1990). Abbreviated manuals of several treatments beyond those mentioned here can be found in a compendium (LeCroy, 1994).

2. *Statistical significance* evaluates the extent to which the results of a study (e.g., differences between groups or changes within groups) are likely due to genuine rather than chance effects. A statistically significant difference (e.g., $p < .05$) indicates that if the experiment were conducted repeatedly, the finding would occur 5 out of 100 times on a chance basis, if there were no real difference between groups (i.e., the null hypothesis is true). *Magnitude of effect* is a measure of the strength of relation between the independent and dependent variable and is quite different from statistical significance. There are many indices or measures of the strength of the relation, including omega^2 (ω^2), eta (η), epsilon^2 (ϵ^2), and Pearson product-moment correlation (r, r^2) and in multiple regression (R, R^2) (see Haase, Ellis, & Ladany, 1989; Kirk, 1996; Rosenthal, 1984; Rosenthal & Rosnow, 1991). As mentioned previously, those most familiar in psychology are effect size (ES or δ) and correlation (r). The relations between statistical significance and magnitude of effect enjoy all the expected permutations (e.g., an effect can be statistically significant but show an extremely small relation, or not be significant statistically but show a quite strong relation, and so on) (see Kazdin, 1998b). Magnitude of effect does not necessarily mean that the effect makes a difference to individuals, is important in some practical way, or can be seen in everyday life. For example, if everyone in the treatment group improves in one or two symptoms (out of several), but everyone in the no-treatment group stays the same or becomes worse, the strength of the relation between treatment and therapeutic change (effect size) might be very large. Yet none of the treated cases may have improved in a way that affects their lives. Clinical significance is reserved for these latter differences and effects.

Chapter 9

1. The term *participants* is currently recommended to refer to the persons who serve as subjects in a study (American Psychological Association, 1994). However, in psychotherapy research participants can include subjects and therapists and both can contribute to the results and the conclusions. For present purposes, the terms *subjects, clients, patients, cases,* and *families* are used to refer to the recipients of treatment (children, adolescents, and their families). Those who deliver the treatment will be referred to as *therapists* or *therapeutic agents.*

2. The level of power that is "adequate" in research is based on convention about the margin of protection one should have against falsely accepting the null hypothesis (i.e., concluding that there are no differences when there really are differences). Cohen (1965) recommended .80 means as the level of power for research; this means that the chances are 8 in 10 that differences will be found if they exist across a series of studies testing for the difference. Although power $\geq.80$ has become a reference point for research, higher levels (.90, .95) are often encouraged (see Friedman, Furberg, & DeMets, 1985).

Chapter 10

1. Another methodological approach provides leads for evaluation in clinical work. Qualitative research methods provide systematic and rigorous ways of examining the individual in detail, using description and inference. In contrast to the anecdotal case study, qualitative research consists of systematic methods for extracting data, for validating inferences, and for replicating effects. Qualitative research methods are rarely taught in psychology, psychiatry, or social work programs, at least in the United States. Although qualitative research methods are beyond the scope of this chapter, the interested reader may wish to consult overviews of applications of qualitative methods to clinical work (Kazdin, 1998b; Krahn, Hohn, & Kime, 1995; Trierweiler & Stricker, 1998) and to child therapy (Webster-Stratton & Spitzer, 1996) or comprehensive descriptions of the methodology (e.g., Denzin & Lincoln, 1994; Miles & Huberman, 1994).

Appendix B

1. Dr. Quickie currently consults and is in private practice. Actually, the practice is a little too private; at this moment, he does not have any clients. Because of the foreclosure of his post office box, please direct all correspondence to him in care of Alan Kazdin. Dr. Quickie gratefully acknowledges grant support from the Rapid Eye Movement Foundation, the Very Brief Psychotherapy Foundation, and the Rapid Transit Authority.

2. The terminology of research design makes no sense. Consider just a few of the problems. If there are true experiments, why aren't there *false* experiments? Also, there are *single*-case designs but no *married*-case designs. Sounds like a clear case of methodological discrimination to me. There are randomized controlled clinical trials galore, but none of the permutations are mentioned in public (e.g., randomized *un*controlled *non*clinical trial [RUNT] or the *non*randomized *un*controlled clinical trial [NUCT]—leaving aside my personal favorite, the *non*randomized *un*controlled *non*clinical trial [or NUNT], and all the others).

References

Achenbach, T.M. (1991). *Manual for the Child Behavior Checklist/4–18 and 1991 Profile.* Burlington: University of Vermont, Department of Psychiatry.

Achenbach, T.M., McConaughy, S.H., & Howell, C.T. (1987). Child/adolescent behavioral and emotional problems: Implications of cross-informant correlations for situational specificity. *Psychological Bulletin, 101,* 213–232.

Addis, M.E. (1997). Evaluating the treatment manual as a means of disseminating empirically validated psychotherapies. *Clinical Psychology: Science and Practice, 4,* 1–11.

Adler, N.E., Boyce, T., Chesney, M.A., Cohen, S., Folkman, S., Kahn, R.L., & Syme, S.L. (1994). Socioeconomic status and health: The challenge of the gradient. *American Psychologist, 49,* 15–24.

Aiken, L.R. (1996). *Rating scales and checklists: Evaluating behavior, personality, and attitude.* New York: Wiley & Sons.

Alexander, J.F., & Parsons, B.V. (1982). *Functional family therapy.* Monterey, CA: Brooks/Cole.

Allport, G.W. (1937). *Personality: A psychological interpretation.* New York: Holt.

Alter, C., & Evens, W. (1990). *Evaluating your practice: A guide to self-assessment.* New York: Springer.

American Academy of Child and Adolescent Psychiatry. (1997). Practice parameters. *Journal of the American Academy of Child and Adolescent Psychiatry, 36* (10, 1s–202s, supplement).

American Academy of Child and Adolescent Psychiatry. (1998). Practice parameters. *Journal of the American Academy of Child and Adolescent Psychiatry, 37* (10, 1s–89s, supplement).

American Psychiatric Association. (1980). *Diagnostic and statistical manual of mental disorders* (3rd ed.). Washington, DC: APA.

American Psychiatric Association. (1987). *Diagnostic and statistical manual of mental disorders* (3rd ed.-revised). Washington, DC: APA.

American Psychiatric Association. (1993). Practice guideline for major depressive disorders in adults. *American Journal of Psychiatry, 150* (4, supplement), v, 1–26.

American Psychiatric Association. (1994a). *Diagnostic and statistical manual of mental disorders* (4th ed.). Washington, DC: APA.

American Psychiatric Association. (1994b). Practice guideline for treatment patients with bipolar disorder. *American Journal of Psychiatry, 152* (12, supplement), iv, 1–36.

American Psychiatric Association. (1995). Practice guidelines for the treatment of patients with substance use disorders: Alcohol, cocaine, opiods. *American Journal of Psychiatry, 152*(11, supplement), 1–59.

American Psychological Association. (1992). Ethical principles of psychologists and code of conduct. *American Psychologist, 47,* 1597–1611.

American Psychological Association. (1994). *Publication manual of the American Psychological Association* (4th ed.). Washington, DC: APA.

American Psychological Association. (1995). *Template for developing guidelines: Interventions for mental disorders and psychosocial aspects of physical disorders.* Washington, DC: APA.

Amir, Y., & Sharon, I. (1991) Replication in behavioral research. In J.W. Neuliep (Ed.), *Replication research in the social sciences* (pp. 51–69). Newbury Park, CA: Sage.

Ammerman, R.T., Last, C.G., & Hersen, M. (Eds.). (1999). *Handbook of prescriptive treatments for children and adolescents* (2nd ed.). Needham Heights, MA: Allyn & Bacon.

Arndorfer, R. E., Allen, K. D., & Aljazireh, L. (1999). Behavioral health needs in pediatric medicine and the acceptability of behavioral solutions: Implications for behavioral psychologists. *Behavior Therapy, 30,* 137–148.

Asher, S.R., & Coie, J.D. (Eds.). (1990). *Peer rejection in childhood.* New York: Cambridge University Press.

Austin, N.K., Liberman, R.P., King, L.W., & DeRisi, W.J. (1976). A comparative evaluation of two-day hospitals: Goal attainment scaling of behavior therapy vs. milieu therapy. *Journal of Nervous and Mental Disease, 163,* 253–262.

Baer, D.M. (1977). Perhaps it would be better not to know everything. *Journal of Applied Behavior Analysis, 10,* 167–172.

Baer, R.A., & Nietzel, M.T. (1991). Cognitive and behavioral treatment of impulsivity in children: A meta-analytic review of the outcome literature. *Journal of Clinical Child Psychology, 20,* 400–412.

Bank, L., Marlowe, J.H., Reid, J.B., Patterson, G.R., & Weinrott, M.R. (1991). A comparative evaluation of parent-training interventions for families of chronic delinquents. *Journal of Abnormal Child Psychology, 19,* 15–33.

Banken, D.M., & Wilson, G.L. (1992). Treatment acceptability of alternative therapies for depression: A comparative analysis. *Psychotherapy, 29,* 610–619.

Barkley, R.A. (1998). Attention-deficit/hyperactivity disorder. In E.J. Mash & R.A. Barkley (Eds.), *Treatment of childhood disorders* (2nd ed., pp. 55–110). New York: Guilford.

Barlow, D.H., Hayes, S.C., & Nelson, R.O. (1984). *The scientist-professional: Research and accountability in clinical and research settings.* Elmsford, NY: Pergamon.

Barlow, D.H., & Hersen, M. (1984). *Single-case experimental designs: Strategies for studying behavior change* (2nd ed.). Elmsford, NY: Pergamon.

Baron, R.M., & Kenny, D.A. (1986). The moderator-mediator variable distinction in social psychological research: Conceptual, strategic, and statistical considerations. *Journal of Personality and Social Psychology, 51,* 1173–1182.

Barrett, C.L., Hampe, I.E., & Miller, L.C. (1978). Research on child psychotherapy. In S.L. Garfield & A.E. Bergin (Eds.), *Handbook of psychotherapy and behavior change: An empirical analysis* (2nd ed., pp. 411–435). New York: Wiley & Sons.

Barrett, P.M., Dadds, M.R., & Rapee, R.M. (1996). Family treatment of childhood anxiety: A controlled trial. *Journal of Consulting and Clinical Psychology, 64,* 333–342.

Barrnett, R.J., Docherty, J.P., & Frommelt, G.M. (1991). A review of psychotherapy research since 1963. *Journal of the American Academy of Child and Adolescent Psychiatry, 30,* 1–14.

Bechterev, V.M. (1993). *General principles of human reflexology: An introduction to the objective study of personality* (E. Murphy & W. Murphy, translators). London: Jarrods.

Bergin, A.E., & Garfield S.L. (Eds.). (1994). *Handbook of psychotherapy and behavior change* (4th ed.). New York: Wiley & Sons.

Bergin, A.E., & Lambert, M.J. (1978). The evaluation of therapeutic outcomes. In S.L. Garfield & A.E. Bergin (Eds.), *Handbook of psychotherapy and behavior change* (2nd ed., pp. 139–189). New York: Wiley & Sons.

Bergin, A.E., & Strupp, H.H. (1972). *Changing frontiers in the science of psychotherapy.* Chicago: Aldine.

Betan, E.J., Roberts, M.C., & McCluskey-Fawcett, K. (1995). Rates of participation for clinical child and pediatric psychology research: Issues in methodology. *Journal of Clinical Child Psychology, 24,* 227–235.

Beutler, L.E. (1997). The psychotherapist as a neglected variable in psychotherapy: An illustration by reference to the role of therapist experience and training. *Clinical Psychology: Science and Practice, 4,* 44–52.

Beutler, L. E. (1998). Identifying empirically supported treatments: What if we didn't? *Journal of Consulting and Clinical Psychology, 66,* 113–120.

Beutler, L.E., Machado, P.P.P., & Neufeldt, S.A. (1994). Therapist variables. In A.E. Bergin & S.L. Garfield (Eds.), *Handbook of psychotherapy and behavior change* (4th ed., pp. 229–269). New York: Wiley & Sons.

Bird, H.R., Yager, T.J., Staghezza, B., Gould, M.S., Canino, G., & Rubio-Stipec, M. (1990). Impairment in the epidemiological measurement of psychopathology in the community. *Journal of the American Academy of Child and Adolescent Psychiatry, 29,* 796–803.

Blanchard, E.B. (1994). Behavioral medicine and health psychology. In A.E. Bergin & S.L. Garfield (Eds.), *Handbook of psychotherapy and behavior change* (4th ed., pp. 701–733). New York: Wiley & Sons.

Bloom, M., & Fischer, J. (1982). *Evaluating practice: Guidelines for the accountable professional.* Englewood Cliffs, NJ: Prentice Hall.

Borkovec, T., & Rachman, S. (1979). The utility of analogue research. *Behaviour Research and Therapy, 17,* 253–261.

Boyle, M.H., Offord, D., Racine, Y.A., Szatmari, P., Fleming, J.E., & Sanford, M.N. (1996). Identifying thresholds for classifying psychiatric disorder: Issues and prospects. *Journal of the American Academy of Child and Adolescent Psychiatry, 35,* 1440–1448.

Brestan, E.V., & Eyberg, S.M. (1998). Effective psychosocial treatment of conductdisordered children and adolescents: 29 years, 82 studies, and 5275 kids. *Journal of Clinical Child Psychology, 27,* 180–189.

Breuer, J., & Freud, S. (1957). *Studies in hysteria.* New York: Basic Books.

Brofenbrenner, U. (1979). *The ecology of human development: Experiments by nature and design.* Cambridge, MA: Harvard University Press.

Brooks, C.H. (1922). *The practice of autosuggestion by the method of Emile Coué.* New York: Dodd, Mead.

Brooks-Gunn, J., & Warren, M.P. (1989). Biological and social contributions to negative affect in young adolescent girls. *Child Development, 60,* 40–55.

Brown, J. (1987). A review of meta-analyses conducted on psychotherapy outcome research. *Clinical Psychology Review, 7,* 1–23.

Brownell, K.D., & Wadden, T.A. (1992). Etiology and treatment of obesity: Toward understanding a serious, prevalent, and refractory disorder. *Journal of Consulting and Clinical Psychology, 60,* 505–517.

Buckner, J.C., & Chesney-Lind, M. (1983). Dramatic cures for juvenile crime: An evaluation of a prisoner-run delinquency prevention program. *Criminal Justice and Behavior, 10,* 227–247.

Campbell, D.T., & Stanley, J.C. (1963). Experimental and quasi-experimental designs for research and teaching. In N.L. Gage (Ed.), *Handbook of research on teaching.* Chicago: Rand McNally.

Caron, C., & Rutter, M. (1991). Comorbidity in child psychopathology: Concepts, issues, and research strategies. *Journal of Child Psychology and Psychiatry, 32,* 1063–1080.

Casey, R.J., & Berman, J.S. (1985). The outcome of psychotherapy with children. *Psychological Bulletin, 98,* 388–400.

Caspi, A., Moffitt, T.E., Newman, D.L., & Silva, P.A. (1996). Behavioral observations at age 3 predict adult psychiatric disorders. *Archives of General Psychiatry, 53,* 1033–1039.

Caspi, A., & Silva, P.A. (1995). Temperamental qualities at age three predict personality traits in young adulthood: Longitudinal evidence from a birth cohort. *Child Development, 66,* 486–498.

Catalano, R.F., Hawkins, J.D., Krenz, C., Gillmore, M., Morrison, D., Wells, E., & Abbott, R. (1993). Using research to guide culturally appropriate drug abuse prevention. *Journal of Consulting and Clinical Psychology, 61,* 804–811.

Cautela, J.R. (1967). Covert sensitization. *Psychological Reports, 20,* 459–468.

Chambless, D.L., Baker, M.J., Baucom, D.H., Beutler, L.E., Calhoun, K.S., Crits-Cristoph, P., Daiuto, A., DeRubeis, R., Detweiler, J., Haaga, D.A.F., Johnson, S.B., McCurry, S., Mueser, K.T., Pope, K.S., Sanderson, W.C., Shoham, V., Stickle, T., Williams, D.A., & Woody, S.R. (1998). Update on empirically validated therapies, II. *Clinical Psychologist, 51* (1), 3–16.

Chambless, D.L., & Hollon, S.D. (1998). Defining empirically supported therapies. *Journal of Consulting and Clinical Psychology, 66,* 7–18.

Chambless, D.L., Sanderson, W.C., Shoham, V., Bennett-Johnson, S., Pope, K.S., Crits-Cristoph, P., Baker, M., Johnson, B., Woody, S.R., Sue, S., Beutler, L., Williams, D.A., & McCurry, S. (1996). An update on empirically validated treatments. *Clinical Psychologist, 49* (2), 5–18.

Chow, S.L. (1988). Significance test or effect size? *Psychological Bulletin, 103,* 105–110.

Christensen, L. (1996). *Diet-behavior relationships: Focus on depression.* Washington, DC: American Psychological Association.

Clark, L.A., Watson, D., & Reynolds, S. (1995). Diagnosis and classification of psychopathology: Challenges to the current system and future directions. *Annual Review of Psychology, 46,* 121–152.

Clarke, G.N., Lewinsohn, P.M., & Hops, H. (1990). *Adolescent Coping with Depression Course: Leader's manual for adolescent groups.* Eugene, OR: Castalia.

Clement, P.W. (1994). Quantitative evaluation of 26 years of private practice. *Professional Psychology: Research and Practice, 25,* 173–176.

Clement, P.W. (1996). Evaluation in private practice. *Clinical Psychology: Science and Practice, 3,* 146–159.

Clement, P.W. (1999). *Outcomes and incomes: How to evaluate, improve, and market your practice by measuring outcomes in psychotherapy.* New York: Guilford.

Cobham, V.E., Dodds, M.R., & Spence, S.H. (1998). The role of parental anxiety in the treatment of childhood anxiety. *Journal of Consulting and Clinical Psychology, 66,* 893–905.

Cohen, J. (1965). Some statistical issues in psychological research. In B.B. Wolman (Ed.), *Handbook of clinical psychology* (pp. 95–121). New York: McGraw-Hill.

Cohen, J. (1988). *Statistical power analysis for the behavioral sciences* (2nd ed.). Hillsdale, NJ: Erlbaum.

Cohen, J. (1992). A power primer. *Psychological Bulletin, 112,* 155–159.

Cohen, L.H., Sargent, M.M., & Sechrest, L.B. (1986). Use of psychotherapy research by practicing psychotherapists. *American Psychologist, 41,* 198–206.

Cohen, P., Cohen, J., Kasen, S., Velez, C.N., Hartmark, C., Johnson, J., Rojas, M., Book, J., & Streuning, E. L. (1993). An epidemiological study of disorders in late childhood and adolescence—I. Age- and gender-specific prevalence. *Journal of Child Psychology and Psychiatry, 34,* 851–867.

Cohen, Y., Spirito, A., & Brown, L.K. (1996). Suicide and suicidal behavior. In R.J. DiClemente, W.B. Hansen, & L.E. Ponton (Eds.), *Handbook of adolescent health risk behavior* (pp. 193–224). New York: Plenum.

Cook, T.D., & Campbell, D.T. (Eds.). (1979). *Quasi-experimentation: Design and analysis issues for field settings.* Chicago: Rand McNally.

Cook, T.D., Cooper, H., Cordray, D.S., Hartmann, H., Hedges, L.V., Light, R.J., Louis, T.A., & Mosteller, F. (1992). *Meta-analysis for explanation: A casebook.* New York: Russell Sage Foundation.

Cooper, J.O., Heron, T.E., & Heward, W.L. (1987). *Applied behavior analysis.* Columbus, OH: Merrill.

Costello, E.J. (1989). Developments in child psychiatric epidemiology. *Journal of the American Academy of Child and Adolescent Psychiatry, 28,* 836–841.

Coué, E. (Ed.). (1922). *Self-mastery through conscious autosuggestion.* New York: American Library Service.

Coué, E. (Ed.). (1923). *How to practice suggestion and autosuggestion.* New York: American Library Service.

Cuijpers, P. (1998). A psychoeducational approach to the treatment of depression: A meta-analysis of Lewinsohn's "Coping with Depression" course. *Behavior Therapy, 29,* 521–533.

Cunningham, C.E., Bremner, R., & Boyle, M. (1995). Large group community-based parenting programs for families of preschoolers at risk for disruptive behaviour disorders: Utilization, cost effectiveness, and outcome. *Journal of Child Psychology and Psychiatry, 36,* 1141–1159.

Dadds, M.R., & McHugh, T.A. (1992). Social support and treatment outcome in behavioral family therapy for child conduct problems. *Journal of Consulting and Clinical Psychology, 60,* 252–259.

Dadds, M.R., Schwartz, S., & Sanders, M.R. (1987). Marital discord and treatment outcome in behavioral treatment of child conduct disorders. *Journal of Consulting and Clinical Psychology, 55,* 396–403.

Davidson, P.O., & Costello, C.G. (Eds.). (1969). *N = 1 experimental studies of single cases.* New York: Van Nostrand Reinhold.

Davison, G.C., & Lazarus, A.A. (1994). Clinical innovation and evaluation: Integrating practice with inquiry. *Clinical Psychology: Science and Practice, 1,* 157–168.

Dawes, R.M. (1994). *House of cards: Psychology and psychotherapy built on myth.* New York: Free Press.

Denzin, N.H, & Lincoln, Y.S. (Eds.). (1994). *Handbook of qualitative research.* Thousand Oaks, CA: Sage.

DiClemente, R.J.. Hansen, W.B., Ponton, L.E. (Eds.). (1996). *Handbook of adolescent health risk behavior.* New York: Plenum.

Dishion, T.J., & Andrews, D.W. (1995). Preventing escalation in problem behaviors with high-risk young adolescents: Immediate and 1-year outcomes. *Journal of Consulting and Clinical Psychology, 63,* 538–548.

Dishion, T.J., & Patterson, G.R. (1992). Age effects in parent training outcomes. *Behavior Therapy, 23,* 719–729.

Dishion, T.J., & Patterson, G.R. (in press). Model building in developmental psychopathology: A pragmatic approach to understanding and intervention. *Journal of Clinical Child Psychology.*

Dishion, T.J., Patterson, G.R., & Kavanagh, K.A. (1992). An experimental test of the coercion model: Linking theory, measurement, and intervention. In J. McCord & R.E. Tremblay (Eds.), *Preventing antisocial behavior* (pp. 253–282). New York: Guilford.

Dobson, K.S., & Shaw, B.F. (1988). The use of treatment manuals in cognitive therapy: Experience and issues. *Journal of Consulting and Clinical Psychology, 56,* 673–680.

Dodge, K.A., Pettit, G.S., & Bates, J.E. (1994) Socialization mediators of the relation between socioeconomic status and child conduct problems. *Child Development, 65,* 649–655.

Dollard, J., & Miller, N.E. (1950). *Personality and psychotherapy: An analysis in terms of learning, thinking, and culture.* New York: McGraw-Hill.

Domar, A.D. (1998, October). *The application of mind/body techniques to infertile women.* Meeting of the American Society of Reproductive Medicine, San Francisco, CA.

Dryfoos, J.G. (1990). *Adolescents at risk: Prevalence and prevention.* New York: Oxford University Press.

Dumas, J.E., & Wahler, R.G. (1983). Predictors of treatment outcome in parent training: Mother insularity and socioeconomic disadvantage. *Behavioral Assessment, 5,* 301–313.

Dumont, F. (1993). Inferential heuristics in clinical problem formulation: Selective review of their strengths and weaknesses. *Professional Psychology: Research and Practice, 24,* 196–205.

Dunne, J.E. (1997). Introduction: History and development of practice parameters. *Journal of the American Academy of Child and Adolescent Psychiatry, 36* (10, supplement), 1–3.

Durlak, J.A., Fuhrman, T., & Lampman, C. (1991). Effectiveness of cognitive-behavioral therapy for maladapting children. *Psychological Bulletin, 110,* 204–214.

Durlak, J.A., Wells, A.M., Cotten, J.K., & Johnson, S. (1995). Analysis of selected methodological issues in child psychotherapy research. *Journal of Clinical Child Psychology, 24,* 141–148.

Eagle, M.N., & Wolitzky, D. L. (1992). Psychoanalytic theories of psychotherapy. In D.K. Freedheim (Ed.), *History of psychotherapy: A century of change* (pp. 109–158). Washington, DC: American Psychological Association.

Edwards, A.L., & Cronbach, L.J. (1952). Experimental design for research in psychotherapy. *Journal of Clinical Psychology, 8,* 51–59.

Eisenberg, L., & Gruenberg, E.M. (1961). The current status of secondary prevention in child psychiatry. *American Journal of Orthopsychiatry, 31,* 355–367.

Elliott, D.S., Huizinga, D., & Ageton, S.S. (1985). *Explaining delinquency and drug use.* Beverly Hills, CA: Sage.

Elliott, D.S., Huizinga, D., & Menard, S. (1988). *Multiple problem youth: Delinquency, substance abuse, and mental health problems.* New York: Springer-Verlag.

Epstein, M.H., Kutash, K., & Duchnowski, A.J. (Eds.). (1998). *Outcomes for children and youth with emotional and behavioral disorders and their families: Programs and evaluation best practices.* Austin, TX: Pro-Ed.

Evidence-Based Mental Health: Linking Research to Practice (1998). *1*(1). London: BMJ Publishing Group, British Medical Association.

Eysenck, H.J. (1952). The effects of psychotherapy: An evaluation. *Journal of Consulting Psychology, 16,* 319–324.

Eysenck, H.J. (1960). The effects of psychotherapy. In H.J. Eysenck (Ed.), *Handbook of abnormal psychology: An experiential approach.* London: Pitman Medical.

Eysenck, H.J. (1966). *The effects of psychotherapy.* New York: International Science Press.

Eysenck, H.J. (1978). An exercise in mega-silliness. *American Psychologist, 33,* 517.

Eysenck, H.J. (1995). The outcome problem in psychotherapy: What have we learned? *Behaviour Research and Therapy, 32,* 477–495.

Falloon, I.R. (1988). Expressed emotion: Current status. *Psychological Medicine, 18,* 269–274.

Farrington, D.P. (1995). The development of offending and antisocial behaviour from childhood: Key findings from the Cambridge Study in delinquent development. *Journal of Child Psychology and Psychiatry, 36,* 929–964.

Farrington, D.P., Loeber, R., & Van Kammen, W.B. (1990). Long-term criminal outcomes of hyperactivity-impulsivity-attention deficit and conduct problems in childhood. In L. Robins & M. Rutter (Eds.), *Straight and devious pathways from childhood to adulthood* (pp. 62–81). New York: Cambridge University Press.

Faulkner & Gray Health Care Information Center. (1997). *The 1997 behavioral outcomes and guidelines sourcebook.* New York: Faulkner & Gray.

Feldman, R.A., Caplinger, T.E., & Wodarski, J.S. (1983). *The St. Louis conundrum: The effective treatment of antisocial youths.* Englewood Cliffs, NJ: Prentice-Hall.

Fensterheim, H., & Raw, S.D. (1996). Psychotherapy research is not psychotherapy practice. *Clinical Psychology: Science and Practice, 3,* 168–171.

Finch, A.J., Jr., Nelson, W.M., & Ott, E.S. (1983). *Cognitive-behavioral procedures with children and adolescents: A practical guide.* Needham Heights, MA: Allyn & Bacon.

Finckenauer, J.O. (1982). *Scared straight! and the panacea phenomenon.* Englewood Cliffs, NJ: Prentice-Hall.

Fiske, D.W. (1977). Methodological issues in research on the psychotherapist. In S. Gurman & A.M. Razin (Eds.), *Effective psychotherapy: A handbook of research* (pp. 23–37). New York: Pergamon.

Fonagy, P., & Target, M. (1994). The efficacy of psychoanalysis for children with disruptive disorders. *Journal of the American Academy of Child Psychiatry, 33,* 45–55.

Forehand, R., & Long, N. (1996). *Parenting the strong-willed child.* Chicago: Contemporary Books.

Forehand, R., & McMahon, R.J. (1981). *Helping the noncompliant child: A clinician's guide to parent training.* New York: Guilford.

Forgatch, M.S. (1991). The clinical science vortex: A developing theory of antisocial behavior. In D.J. Pepler & K.H. Rubin (Eds.), *The development and treatment of childhood aggression* (pp. 291–315). Hillsdale, NJ: Erlbaum.

Forgatch, M., & Patterson, G. (1989). *Parents and adolescents living together—Part 2: Family problem solving.* Eugene, OR: Castalia.

Foxx, R.M., Bremer, B.A., Schutz, C., Valdez, J., & Johndrow, C. (1996). Increasing treatment acceptability through video. *Behavioral Interventions, 11,* 171–180.

Frame, C.L., & Strauss, C.C. (1987). Parental informed consent and sample bias in grade-school children. *Journal of Social and Clinical Psychology, 5,* 227–236.

Frank, E., Johnson, S., & Kupfer, D.J. (1992). Psychological treatments in prevention of relapse. In S.A. Montgomery & F. Rouillon (Eds.), *Long-term treatment of depression* (pp. 197–228). Chichester, England: Wiley & Sons.

Frank, E., Kupfer, D.J., Perel, J.M., Cornes, C., Mallinger, A.G., Thase, M.E., McEachran, A.B., & Grochocinski, V.J. (1993). Comparison of full-dose versus half-dose pharmacotherapy in the maintenance treatment of recurrent depression. *Journal of Affective Disorders, 27,* 139–145.

Frank, E., Kupfer, D.J., Wagner, E.F., McEachran, A.B., & Cornes, C. (1991). Efficacy of interpersonal psychotherapy as a maintenance treatment for recurrent depression. *Archives of General Psychiatry, 48,* 1053–1059.

Frank, J.D., & Frank, J.B. (1991). *Persuasion and healing* (3rd ed.). Baltimore, MD: Johns Hopkins University Press.

Freud, S. (1933). *New introductory lectures in psychoanalysis.* (W.J.H. Sprott, translator). New York: Norton.

Friedman, L.M., Furberg, C.D., & DeMets, D.L. (1985). *Fundamentals of clinical trials* (2nd ed.). Littleton, MA: PSG.

Gagnon, R., & Gaston, L. (1996). The role of process research in manual development. *Clinical Psychology: Science and Practice, 3,* 13–24.

Garb, H.N. (1997). Race bias, social class bias, and gender bias in clinical judgment. *Clinical Psychology: Science and Practice, 4,* 99–120.

Garfield, S.L. (1980). *Psychotherapy: An eclectic approach.* New York: Wiley & Sons.

Garfield, S.L. (1982). Eclecticism and integration in psychotherapy. *Behavior Therapy, 13,* 610–623.

Garfield, S.L. (1983). Meta-analysis and psychotherapy: Introduction to special section. *Journal of Consulting and Clinical Psychology, 51,* 3.

Garfield, S.L. (1996). Some problems associated with "validated" forms of psychotherapy. *Clinical Psychology: Science and Practice, 6,* 218–229.

Garfield, S.L. (1998). Some comments on empirically supported treatments. *Journal of Consulting and Clinical Psychology, 66,* 121–125.

Gaw, A.C. (Ed.). (1993). *Culture and ethnicity and mental illness.* Washington, DC: American Psychiatric Press.

Gorman, B.S., Primavera, L.H., & Allison, D.B. (1995). POWPAL: A program for estimating effect sizes, statistical power, and sample sizes. *Educational and Psychological Measurement, 55,* 773–776.

Gotlib, I.H., Lewinsohn, P.M., & Seeley, J.R. (1995). Symptoms versus a diagnosis of depression: Differences in psychosocial functioning. *Journal of Consulting and Clinical Psychology, 63,* 90–100.

Gottman, J. (1981). *Time-series analysis: A comprehensive introduction for social scientists.* Cambridge: Cambridge University Press.

Graber, J.A., Lewinsohn, P.M., Seeley, J.R., & Brooks-Gunn, J. (1997). Is psychopathology associated with the timing of pubertal development. *Journal of the American Academy of Child and Adolescent Psychiatry, 36,* 1768–1776.

Graziano, A.M., & Diament, D.M. (1992). Parent behavioral training: An examination of the paradigm. *Behavior Modification, 16,* 3–38.

Greenbaum, P.E., Foster-Johnson, L., & Petrila, A. (1996). Co-occurring addictive and mental disorders among adolescents: Prevalence research and future directions. *American Journal of Orthopsychiatry, 66,* 52–60.

Greenhill, L.L. (1998). Childhood attention deficit hyperactivity disorder: Pharmacological treatments. In P.E. Nathan & J.M. Gorman (Eds.), *A guide to treatments that work* (pp. 42–64). New York: Oxford University Press.

Grissom, R.J. (1996). The magical number .7 $\pm$ .2: Meta-meta analysis of the probability of superior outcome in comparisons involving therapy, placebo, and control. *Journal of Consulting and Clinical Psychology, 64,* 973–982.

Grych, J.H., & Fincham, F.D. (1990). Marital conflict and children's adjustment: A cognitive-contextual framework. *Psychological Bulletin, 108,* 267–290.

Haase, R.F., Ellis, M.V., & Ladany, N. (1989). Multiple criteria for evaluating the magnitude of experimental effects. *Journal of Counseling Psychology, 4,* 511–516.

Hammen, C. (1991). *Depression runs in families. The social context of risk and resilience in children of depressed mothers.* New York: Springer-Verlag.

Hammen, C., & Rudolf, K.D. (1996). Childhood depression. In E.J. Mash & R.A. Barkley (Eds.), *Child psychopathology* (pp. 153–195). New York: Guilford.

Hanf, C. (1969, April). *A two-stage program for modifying maternal controlling during mother-child interaction.* Paper presented at the meeting of the Western Psychological Association, Vancouver, British Columbia.

Hayes, S.C. (1981). Single-case experimental design and empirical clinical practice. *Journal of Consulting and Clinical Psychology, 49,* 193–211.

Hayes, S.C., Follette, V.M., Dawes, R.M., & Grady, K.E. (1995). *Scientific standards of psychological practice. Issues and recommendations.* Reno, NV: Context.

Haynes, S.N., Lemsky, C., & Sexton-Radek, K. (1987). Why clinicians infrequently do research. *Professional Psychology: Research and Practice, 18,* 515–519.

Hazelrigg, M.D., Cooper, H.M., & Borduin, C.M. (1987). Evaluating the effectiveness of family therapies: An integrative review and analysis. *Psychological Bulletin, 101,* 428–442.

Hedges, L.V., & Olkin, I. (1985). *Statistical methods for meta-analysis.* New York: Academic.

Heimberg, R.G., & Becker, R.E. (1984). Comparative outcome research. In M. Hersen, L. Michelson, & A.S. Bellack (Eds.), *Issues in psychotherapy research* (pp. 251–283). New York: Plenum.

Heinicke, C. M., & Goldman, A. (1960). Research on psychotherapy with children: A review and suggestions for further study. *American Journal of Orthopsychiatry, 30,* 483–494.

Heinicke, C.M., & Ramsey-Klee, D.M. (1986). Outcome of child psychotherapy as a function of frequency of session. *Journal of the American Academy of Child Psychiatry, 25,* 247–253.

Heinicke, C.M., & Strassman, L.H. (1975). Toward more effective research on child psychotherapy. *Journal of the American Academy of Child Psychiatry, 3,* 561–588.

Heller, K. (1971). Laboratory interview research as an analogue to treatment. In A.E. Bergin & S.L. Garfield (Eds.), *Handbook of psychotherapy and behavior change: An empirical analysis* (pp. 126–153). New York: Wiley & Sons.

Henggeler, S.W., Melton, G.B., Brondino, M.J., Scherer, D.G., & Hanley, J.H. (1997). Multisystemic therapy with violent and chronic juvenile offenders and their families:

The role of treatment fidelity in successful dissemination. *Journal of Consulting and Clinical Psychology, 65,* 821–833.

Henggeler, S.W., Schoenwald, S.K., Borduin, C.M., Rowland, M.D., &. Cunningham, P.B. (1998). *Multisystemic treatment of antisocial behavior in children and adolescents.* New York: Guilford.

Herink, R. (Ed.). (1980). *The psychotherapy handbook: The A to Z guide to more than 250 different therapies in use today.* New York: New American Library.

Hibbeln, J.R. (1998, September). *Essential fatty acid status and markers of serotonergic neurotransmission, in alcoholism and suicide.* Paper presented at the National Institutes of Health Workshop on Omega-3 Essential Fatty Acids and Psychiatric Disorders, Bethesda, Maryland.

Hibbs, E., & Jensen, P. (Eds.). (1996). *Psychosocial treatment research of child and adolescent disorders: Empirically based strategies for clinical practice.* Washington, DC: American Psychological Association.

Hoag, M.J., & Burlingame, G.M. (1997). Evaluating the effectiveness of child and adolescent group treatment: A meta-analytic review. *Journal of Clinical Child Psychology, 26,* 234–246.

Hoagwood, K., Hibbs, E., Brent, & Jensen, P.J. (1995). Efficacy and effectiveness in studies of child and adolescent psychotherapy. *Journal of Consulting and Clinical Psychology, 63,* 683–687.

Holmbeck, G.N. (1997). Toward terminological, conceptual, and statistical clarity in the study of mediators and moderators: Examples from the child-clinical and pediatric psychology literatures. *Journal of Consulting and Clinical Psychology, 65,* 599–610.

Hood-Williams, J. (1960). The results of psychotherapy with children: A reevaluation. *Journal of Consulting Psychology, 24,* 84–88.

Horgen, K.B., & Brownell, K.D. (1998). Policy change as a means for reducing the prevalence and impact of alcoholism, smoking, and obesity. In W.R. Miller & N. Heather (Eds.), *Treating addictive behaviors* (2nd ed., pp. 105–118). New York: Plenum.

Horne, A.M., & Sayger, T.V. (1990). *Treating conduct and oppositional disorders in children.* Elmsford, NY: Pergamon.

Howard, B., & Kendall, P.C. (1996). Cognitive-behavioral family therapy for anxiety-disordered children: A multiple-baseline evaluation. *Cognitive Therapy and Research, 20,* 423–443.

Howard, K.I., Krause, M.S., & Orlinsky, D.E. (1986). The attrition dilemma: Toward a new strategy for psychotherapy research. *Journal of Consulting and Clinical Psychology, 54,* 106–110.

Hsu, L.M. (1989). Random sampling, randomization, and equivalence of contrasted groups in psychotherapy outcome research. *Journal of Consulting and Clinical Psychology, 57,* 131–137.

Ingersoll, B.D., & Goldstein, S. (1993). *Attention deficit disorder and learning disabilities: Realities, myths, and controversial treatments.* New York: Doubleday.

Institute of Medicine. (1989). *Research on children and adolescents with mental, behavioral, and developmental disorders.* Washington, DC: National Academy Press.

Jacobson, N.S. (1991). Behavioral versus insight-oriented marital therapy: Labels can be misleading. *Journal of Consulting and Clinical Psychology, 59,* 142–145.

Johnston, J.M., & Pennypacker, H.S. (1980). *Strategies and tactics of human behavioral research.* Hillsdale, NJ: Erlbaum.

Johnston, L.D. (1996, December). *The rise of drug use among American teens contin-ues in 1996: Monitoring the Future Study*. Ann Arbor: University of Michigan.

Jones, E.E., Ghannam, J., Nigg, J.T., & Dyer, J.F.P. (1993). A paradigm for single-case research: The time series study of a long-term psychotherapy for depression. *Journal of Consulting and Clinical Psychology, 61,* 381–394.

Jones, M.C. (1924a). The elimination of children's fears. *Journal of Experimental Psychology, 7,* 382–390.

Jones, M.C. (1924b). A laboratory study of fear: The case of Peter. *Pedagogical Seminary, 31,* 308–315.

Kanfer, F.H., & Schefft, B.K. (1988). *Guiding the process of therapeutic change.* Champaign, IL: Research.

Karasu, T. B. (1985). Personal communication, March 1, 1985.

Kaslow, N.J., & Thompson, M.P. (1998). Applying the criteria for empirically supported treatments to studies of psychosocial interventions for child and adolescent depres-sion. *Journal of Clinical Child Psychology, 27,* 146–155.

Kazdin, A.E. (1978a). Evaluating the generality of findings in analogue therapy re-search. *Journal of Consulting and Clinical Psychology, 46,* 673–686.

Kazdin, A.E. (1978b). *History of behavior modification: Experimental foundations of contemporary research.* Baltimore, MD: University Park Press.

Kazdin, A.E. (1981). Drawing valid inferences from case studies. *Journal of Consulting and Clinical Psychology, 49,* 183–192.

Kazdin, A.E. (1982). *Single-case research designs: Methods for clinical and applied set-tings.* New York: Oxford University Press.

Kazdin, A.E. (1985). *Treatment of antisocial behavior in children and adolescents.* Homewood, IL: Dorsey Press.

Kazdin, A.E. (1986). Acceptability of psychotherapy and hospitalization for disturbed children: Parent and child perspectives. *Journal of Clinical Child Psychology, 15,* 333–340.

Kazdin, A.E. (1988). *Child psychotherapy: Developing and identifying effective treat-ments.* Elmsford, NY: Pergamon.

Kazdin, A.E. (1989). Identifying depression in children: A comparison of alternative se-lection criteria. *Journal of Abnormal Child Psychology, 17,* 437–455.

Kazdin, A.E. (1993a). Changes in behavioral problems and prosocial functioning in child treatment. *Journal of Child and Family Studies, 2,* 5–22.

Kazdin, A.E. (1993b). Evaluation in clinical practice: Clinically sensitive and system-atic methods of treatment delivery. *Behavior Therapy, 24,* 11–45.

Kazdin, A.E (1994a). *Behavior modification in applied settings* (5th ed.). Pacific Grove, CA: Brook/Cole.

Kazdin, A.E. (1994b). Informant variability in the assessment of childhood depression. In W.M. Reynolds & H. Johnston (Eds.), *Handbook of depression in children and adolescents* (pp. 249–271). New York: Plenum.

Kazdin, A.E. (1995a). Child, parent, and family dysfunction as predictors of outcome in cognitive-behavioral treatment of antisocial children. *Behaviour Research and Therapy, 33,* 271–281.

Kazdin, A.E. (1995b). *Conduct disorder in childhood and adolescence* (2nd ed.). Thousand Oaks, CA: Sage.

Kazdin, A.E. (1995c). Scope of child and adolescent psychotherapy research: Limited sampling of dysfunctions, treatments, and client characteristics. *Journal of Clinical Child Psychology, 24,* 125–140.

Kazdin, A.E. (1996a). Combined and multimodal treatments in child and adolescent psychotherapy: Issues, challenges, and research directions. *Clinical Psychology: Science and Practice, 3,* 69–100.

Kazdin, A.E. (1996b). Dropping out of child therapy: Issues for research and implications for practice. *Clinical Child Psychology and Psychiatry, 1,* 133–156.

Kazdin, A.E. (1996c). Problem solving and parent management in treating aggressive and antisocial behavior. In E.D. Hibbs & P.S. Jensen (Eds.), *Psychosocial treatments for child and adolescent disorders: Empirically based strategies for clinical practice.* (pp. 377–408). Washington, DC: American Psychological Association.

Kazdin, A.E. (1998a). Psychosocial treatments for conduct disorder in children. In P.E. Nathan & J.M. Gorman (Eds.), *A guide to treatments that work* (pp. 65–89). New York: Oxford University Press.

Kazdin, A.E. (1998b). *Research design in clinical psychology* (3rd ed.). Needham Heights, MA: Allyn & Bacon.

Kazdin, A.E. (1999). The meanings and measurement of clinical significance. *Journal of Consulting and Clinical Psychology, 67,* 332–339.

Kazdin, A.E. (in press). Adolescent development, mental disorders, and decision making of delinquent youths. In T. Grisso & R. Schwartz (Eds.), *Youth on trial.* Chicago: University of Chicago Press.

Kazdin, A.E., & Bass, D. (1989). Power to detect differences between alternative treatments in comparative psychotherapy outcome research. *Journal of Consulting and Clinical Psychology, 57,* 138–147.

Kazdin, A.E., Bass, D., Ayers, W.A., & Rodgers, A. (1990). The empirical and clinical focus of child and adolescent psychotherapy research. *Journal of Consulting and Clinical Psychology, 58,* 729–740.

Kazdin, A.E., Bass, D., Siegel, T., & Thomas, C. (1989). Cognitive-behavioral treatment and relationship therapy in the treatment of children referred for antisocial behavior. *Journal of Consulting and Clinical Psychology, 57,* 522–535.

Kazdin, A.E., & Crowley, M.J. (1997). Moderators of treatment outcome in cognitively based treatment of antisocial children. *Cognitive Therapy and Research, 21,* 185–207.

Kazdin, A.E., French, N.H., & Sherick, R.B. (1981). Acceptability of alternative treatments for children: Evaluations by inpatient children, parents, and staff. *Journal of Consulting and Clinical Psychology, 49,* 900–907.

Kazdin, A.E., Holland, L., & Crowley, M. (1997). Family experience of barriers to treatment and premature termination from child therapy. *Journal of Consulting and Clinical Psychology, 65,* 453–463.

Kazdin, A.E., Kraemer, H.C., Kessler, R.C., Kupfer, D.J., & Offord, D.R. (1997). Contributions of risk-factor research to developmental psychopathology. *Clinical Psychology Review, 17,* 375–406.

Kazdin, A.E., & Marciano, P.L. (1998). Childhood and adolescent depression. In E.J. Mash & R.A. Barkley (Eds.), *Treatment of childhood disorders* (2nd ed., pp. 211–248). New York: Guilford.

Kazdin, A.E., Mazurick, J.L., & Bass, D. (1993). Risk for attrition in treatment of antisocial children and families. *Journal of Clinical Child Psychology, 22,* 2–16.

Kazdin, A.E., Mazurick, J.L., & Siegel, T.C. (1994). Treatment outcome among children with externalizing disorder who terminate prematurely versus those who complete psychotherapy. *Journal of the American Academy of Child and Adolescent Psychiatry, 33,* 549–557.

Kazdin, A.E., Siegel, T.C., & Bass, D. (1990). Drawing upon clinical practice to inform research on child and adolescent psychotherapy: A survey of practitioners. *Professional Psychology: Research and Practice, 21,* 189–198.

Kazdin, A.E., Stolar, M.J., & Marciano, P.L. (1995). Risk factors for dropping out of treatment among White and Black families. *Journal of Family Psychology, 9,* 402–417.

Kazdin, A.E., & Tuma, A.H. (Eds.). (1982). *New directions for methodology of social and behavioral sciences: Single-case research designs.* San Francisco: Jossey-Bass.

Kazdin, A.E., & Wassell, G. (1998). Treatment completion and therapeutic change among children referred for outpatient therapy. *Professional Psychology: Research and Practice, 29*

Kazdin, A.E., & Wassell, G. (1999). Barriers to treatment participation and therapeutic change among children referred for conduct disorder. *Journal of Clinical Child Psychology, 28,* 160–172.

Kazdin, A.E., & Weisz, J.R. (1998). Identifying and developing empirically supported child and adolescent treatments. *Journal of Consulting and Clinical Psychology, 66,* 19–36.

Kazdin, A.E., & Wilson, G.T. (1978a). Criteria for evaluating psychotherapy. *Archives of General Psychiatry, 35,* 407–416.

Kazdin, A.E., & Wilson, G.T. (1978b). *Evaluation of behavior therapy: Issues, evidence, and research strategies.* Cambridge, MA: Ballinger.

Kazrin, A., Durac, J., & Agteros, T. (1979). Meta-meta analysis: A new method for evaluating therapy outcome. *Behaviour Research and Therapy, 17,* 397–399.

Kendall, P.C. (1994). Treating anxiety disorders in children: Results of a randomized clinical trial. *Journal of Consulting and Clinical Psychology, 62,* 100–110.

Kendall, P.C. (1999). Special section: Clinical significance. *Journal of Consulting and Clinical Psychology, 67,* 283–339.

Kendall, P.C., Butcher, J.N., &. Holmbeck, G.N. (Eds.). (1999). *Handbook of research methods in clinical psychology* (2nd ed.). New York: Wiley & Sons.

Kendall, P.C., & Chambless, D.L. (Eds.). (1998). Special section: Empirically supported psychological therapies. *Journal of Consulting and Clinical Psychology, 66,* 3–167.

Kendall, P.C., Chansky, T.E., Kane, M.T., Kim, R., Kortlander, E., Ronan, K.R., Sessa, F.M., & Siqueland, L. (1992). *Anxiety disorders in youth: Cognitive-behavioral interventions.* Needham Heights, MA: Allyn & Bacon.

Kendall, P.C., Flannery-Schroeder, E., Panichelli-Mindel, S.M., Southam-Gerow, M.A., Henin, A., & Warman, M. (1997). Therapy for youths with anxiety disorders: A second randomized clinical trial. *Journal of Consulting and Clinical Psychology, 65,* 366–380.

Kendall, P.C., Kane, M., Howard, B., & Siqueland, L. (1990). *Cognitive-behavioral therapy for anxious children: Treatment manual.* Philadelphia: Department of Psychology, Temple University.

Kendall, P.C., Panichelli-Mindel, S.M., Sugarman, A., & Callahan, S.A. (1997). Exposure to child anxiety: Theory, research, and practice. *Clinical Psychology: Science and Practice, 4,* 29–39.

Kendall, P.C., & Southam-Gerow, M.A. (1996). Long-term follow-up of a cognitive-behavioral therapy for anxiety-disordered youth. *Journal of Consulting and Clinical Psychology, 64,* 724–730.

Kendall, P.C., & Treadwell, K.R.H. (1996). Cognitive-behavioral group treatment for socially anxious youth. In E.D. Hibbs & P. Jensen (Eds.), *Psychosocial treatment re-*

search of child and adolescent disorders: Empirically based strategies for clinical practice (pp. 23–41). Washington, DC: American Psychological Association.

Kernberg, P.F., & Chazan, S.E. (1991). Children with conduct disorders: A psychotherapy manual. New York: Basic Books.

Ketterlinus, R.D., & Lamb, M.E. (Eds.). (1994). Adolescent problem behaviors: Issues and research. Hillsdale, NJ: Erlbaum.

Kiesler, D.J. (1966). Some myths of psychotherapy research and the search for a paradigm. Psychological Bulletin, 65, 110–136.

Kiesler, D.J. (1971). Experimental designs in psychotherapy research. In A.E. Bergin & S.L. Garfield (Eds.), Handbook of psychotherapy and behavior change: An empirical analysis (pp. 36–74). New York: Wiley & Sons.

King, C.A., & Kirschenbaum, D.S. (1992). Helping young children develop social skills: The social growth program. Pacific Grove, CA: Brooks/Cole.

Kiresuk, T.J., & Garwick, G. (1979). Basic goal attainment scaling procedures. In B.R. Compton & B. Gallaway (Eds.), Social work processes (Rev ed., pp. 412–420). Homewood, IL: Dorsey.

Kirk, R.E. (1996). Practical significance: A concept whose time has come. Educational and Psychological Measurement, 56, 746–759.

Klein, R.G., & Last, C.G. (1989). Anxiety disorders in children. Newbury Park, CA: Sage.

Kleinmuntz, B. (1990). Why we still use our heads instead of the formulas: Toward an integrative approach. Psychological Bulletin, 107, 415–419.

Klosko, J.S., Barlow, D.H., Tassinari, R., & Cerny, J.A. (1990). A comparison of Alprazolam and behavior therapy in the treatment of panic disorder. Journal of Consulting and Clinical Psychology, 58, 77–84.

Koocher, G.P., & Pedulla, B.M. (1977). Current practices in child psychotherapy. Professional Psychology, 8, 275–287.

Kolvin, I., Garside, R.F., Nicol, A.E., MacMillan, A., Wolstenholme, F., & Leitch, I.M. (1981). Help starts here: The maladjusted child in the ordinary school. London: Tavistock.

Krahn, G.L., Hohn, M.F., & Kime, C. (1995). Incorporating qualitative approaches into clinical child psychology research. Journal of Clinical Child Psychology, 24, 204–213.

Kratochwill, T.R., & Piersel, W.C. (1983). Time-series research: Contributions to empirical clinical practice. Behavioral Assessment, 5, 165–176.

Krishef, C.H. (1991). Fundamental approaches to single subject design and analysis. Malabar, FL: Kreiger.

Kroll, L., Harrington, R., Jayson, D., Frazer, J., & Gowers, S. (1996). Pilot study of continuation cognitive-behavior therapy for major depression in adolescents. Journal of the American Academy of Child and Adolescent Psychiatry, 35, 1156–1161.

Kupfer, D.J., Frank, E., Perel, J.M., Cornes, C., Mallinger, A.G., Thase, M.E., McEachran, A.B., & Grochocinski, V.J. (1992). Five-year outcome for maintenance therapies in recurrent depression. Archives of General Psychiatry, 49, 769–773.

Kupfersmid, J. (1988). Improving what is published: A model in search of an editor. American Psychologist, 43, 635–642.

LaGreca, A.M. (Ed.). (1990). Through the eyes of the child: Obtaining self-reports from children and adolescents. Needham Heights, MA: Allyn & Bacon.

Lambert, M.J. (1983). Introduction to assessment of psychotherapy outcome: Historical perspective and current issues. In M.J. Lambert, E.R. Christensen, & S.S. DeJulio

(Eds.), *The assessment of psychotherapy outcome* (pp. 3–32). New York: Wiley & Sons.

Lambert, M.J., & Brown, G.S. (1996). Data-based management for tracking outcome in private practice. *Clinical Psychology: Science and Practice, 3,* 172–178.

Lazarus, A.A., & Davison, G.C. (1971). Clinical innovation in research and practice. In A.E. Bergin & S.L. Garfield (Eds.), *Handbook of psychotherapy and behavior change: An empirical analysis* (pp. 196–213). New York: Wiley & Sons.

Leaf, R.C., DiGiuseppe, R., Mass, R., & Alington, D.E. (1993). Statistical methods for analysis of incomplete clinical service records: Concurrent use of longitudinal and cross-sectional data. *Journal of Consulting and Clinical Psychology, 61,* 495–505.

LeCroy, C.W. (1994). *Handbook of child and adolescent treatment manuals.* New York: Lexington.

Lee, T.M., Chen, E.Y.H., Chan, C.C.H., Paterson, J.G., Janzen, H.L., & Blashko, C.A. (1998). Seasonal affective disorder. *Clinical Psychology: Science and Practice, 5,* 275–290.

Lerner, R.M. (1991). Changing organism-context relations as the basic process of development: A developmental contextual perspective. *Developmental Psychology, 27,* 27–32.

Levin, J.S. (1994). Religion and health: Is there an association, is it valid, is it causal? *Social Science & Medicine, 38,* 1475–1482.

Levitt, E.E. (1957). The results of psychotherapy with children: An evaluation. *Journal of Consulting Psychology, 21,* 189–196.

Levitt, E.E. (1963). Psychotherapy with children: A further evaluation. *Behaviour Research and Therapy, 60,* 326–329.

Lewinsohn, P.M., & Clarke, G.N. (1999). Psychosocial treatments for adolescent depression. *Clinical Psychology Review, 19,* 329–342.

Lewinsohn, P.M., Clarke, G.N., Hops, H., & Andrews, J. (1990). Cognitive-behavioral treatment for depressed adolescents. *Behavior Therapy, 21,* 385–401.

Lewinsohn, P.M., Clarke, G.N., & Rohde, P. (1994). Psychological approaches to the treatment of depression in adolescents. In W.M. Reynolds & H.F. Johnston (Eds.), *Handbook of depression in children and adolescents* (pp. 309–344). New York: Plenum.

Lewinsohn, P.M., Clarke, G.N., Rohde, P., Hops, H., & Seeley, J.R. (1996). A course in coping: A cognitive-behavioral approach to the treatment of adolescent depression. In E.D. Hibbs & P. Jensen (Eds.), *Psychosocial treatment research of child and adolescent disorders: Empirically based strategies for clinical practice* (pp. 109–135). Washington, DC: American Psychological Association.

Lewinsohn, P.M., Hops, H., Teri, L., & Hautzinger, M. (1985). An integrative theory of depression. In S. Reiss & R. Bootzin (Eds.), *Theoretical issues in behavior therapy* (pp. 331–359). San Diego, CA: Academic Press.

Lipman, E.L., Offord, D.R., & Boyle, M.H. (1994). Relation between economic disadvantage and psychosocial morbidity in children. *Canadian Medical Association Journal, 151,* 431–437.

Little, R.J.A., & Rubin, D.B. (1987). *Statistical analysis with missing data.* New York: Wiley & Sons.

London, P. (1986). *The modes and morals of psychotherapy* (2nd ed.). New York: Hemisphere.

Long, P., Forehand, R., Wierson, M., & Morgan, A. (1994). Does parent training with young noncompliant children have long-term effects? *Behaviour Research and Therapy, 32,* 101–107.

Lonigan, C.J., & Elbert, J.C. (Eds.). (1998). Special issue on empirically supported psychosocial interventions for children. *Journal of Clinical Child Psychology, 27,* 138–226.

Lonigan, C.J., Elbert, J.C., & Johnson, S.B. (1998). Empirically supported psychosocial interventions for children: An overview. *Journal of Clinical Child Psychology, 27,* 138–145.

Lopiano, D.A. (1998). *The importance of sport opportunities for our daughters.* New York: Women's Sports Foundation.

Lord, J.P. (1985). *A guide to individual psychotherapy with school-age children and adolescents.* Springfield, IL: Charles C. Thomas.

Lovaas, O.I. (1987). Behavioral treatment and normal educational/intellectual functioning in young autistic children. *Journal of Consulting and Clinical Psychology, 55,* 3–9.

Luborsky, L., Crits-Cristoph, P., Mintz, J., & Auerbach, A. (1988). *Who will benefit from psychotherapy? Predicting therapeutic outcomes.* New York: Basic Books.

Luborsky, L., Diguer, L., Seligman, D.A., Rosenthal, R., Krause, E.D., Johnson, S., Halperin, G., Bishop, M., Berman, J.S., & Schweizer, E. (1999). The researcher's own therapy allegiances: A "wild card" in comparisons of treatment efficacy. *Clinical Psychology: Science and Practice, 6,* 95–106.

Luborsky, L., McLellen, T., Diguer, L., Woody, G., & Seligman, D.A. (1997). The psychotherapist matters: Comparison of outcomes across twenty-two therapists and seven patient samples. *Clinical Psychology: Science and Practice, 4,* 53–65.

Luborsky, L., Singer, B., & Luborsky, L. (1975). Comparative studies of psychotherapies: Is it true that "everyone has won and all must have prizes"? *Archives of General Psychiatry, 32,* 995–1008.

Luster, T. (1998). Individual differences in the caregiving behavior of teenage mothers. *Clinical Child Psychology and Psychiatry, 3,* 341–360.

Luthar, S.S. (1999). *Children in poverty: Risk and protective forces in adjustment.* Thousand Oaks, CA: Sage.

Lynam, D., Moffitt, T., & Stouthamer-Loeber, M. (1993). Explaining the relation between IQ and delinquency: Class, race, test motivation, school failure, or self-control? *Journal of Abnormal Psychology, 102,* 187–196.

Maddahian, E., Newcomb, M.D., & Bentler, P.M. (1988). Risk factors for substance use: Ethnic differences among adolescents. *Journal of Substance Abuse, 1,* 11–23.

Magnusson, D., Klinteberg, B.A., & Station, H. (1994). Juvenile and persistent offenders: Behavioral and physiological characteristics. In R.D. Ketterlinus & M.E. Lamb (Eds.), *Adolescent problem behaviors: Issues and research* (pp. 81–91). Hillsdale, NJ: Erlbaum.

Maletzky, B.M. (1980). Self-referred versus court-referred sexually deviant patients. *Behavior Therapy, 11,* 306–314.

Maletzky, B.M. (1991). *Treating the sexual offender.* Newbury Park, CA: Sage.

Mann, B.J., Borduin, C.M., Henggeler, S.W., & Blaske, D.M. (1990). An investigation of systemic conceptualizations of parent-child coalitions and symptom change. *Journal of Consulting and Clinical Psychology, 58,* 336–344.

Marks, I., Shaw, S., & Parkin, R. (1998). Computer-aided treatments of mental health problems. *Clinical Psychology: Science and Practice, 5,* 151–170.

Marquis, J.N. (1991). A report on seventy-eight cases treated by eye movement desensitization. *Journal of Behavior Therapy and Experimental Psychiatry, 22,* 187–192.

Marrs, R.W. (1995). A meta-analysis of bibliotherapy studies. *American Journal of Community Psychology, 23,* 843–870.

Maser, J.D., Kaelber, C., & Weise, R.E. (1991). International use and attitudes toward DSM-III and DSM-III-R: Growing consensus in psychiatric classification. *Journal of Abnormal Psychology, 100,* 271–279.

Mash, E.J., & Barkley, R. (Eds.). (1996). *Child psychopathology.* New York: Guilford.

Mash, E.J., & Barkley, R. (Eds.). (1998). *Treatment of childhood disorders* (2nd ed.). New York: Guilford.

Mash, E.J., & Terdal, L.G. (Eds.). (1997). *Assessment of childhood disorders* (3rd ed.). New York: Guilford.

Matt, G.E. (1989). Decision rules for selecting effect sizes in meta-analysis: A review and reanalysis of psychotherapy outcome studies. *Psychological Bulletin, 105,* 106–115.

Matt, G.E., & Navarro, A.M. (1997). What meta-analyses have and have not taught us about psychotherapy effects: A review and future directions. *Clinical Psychology Review, 17,* 1–32.

Matthey, S. (1998). $p < .05$—But is it clinically significant? Practical examples for clinicians. *Behaviour Change, 15,* 140–146.

McCullough, M.E. (1995). Prayer and health: Conceptual issues, research review, and research agenda. *Journal of Psychology and Theology, 23,* 15–29.

McEachin, J.J., Smith, T., & Lovaas, O.I. (1993). Outcome in adolescence of autistic children receiving early intensive behavioral treatment. *American Journal of Mental Retardation, 97,* 359–372.

Measelle, J.R., Ablow, J.C., Cowan, P.A., & Cowan, C.P. (1998). Assessing young children's views of their academic, social, and emotional lives: An evaluation of the self-perception scales of the Berkeley Puppet Interview. *Child Development, 69,* 1556–1576.

Meehl, P. (1954). *Clinical versus statistical prediction: A theoretical analysis and a review of the evidence.* Minneapolis: University of Minnesota Press.

Meehl, P. (1978). Theoretical risks and tabular asterisks: Sir Karl, Sir Ronald, and the slow progress of soft psychology. *Journal of Consulting and Clinical Psychology, 46,* 806–834.

Meehl, P. (1997). Credentialed persons, credentialed knowledge. *Clinical Psychology: Science and Practice, 4,* 91–98.

Metcalf, L. (1998). *Solution focused group therapy: Ideas for groups in private practice, schools, agencies, and treatment programs.* New York: Free Press.

Meyers, A.W., Graves, T.J., Whelan, J.P., & Barclay, D. (1996). An evaluation of television-delivered behavioral weight loss program. Are the ratings acceptable? *Journal of Consulting and Clinical Psychology, 64,* 172–178.

Michelson, L. (1985). Editorial: Introduction and commentary. *Clinical Psychology Review, 5,* 1–2.

Michelson, L., Sugai, D.P., Wood, R.P., & Kazdin, A.E. (1983). *Social skills assessment and training with children.* New York: Plenum.

Milberger, S., Biederman, J., Faraone, S.V., & Jones, J. (1998). Further evidence of an association between maternal smoking during pregnancy and attention deficit hyperactivity disorder: Findings from a high-risk sample of siblings. *Journal of Clinical Child Psychology, 27,* 352–358.

Miles, M.B., & Huberman, A.M. (1994). *Qualitative data analysis* (2nd ed.). Thousand Oaks, CA: Sage.

Milin, R., Halikas, J.A., Meller, J.E., & Morse, C. (1991). Psychopathology among substance abusing juvenile offenders. *Journal of the American Academy of Child and Adolescent Psychiatry, 30,* 569–574.

Miller, G.E., Dopp, J.M., Myers, H.F., & Fahey, J.L. (1997, April). *Affective responses to marital conflict and their cardiovascular, neuroendocrine, and immunologic sequelae.* Paper presented at the meeting of the Society of Behavioral Medicine, San Francisco, CA.

Miller, G.E., & Prinz, R.J. (1990). Enhancement of social learning family interventions for child conduct disorder. *Psychological Bulletin, 108,* 291–307.

Moffitt, T.E. (1993). Adolescence-limited and life-course persistent antisocial behavior: A developmental taxonomy. *Psychological Review, 100,* 674–701.

Morris, R.J., & Kratochwill, T.R. (Eds.). (1998). *The practice of child therapy* (3rd. ed.). Needham Heights, MA: Allyn & Bacon.

Nathan, P.E., &. Gorman, J.M. (Eds.). (1998). *Treatments that work.* New York: Oxford University Press.

National Institute of Mental Health. (1975). *Research in the service of mental health.* (DHEW Publication No. (ADM) 75–236.) Rockville, MD: DHEW.

Needleman, H.L. (Ed.). (1988). *Low level of lead exposure: The clinical implications of current research.* New York: Raven.

Needleman, H.L., & Gatsonis, C.A. (1990). Low-level led exposure and the IQ of children: A meta-analysis of modern studies. *Journal of the American Medical Association, 263,* 673–678.

Needleman, H.L., Schell, A.S., Bellinger, D., Leviton, A., & Alldred, E.N. (1990). The long-term effects of exposure to low doses of lead in childhood: An 11-year follow-up report. *New England Journal of Medicine, 322,* 83.

Newcomb, M.D., & Bentler, P.M. (1988). *Consequences of adolescent drug use: Impact on the lives of young adults.* Newbury Park, CA: Sage.

Newcomb, M.D., & Bentler, P.M. (1989). Substance use and abuse among children and teenagers. *American Psychologist, 44,* 242–248.

Newman, M.G., Consoli, A., & Taylor, C.B. (1997). Computers in assessment and cognitive behavioral treatment of clinical disorders: Anxiety as a case in point. *Behavior Therapy, 28,* 211–235.

Newman, M.G., Kenardy, J., Herman, S., & Taylor, C.B. (1997). Comparison of palm-top-computer-assisted brief cognitive-behavioral treatment to cognitive-behavioral treatment for panic disorder. *Journal of Consulting and Clinical Psychology, 65,* 178–183.

Nezu, A.M., & Nezu, C.M. (Eds.) (1989). *Clinical decision making in behavior therapy: A problem-solving perspective.* Champaign, IL: Research Press.

Nicholson, R.A., & Berman, J.S. (1983). Is follow-up necessary in evaluating psychotherapy? *Psychological Bulletin, 93,* 555–565.

O'Donnell, C.R. (1992). The interplay of theory and practice in delinquency prevention: From behavior modification to activity settings. In J. McCord & R.E. Tremblay (Eds.), *Preventing antisocial behavior* (pp. 209–232). New York: Guilford.

Offord, D., Boyle, M.H., Racine, Y.A., Fleming, J.E., Cadman, D.T., Blum, H.M., Byrne, C., Links, P.S., Lipman, E.L., MacMillan, H.L., Rae Grant, N.I., Sanford, M.N., Szatmari, P., Thomas, H., & Woodward, C.A. (1992). Outcome, prognosis, and risk in a longitudinal follow-up study. *Journal of the American Academy of Child and Adolescent Psychiatry, 31,* 916–923.

Offord, D., Boyle, M.H., Racine, Y.A., Szatmari, P., Fleming, J.E., Sanford, M.N., &

Lipman, E.L. (1996). Integrating assessment data from multiple informants. *Journal of the American Academy of Child and Adolescent Psychiatry, 35,* 1078–1085.

Offord, D.R., Kraemer, H.C., Kazdin, A.E., Jensen, P.J., & Harrington, R. (1998). Lowering the burden of suffering from child psychiatric disorder: Trade-offs among clinical, targeted, and universal interventions. *Journal of the American Academy of Child and Adolescent Psychiatry, 37,* 686–694.

Ollendick, T.H., & Hersen, M. (Eds.). (1993). *Handbook of child and adolescent assessment.* Needham Heights, MA: Allyn & Bacon.

Ollendick, T.H., & King, N.J. (1998). Empirically supported treatments for children with phobic and anxiety disorders. *Journal of Clinical Child Psychology, 27,* 156–167.

O'Malley, S.S., Foley, S.H., Rounsaville, B.J., Watkins, J.T., Sotsky, S.M., Imber, S.D., & Elkin, I. (1988). Therapist competence and patient outcome in interpersonal psychotherapy of depression. *Journal of Consulting and Clinical Psychology, 56,* 496–501.

OPTAIO™ Provider's desktop. (1997). San Antonio, TX: The Psychological Corporation.

Orlinsky, D.E., Grawe, K., & Parks, B.K. (1994). Process and outcome in psychotherapy. In A.E. Bergin & S.L. Garfield (Eds.), *Handbook of psychotherapy and behavior change* (4th ed., pp. 270–376). New York: Wiley & Sons.

Otto, R.K., Greenstein, J.J., Johnson, M.K., & Friedman, R.M. (1992). Prevalence of mental disorders among youths in the juvenile justice system. In J.J. Cocozza (Ed.), *Responding to the mental health needs of youths in the juvenile justice system* (pp. 7–48). Seattle, WA: National Coalition for the Mentally Ill in the Criminal Justice System.

Parsonson, B.S., & Baer, D.M. (1978). The analysis and presentation of graphic data. In T.R. Kratochwill (Ed.), *Single-subject research: Strategies for evaluating change* (pp. 101–165). New York: Academic.

Patterson, G.R. (1976). *Living with children: New methods for parents and teachers* (Revised ed.). Champaign, IL: Research.

Patterson, G.R. (1982). *Coercive family process.* Eugene, OR: Castalia.

Patterson, G.R., & Chamberlain, P. (1994). A functional analysis of resistance during parent training therapy. *Clinical Psychology: Science and Practice, 1,* 53–70.

Patterson, G.R., Dishion, T.J., & Chamberlain, P. (1993). Outcomes and methodological issues relating to treatment of antisocial children. In T.R. Giles (Ed.), *Handbook of effective psychotherapy* (pp. 43–87). New York: Plenum

Patterson, G.R., & Forgatch, M. (1987). *Parents and adolescents living together—Part 1: The basics.* Eugene, OR: Castalia.

Patterson, G.R., Reid, J.B., & Dishion, T.J. (1992). *Antisocial boys.* Eugene, OR: Castalia.

Patzer, G.L., & Burke, D.M. (1988). Physical attractiveness and childhood adjustment. In B.B. Lahey & A.E. Kazdin, (Eds.), *Advances in clinical child psychology* (Vol. 11, pp. 325–368). New York: Plenum.

Paul, G.L. (1967). Outcome research in psychotherapy. *Journal of Consulting Psychology, 31,* 109–118.

Pavlov I.P. (1927). *Conditioned reflexes: An investigation of the physiological activities of the cerebral cortex.* London: Oxford University Press.

Peet, M. (1998, September). *Intervention trials of EFAs in schizophrenia.* Paper presented at the National Institutes of Health Workshop on Omega-3 Essential Fatty Acids and Psychiatric Disorders, Bethesda, MD.

Pelham, W.E., Jr., Wheeler, T., & Chronis, A. (1998). Empirically supported psychosocial treatments for attention deficit hyperactivity disorder. *Journal of Clinical Child Psychology, 27,* 190–205.

Persons, J.B., & Silberschatz, G. (1998). Are results of randomized controlled clinical trials useful to psychotherapists? *Journal of Consulting and Clinical Psychology, 66,* 126–135.

Peterson, L., & Bell-Dolan, D. (1995). Treatment outcome research in child psychology: Realistic coping with the "Ten Commandments of Methodology." *Journal of Clinical Child Psychology, 24,* 149–162.

Phillips, E.L. (1985). *Psychotherapy revised: New frontiers in research and practice.* Hillsdale, NJ: Erlbaum.

Prinz, R.J., & Miller, G.E. (1994). Family-based treatment for childhood antisocial behavior: Experimental influences on dropout and engagement. *Journal of Consulting and Clinical Psychology, 62,* 645–650.

Prioleau, L., Murdock, M., & Brody, N. (1983). An analysis of psychotherapy versus placebo studies. *Behavioral and Brain Sciences, 6,* 275–310.

Prout, H.T., & DeMartino, R.A. (1986). A meta-analysis of school-based studies of psychotherapy. *Journal of School Psychology, 24,* 285–292.

Prout, S.M., & Prout, H.T. (1998). A meta-analysis of school-based studies of counseling and psychotherapy: An update. *Journal of School Psychology, 36,* 121–136.

Rachman, S.J., & Wilson, G.T. (1980). *The effects of psychological therapy* (2nd ed.). Oxford: Pergamon.

Regier, D.A., Myers, J.K., Kramer, M., Robins, L.N., Blazer, D.G., Hough, R.L., Eaton, W.W., & Locke, B.Z. (1984). The NIMH Epidemiologic Catchment Area program: Historical context, major objectives, and study population characteristics. *Archives of General Psychiatry, 41,* 934–941.

Reimers, T.M., Wacker, D.P., Cooper, L.J., & DeRaad, A.O. (1992). Clinical evaluation of the variables associated with treatment acceptability and their relation to compliance. *Behavioral Disorders, 18,* 67–76.

Robins, L.N. (1978). Sturdy childhood predictors of adult antisocial behavior: Replications from longitudinal studies. *Psychological Medicine, 8,* 611–622.

Robins, L.N., Helzer, J., Weissman, M., Orvaschel, H., Gruenberg, E., Bruche, J., & Regier, D. (1984). Lifetime prevalence of specific psychiatric disorders in three sites. *Archives of General Psychiatry, 41,* 949–958.

Robins, L.N., & Regier, D.A. (1991). *Psychiatric disorders in America: The Epidemiologic Catchment Area Study.* New York: Free Press.

Robins, L., & Rutter, M. (Eds.). (1990). *Straight and devious pathways from childhood to adulthood.* Cambridge: Cambridge University Press.

Rogers, S.J. (1998). Empirically supported treatment for young children with autism. *Journal of Clinical Child Psychology, 27,* 168–179.

Rosen, G.M. (1987). Self-help treatment books and the commercialization of psychotherapy. *American Psychologist, 42,* 46–51.

Rosenthal, R. (1984). *Meta-analytic procedures for social research.* Beverly Hills, CA: Sage.

Rosenthal, R., & Rosnow, R.L. (1991). *Essentials of behavioral research: Methods and data analysis* (2nd ed.). New York: McGraw-Hill.

Rossi, J.S. (1990). Statistical power of psychological research: What have we gained in 20 years. *Journal of Consulting and Clinical Psychology, 58,* 646–656.

Roth, A., & Fonagy, P. (1996). *What works for whom: A critical review of psychotherapy research.* New York: Guilford.

Rounsaville, B.J., O'Malley, S., Foley, S., & Weissman, M. (1988). Role of manual-guided training in the conduct and efficacy of interpersonal psychotherapy of depression. *Journal of Consulting and Clinical Psychology, 56,* 681–688.

Rowan, T., & O'Hanlon, B. (1999). *Solution-oriented therapy for chronic and severe mental illness.* New York: Wiley & Sons.

Ruma, P.R., Burke, R.V., & Thompson, R.W. (1996). Group parent training: Is it effective for children of all ages? *Behavior Therapy, 27,* 159–169.

Rutter, M., & Casaer, P. (Eds.). (1991). *Biological risk factors for psychosocial disorders.* Cambridge: Cambridge University Press.

Rutter, M., Harrington, R., Quinton, D., & Pickles, A. (1994). Adult outcome of conduct disorder in childhood: Implications for concepts and definitions and patterns of psychopathology. In R.D. Ketterlinus & M.E. Lamb (Eds.), *Adolescent problem behaviors: Issues and research* (pp. 57–80). Hillsdale, NJ: Erlbaum.

Rutter, M., & Rutter, M. (1993). *Developing minds: Challenge and continuity across the life span.* New York: Basic Books.

Rutter, M., Yule, W., & Graham, P. (1973). Enuresis and behavioural deviance: Some epidemiological considerations. In I. Kolvin, R. MacKeith, & S.R. Meadow (Eds.), *Bladder control and enuresis: Clinics in Developmental Medicine* (Vol. 48/49). London: Heinemann/SIMP.

Saile, H., Burgmeier, R., & Schmidt, L.R. (1988). A meta-analysis of studies on psychological preparation of children facing medical procedures. *Psychology and Health, 2,* 107–132.

Salter, A. (1949). *Conditioned reflex therapy: The direct approach to the reconstruction of personality.* New York: Creative Age.

Sanders, M.R., & Dadds, M.R. (1993). *Behavioral family intervention.* Needham Heights, MA: Allyn & Bacon.

Sanford, M.N., Offord, D.R., Boyle, M.H., Peace, A., & Racine, Y.A. (1992). Ontario Child Health Study: Social and school impairments in children aged 6–16 years. *Journal of the American Academy of Child and Adolescent Psychiatry, 31,* 60–67.

Santisteban, D.A, Szapocznik, J., Perez-Vidal, A., Kurtines, W.H, Murray, E.J., & LaPerriere, A. (1996). Efficacy of intervention for engaging youth and families into treatment and some variables that may contribute to differential effectiveness. *Journal of Family Psychology, 10,* 35–44.

Santrock, J.W., Minnett, A.M., & Campbell, B.D. (1994). *The authoritative guide to self-help books.* New York: Guilford.

Satterfield, J.H., Satterfield, B.T., & Schell, A.M. (1987). Therapeutic interventions to prevent delinquency in hyperactive boys. *Journal of the American Academy of Child and Adolescent Psychiatry, 26,* 56–64.

Schering-Plough, Inc. (© 1996). Coppertone™ Gold (SPF 4)—Dark tanning oil. (Product description from the back of the 8 oz. bottle.)

Schmidt, F.L. (1996). Statistical significance testing and cumulative knowledge in psychology: Implications for training of researchers. *Psychological Methods, 1,* 115–129.

Sechrest, L., West, S.G., Phillips, M.A., Redner, R., & Yeaton, W. (1979). Some neglected problems in evaluation research: Strength and integrity of treatments. In L. Sechrest, S.G. West, M.A. Phillips, R. Redner, & W. Yeaton (Eds.), *Evaluation studies: Review annual* (Vol. 4, pp. 15–35). Beverly Hills: Sage.

Sederer, L.I., & Dickey, B. (Eds.). (1994). *Outcomes assessment in clinical practice.* Baltimore, MD: Williams & Wilkins.

Sedlmeier, P., & Gigerenzer, G. (1989). Do studies of statistical power have an effect on the power of studies? *Psychological Bulletin, 105,* 309–316.

Serketich, W.J., & Dumas, J.E. (1996). The effectiveness of behavioral parent training to modify antisocial behavior in children: A meta-analysis. *Behavior Therapy, 27,* 171–186.

Shadish, W.R., Matt, G.E., Navarro, A.M., Siegle, G., Cris-Christoph, P., Hazelrigg, M.D., Jorm, A.F., Lyons, L.C., Nietzel, M.T., Prout, H.T., Robinson, L., Smith, M.L., Svartberg, M., & Weiss, B. (1997). Evidence that therapy works in clinically representative conditions. *Journal of Consulting and Clinical Psychology, 65,* 355–365.

Shadish, W.R., Montgomery, L.M., Wilson, P., Wilson, M.R., Bright, I., & Okwumabua, T. (1993). Effects of family and marital psychotherapies: A meta-analysis. *Journal of Consulting and Clinical Psychology, 61,* 992–1002.

Shadish, W.R., & Ragsdale, K. (1996). Random versus nonrandom assignment in controlled experiments: Do you get the same answer? *Journal of Consulting and Clinical Psychology, 64,* 1290–1305.

Shapiro, D.A., Firth-Cozens, J., & Stiles, W.B. (1989). Therapists' differential effectiveness: A Sheffield Psychotherapy Project addendum. *British Journal of Psychiatry, 154,* 383–385.

Shapiro, D.A., & Shapiro, D. (1982). Meta-analysis of comparative therapy outcome research: A replication and refinement. *Psychological Bulletin, 92,* 581–604.

Shapiro, M.B. (1957). Experimental method in the psychological description of the individual psychiatric patient. *International Journal of Social Psychiatry, 3,* 89–102.

Shapiro, M.B. (1964). The measurement of clinically relevant variables. *Journal of Psychosomatic Research, 8,* 245–254.

Sheinkopf, S.J., & Siegel, B. (1998). Home based behavioral treatment of young children with autism. *Journal of Autism and Developmental Disabilities, 28,* 15–23.

Sidman, M. (1960). *Tactics of scientific research.* New York: Basic Books.

Skinner, B.F. (1938). *The behavior of organisms: An experimental analysis.* New York: Appleton-Century.

Skinner, B.F. (1957). The experimental analysis of behavior. *American Scientist, 45,* 343–371.

Sloane, R.B., Staples, F.R., Cristol, A.H., Yorkston, N.J., & Whipple, K. (1975). *Psychotherapy versus behavior therapy.* Cambridge, MA: Harvard University Press.

Smith, D., & Dumont, F. (1997). Eliminating overconfidence in psychodiagnosis: Strategies for training and practice. *Clinical Psychology: Science and Practice, 4,* 335–345.

Smith, M.L., & Glass, G.V. (1977). Meta-analysis of psychotherapy outcome studies. *American Psychologist, 32,* 752–760.

Smith, M.L., Glass, G.V., & Miller, T.I. (1980). *The benefits of psychotherapy.* Baltimore, MD: Johns Hopkins University Press.

Smith, T. (1999). Outcome of early intervention for children with autism. *Clinical Psychology: Science and Practice, 6,* 33–49.

Smyrnios, K.X., & Kirkby, R.J. (1993). Long-term comparison of brief versus unlimited psychodynamic treatments with children and their parents. *Journal of Consulting and Clinical Psychology, 61,* 1020–1027.

Smyth, J.M. (1998). Written emotional expression: Effect sizes, outcome types, and moderating variables. *Journal of Consulting and Clinical Psychology, 66,* 174–184.

Snyder, D.K., & Wills, R.M. (1989). Behavioral versus insight-oriented marital therapy:

Effects on individual and interspousal functioning. *Journal of Consulting and Clinical Psychology, 57,* 39–46.

Snyder, D.K., Wills, R.M., & Grady-Fletcher, A. (1991). Long-term effectiveness of behavioral versus insight-oriented marital therapy: A 4-year follow-up study. *Journal of Consulting and Clinical Psychology, 59,* 138–141.

Sorenson, R.L., Gorsuch, R.L., & Mintz, J. (1985). Moving targets: Patients' changing complaints during psychotherapy. *Journal of Consulting and Clinical Psychology, 53,* 49–54.

Spiegel, D., Bloom, J.R., Kraemer, H.C., & Gottheil, E. (1989). Effect of psychosocial treatment on survival of patients with metastatic breast cancer. *Lancet, 2* (8668), 888–891.

Stake, R.E. (1995). *The art of case study research.* Thousand Oaks, CA: Sage.

Statistical Solutions. (1995). *nQuery Advisor™.* Boston: Statistical Solutions.

Stiles, W.B., Shapiro, D.A., & Elliott, R. (1986). "Are all psychotherapies equivalent?" *American Psychologist, 41,* 165–180.

Stoff, D.M., Breiling, J., & Maser, J.D. (Eds.). (1997). *Handbook of antisocial behavior.* New York: Wiley & Sons.

Stoll, A. (1998, September). *Bipolar disorder: Observational and interventional studies.* Paper presented at the National Institutes of Health Workshop on Omega-3 Essential Fatty Acids and Psychiatric Disorders, Bethesda, MD.

Stricker, G., & Keisner, R.H. (Eds.). (1985). *From research to clinical practice: The implications of social and developmental research for psychotherapy.* New York: Plenum.

Strupp, H.H., & Anderson, T. (1997). On the limitations of manuals. *Clinical Psychology: Science and Practice, 4,* 76–82.

Strupp, H.H., & Hadley, S.W. (1977). A tripartite model of mental health and therapeutic outcomes. *American Psychologist, 32,* 187–196.

Sugden, D.A., & Wright, H.A. (1998). *Motor coordination disorders in children.* Thousand Oaks, CA: Sage.

Szapocznik, J., Kurtines, W.H., Foote, F.H., Perez-Vidal, A., & Hervis, O. (1986). Conjoint versus one person family therapy: Further evidence for the effectiveness of conducting family therapy through one person. *Journal of Consulting and Clinical Psychology, 54,* 395–397.

Szapocznik, J., Perez-Vidal, A., Brickman, A., Foote, F.H., Santisteban, D.A., Hervis, O., & Kurtines, W.H. (1988). Engaging adolescent drug abusers and their families into treatment: A strategic structural systems approach. *Journal of Consulting and Clinical Psychology, 56,* 552–557.

Szapocznik, J., Rio, A., Murray, E., Cohen, R., Scopetta, M., Rivas-Vasquez, A., Hervis, O., Posada, V., & Kurtines, W. (1989). Structural family versus psychodynamic child therapy for problematic Hispanic boys. *Journal of Consulting and Clinical Psychology, 57,* 571–578.

Talley, P.F., Strupp, H.H., & Butler, S.F. (Eds.). (1994). *Psychotherapy research and practice: Bridging the gap.* New York: Basic Books.

Tarnowski, K.J., & Simonian, S.J. (1992). Assessing treatment acceptance: The Abbreviated Acceptability Rating Profile. *Journal of Behavior Therapy and Experimental Psychiatry, 23,* 101–106.

Tarrier, N., & Barrowclough, C. (1990) Family interventions for schizophrenia. Special Issue: Recent developments in the behavioral treatment of chronic psychiatric illness. *Behavior Modification, 14,* 408–440.

Task Force on Promotion and Dissemination of Psychological Procedures. (1995). Training in and dissemination of empirically validated psychological treatments: Report and recommendations. *Clinical Psychologist, 48* (1), 3–23.

Tharp, R.G. (1991). Cultural diversity and treatment of children. *Journal of Consulting and Clinical Psychology, 59,* 799–812.

Thigpen, C.H., & Cleckley, H.M. (1954). A case of multiple personality. *Journal of Abnormal and Social Psychology, 49,* 135–151.

Thigpen, C.H., & Cleckley, H.M. (1957). *Three faces of Eve.* New York: McGraw-Hill.

Thompson, R.W., Ruma, P.R., Schuchmann, L.F., & Burke, R.V. (1996). A cost-effectiveness evaluation of parent training. *Journal of Child and Family Studies, 5,* 415–429.

Thoresen, C.E., & Powell, L.H. (1992). Type A behavior pattern: New perspectives on theory, assessment, and intervention. *Journal of Consulting and Clinical Psychology, 60,* 595–604.

Todd, D.M., Jacobus, S.J., & Boland, J. (1992). Uses of a computer database to support research-practice integration in a training clinic. *Professional Psychology: Research and Practice, 23,* 52–58.

Tracy, P.E., Wolfgang, M.E., & Figlio, R.M. (1990). *Delinquency careers in two birth cohorts.* New York: Plenum.

Trierweiler, S.J., & Stricker, G. (1998). *The scientific practice of professional psychology.* New York: Plenum.

U.S. Bureau of Census, Current Population Reports. (1993). *U.S. population estimates by age, sex, race, and Hispanic origin: 1980–1991.* (P25–1095). Washington, DC: U.S. Government Printing Office.

U.S. Congress, Office of Technology Assessment. (1986). *Children's mental health: Problems and services—A background paper.* (OTA-BP-H-33). Washington, DC: U.S. Government Printing Office.

U.S. Congress, Office of Technology Assessment. (1991). *Adolescent health.* (OTA-H-468). Washington, DC: U.S. Government Printing Office.

U.S. Department of Health and Human Services, National Institutes of Health, Office for Protection from Research Risks. (1983). *Code of federal regulations: Part 46: Protection of human subjects.* Washington, DC: U.S. Government Printing Office.

Wade, S.L., Taylor, H.G., Drotar, D., Stancin, T., & Yeates, K.O. (1998). Family burden and adaptation during the initial year after traumatic brain injury in children, *Pediatrics, 102,* 110–116.

Wahler, R.G. (1980). The insular mother: Her problems in parent-child treatment. *Journal of Applied Behavior Analysis, 13,* 207–219.

Walrond-Skinner, S. (1986). *Dictionary of psychotherapy.* London: Routledge & Kegan Paul.

Waltz, J., Addis, M., Koerner, K., & Jacobson, N.S. (1993). Testing the integrity of a psychotherapy protocol: Assessment of adherence and competence. *Journal of Consulting and Clinical Psychology, 61,* 620–630.

Watson, J.B., & Rayner, R. (1920). Conditioned emotional reactions. *Journal of Experimental Psychology, 3,* 1–14.

Webster-Stratton, C. (1985). Predictors of treatment outcome in parent training for conduct disordered children. *Behavior Therapy, 16,* 223–243.

Webster-Stratton, C. (1996). Early intervention with videotape modeling: Programs for families of children with oppositional defiant disorder or conduct disorder. In E.D. Hibbs & P. Jensen (Eds.), *Psychosocial treatment research of child and adolescent disorders: Empirically based strategies for clinical practice* (pp. 435–474). Washington, DC: American Psychological Association.

Webster-Stratton, C. (1998). Preventing conduct problems in Head Start children: Strengthening parenting competencies. *Journal of Consulting and Clinical Psychology, 66,* 715–730.

Webster-Stratton, C., & Hammond, M. (1990). Predictors of treatment outcome in parent training for families with conduct problem children. *Behavior Therapy, 21,* 319–337.

Webster-Stratton, C., & Spitzer, A. (1996). Parenting of a young child with conduct problems: New insights using qualitative methods. In T.H. Ollendick & R.J. Prinz (Eds.), *Advances in clinical child psychology* (Vol. 18, pp. 1–62). New York: Plenum.

Weinberg, N.Z., Rahdert, E., Colliver, J.D., & Glanz, M.D. (1998). Adolescent substance abuse: A review of the past 10 years. *Journal of the American Academy of Child and Adolescent Psychiatry, 37,* 252–261.

Weinberger, D.A., Tublin, S.K., Ford, M.E., & Feldman, S.S. (1990). Preadolescents' social-emotional adjustment and selective attention in family research. *Child Development, 61,* 1374–1386.

Weiss, G., & Hechtman, L.T. (1986). *Hyperactive children grown up.* New York: Guilford.

Weisz, J.R., Donenberg, G.R., Han, S.S., & Kauneckis, D. (1995). Child and adolescent psychotherapy outcomes in experiments and in clinics: Why the disparity? *Journal of Abnormal Child Psychology, 23,* 83–106.

Weisz, J.R., Donenberg, G.R., Han, S.S., & Weiss, B. (1995). Bridging the gap between lab and clinic in child and adolescent psychotherapy. *Journal of Consulting and Clinical Psychology, 63,* 688–701.

Weisz, J.R., & Hawley, K.M. (1998). Finding, evaluating, refining, and applying empirically supported treatments for children and adolescents. *Journal of Clinical Child Psychology, 27,* 206–216.

Weisz, J.R., Huey, S.J., & Weersing, V.R. (1998). Psychotherapy outcome research with children and adolescents. In T.H. Ollendick & R.J. Prinz (Eds.), *Advances in clinical child psychology* (Vol. 20, pp. 49–91). New York: Plenum.

Weisz, J.R., & Weiss, B. (1993). *Effects of psychotherapy with children and adolescents.* Newbury Park, CA: Sage.

Weisz, J.R., Weiss, B., Alicke, M.D., & Klotz, M.L. (1987). Effectiveness of psychotherapy with children and adolescents: A meta-analysis for clinicians. *Journal of Consulting and Clinical Psychology, 55,* 542–549.

Weisz, J.R., Weiss, B., & Donenberg, G.R. (1992). The lab versus the clinic: Effects of child and adolescent psychotherapy. *American Psychologist, 47,* 1578–1585.

Weisz, J.R., Weiss, B., Han, S.S., Granger, D.A., & Morton, T. (1995). Effects of psychotherapy with children and adolescents revisited: A meta-analysis of treatment outcome studies. *Psychological Bulletin, 117,* 450–468.

Werner, E.E., & Smith, R.S. (1992). *Overcoming the odds: High risk children from birth to adulthood.* Ithaca, NY: Cornell University Press.

Wierzbicki, M., & Pekarik, G. (1993). A meta-analysis of psychotherapy dropout. *Professional Psychology: Research and Practice, 24,* 190–195.

Wiger, D.E. (1999). *The psychotherapy documentation primer.* New York: Wiley & Sons.

Williams, C.L., Butcher, J.N., Ben-Porath, Y.S., & Graham, J.R. (1992). *MMPI-A con-*

tent scales: Assessing psychopathology in adolescents. Minneapolis: University of Minnesota Press.

Williams, G.M., O'Callaghan, M., Najman, J.M., Bor, W., Anderson, M.J., & Richards, D. (1998). Maternal cigarette smoking and child psychiatric morbidity: A longitudinal study. *Pediatrics, 102,* e 11.

Wilson, G.T. (1998). Manual-based treatment and clinical practice. *Clinical Psychology: Science and Practice, 5,* 363–375.

Windle, M., Shope, J.T., & Bukstein, O. (1996). Alcohol use. In R.J. DiClemente, W.B. Hansen, & L.E. Ponton (Eds.), *Handbook of adolescent health risk behavior* (pp. 115–159). New York: Plenum.

Wolfe, V.V., Gentile, C., Michienzi, T., Sas, L., & Wolfe, D. (1991). The Children's Impact on Traumatic Events Scale: A measure of post-sexual-abuse PTSD symptoms. *Behavioral Assessment, 13,* 359–383.

Wolfe, V.V., Gentile, C., & Wolfe, D. (1989). The impact of sexual abuse on children: A PTSD formulation. *Behavior Therapy, 20,* 215–228.

Wolpe, J. (1958). *Psychotherapy by reciprocal inhibition.* Stanford, CA: Stanford University Press.

Wolraich, M.R., Wilson, D.B., & White, J.W. (1995). The effect of sugar on behavior or cognition in children: A meta-analysis. *Journal of the American Medical Association, 274,* 1617–1621.

World Health Organization. (1992). *The ICD-10 classification of mental disorders.* Geneva: WHO.

Yates, B.T. (1995). Cost-effectiveness analysis, cost-benefit analysis, and beyond: Evolving models for the scientist-manager-practitioner. *Clinical Psychology: Science and Practice, 2,* 385–398.

Yin, R.K. (1994). *Case study research: Design and methods* (2nd ed.). Thousand Oaks, CA: Sage.

Zhu, S., Stretch, V., Balabanis, M., Rosbrook, B., Sadler, G., & Pierce, J.P. (1996). Telephone counseling for smoking cessation: Effects of single-session and multiple-session interventions. *Journal of Consulting and Clinical Psychology, 64,* 202–211.

Zill, N., & Schoenborn, C.A. (1990, November). *Developmental, learning, and emotional problems: Health of our nation's children, United States 1988.* Advance Data, 190. Washington, DC: National Center for Health Statistics.

Author Index

Subject Index